The Bronze Age Civilization
of Central Asia

RECENT SOVIET DISCOVERIES

Edited with an Introduction by Philip L. Kohl
Afterword by C. C. Lamberg-Karlovsky

M. E. Sharpe, Inc.
Armonk, New York

The essays translated in this volume come from the sources listed below and are published by arrangement with VAAP, the Soviet Copyright Agency. "Manuscripts" were written expressly for this collection.

Chapter 1: "Mogil'nik epokhi rannei bronzy Parkai II," manuscript.
Chapter 2: "Namazga-tepe i ephokha pozdnei bronzy Iuzhnoi Turkmenii," abstract of candidate's dissertation, Leningrad, "Nauka" Publishers, 1978.
Chapter 3: "Altyn-depe v epokhu eneolita," *Sovetskaia arkheologiia*, 1977, no. 4.
Chapter 4: "Problemy proiskhozhdenii kul'tury rannei bronzy Iuzhnoi Turkmenii," *Izvestiia Akademii nauk Turkmenskoi SSR*, 1976, no. 6.
Chapter 5: "Chelovek na zare urbanizatsii," *Priroda*, 1976, no. 4.
Chapter 6: "Gorodskie tsentry ranneklassovykh obshchestv," *Istoriia i arkheologiia Srednei Azii*, Ashkhabad, "Ylym" Publishers, 1978.
Chapter 7: "Pechati protoindiiskogo tipa iz Altyn-depe," *Vestnik drevnei istorii*, 1977, no. 4.
Chapter 8: "Margiana v ephokhu bronzy," manuscript.
Chapter 9: "Izuchenie pamiatnikov epokhi bronzy nizov'ev Murgaba," *Sovetskaia arkheologiia*, 1979, no. 1.
Chapter 10: "Pechati-amulety murgabskogo stilia," *Sovetskaia arkheologiia*, 1976, no. 1.
Chapter 11: "Iuzhnii Uzbekistan vo II tysiacheletii do n.e.," manuscript.
Chapter 12: "Raskopki pamiatnika epokhi bronzy na poselenii Sarazm," manuscript.
Chapter 13: "Pamiatniki epokhi bronzy na territorii Iuzhnogo Tadzhikistana," manuscript.
Chapter 14: "Istoriia metalloobrabatyvaiushchego proizvodstva u drevnikh zemledel'tsev Iuzhnoi Turkmenii," abstract of candidate's dissertation, Moscow, Laboratoriia NTI Instituta istorii SSSR AN SSSR, 1975.
Chapter 15: "Drevneishie zhatvennye orudiia i ikh proizvoditel'nost' (v svete eksperimental'no-trasologicheskogo izucheniia)," *Sovetskaia arkheologiia*, 1978, no. 4.
Chapter 16: "Istoriia oroshaemogo zemledeliia v Iuzhnoi Turkmenii (rannezemledel'-cheskaia epokha)," *Uspekhi sredneaziatskoi arkheologii*, issue 1, 1972 (Leningrad, "Nauka" Publishers).
Chapter 17: "Ekologicheskie predposylki rannego zemledeliia na iuge Turkmenii," manuscript.

Translated by Philip L. Kohl and William Mandel.

Published simultaneously as Vol. XIX, Nos. 1-2 and 3-4 of *Soviet Anthropology and Archeology*, edited by Stephen P. Dunn.

Library of Congress Cataloging in Publication Data
Main entry under title:

Includes bibliographical references.
1. Bronze age—Soviet Central Asia. 2. Soviet Central Asia—Antiquities.
3. Excavations (Archaeology)—Soviet Central Asia. I. Kohl, Philip L., 1946-
GN778.32.S65B76   957   80-5454
ISBN 0-87332-169-3   AACR2   83 - 7720

Printed in the United States of America.

TABLE OF CONTENTS

Part Three
Margiana and Settlements in Southeastern
Central Asia

Part Four
Reproduction of Productive Activities:
Techniques and Analysis

The Namazga Civilization:
An Overview

PHILIP L. KOHL

It became apparent during two exchange visits to the Soviet Union in 1978 and 1979[1] that the only major English summaries of the Aeneolithic and Bronze Age remains from Central Asia[2] were dated and did not include adequate descriptions of major discoveries, such as the Murghab Delta sites. An immediate solution to this problem suggested itself: a collection of translated articles which both presented the latest discoveries in the area and illustrated current techniques and methods of analysis used by Soviet archeologists. In December 1978 I discussed the idea of such a publication with V. M. Masson, Director of the Central Asia and Caucasus Section of the Leningrad Branch of the Institute of Archeology, USSR Academy of Sciences, who agreed that such a publication was needed. He kindly provided me with a list of articles that he considered representative of current work in southern Central Asia.[3] Although several articles were commissioned especially for this volume and every attempt was made to present the most recent findings, the pace of investigations has been so rapid that major studies have already appeared that have not been included in this volume.[4] This preface will attempt to evaluate the significance of this recent work by analyzing the ecological setting and assessing the scale of Bronze Age developments in southern Central Asia. First, it will summarize previous work in the area and then analyze the gradual and largely indigenous development of a uniform and distinctive Bronze Age civilization that arose in what has been termed "the northeastern frontier of the ancient Near East."

Philip L. Kohl

1. Archeological Investigations in
Southern Central Asia

Systematic archeological investigations in southern Central Asia
began with the excavations of Pumpelly at Anau in 1904.[5] For two
decades after these investigations Western scholars emphasized
the importance of the Anau civilization[6] and treated it almost as
the equal of those that appeared in more famous areas, such as
southern Mesopotamia and Khuzestan. This initial perspective,
however, was radically altered and deemphasized due to the cessation of Western investigations in the area and to the discovery and
elaboration of complex developments, such as the Harappan civilization, in contiguous zones.[7] Western interest declined as the
young Soviet Union consolidated its rule; indications of extensive
Bronze Age remains in the northeastern frontier, as suggested,
for example, by T. J. Arne's discovery of scores of prehistoric
sites on the Gorgan Plain of northeastern Iran, largely went un-
noticed.

Initial Soviet investigations in southern Turkmenistan[8] were
conducted on a small scale by amateurs, such as D. D. Bukinich,
an irrigation engineer, who discovered Namazga-depe in 1916 and
conducted exploratory soundings at it and other sites during the
twenties. The work in the piedmont belt of the Kopet Dagh was extended by A. A. Marushchenko in the thirties, but the first significant systematic investigations in Turkmenia were initiated by S. P.
Tolstov in Khoresmia or the delta of the Amu Darya and surrounding area immediately south of the Aral Sea in 1937. The Khores-
mian project, which is still going on under the direction of M. A.
Itina, has concentrated largely on later historical periods and
documented the development of large-scale irrigation works in
this fertile alluvial plain.[9] Work on the emergence and development of sedentary food-producing communities in Central Asia
began with the formation of the Combined Archeological Expedition
to Southern Turkmenistan (IuTAKE) at the end of World War II.
The prehistoric sequence was extended by B. A. Kuftin in 1952[10]
through a series of deep soundings at Namazga-depe. Kuftin's investigations, coupled with the work of A. P. Okladnikov on Palae-
olithic and Mesolithic sites on or near the Krasnovodsk Peninsula[11]
and of V. M. Masson at Djeitun on the southern edge of the Kara
Kum northwest of Ashkhabad[12] conclusively demonstrated the local
development of a food-producing economy in southern Turkmenistan. From 1955 to 1962 the Fourteenth Division of IuTAKE in-

vestigated eleven sites: nine as part of a salvage operation in the Geoksyur Oasis of the Tedjen River; [13] Kara-depe near Artykh; [14] and Djeitun. Large-scale excavations at Altyn-depe started in 1965, and this work refined Kuftin's sequence from Namazga-depe and, more importantly, documented the emergence and nature of a complex urban society in the piedmont belt of the Kopet Dagh Mountains during the Late Bronze Age. The initial explorations along the middle Sumbar River in southwestern Turkmenistan and the formation of the Soviet-Afghan Archeological Expedition occurred in 1969. The latter prehistoric investigations, headed by V. I. Sarianidi, documented the Central Asian colonization of the south Bactrian plain. Similar materials were recovered by the Murghab Expedition of the Institute of Archeology in Moscow, which was formed in 1972 and also directed by Sarianidi, and the Murghab Expedition of the Institute of History in Ashkhabad, which began in 1974 under the leadership of I. S. Masimov; together their discoveries added a new dimension to the scale and complexity of sedentary life on the Central Asian plains during the Bronze Age. At the same time, the work of A. Askarov and his colleagues in southern Uzbekistan (northern Bactria) at the sites, particularly, of Sapalli-tepe and Djarkutan has documented the presence of fortified Bronze Age settlements, closely related to the south Turkmenian sites, in the east at least as far as the narrow mountain valleys of southern Tadjikistan.

Recent non-Soviet investigations in Iran, Afghanistan, and Pakistan have supported the existence of a complex Bronze Age civilization in southern Central Asia. Excavations on the Iranian plateau at Tepe Sang-e Caxmaq by S. Masuda[15] have reconfirmed the earlier discovery at Yarim Tepe near Gonbad-i Gabus of a Neolithic Djeitun horizon in northeastern Iran; when recalibrated, a reported radiocarbon date of "about 7800 B.P." from the third of five levels in the site's western mound extends the emergence of sedentary Neolithic Djeitun-related sites back to the midseventh millennium. Surveys conducted by the Hiroshima University Scientific Expedition to Iran in the western Gorgan Plain have recorded over one hundred sites that date to the Bronze and Early Iron Age; [16] a similar dense concentration of Bronze Age settlements for the eastern Gorgan Plain has been documented by the Iranian Archeological Service under Y. Kiani.[17] Surveys and a sounding at Yom Tepe in the Upper Atrek Valley conducted by Turin University in 1976-78[18] discovered Aeneolithic, Bronze, and Iron Age materials in northern Iranian Khorassan that were identical to those from southern

Turkmenia; similar results were obtained in 1978 for the Darreh Gaz Plain immediately south of Kara-depe and Namazga-depe in Iran.[19]

Further east the discovery in 1975 of Harappan settlements on the Shortugai Plain northeast of Ai Khanoum in Badakhshan, Afghanistan, has received considerable, well-deserved attention;[20] the terminal Central Asian Vaksh- and Beshkent-related occupations of the Shortugai sites raise significant problems as to the date and nature of the "steppe" cultures of southern Tadjikistan.[21] Perhaps even more important are the recent discoveries of a Late Bronze Central Asian cemetery and settlement, Sibri Damb, at the foot of the Bolan Pass in northern Pakistan. This recent discovery, made during the excavations at Mehrgarh by the French Archeological Mission,[22] suggests a possibly substantial influx of peoples south from Central Asia into Baluchistan whose material culture closely resembles that from late Namazga V levels in sites located along the Kopet Dagh piedmont strip and in the northwesternmost oases of the former Murghab Delta. Their work undoubtedly will force archeologists to reevaluate late third millennium materials from southeastern Iran and from sites and cemeteries in Baluchistan, which were originally sampled by Stein. The presence of a Harappan settlement, Nowsharo, in immediate proximity to the Central Asian site also promises to supplement considerably our sketchy understanding of the chronological and economic and social relationships that existed between these two Bronze Age civilizations.[23]

2. Ecological Setting

Our current understanding of cultural evolution in the "northeastern frontier of the ancient Near East" is best documented along the narrow piedmont strip or atak (skirt) formed by the Kopet Dagh Mountains that separate Iranian Khorassan and the Iranian plateau from the Kara Kum Desert. This zone is watered by seasonal runoff from streams flowing down from the Kopet Dagh which are fed mostly by ground waters with a relatively stable discharge.[24] Meters of alluvial deposit that have been carried down by these streams into the Kara Kum have buried the earliest levels of major sites, such as Altyn and Namazga-depe, and undoubtedly obliterated the remains of smaller Neolithic and Aeneolithic sites. One sounding at Altyn-depe revealed cultural deposits extending eight meters below the contemporary level of the plain, a fact that must be remembered when assessing settlement patterns in the piedmont zone. Both from a geomorphological and cultural perspective, the atak can be divided into three sections:[25] the Atak-i-Kelat, an eastern section stretching from the Ab-i Khur or stream that waters the district of Chacha west to Dushak; a central section, the Darreh Gaz Atak, stretching from the Ab-i Archingar and the region of Kaakha west to Gawars; and the western, Akhal Atak, which extends from Anau to Kyzyl Arvat. The Darreh Gaz or central section is the only area to have an extensive upland plain, which is now in Iran and is known to contain at least four sites with prehistoric materials identical to those from Kara-depe and Namazga-depe. It is important to note the physical separation of the western, Akhal Atak, section. The streams that water it are less numerous than those to the east and, more significantly, are more removed from the former broad terminal fan of the Tedjen River. The desert to the north always was a much more immediate and untempered reality the further west one proceeded along the piedmont strip. Moreover, tributaries, such as the Sumbar, that flow into the Lower Atrek readily connect this western section with the Meshed-Misrian and Gorgan plains to the west.

The prehistoric investigations of R. Biscione, from Turin University, in the Upper Atrek Valley, roughly between Quchan and Shirvan led to the discovery of Neolithic through Iron Age sites with material remains identical to those from south-central and southeastern Turkmenistan. This discovery is of cardinal importance, for it strongly suggests that the valley formed by the Kashaf Rud, which flows past Meshed before entering the Tedjen River, likewise should contain prehistoric settlements relating to the Namazga and Altyn sequences and not to those documented further west on the Iranian plateau (Sialk-Hissar) or on the Gorgan Plain (Tureng-tepe, Shah-tepe). That is, present evidence suggests that most of northern Iranian Khorassan, which primarily consists of high intermontane valleys, developed from the beginnings of settled life through the advent of the Iron Age in close association with the major settled communities of the northern piedmont strip.

Investigations in the Geoksyur Oasis in southeastern Turkmenistan and in the former terminal fan of the Murghab River, which extended as far as 120 kilometers north-northwest of Mari, have revealed substantial evidence for occupation of a lowland zone watered by the Tedjen and Murghab rivers. These rivers effectively formed a "little Central Asian Mesopotamia"[26] that was con-

sidered a most prosperous and fertile area even in antiquity.[27]
Satellite LANDSAT imagery for the area shows an extensive takyr
(i.e., an alkaline soil formation consisting of clays with algae and
lichens) front extending west nearly to Geok-tepe, roughly 50 km
west of Ashkhabad; this front presumably was formed by the northern and western extension of the Tedjen and Murghab rivers.
Maps compiled in the nineteenth century, when the area was much
more sparsely occupied and the waters of these rivers far less
utilized than today, frequently depict the extension of the Murghab
and Tedjen far to the northwest, deep into the Kara Kum.[28] Figure 1, which maps sites mentioned in this chapter, outlines from
the satellite imagery the rough extension of these clay deposits.
It is significant that the northern and eastern edges of this takyr
front correspond almost precisely with the locations of Bronze Age
settlements along the Lower Murghab. Moreover, it is possible
that several of the Early Neolithic Djeitun sites, including Djeitun
itself, were situated not exclusively along seasonal streams flowing
down from the Kopet Dagh, as has been assumed, but on the edge
of terminal swamps created by the Tedjen. An additional implica-
tion of this front is that a vast lowland zone — a "little Central
Asian Mesopotamia" — exists immediately north of the piedmont
strip, which remains virtually unexplored by archeologists.[29] Similar lowland plains, only slightly better documented, are situated
further west bordering the Caspian, e.g., the Meshed-Misrian and
Gorgan plains.

Thus it is possible to refer to three major regions that formed
the setting for the development of the Namazga civilization: (a) a
fertile piedmont skirt with relatively reliable water sources; (b)
the highland intermontane valleys of northern Iranian Khorassan;
and (c) lowland plains formed chiefly by the former extended fans
of the Murghab and Tedjen rivers. Only the first region has received adequate investigation. The interrelationship between these
regions, such as a possible interregional exchange of highland resources from Khorassan to the lowland, more densely settled communities situated in the piedmont strip or in oases along former
courses of the Tedjen and Murghab, should form a major theme
for future research. The extent of prehistoric settlements in southern Central Asia, now graphically demonstrated by the recent Murghab discoveries, is only beginning to be appreciated. What is
certain is that these Namazga-related sites were situated in a natural setting that allowed densely concentrated sedentary populations to subsist by practicing relatively simple forms of irrigation

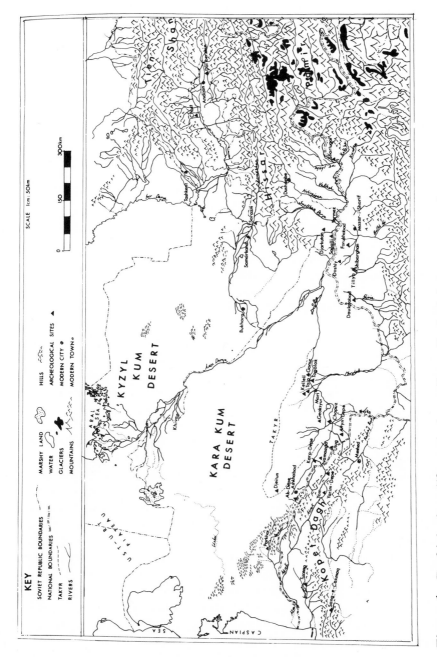

Figure 1. Prehistoric settlements in southern Central Asia: a general map.

agriculture; few regions in inner or outer (Turan) Iran offered a similar potential.[30]

3. Neolithic and Aeneolithic Developments

The earliest stages of the Neolithic or Djeitun period still remain to be investigated, although, as already mentioned, work at Tepe Sang-e Caxmaq on the Iranian plateau near Shahrud extends the sequence back possibly to the midseventh millennium. Soviet archeologists divide the Djeitun period into early, middle, and late subperiods, which, in turn, are further subdivided.[31] Two features should be emphasized. First, present evidence supports an exceptionally broad distribution of sedentary food-producing Djeitun-related communities that extends from southeastern Turkmenistan west nearly to Shahrud on the Iranian plateau; additional analyses are needed to confirm the apparent uniformity of this distribution. Second, the earliest Djeitun sites in southern Turkmenistan cluster near Geok-tepe northwest of Ashkhabad along the western edge of the takyr front representing the terminal extension of the Tedjen River; their spatial distribution may resemble the oases-centered settlements characteristic of later periods (Geoksyur, Lower Murghab). In other words, this Neolithic cluster of sites may have been related to the former terminal fan of the Tedjen and not have been exclusively dependent on runoff from the Kopet Dagh.

Following the interpretation of G. N. Lisitsina, M. Tosi[32] has noted that sites of the Djeitun Culture are situated in the area of the wild distribution of Aeqilops squarrosa, a weed supposed to have hybridized with Triticum boeticum to form T. aestivum, or bread wheat. That is, bread wheat, which is first recognized at a surprisingly late date in West Asia,[33] may first have been domesticated by Djeitun-related peoples in northeastern Iran or southwestern Turkmenistan. Actual carbonized seed remains of T. aestivum have been identified in the Late Djeitun site of Chagylly-depe, although their absence in earlier Djeitun sites may reflect more the methods of retrieval, particularly the nonutilization of flotation, than the actual period when bread wheat first appeared in the area. It also should be noted that camel bones have been found in the basal Aeneolithic levels of the northern mound at Anau,[34] which should date at least to the early fifth millennium.

The type site, Djeitun, was excavated totally; Soviet investigators believe that about thirty nuclear families lived at the site in small single-roomed houses of standardized plan, and that they practiced a simple form of irrigation agriculture while continuing to hunt gazelles. The currently known — though far from complete — distribution of Djeitun settlements in southern Turkmenistan suggests a gradual movement west to east of such food-producing sedentary communities; this move or expansion is perhaps associated both with environmental changes and with improvements in water-management techniques for utilizing the "heavier" water from rivers further upstream to the southeast.

The subsequent Aeneolithic period (Namazga I-III) continues the sequence to the latter part of the fourth millennium and witnesses the beginning of a regionalization or differentiation into distinct cultural zones from the common Djeitun base. Specifically, it is during this period that one first recognizes the basic division into a western cultural zone linking southwestern Turkmenistan (west of Ashkhabad), the Sumbar Valley, and the Meshed-Misrian and Gorgan plains and an eastern zone extending from south-central Turkmenistan to the Geoksyur Oasis and including the Darreh Gaz Plain and the Upper Atrek Valley of northeastern Iran. Analysis of the material remains, such as the prevalence, nature, and date of occurrence of polychrome pottery, suggests the beginnings of further differentiation within the eastern cultural zone, separating the central piedmont strip and northern Khorassan west of the Kashaf Rud, on the one hand, from the southeastern piedmont strip, including Altyn-depe,[35] and the lowland Geoksyur Oasis, on the other. With the possible exception of the still poorly understood Anau IA period, this Aeneolithic sequence seems to represent a continuous and uninterrupted development. It also should be noted that shifts in settlement distribution at the end of the Aeneolithic reveal patterns of the nucleation or consolidation of medium-sized (roughly 12 hectare) settlements, such as Altyn-depe and Ilginli-depe, into major urban centers. Documentation for the Aeneolithic sequence is derived primarily from two sources: excavations at the central piedmont site of Kara-depe and salvage work undertaken at nine sites in the Geoksyur Oasis of the Tedjen River. Our understanding of the Middle and Late Aeneolithic (Namazga II-III) is far more complete than for the earlier Namazga I period, which remains relatively undifferentiated despite deposits ranging in thickness from 6 to 12 meters. Excavations at Kara-depe have revealed a detailed sequence of six levels, the lower five of which relate to the Namazga II period; similarly the Geoksyur Oasis is best defined for the Yalangach (late Namazga II-III) and subsequent Geoksyur phase.

Sites in this oasis are analogous to the later Bronze Age settlements in the Murghab Delta and in northwestern Afghanistan in
that they are clustered along the terminal courses of rivers disappearing into the desert; even more striking is the resemblance
between the fortified "capital" Geoksyur 1 settlement and the later
principal settlements, such as Gonur 1, in the separate oases of
the Murghab Delta. Thus the Geoksyur pattern of a discrete cluster of sites with a central settlement represents a successful adaptation to a specific lowland setting that may have originated much
earlier during Djeitun times and continued on a larger scale during
the Bronze Age. These Geoksyur settlements differ from those
described by Masimov and Sarianidi for the Murghab Delta in one
important respect: their cultural levels are thicker (e.g., Geoksyur 1 with roughly a 10 meter deposit) than those in the Murghab
or Bactrian oases, suggesting much longer occupation. Clearly
more water was available for a longer period in the Geoksyur
Oasis, which was located south and actually east of the terminal
main course of the Tedjen; the east to west shift of the branch of
the Tedjen that watered the oasis, which was proposed by Lisitsina
to explain the abandonment of settlements in the late fourth millennium,[36] probably represents a more episodic phenomenon than the
long-term retraction of the headwaters of the Murghab, which is
suggested by the continuous shift of the Late Bronze and Early
Iron Age settlements to the southeast.

4. The Bronze Age and Methods of Analysis

Nearly all the articles in this volume are concerned with work
relating to the appearance and evolution of urban Bronze Age societies that share numerous material culture traits. The first
section consists of two articles dealing with discoveries chiefly
in southwestern Turkmenistan and northeastern Iran. The article
by I. N. Khlopin presents materials from the recently discovered
Early Bronze Age cemetery, Parkhai II, near Kara Q'ala on the
middle Sumbar River. This material clearly shows the close ties
between southwestern Turkmenistan and the Gorgan Plain of Iran.
The so-called Gorgan graywares, first identified by T. J. Arne,[37]
dominate the materials from the Middle Sumbar, demonstrating
that the major prehistoric cultural division in the area did not
follow the contemporary political border that splits the area into
northern and southern halves but separated the area, as previously

mentioned, into more natural western and eastern zones. The
former included the fertile eastern plains of the Caspian, intermontane valleys formed by the Gorgan, Lower Atrek, and its tributaries, and the narrow, more sparsely watered western atak.
The decrease in proportions of these graywares as one proceeds
east along the piedmont strip is striking. At Parkhai II graywares
represent the characteristic ceramic type; at Ak-depe near Ashkhabad identical carinated vessels are found in nearly equal proportions with painted Namazga III-IV wares;[38] further east at
Kara-depe such wares constitute less than 10 percent of the ceramic corpus, while only isolated sherds have been uncovered at Altyn-
depe. Although other traits of material culture must be correlated
with this distributional patterning of functionally identical ceramic
wares to support our proposed division into eastern and western
cultural zones, it is unlikely that such marked spatial variation
can be explained in functional terms.

Dr. Khlopin's article presents a sociological explanation for
the transformation from the earlier collective vault tombs to
the later single catacomb graves in separate cemeteries. His
comments on the presence of collective vaults within habitation
sites in the lowlands and piedmont belt, on the one hand, and their
occurrence in cemeteries in narrow intermontane valleys, on the
other hand, also are most important and underscore the relative difficulty of locating settlements in mountainous regions where tepes
(mounds) were not formed by the gradual buildup and decay of mud-
brick architecture. This difficulty undoubtedly skews our understanding of early settlement distribution in mountainous regions
such as southern Tadjikistan and Badakhshan.[39]

L. I. Khlopina's dissertation abstract summarizes the Late
Bronze or Namazga VI excavations on the "tower" or summit of
Namazga-depe and relates them to other Late Bronze Age remains
in the area. She also presents detailed arguments for a low absolute dating of the Namazga sequence. It should be noted that these
dates are several hundred years lower than those proposed by other
Soviet investigators, such as V. I. Sarianidi and A. Askarov; but
there is no official Soviet chronology, and Dr. Khlopina's dates are
internally consistent and demand careful evaluation. Arguments
based largely on correspondences of the Central Asian materials
with remains to the south in Iran, Afghanistan, and Pakistan and
on calibrated radiocarbon dates are presented in Part 5 of the
introduction; here we only note possible explanations for the ex-
treme discrepancies — nearly a millennium — between Dr. Khlo-

pina's dates and ours. The most easily resolvable problem concerns her late dating for the advent of the Early Iron Age in Iran; following Dyson's interpretation of corrected dates for Hasanlu and Dinkha Tepe,[40] this period should begin around 1500 B.C. Second, a major difficulty concerns how representative and complete the Namazga VI occupation at Namazga-depe is for the Late Bronze Age of the area as a whole. Work in the Murghab Delta, northern Afghanistan, and southern Uzbekistan has defined distinct subphases for this terminal Bronze Age period; it is hardly conceivable that similar refinements will not be found for contemporaneous developments in the western zone or that area linking the western atak, the Sumbar Valley, and the Meshed-Misrian and Gorgan plains. We already know that dozens of Gorgan grayware sites dot the Gorgan Plain, and future work will undoubtedly define new divisions of this material. We simply are not in a position to determine how specific or diagnostic the parallels Dr. Khlopina cites are for restricting the Late Bronze period to a limited horizon immediately prior to the appearance of sites containing iron artifacts.[41]

Exploratory surveys and soundings have been conducted on a limited scale in northeastern Iran during the last six years. Somewhat unexpectedly, this work has linked northern Iranian Khorassan not with the western zone or area dominated by the presence of the so-called Gorgan graywares but with Namazga-depe, Kara-depe, and sites further to the southeast in Turkmenistan. Future work in the Kashaf Rud will undoubtedly document a similar correspondence and support the existence of a highland component to the Namazga culture which, at least at a site such as Yom Tepe in the fertile Upper Atrek Valley, may have prospered without the aid of the water management techniques that were necessary on the lower skirt or terminal oases of the Kara Kum. What remains unknown, however, is the nature and extent of the interaction between these lowland and highland communities. Only future investigations can determine whether the Namazga-related sites of northern Khorassan exchanged locally available raw materials, such as turquoise and copper ores, for finished goods produced in the larger urban settlements of southeastern Turkmenistan.

Part II presents five articles detailing results of the excavations at Altyn-depe, the second largest and most accessible of the prehistoric centers in the piedmont zone. It is a mound of about 30 hectares, with nearly 30 meters of cultural deposit, and is situated near the village of Meana in southeastern Turkmenistan. The current excavations at the site, which began in 1965 (under the sole direction of V. M. Masson since 1967), not only have refined the Namazga I-V sequence but also have extensively documented the advent of urban life in Central Asia. From a Western perspective one of the most impressive features of these excavations has been their scope and careful planning. Thirteen major excavation units, one of which alone (excavation 9) extends over 6,000 square meters, and three stratigraphic soundings have revealed the architecture, activities, and social structure of this third millennium urban community. Few Near Eastern or South Asian sites of comparable date can duplicate this exposure; and, as Dr. Masson reminds us in Chapters 5 and 6, this work did not concentrate on a single central area but deliberately exposed different quarters to reveal distinct activity and residential areas. Excavations in the craftsmen's quarters (excavation 10), the sacred or ceremonial precinct (excavation 7), the so-called elite quarter (9), and a residential area for relatively prosperous and seemingly self-sufficient burghers (5) have revealed the presence of separate social groups or classes that performed distinct functions and lived and accumulated wealth differentially.

Chapter 3, by V. M. Masson, and Chapter 4, by L. B. Kircho, present the Aeneolithic through Early Bronze sequence at the site. Both articles stress the indigenous and continuous nature of this development. The fifth article, by V. M. Masson and T. P. Kiiatkina, originally appeared in the popular scientific periodical Priroda (Nature); it presents a general overview of the excavations plus a preliminary analysis of several hundred skeletal remains from the site. The next article, "Urban Centers of Early Class Society," by V. M. Masson, reiterates the same conclusions in slightly greater detail; readers may find particularly interesting a description of the excavation techniques employed at the site. Finally, Masson's extended discussion of the discovery of two "proto-Indian" stamp seals in Chapter 7 represents an imaginative — if problematic — reconstruction of the ethnic and linguistic affiliations of the Bronze Age inhabitants of southern Central Asia and the Indian subcontinent prior to the dawn of more complete and decipherable written records. Suffice it to say that these seals are unique finds from Altyn-depe and that the example with the swastika motif, a common design on later Bactrian materials, may or may not indicate contact with South Asia.

The third section presents remarkable new materials from the former Murghab Delta and the northern Bactrian plain which are

probably less familiar to Western readers. Current investigations
in Margiana began in the early seventies. This work, conducted
both by an expedition from Moscow and one from Ashkhabad, considerably amplifies and extends the rich Bactrian discoveries of
the Soviet Archeological Expedition to Afghanistan.[42] In fact the
Bronze Age sites of the Lower Murghab, which extend as far as
about 120 km north-northwest of the contemporary center of Mari,
are larger and more numerous than the closely related Bactrian
settlements. The Soviet investigators define a chronological gra-
dient that stretches from northwest to southeast and is associated
with the gradual retraction of the Murghab. The large-scale colonization of the Murghab oases appears to have occurred near the
end of the Namazga V period, although small Aeneolithic surface
scatters (Namazga III) — possibly associated with the abandonment
of the Geoksyur Oasis — have been located in the northernmost
Kelleli Oasis. Settlements are clustered in groups and typically
are centered around a major site or capital that is frequently fortified; the same patterning occurs on the southern Bactrian Plain
and, as already noted, is reminiscent of the earlier clustering in
the Geoksyur Oasis further south along the Tedjen.

Dr. Sarianidi's first article, "Margiana in the Bronze Age,"
presents a very useful overview of these discoveries and attempts
to reconstruct the historical development and political structure
of the lands of Margush. It should be noted that at least one aspect
of Dr. Sarianidi's reconstruction of tribal movements or migrations
west to east for explaining the colonization of Margiana and Bactria
is open to question, i.e., developments in northern Iranian Khorassan now appear to parallel those along the northern piedmont strip
of the Kopet Dagh and are best lumped together into a single cultural zone. One need not propose a chain reaction of tribal movements stretching from the Damghan and Gorgan plains east, but
can conceptualize a general colonization from a single core area
of high demographic potential and equally high agricultural instability (southern Turkmenistan and Iranian Khorassan) east onto
the Bactrian Plain and south into Baluchistan. The time-honored
question of parallel movements from the Gorgan Plain west onto
the Iranian plateau can only be resolved with more intensive investigations in northern Iran. Doubtless some movement, possibly
associated with more efficient water-management techniques, actually occurred. The Murghab settlements, like their Bactrian
counterparts, appear in areas that surveys have shown were previously unoccupied and do not exhibit long developmental sequences.

Those that have been excavated, such as Sapalli-tepe further east in northern Bactria or the Dashly sites in Afghanistan, present unequivocal evidence for planning, and preliminary soundings on the Murghab sites suggest a similar degree of rapid but controlled development.

I. S. Masimov's article summarizes the investigations of the northern Murghab settlements in the Kelleli, Taip, Adzhi-kui, and Adam Basan oases. Since this article was written, Masimov has mapped additional sites in these oases and conducted a series of soundings; work in the fortress of the capital Taip-depe 1 settlement, in particular, has yielded remarkable results, including the recovery of four distinctive cylinder seals and one cylinder seal impression. The iconography of these seals is as rich and distinctive as that which appears on the Murghab stamp seal amulets, which are described by Sarianidi in Chapter 10.[43] Sarianidi's discussion of these amulets stresses their unique character and attempts to interpret their symbolic content in part through a discussion of later Sanskrit texts and features of Zoroastrian mythology; significantly, he observes the close similarity of these amulets with those found in the Jhukar or post-Harappan levels at Chanhu-daro and also sees a distant parallel to the Hittite seals of Anatolia.[44]

Dr. A. Askarov's contribution summarizes Bronze Age investigations in southern Uzbekistan. As he correctly observes, our entire conception of the depth and complexity of sedentary agricultural communities on the Bactrian Plain has been completely transformed during the past decade. The investigations of the Soviet-Afghanistan expedition and his own work at Sapalli-tepe and Djarkutan have exploded Foucher's frustrated conception of a Bactrian "mirage" or the lack of developed society until much later in historic times. Careful, exhaustive surveys undertaken in southern Uzbekistan clearly reveal the sudden appearance of sedentary planned communities, such as Sapalli-tepe, on the north Bactrian Plain and suggest deliberate colonization from the west. Northern Bactria contains fewer Bronze Age sites than the larger and more fertile plain south of the Amu Darya, and it should be emphasized that this pattern prevails until a pronounced increase in settlements in northern Bactria is observed for the Kushan period.[45] Dr. Askarov's description of his material is lucid and straightforward, though he only refers briefly to the cardinal discovery of silk in graves at Sapalli-tepe.[46] While it is apparently true that silkworms are indigenous to southern Central Asia, this

discovery immediately raises the question of contacts with East
Asia, since cocoons of silkworms have been found in fifth millennium Yang-shao sites in northwestern China.[47] Intriguingly, intricate compartmented bronze seals, which clearly developed from
earlier drilled stone amulets and occur repeatedly on Middle and
Late Bronze Age sites in Central Asia, closely resemble seals
collected by Christian missionaries in the 1920s in the Ordos region of northwestern China (Figures 2a and 2b).[48] Final determination of the historical relationship, if any, between these Chinese
seals and the compartmented Bronze Age seals of Central Asia
must, of course, await their discovery in an undisturbed archeological context in westernmost China (Xinjiang).

The existence of East to Central Asian Bronze Age connections
is perhaps strengthened by the discovery of an extensive Late
Aeneolithic (?) to Early Bronze Age (Namazga IV) settlement,
Sarazm, along the left bank of the Middle Zeravshan River, roughly
midway between Pendjikent and Samarkand. The preliminary report of the recent excavations at this site by A. I. Isakov illustrates
the materials used to synchronize this original and distinctive culture with the southern Turkmenian sequence. If the parallels,
particularly in rare painted sherds, truly allow us to establish an
early third millennium date for the site, then it is clear that southern Turkmenistan did not simply represent "the northeastern
frontier of the ancient Near East" or the final area affected by the
Neolithic and urban revolutions of West Asia, for the simple reason that it too transmitted the innovations associated with these
processes further to the northeast. In other words, the Kara Kum
Desert was not a totally effective barrier for preventing the spread
of food-producing communities north into the eastern intermontane
valleys of Central Asia. The site, which extends for several hundred meters in all directions, was discovered accidentally; it is
not a tepe or mound with an extensive cultural deposit but a low-
lying site with remains of structures and artifacts strewn inter-
mittently across a broad area. In mountainous areas such sites
are more difficult to detect than the classic mounds of broader
valleys and plains, and it is for this reason that we must constantly
remind ourselves of the lacunae in the archeological record. The
only prior indication of agricultural, Namazga-related communities
along the Zeravshan came from the site of Zamanbaba near the
Bukhara Oasis; although its distinctive mixture of "steppe" and
Kelteminar elements with southern Turkmenian traits appears to
be later than Sarazm, its close links with the southern Bactrian

materials, particularly those from the Farukhabad and Nichkin oases, suggest considerable interaction in the early second millennium, if not, as Sarianidi[49] argues, the movement of peoples south to north into the classical center of Central Asian civilization. The discovery of Sarazm also raises the question of whether the origin and beginning date for the food-producing Chust Culture of the Fergana Valley is fully resolved;[50] it is useful to recall J.-M. Casal's belief[51] that Chust or Chust-related peoples were responsible for the demise of Mundigak V, a theory that implies an earlier than late-second-millennium date for the beginnings of this culture. Present evidence is far from conclusive but suggests that food-producing cultures of the "Middle Eastern type" may have spread from southern Turkmenia to the borders of Xinjiang, China, as early as the third millennium B.C. and may have provided the backdrop for the exchange of materials, such as silk and metals, between two major cultural areas.

A similar problem of the possibly unrepresentative and limited nature of present evidence is implicit in L. T. P'iankova's useful summary of Bronze Age materials from southern Tadjikistan. New discoveries of habitation sites in southern Tadjikistan[52] suggest the presence of, at least, semipermanent agricultural communities alongside the extensive burial mounds usually attributed to nomadic pastoralists; more complete documentation of such sites will undoubtedly emerge when the current surveys by Vinogradova and P'iankova are completed in the Lower Kyzyl Su Valley, an area almost directly north of the Bronze Age discoveries on the Shortugai Plain in northeastern Afghanistan. As the excavator H.-P. Francfort has shown,[53] the terminal occupations of the Shortugai sites are closely related to the so-called Vakhsh and Beshkent cultures of southern Tadjikistan and raise questions as to their exclusively pastoral character. That is, the extensively excavated dispersed cemetery sites of southern Tadjikistan probably should not be interpreted as separate "archeological cultures" of steppe pastoralists but as possibly seasonal components of larger, more complex systems that maintained habitation sites, practiced agriculture, and processed locally available resources.

The fourth section of the book consists of articles illustrating the utilization of natural and physical scientific techniques and experimental methods for Central Asian prehistory. All the articles are concerned with documenting basic productive activities: irrigation agriculture, metallurgy, and harvesting practices.

N. N. Terekhova's contribution on the nature of early metallurgical

Figure 2a.

Figure 2b.

production in Central Asia summarizes the results of her candidate's dissertation, the substantive and detailed results of which have been published in a much longer article.[54] In this abstract Terekhova presents the largely indigenous development of the Central Asian metallurgical industry from Anau IA times through the Late Bronze Age as reconstructed from the analyses of about 300 artifacts. Noteworthy are specific features, such as the utilization of cast blanks or rods that were further worked and the initial exploitation of plumbous copper followed by the later deliberate alloying of lead with copper, which both distinguish this metallurgical tradition and link it to historically related industries, such as that at Shahr-i Sokhta in the Iranian Seistan.[55] Terekhova believes that the earliest stages in metalworking developed further west, but she stresses the early appearance of casting and other complex techniques in the Central Asian sequence. This elaboration is particularly significant if we revise upward her absolute dates to correspond with recalibrated C14 determinations and the synchronisms proposed below. In what way and to what extent the further elaboration of this industry, reflected now in the rich Bactrian finds of the Late Bronze Age, influenced or affected the development of metalworking techniques in South or even in East Asia are questions that must await additional research.

Although G. F. Korobkova's impressive investigation on the productivity of the earliest harvesting tools in the USSR goes somewhat beyond the spatial and temporal limits of this volume, it illustrates the use of experimental studies in Soviet archeology. A student and colleague of the late S. A. Semenov, who pioneered microscopic tracewear analysis, Korobkova shows how his method can be extended to answer different questions, such as the size of field plots for the early agriculturalists. Assumptions in her calculations for Djeitun are problematic (e.g., complete recovery or the utilization of all harvesting knives within a single year), but the potential value of her study must be acknowledged. As she argues, her results should be compared with those derived by totally independent methods, and when they coincide, as in the Djeitun example, should be accepted with greater confidence. Study of the productivity of the harvesting implements also can help determine which traits have cultural (e.g., shape of the handle) and which technological (inset flaking) significance.

Lisitsina's article[56] presents a summary evolutionary model for the development of water-management techniques in prehistoric Central Asia. Her claim that the earliest sedentary sites are associ-

ated exclusively with runoff from the Kopet Dagh Mountains may
need to be revised in light of previously cited evidence for the extension of the Tedjen River far to the northwest; as Dr. Lisitsina
notes, it is unfortunate that the earliest irrigation works for sites
in the piedmont belt cannot be traced due to later alluvial deposits.
The investigations of the Aeneolithic settlements in the Geoksyur
Oasis of the Tedjen have provided the most complete record for
early irrigation systems in the area, which are now complemented
and amplified by the rich discoveries of Late Bronze Age sites in
the Lower Murghab. As is to be expected, the best evidence for extensive irrigation networks comes from the lowland plains, such
as the Meshed-Misrian Plain, which slopes down toward the Caspian, or along the terminal extensions of the Murghab and Tedjen
rivers. When large-scale extensive irrigation systems, such as
those of the Early Iron Age Dakhistan complex that apparently drew
off and conserved waters from the distant Sumbar and Atrek rivers,[57] or the qanat network unequivocally attested at Ulug-depe,[58]
first began and to what extent they radically modified the natural
landscape and led to the retreat or diminution of water courses
further downstream remain important unresolved questions. While
Dr. Lisitsina does not refer to such standardized procedures for
obtaining quantitative palaeobotanical data as flotation, she and
other Soviet investigators interested in the development of subsis-
tence practices in Central Asia[59] have examined available aerial
photos to trace the remains of ancient irrigation canals, which
they have then visited, measured, and excavated in order to determine their date and reason for abandonment. Data on the scale
and development of Central Asian irrigation technology are exceptionally complete and provide a marvelous source for comparison
with Mesopotamian and other well-known developmental sequences.
   Dr. Dolukhanov's article (a manuscript received just as this
volume was going to press) presents a detailed summary of the
environmental features that helped shape the Bronze Age civilization of southern Turkmenia. His emphasis on the relatively stable
water sources for the piedmont strip compared to the tremendous
variability in the discharge of the Murghab and Tedjen rivers has
profound implications for prehistoric settlements in the area and
supports our distinction between lowland and piedmont sites. Likewise significant is his observation that the amount of water reaching southern Turkmenia from the Tedjen depends partly on the
utilization of this river upstream in Iran and Afghanistan. Some
day it might be possible to document how settlements along the

Kashaf Rud, a major upstream tributary, affected settlements in
the lowland plains of southern Turkmenia. Dr. Dolukhanov correctly insists that the earliest food-producing sites in southern
Turkmenistan developed from an even earlier base, presumably
in northern Iran, and presents the traditional Soviet interpretation
for the setting of the western cluster of Neolithic sites, which con-
flicts with our suggestion, based upon the satellite data, that these
sites also may have been exploiting the terminal waters of the
Tedjen. This problem demands further study, but it should be
noted that the type of small-scale liman or estuary irrigation and
damming techniques postulated for these sites also could have
been employed to control and modify slightly the swamps and
marshes formed by the lower reaches of the Tedjen.

Finally, the afterword by C. C. Lamberg-Karlovsky places the
recent Soviet discoveries in Central Asia in the broader context
of archeological investigations from Mesopotamia to the Indus
Valley. His demonstration of shared beliefs or mutually understood, complex symbols between widely disparate areas conclusively shows that ideas diffused together with materials and techniques, and it echoes the Soviet interpretations of Sarianidi on the
Murghab seals and Masson on cult objects from Altyn-depe. Although the dichotomy between ideological bonds and economic practices seems forced and the assertion that intercultural relations
were not economically significant is problematic, his comments
eloquently correct the archeological bias of emphasizing material
remains while neglecting the more subtle, meaningful adoption of
complex patterns of communication. The transfer of ideas as well
as goods had profound consequences for the simple reason that
firmly held beliefs also help shape and direct man's productive
activities.

5. Chronology

For several years Western archeologists working in Iran and
Palestine have questioned the low Soviet dating advanced by Masson
and Sarianidi in their English monograph Central Asia: Turkmenia
before the Achaemenids.[60] It is important to realize that there is
no universally accepted or orthodox Soviet dating system; as discussed above, the Khlopins favor an even later date for the end of
the Bronze Age sequence in southern Turkmenia, while Masson
now appears ready to accept earlier absolute dates, at least for the
Middle and Late Aeneolithic periods. This dating problem cannot

be discussed in detail in this introductory chapter;[61] however, it must be mentioned that the recalibration of Soviet carbon dates and their correlations with recent excavations in Iran, Afghanistan, and Pakistan support an even higher chronology than previously proposed.

The only Soviet review of radiocarbon determinations from Central Asia appeared in 1972 and does not include more recently obtained dates, particularly those from Bactria.[62] If one assembles all the dates reported in the literature, adjusts them to the 5730 half-life, and applies the correction factors advocated by the MASCA Laboratories in Philadelphia, a fairly consistent sequence of nearly fifty dates is obtained that pushes the Central Asian sequence back even slightly earlier than Western archeologists have favored. Dates for the Neolithic and Aeneolithic periods are particularly incomplete, though the cited date from the Djeitun-related site of Tepe Sang-e Caxmaq in northern Iran would push the beginnings of this sequence back as early as the midseventh millennium. Dates are more complete for the Late Aeneolithic period (Namazga III) and suggest a range extending roughly from 3600 to 3000 B.C. The Early Bronze or Namazga IV period follows with three determinations suggesting a date ranging from 3000 to 2600 B.C. Dates for the important Namazga V period are less consistent but would support an extension of the sequence down to about 2200-2100 B.C. The initial expansion of Central Asian settlements into the Lower Murghab and onto the northern and southern Bactrian Plain would then have occurred in the last centuries of the third millennium; and the development of this culture, particularly in southern Bactria, and the abandonment of the piedmont belt (Namazga VI) would have continued throughout the first half of the second millennium, or down to the beginnings of the Early Iron Age (Yaz I); this period in turn would correlate more or less precisely with the advent of the Early Iron Age in northwestern Iran. Refinement of the Late Bronze or Namazga VI period in particular is needed; this process has begun for Margiana and Bactria but is still urgently required for the piedmont strip and southwestern Turkmenistan.

This proposed sequence, derived from the recalibration of radiocarbon dates, corresponds well with correlations established by recent excavations in Iran, Pakistan, and Afghanistan. Both Tosi[63] and Biscione[64] have hypothesized that the initial settlement of Shahr-i Sokhta and Iranian Seistan was related to a movement south from Turkmenistan in terminal Geoksyur times, a migration that also possibly can be observed further east with the appearance of

the so-called Quetta wares.[65] The earliest settlement of Shahr-i
Sokhta contains proto-Elamite sealings and a single tablet[66] and
can be equated to the proto-Elamite or IVC occupation at Tepe
Yahya,[67] which can be firmly dated to the beginning of the third
millennium, about 3000-2900 B.C. Similarly, the reexcavations
of Tepe Hissar in 1976 have yielded a consistent series of radiocarbon dates that support a high chronology for this troublesome
site, including a terminal fourth–early third mellennium date for
Schmidt's Hissar IIB period.[68]

The exceptionally important and productive excavations at Mehrgarh at the foot of the Bolan Pass in Pakistani Baluchistan soon
will help determine the date for a second major southern expansion
of Central Asian-related settlements. A separate "Central Asian"
site, Sibri Damb, with pottery identical to late Namazga V–early
Namazga VI wares and figurines resembling those from the Kelleli
Oasis in the Lower Murghab, was discovered a few kilometers
south of Mehrgarh in close proximity to a large Harappan mound,
Nowsharo.[69] A "Central Asian" cemetery with late Namazga V
materials completely foreign to the Mehrgarh sequence (which apparently ends about 2500 B.C.) has been partially excavated on the
outskirts of Mehrgarh. The exact chronological and functional interrelationship between the Harappans and "Central Asians" will
have to be determined through future excavations; current evidence,
however, supports a late third millennium date for the advent of
the Namazga-related peoples. Recalibrated dates for the terminal
Shortugai IV or Vakhsh-related culture of northeastern Afghanistan suggests occupation at the end of the third and beginning of
the second millennium, a date that correlates well with a corrected determination from a kurgan at the slightly later Tigrovaia
Balkh cemetery of 1870-1600 B.C. (LE 715).

The table on page xxxi summarizes the chronology proposed in
this chapter for the Central Asian sequence.

6. Conclusion

Since the end of World War II Soviet archeologists have uncovered
an extensive Bronze Age civilization in southern Central Asia; the
scale and significance of this civilization that formed in the intermontane valleys of Iranian Khorassan, along the fertile atak or
northern slopes of the Kopet Dagh Mountains and in the lowland
plains, watered, in particular, by the Tedjen and Murghab rivers,
are just now beginning to be appreciated; later the eastern mani-

Period	Archeological sites	Dates B.C.
Namazga III	Altyn 9-10, Geoksyur 1, Kara-depe 1, Chong-depe (terminal NMG III: Yahya IVC, Shahr-i Sokhta I (10-9) Damb Sadaat II, Hissar IIB)	3600-3000
Namazga IV	Altyn 4-8, Ulug-depe, Ak-depe, Parkhai II, Sarazm, Khapuz-depe (III-XII) (Shahr-i Sokhta II (7-5), Mundigak IV, 1-2)	3000-2600
Namazga V	Altyn 1-3, Khapuz-depe (I-II), Namazga-depe (Mehrgarh cemetery (?), Mundigak IV, 3, Shahr-i Sokhta III (4-3), Hissar IIIB, Shortugai I (?)	2600-2200
Namazga V-VI (Kelleli phase)	Kelleli, Girdai-depe(?), Sapalli (Sibri Damb (?), Shortugai II-III, Shahr-i Sokhta IV (2-0), Hissar IIIC (?)	2300-2100
Namazga VIa (Gonur phase)	Gonur, Taip-depe, early Dashly (?), Djarkutan (Shortugai IV)	2100-1800
Namazga VIb (Togolok phase)	Togolok, Takhirbai, late Dashly(?), Farukhabad, Vakhsh, Molali, Sumbar, Namazga "Tower," Zamanbaba	1800-1500

festation of this civilization spread east and south to interact with
complex cultures emerging in South and, possibly, East Asia. The
Bronze Age or Namazga civilization of Central Asia assumed a
distinctive and characteristic form that was shaped by its peculiarly unstable ecological setting along rivers that drained into the
sands of the Kara Kum. Sites were clustered in separate oases
along these terminal courses at least as early as the Aeneolithic
period. Similarly, the location of this culture between the complex
riverine civilizations of the Near East to the south and the densely
settled but poorly developed Aeneolithic and hunting and gathering
cultures to the north[70] exercised a profound influence on its internal development. The Namazga peoples had extensive ceramic and
metallurgical industries and utilized wheel transport in the form
of Bactrian camels harnessed to carts as early as the beginning of
the third millennium. Archeological evidence supports a possible
movement from southern Turkmenistan south to the Seistan and
the Quetta Valley in terminal Namazga III times; a more substantial and better-documented expansion east across the Bactrian
Plain and south into Baluchistan appears to have occurred at the
end of the Namazga V period. Whether this movement, which may
have been associated with the rise of mounted pastoral nomadism
among the "steppe" cultures to the north, marked the beginning of
the well-known historical pattern for the penetration of peoples
from Central Asia into the Middle East and the Indian subcontinent
must await future research. In any event it is undeniable that some
colonization of Bactria and some replacement of indigenous cultures
in Baluchistan took place, and this had a profound impact on the
subsequent history of the area. A parallel and roughly contemporaneous spread westward across northern Iran from the Gurgan
and Meshed-Misrian plains and the southwestern atak remains a
viable hypothesis that deserves further investigation.

Excavations in Central Asia raise significant evolutionary and
historical questions. A detailed comparison of the Central Asian
developmental sequence with those from the other, more strictly
riverine civilizations of the Old World would provide striking parallels and contrasts. Why the Namazga peoples largely abandoned
the piedmont strip and settled in new areas throughout most of the
first half of the second millennium is a question that cannot be answered solely from traditional archeological evidence; more so-
phisticated cooperation with specialists in the natural sciences is
needed to distinguish natural from human-induced environmental
changes. Much work needs to be done, but it is clear that system-

atic investigations in Central Asia, which began scarcely thirty years ago, already have documented an important chapter in the prehistory of the greater Near East. It is hoped that this volume of translations will make available some of this recent work to a broader scholarly community and help facilitate additional cooperation between archeologists of various nations. Our understanding of cultural evolution, in general, and of the unique and pivotal role of southern Central Asia, in particular, can only increase and benefit from such cooperation.

Notes

1. From November 13, 1978, to February 9, 1979, the author visited Moscow, Leningrad, Dushanbe, and Ashkhabad on the U.S. National Academy of Sciences exchange program with the Soviet Academy of Sciences; from March 25 to June 10, 1979, the author worked in Leningrad and in Uzbekistan on the International Research and Exchanges Board (IREX) Senior Scholar exchange program with the Soviet Ministry of Higher Education and the Office of Foreign Affairs (Inotdel) at Tashkent State University. The help of all relevant agencies, both Soviet and American, is gratefully acknowledged; I would particularly like to thank Mr. Robert Forcey, formerly of the Section on the USSR and Eastern Europe at the U.S. National Academy of Sciences, and Ms. Carolyn Rodgers at IREX for patiently fulfilling numerous requests.

2. V. M. Masson and V. I. Sarianidi, Central Asia: Turkmenia before the Achaemenids, London, Thames and Hudson, 1972; S. P. Gupta, Archaeology of Soviet Central Asia and the Iranian Borderlands, Delhi, B. R. Publishing Corporation, 1979. An additional major synthesis of Central Asian prehistory, which usefully outlines the ecological features of the area, also, unfortunately, does not include the most recent Bronze Age discoveries on the Central Asian plains; see M. Tosi, "The Northeastern Frontier of the Ancient Near East," Mesopotamia, 1973-74, vol. 13-14.

3. Dr. Masson recommended all the articles on Altyn-depe in Part II (Chapters 4-8), Chapters 10 and 11 in Part III, and all the articles in Part IV (Chapters 14-17).

4. For example, a detailed analysis of metal objects from Altyn-depe by L. B. Kircho, "Metallicheskie izdeliia epokhi eneolita i bronzy Altyn-depe," Sovetskaia arkheologiia, 1980, no. 1, pp. 158-74; short reports of new discoveries in Central Asia in Uspekhi sredneaziatskoi arkheologii, 1979, no. 4, pp. 79-85; and major articles by Masson, Sarianidi, and Askarov in Etnografiia i arkheologiia Srednei Azii, Moscow, 1979.

5. R. Pumpelly, Explorations in Turkestan, vols. 1 and 2, Carnegie Institute, Washington, 1905, 1908.

6. See H. Frankfort, Early Studies of the Pottery of the Near East, 1924, pp. 76-84.

7. Contrast, for example, the interpretation of L. W. King in A History of Sumer and Akkad, pp. 356 ff., or the more reasoned views of Frankfort in Early Studies, with the rather cursory discussion by Schaeffer in Stratigraphie Comparee et Chronologie de l'Asie Occidentale, Oxford, 1948, p. 598, or of Childe

in the final edition of New Light on the Most Ancient East, pp. 193 ff.

8. See E. Atagarryev and O. Berdyev, "The Archaeological Exploration of Turkmenistan in the Years of Soviet Power," East and West, XX, pp. 285-306.

9. See, however, M. A. Itina, Istoriia stepnykh plemen iuzhnogo priaral'ia, Moscow, 1977, and A. V. Vinogradov and E. D. Mamedov, Pervobytnyi Liavliakan, Moscow, 1975, for documentation of earlier materials in Khoresmia and the Kyzyl Kum.

10. B. A. Kuftin, "Polevoi otchet: o rabote XIV otriada IuTAKE po izucheniiu kul'tury pervobytno-oshchinykh osedlozemledel'cheskikh poselenii epokhy medy i bronzy v 1952 g.," Trudy IuTAKE, vol. 7, Ashkhabad, 1956.

11. A. P. Okladnikov, "Drevneishie arkheologicheskie pamiatniki Krasnovod-skogo poluostrova," Trudy IuTAKE, vol. 2, Ashkhabad, 1947; "Peshchera Dzhebel — pamiatnik drevnei kul'tury prikaspiiskikh plemen Turkmenii," Trudy IuTAKE, vol. 7, Ashkhabad, 1956.

12. V. M. Masson, Poselenie Dzheitun, MIA, no. 180, Leningrad, 1971.

13. I. N. Khlopin, "Dashlidzhy-depe i eneoliticheskie zemledel'tsy iuzhnogo Turkmenistana," vol. 10, Trudy IuTAKE, Ashkhabad, 1961, pp. 134-224; Eneolit iuzhnykh oblastei Srednei Azii, Arkheologiia SSSR svod arkheologicheskikh isto-chnikov, B 3-8, Moscow-Leningrad, 1963; Geoksiurskaia gruppa poselenii epokhi eneolita, Leningrad, 1964; "Aeneoliticheskoe poselenie Geokiur (rezultaty rabot 1956-1957 gg.)," vol. 10, Trudy IuTAKE, pp. 225-318; Pamiatniki pozdnego eneolita iugo-vostochnoi Turkmenii, Arkheologiia SSSR, Moscow, 1965; V. M. Masson, Eneolit iuzhnykh oblastei Srednei Azii, Moscow-Leningrad, 1962.

14. V. M. Masson, "Kara-depe u Artyka," Trudy IuTAKE, vol. 10, pp. 319-463, Ashkhabad, 1961.

15. S. Masuda, "Tepe Sang-e Caxmaq," Iran, vol. 12, 1974, pp. 222-23, and "Report of the Archaeological Investigations at Sahrud 1975," in Proceedings of the IVth Annual Symposium on Archaeological Research in Iran, Teheran, 1976, pp. 63-70.

16. H. Shiomi, Archaeological Map of the Gorgan Plain, Iran no. 1, Hiro-shima, 1976; Archaeological Map of the Gorgan Plain, Iran no. 2, Hiroshima, 1978.

17. I am indebted to Michael Ingraham, who accompanied Dr. Kiani to the Gurgan Plain in fall 1978, for this information.

18. R. Biscione, "Prehistoric Connections between Central Asia and the Iranian Plateau and the Role of the Upper Atrek Valley," in Proceedings of the Vth Symposium on Archaeological Research in Iran, Teheran, in press; and "The Sondage at Tappeh Yam," Proceedings of the VIth Symposium on Archaeological Research in Iran, Teheran, in press.

19. D. L. Heskel and P. L. Kohl, "Archaeological Reconnaissances in the Darreh Gaz Plain: A Short Report," Iran, 1980, XVIII, pp. 160-72.

20. H.-P. Francfort and M.-H. Pottier, "Sondage Preliminaire sur l'etablis-sement protohistorique Harapeén et post-Harapeén de Shortugai (Afghanistan du N.-E.)," Arts Asiatiques, 1978, vol. 34, pp. 29-79.

21. Problems with the interpretation of the late periods at Shortugai were discussed by H.-P. Francfort in a stimulating paper presented at the Fifth Inter-national Conference of the Association of South Asian Archeologists in Western Europe in Berlin (Federal Republic), July 1979. For the distribution of Bronze Age and later settlements in northeastern Afghanistan, see the recent detailed publication by J.-C. Gardin and B. Lyonnet, "La Prospection Archeologique de la Bactriane Orientale (1974-1978: Premier Resultats)," Mesopotamia, 1978-79, vol. 13-14, pp. 99-154.

22. For a summary of these incredibly important excavations which document a Neolithic transition for the Indus plain, see J.-F. Jarrige and M. Lechevallier, "Excavations at Mehrgahr, Baluchistan: Their Significance in the Prehistorical Context of the Indo-Pakistani Borderlands," in South Asian Archaeology 1977, ed. by M. Taddei, Naples, Fla., 1979, pp. 463-535; and J. F. Jarrige and R. H. Meadow, "The Antecedents of Civilization in the Indus Valley," Scientific American, August 1980, pp. 122-33.

23. The results of the 1979-80 campaign at Mehrgarh were presented at a seminar at Harvard University in April 1980 by Dr. J.-F. Jarrige. I am grateful to Dr. Jarrige and his wife Catherine for discussing at length with me their tantalizing "Central Asian" materials.

24. In a recent article, "Ecological Prerequisites of Early Farming in Southern Turkmenia" (ms.), Dr. P. M. Dolukhanov, a geomorphologist at the Leningrad Sector of the Institute of Archaeology, contrasts the stability of the piedmont streams with the fluctuating discharge of the Murghab and Tedjen rivers, which depend on rainfall. Agriculture is a much more uncertain undertaking along the terminal fans of these latter rivers.

25. G. C. Napier, "Extracts from a Diary of a Tour in Khorassan and Notes on the Eastern Alborz Tract," Journal of the Royal Geographical Society, 1876, vol. 46, pp. 138-39; and V. M. Masson and V. I. Sarianidi, Central Asia: Turkmenia before the Achaemenids, p. 56.

26. The "major" or "large Central Asian Mesopotamia," of course, refers to the area between the Amu Darya and Syr Darya. The analogy to Mesopotamia is remote, and further study should focus on the differences rather than the similarities between the lowland zone of southern-central and southern Iraq. For comparison, however, we note that the Tedjen, "the Euphrates" of the system, today extends for roughly 1,150 km, with its headwaters above Herat, and drains about 70,600 sq km; the Murghab or "Tigris," which peaks earlier, is roughly 978 km long and drains 46,900 sq km. One obvious contrast with Mesopotamia is that the longer Tedjen has larger and more numerous tributaries and has a catchment area nearly half again as large as that drained by the Murghab. See A. V. Platsev and B. A. Chekmarev, Gidrografiia SSSR, Leningrad, 1978, pp. 182-84.

27. Citing as his sources Pliny and Strabo, Sir H. Rawlinson believed that a southern tributary of the Oxus River, which was known as the Ochus and distinct from the Uzboi tributary, flowed immediately north of the atak or piedmont strip and west into the Uzboi and ultimately the Caspian Sea. He wrote:

> When that river was running, the whole of what was now desert
> formed one of the richest parts of Asia. It was the home of the
> Nisaea horses, which took their name from the town of Nissa,
> near Ashkhabad. It was the cradle indeed of the Parthian race;
> for the Parthians were not mere desert warriors, but possessed
> a very fertile country; and it was from the strength of these
> resources that they were able to conquer all Persia and found
> the great Parthian Empire.

Reprinted in The Country of the Turkomans: An Anthology of Exploration from the Royal Geographical Society, Oguz Press, 1977, p. 170. See also Rawlinson's "Map of the Turcoman Steppe and Northern Khorassan," for his article "The Road to Merv" reprinted in the same volume. Incredibly, LANDSAT imagery reveals a southern tributary of the Oxus that flows north of the westward extension of the Tedjen and the atak before joining the Uzboi south of the Balkhan Mountains to debouch into the Caspian. Only field work, of course, can document

Philip L. Kohl

whether this tributary flowed in antiquity; if it did not, the area's reported fertility could have related simply to the former westward extension of the Tedjen.

28. For example, the map in The Merv Oasis, vol. 2, by E. O'Donovan, New York, 1883, and the author's description of the Tedjen swamp, pp. 448-49.

29. A long article currently is being prepared by M. Tosi and P. L. Kohl, tentatively entitled "The Lands of Prehistoric Turkmenia," which will present this evidence in greater depth.

30. The Kur River basin in Fars Province of southern Iran possibly represents an area on the plateau conducive to such a dense settlement pattern. See W. M. Sumner, "The Malyan Project: Introduction," Problems of Large-Scale, Multi-Disciplinary Regional Archaeological Research: The Malyan Project, ed. by W. M. Sumner, a symposium presented at the Society for American Archaeology meetings, Philadelphia, May 1980.

31. O. K. Berdyev, "Nekotorye rezultaty izucheniia drevnezemledel'cheskikh poselenii," KDI, vol. 3, Ashkhabad, 1970, pp. 27-32.

32. M. Tosi, "The Northeastern Frontier of the Ancient Near East," Mesopotamia; 1973-74, vol. 8-10, p. 27. Also see J. R. Harlan, "The Plants and Animals That Nourish Man," Scientific American, September 1976, p. 93.

33. H. Helbaek, "The Plant Husbandry of Hacilar," in Excavations at Hacilar, vol. 1, ed. by J. Mellaart, Edinburgh, 1970, pp. 211-14. L. Constantini has identified bread wheat (T. durum or T. aestivum) at Merhgarh in period 1 or in levels that are at least as early as those for its first documented occurrence in Central Asia; see Jarrige and Meadow, op. cit., p. 122. Future studies, utilizing standard retrieval techniques, will determine whether Baluchistan and southern Central Asia were separate or related centers for early bread wheat cultivation.

34. S. A. Ershov, "Severnyi kholm Anau," Trudy Instituta istorii, arkheologii i ethnografii, Akademii nauk Turkm. SSR, vol. 2, 195, p. 34.

35. See Chapter 4, V. M. Masson, "Altyn-depe in the Aeneolithic Period," in this volume, pp. 00-00.

36. G. N. Lisitsina, "The Earliest Irrigation in Turkmenia," Antiquity, 1969, vol. 43, pp. 279-88.

37. T. J. Arne, Excavations at Shah Tepe, Iran, Sino-Swedish Expedition, no. 27, Stockholm.

38. V. I. Sarianidi, "Material'naia kul'tura iuzhnogo Turkmenistana v period rannei bronzy," Pervobytnyi Turkmenistan, Ashkhabad, 1976, pp. 82-111.

39. P. L. Kohl, "Archaeological Reconnaissances in Eastern Afghanistan, 1975-1976," Annali, 1978, pp. 63-74.

40. R. H. Dyson, Jr., "Architecture of the Iron I period at Hasanlu in Western Iran and Its Implications for Theories of Migration on the Iranian Plateau," in Le Plateau Iranien et l'Asie Centrale des Origines a la Conquete Islamique, Paris, CNRS, ed. by J. Deshayes, 1977, pp. 00-00. A more complete and illustrated presentation of materials supporting the low chronology of Dr. Khlopina appears in I. N. Khlopin's article in the same volume: "Sumbarskie mogil'niki — kliuch dlia sinkhronizatsii pamiatnikov epokhi bronzy iuga Srednei Azii i Irana," pp. 143-54.

41. It also should be noted that the utilization of iron on a limited scale is unequivocally documented for late third millennium communities in southern Afghanistan. See J. Shafer, "Bronze Age Iron from Afghanistan: Its Implications for South Asian Protohistory," in Studies in South Asian Art and Archaeology, ed. by A. K. Narain and K. A. R. Kennedy, Delhi, 1980.

42. Several reports of the prehistoric investigations in Afghanistan have been translated into English: see V. I. Sarianidi, "Bactria in the Bronze Age," Soviet

Anthropology and Archeology, Summer 1977, pp. 49-83; "Ancient Horassan and
Bactria," in Le Plateau Iranien, pp. 129-42; "Bactrian Centre of Ancient Art,"
Mesopotamia, 1977, vol. 12, pp. 97-110; and "New Finds in Bactria and Indo-
Iranian Connections," in South Asian Archaeology, 1977, vol. 2, pp. 643-60.

43. Summary accounts of the Taip-depe excavations have appeared in Arkheologicheskie otkrytiia 1977, pp. 546-47, and Arkheologicheskie otkrytiia 1978,
p. 568.

44. See E. J. H. Mackay, Chanhu-daro Excavations 1935-36, pls. XLIX-L,
New Haven, American Oriental Society, 1943; and D. G. Hogarth, Hittite Seals,
pls. III-V, Oxford, 1920.

45. E. V. Rtveladze of the Institute of Fine Arts, USSR Academy of Sciences
in Tashkent, provided me with the following data on settlements in Surkhandaria
Province of southern Uzbekistan:

No. of Sites	Period
c. 10	Bronze Age
3	Iron Age
18	Achaemenid
123	Kushan
220	Early Middle Ages

Although A. S. Sagdullaev reports a total of 42 Bronze and Iron Age sites in
Surkhandaria (35 settlements and 7 cemeteries), the dramatic and sharp increase
of settlements in Kushan times remains noteworthy and cannot be explained as
the product of gradual, continuous natural growth. See A. S. Sagdullaev, "Kul'-
tura severnoi Baktrii v epokhu pozdnei bronzy i rannego zheleza," abstract of
candidate's dissertation, Leningrad, 1978, p. 3.

46. For a more detailed report of this discovery and a description of the microscopic analysis of the material, see A. Askarov, Sapallitepe, Tashkent, 1973,
pp. 133-34.

47. K. C. Chang, The Archaeology of Ancient China, New Haven, 3rd edition,
1977, p. 95.

48. L. Hambis, "A propos des sceaux-amulettes 'Nestoriens,'" Arts Asiatiques, 1956, vol. 3, pp. 279-86; P. Pelliot, "Sceaux-amulettes de bronze avec
croix et colombes provenant de la boucle du fleuve jaune," Revue des Arts
Asiatiques, 1931-32, vol. 7, pp. 1-3. Unfortunately these seals or pendants lack
archeological context; because of their frequently recurring cross motifs, they
were assumed to be relics of Nestorian Christians who lived in western China
in the eleventh through fourteenth centuries. Hambis, however, raised the possibility of a much earlier origin and concluded his study:

... il semble que l'art de la steppe art donne deux grands courants
qui ont abouti a des formes et des techniques semblables aux deux
extremités de l'Eurasie, a moins qu'il ne faille chercher pour les
bronzes une origine beaucoup plus ancienne, dans les civilisations
sedentaires qui se sont epanouies entre l'Indus et la Mesopotamie
plusieurs millenaires avant l'ere chretienne.

49. V. I. Sarianidi, "K voprosu o kul'ture Zamanbaba," Etnografiia i arkheologiia Srednei Azii, Moscow, 1979, pp. 23-28.

50. Iu. A. Zadneprovskii, who excavated the type site of Dal'verzin, admits
the difficulty of determining the beginning or initial date for this culture: Drevnezemledel'cheskaia kul'tura Fergany, MIA, no. 118, 1962, pp. 65, 200. A recalibrated radiocarbon determination (LE 323) for a lower level at Dal'verzin
yields a date ranging between 1540 and 1190 B.C.

51. J.-M. Casal, Fouilles de Mundigak, vol. 1, 1961, p. 104, Memoires de la

Philip L. Kohl

Delegation Archeologique Française en Afghanistan, vol. 17.

52. N. M. Vinogradova et al., "Raskopki zemledel'cheskogo poseleniia epokhi bronzy na iuge Tadzhikistana," Arkheologicheskie otkrytiia 1978, p. 576.

53. H.-P. Francfort, "The Late Periods of Shortugai and the Problem of the Bishkent Culture," preliminary paper presented at the Fifth International Conference of the Association of South Asian Archaeologists in Western Europe, July 1979.

54. N. N. Terekhova, "Metallobrabotivaiushchee proizvodstvo u drevneishikh zemledel'tsev Turkmenii," in Ocherki tekhnologii drevneishikh proizvodstv, ed. by B. A. Kolchin, Moscow, 1975, pp. 14-75.

55. P. L. Kohl, "A Note on Chlorite Artifacts from Shahr-i Sokhta," East and West, 1977, pp. 124-25.

56. The model presented in this short contribution is elaborated in far greater detail in her recent synthesis, Stanovlenie i razvitie oroshaemogo zemeledeliia v iuzhnoi Turkmenii, Moscow, 1978.

57. Ibid., pp. 135-37.

58. Ibid., pp. 214-15.

59. See, particularly, B. V. Andrianov, Drevnie orositel'nye sistemy priaral'-ia, Moscow, 1969.

60. G. Dales, "Review of 'Central Asia: Turkmenia before the Achaemenids,'" The Art Bulletin, vol. 57, pp. 571-73; C. C. Lamberg-Karlovsky, "Prehistoric Central Asia: A Review," Antiquity, 1973, vol. 46, pp. 43-46.

61. The author is preparing a complete review of the Central Asian chronology for the new edition of Chronologies in Old World Archaeology, ed. by R. W. Ehrich (in preparation).

62. E. E. Romanova, A. A. Sementsov, and V. I. Timofeev, "Radiouglerodnye daty obraztsov iz Srednei Azii i Kazakhstana laboratorii LOIA, AN SSSR," Uspekhi sredneaziatskoi arkheologii, no. 2, Leningrad.

63. M. Tosi, "Early Urban Evolution and Settlement Patterns in the Indo-Iranian Borderland," in The Explanation of Culture Change: Models in Prehistory, ed. by C. Renfrew, 1973, pp. 429-46.

64. R. Biscione, "Dynamics of an Early South Asian Urbanization: The First Period of Shahr-i Sokhta and Its Connection with Southern Turkmenia," in South Asian Archaeology, ed. by N. Hammond, 1973, pp. 105-18.

65. S. Piggott, "A New Prehistoric Ceramic from Baluchistan," Ancient India, vol. 3; and W. A. Fairservis, Excavations in the Quetta Valley, West Pakistan, vol. 45, part 2, Anthropological Papers of the American Museum of Natural History, New York.

66. P. Amiet and M. Tosi, "Phase 10 at Shahr-i Sokhta: Excavations in Square XDV and the Late Fourth Millennium B.C. Assemblages of Seistan," East and West, 1978, vol. 28, pp. 9-31.

67. C. C. Lamberg-Karlovsky and M. Tosi, "Shahr-i Sokhta and Tepe Yahya: Tracks on the Earliest History of the Iranian Plateau," East and West, 1973, vol. 23, pp. 21-57.

68. Susan Howard and R. H. Dyson, Jr., personal communication.

69. J.-F. Jarrige, personal communication.

70. For example, over 500 surface scatters of relatively primitive Aeneolithic food producers have been recorded in a roughly 84 sq km area near the former Lake Liavliakan in the Kyzyl Kum, which date primarily from the fourth through the first half of the second millennia; see A. V. Vinogradov and E. D. Mamedov, Pervobytnyi Liavliakan, map 2, pp. 216-28.

Acknowledgments

Numerous people have helped in the preparation of this work. Although the list is far from complete, I would like to acknowledge a special debt of gratitude to the following Soviet scholars: V. M. Masson, L. B. Kircho, I. N. Khlopin, L. I. Khlopina, A. Ia. Shchetenko, G. F. Korobkova, P. M. Dolukhanov, V. A. Alekshin, Iu. A. Zadneprovskii, and I. N. Medvedskaia in Leningrad; V. I. Sarianidi, N. M. Vinogradova, B. V. Andrianov, M. A. Itina, A. V. Vinogradov, G. N. Lisitsina, and V. V. Volkov in Moscow; V. A. Ranov, L. T. P'iankova, T. P. Kiiatkina, M. A. Bubovna, and V. S. Solov'ev in Dushanbe; A. I. Isakov in Pendjikent; I. S. Masimov and Kh. Iu. Iusupov in Ashkhabad; A. S. Sagdullaev and L. I. Albaum in Tashkent; and A. Askarov and B. Abdullaev in Samarkand. This volume simply would not have been produced without the assistance and information they generously provided. Successful scientific work often generates more questions than it answers; it is a reflection of the healthy state of Central Asian archeology that various opinions exist which occasionally differ in critical respects from the interpretations advanced in my introduction. My respect for the Soviet achievement in documenting this rich and important evolutionary sequence is profound.

I would also like to extend thanks to Mr. William Mandel for his translations of Chapters 2, 4, 7, 13, 14, 15, and 16 and to Mr. Joe Hollander at M. E. Sharpe for his attention, encouragement, and indispensable editorial assistance. Numerous Western colleagues have assisted me in both direct and subtle ways; I would particularly like to thank M. Tosi and R. Biscione for teaching at Wellesley College in my absence and A. Shimony for her patience and encouragement; J.-C. Gardin, J.-F. Jarrige, and H.-P. Francfort at the Museé Guimet and V. Elisseeff at the Museé Cernuschi in Paris shared their materials willingly and extended gracious hospitality on my trips to and from the Soviet Union. Work in Iran in late 1978 was difficult and could not have been conducted without the help of several scholars, including D. Stronach, then Director at the British Institute; I thank D. L. Heskel for his understanding and admire the survey he completed alone in the Darreh Gaz Plain in early September of 1978. Colleagues at Harvard University have provided a constant source of stimulation over the years; C. C. Lamberg-Karlovsky, in particular, deserves thanks for his willingness to criticize and, occasionally, praise my work.

Barbara Gard has tolerated my long absences and devotion to a remote and specilized field; her constant encouragement has helped me in ways both profound and simple. The recent birth of our son, Owen, also helped maintain a critical and realistic perspective for completing this work.

List of Abbreviations

AO	Arkheologicheskie otkrytiia	Archeological Discoveries
IMKU	Istoriia material'noi kul'tury Uzbekistana	History of the Material Culture of Uzbekistan
IuTAKE	Iuzhno-Turkmenistanskoi arkheologicheskoi kompleksnoi ekspeditsii	Southern-Turkmenistan Complex Archeological Expedition
KD	Karakumskie drevnosti	Kara Kum Antiquities
KSIA	Kratkie soobshcheniia Instituta arkheologii	Brief Reports of the Institute of Archeology
KSIIMK	Kratkie soobshcheniia Instituta material'noi kul'tury	Brief Reports of the Institute of Material Culture
MDAFA	Memoires de la Délegation Archaeologique Française en Afghanistan	Reports of the French Archeological Delegation in Afghanistan
MIA	Materialy i issledovaniia po arkheologii	Materials and Studies in Archeology
MIuTAKE	Materialy Iuzhno-Turkmenistanskoi arkheologicheskoi kompleksnoi ekspeditsii	Materials of the Southern Turkmenistan Complex Archeological Expedition
SA	Sovetskaia arkheologiia	Soviet Archeology
SAI	Svod arkheologicheskikh istochnikov	Digest of Archeological Sources
SE	Sovetskaia etnografiia	Soviet Ethnography
TIuTAKE	Trudy Iuzhno-Turkmenistanskoi arkheologicheskoi kompleksnoi ekspeditsii	Works of the Southern Turkmenistan Complex Archeological Expedition
USA	Uspekhi Sredneaziatskoi arkheologii	Achievements of Central Asian Archeology
VDI	Vestnik drevnei istorii	Bulletin of Ancient History
VI	Vestnik istorii	Bulletin of History

PART ONE

Southwestern Turkmenistan
and the Late Bronze Age

The Early Bronze Age Cemetery of Parkhai II: The First Two Seasons of Excavations: 1977-78

I. N. KHLOPIN

The Sumbar Archeological Expedition of the Leningrad Sector of the Institute of Archeology, USSR Academy of Sciences, began intensive excavations along the middle course of the Sumbar River, a tributary of the Atrek that joins it on its right side, in 1969 with excavations of the Iron Age settlement Parkhai-tepe.[1] Then for six field seasons, 1972-77, the expedition investigated the Late Bronze Age cemeteries: Sumbar I, Sumbar II, and Parkhai I; information about this work has appeared in numerous scientific publications.[2] A full report of these excavations with an interpretation of the materials from all the investigated levels is now ready to be published. Having finished our study of the Late Bronze Age cemeteries, we shifted our focus to cemeteries of earlier periods.

In summer 1977 the cemetery Parkhai II was discovered along the northern edge of the Sumbar Valley close to the western outskirts of the contemporary town of Kara Q'ala. The cemetery was located on a hill ten meters above the valley floor. A natural rise or outlier forms the mound, and its deposit contains traces of its use as a burial ground from the Early Bronze Age to the Late Middle Ages. It was subjected to excavations which revealed its important scientific interest and showed the necessity for conducting several seasons of standardized investigations on it.[3] The first full season at this site was conducted in 1978.

Thus during 1977 and 1978, 27 burial vaults (Figure 1) were excavated that together contained the remains of about 450 burials, roughly 300 vessels, and numerous stone and bronze objects. This

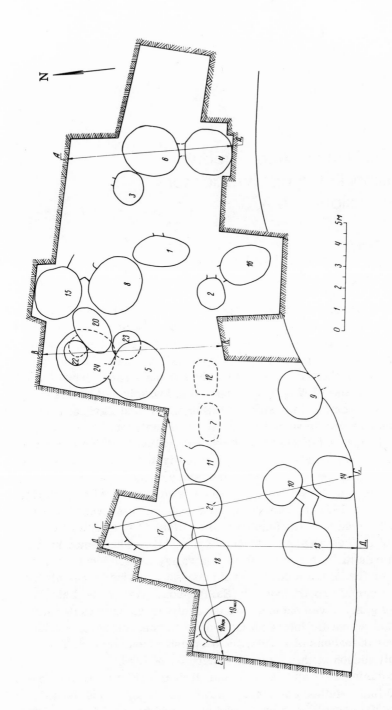

Figure 1. The Parkhai II Cemetery: plan of the excavations.

article presents a preliminary summary of these finds and also attempts to draw the historical conclusions that can be deduced from this material. These conclusions will utilize known archeological materials from sites situated in the northern foothills of the Kopet Dagh and in northern Iran, as well as the virtually unpublished materials from the Sumbar cemeteries of the Late Bronze Age. Naturally these conclusions are not definitive, since excavations of the Sumbar sites have just begun.

Preliminarily we can divide the excavated funerary chambers into three types. The first type consists of a burial construction lacking the piles of bones from skeletons that were pushed into the chamber; the second contains only piles of disarticulated bones without the skeleton of the final burial; and the third refers to a chamber containing the final disturbed burial and a pile of skeletal remains pushed deep within it.

Three chambers (nos. 1, 7, 12) belong to the first type. The interred skeletons are placed on their side in a tightly contracted position. The heel bones almost touch the pelvis, and the knees are placed near the chin. One cannot say that men were put on one side and women on the other, since all possibilities occur. This type of funeral chamber raises more questions than it answers. The quantity of material gifts varies greatly: in chamber 1 thirteen vessels were found beside two skeletons; in chamber 7 only two vessels were found beside the head of a second female skeleton (Figures 2 and 3); and chamber 12 did not contain any gifts or offerings.

Four chambers (nos. 2, 11, 22, and 23) belong to our second type. They are distinguished by their relatively small size, with a diameter of 110-130 centimeters. An entrance covered by a vertically set stone slab on a mud brick was preserved at only one of these chambers. Although a final undisturbed skeleton was not found in this type of chamber, ceramics were discovered near the pile of earlier burials and, in one case (no. 11), even a bronze spiral-headed pin (Figure 21, 5).

The third or basic type consists of the remaining twenty constructions. For this reason we will discuss several of the most interesting burials separately, even though they all share many features.

Chamber 4 was nearly circular with a roughly 2 meter diameter (Figure 4). Its entrance opens from the north-northeast, and the burial of a young boy about 8-9 years of age, which was placed

Figure 2. The Parkhai II Cemetery: chamber 7.

on its left side in a contracted position, was preserved inside on the floor. Decomposed traces of a soft fabric or textile were still preserved on the thorax and shoulders, which were twisted backward toward the spine. The right arm extended along the body, while the left was bent at the elbow, with his hand spread across the breast. The head of the dead person had been placed on a stone but had slipped off. A beautifully ornamented decanter was placed near his left temple. The rest of the chamber was filled with piles of bones which were raised 60 cm above the floor at the small wall opposite the entrance. This assortment contained the remains of no fewer than 38 burials (calculated from the number of skulls) of both sexes and various ages. Twenty-two vessels were found among these bones (Figure 5), including: six beakers, one goblet with a tubular foot, three cups, four sphero-conical vessels, three pear-shaped vessels, four cylindrical vessels, a spherical vessel, and fragments of two rectangular vessels on pedestals with sculpted heads of bulls and some undetermined animal. The

Figure 3. The Parkhai II Cemetery: chamber 7, ceramics.

Figure 4. The Parkhai II Cemetery: chamber 4.

7

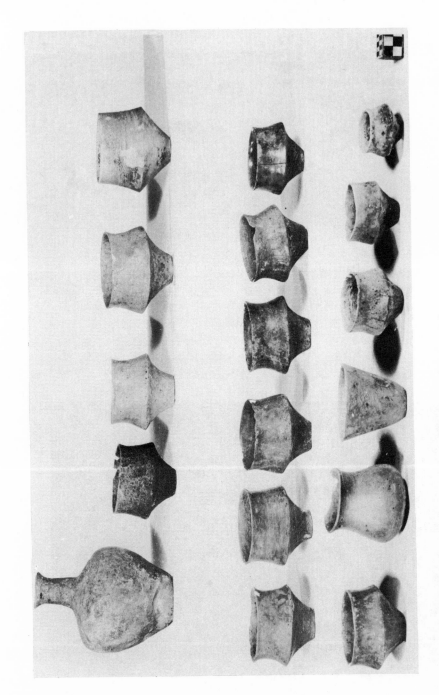

Figure 5. The Parkhai II Cemetery: chamber 4, ceramics.

8

bones of a ram, presumably the remains of a funeral meal, were found among the human bones.

Chamber 8 is 2.6 m in diameter; its entrance opens from the north-northeast and was built with stones and mud bricks. It twice functioned as a burial vault, with some chronological gap separating its periods of utilization. An undisturbed burial of a woman of about 40-45 was preserved in the lower vault (Figure 6); the contracted skeleton lay on its left side with its back to the entrance and its head, which was placed on a stone, directed toward the

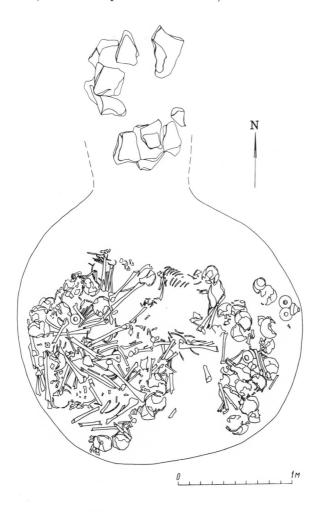

N

0   1M

Figure 6. The Parkhai II Cemetery: chamber 8, lower vault, plan.

east. No objects were found beside this burial. A pile of bones, which contained 29 male and female skulls of various ages, was cleared between the final burial and the back walls of the chamber. Thirty-one vessels (Figure 7) were found among these bones, including: twenty-two small goblets, two cups, one sphero-conical vessel, a carafe or decanter, a vase, a conical cup, and a small bucket with a handle and spout. A bronze spiral-headed pin (Figure 21, 1), a pierced needle (Figure 21, 3), a bracelet with a circular section (Figure 21, 9) that wound over on itself one and a half times, a ring, and a necklace with 174 small limestone beads and one turquoise bead were also found.

A level without bones but containing stones and fragments of large gray vessels was located between the upper and lower vaults. An undisturbed skeleton was not found in the upper vault (Figure 8), a situation probably caused by the burrowing of a large animal into the funeral chamber. However, the location of the pile of bones and its scattering toward the entrance prove that the opening into the chamber was in the same place. It was demonstrated that no fewer than 20 individuals of both sexes and different ages were interred in this vault. Seventeen vessels (Figure 9) were found, including: fourteen goblets, a conical cup, a pear-shaped vessel, and a decanter. A bronze knife 14 cm long (Figure 21, 12) also was discovered.

Chamber 10 had a circular plan 1.9 m in diameter (Figure 10) with its entrance opening from the south-southwest. In front of the entrance a male skeleton 25-30 years old lay on its right side. Its face was turned toward the entrance and its head directed south. The legs were bent at the knees so that the heel bones pressed against the pelvis. It was not possible to trace the arms, but the left probably extended along the body and the right bent at the elbow. The remains of no fewer than 36 individuals of both sexes and different ages were found between the final burial and the back walls of the vault. Nine vessels (Figure 11) were found, including: two goblets, two spherical cups, two sphero-conical vessels, a cylindrical vessel, and the fragments of two twin vessels. A small bronze ring, a nail, and a spiral-headed pin (Figure 21, 8) also were found.

Chamber 16 (Figure 12) had an oval plan 1.5 × 2.2 m. Its entrance opened from the northwest, and the remains of a circular hole of a column 16 cm in diameter were found in the middle of

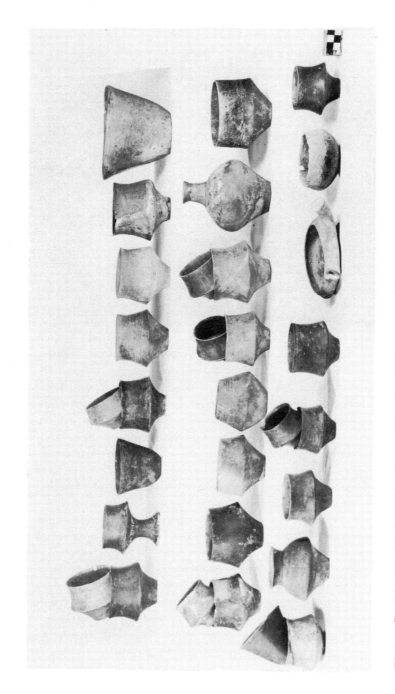

Figure 7. The Parkhai II Cemetery: chamber 8, lower vault, ceramics.

11

Figure 8. The Parkhai II Cemetery: chamber 8, upper vault.

the eastern wall of the chamber. Four skeletons with their
heads oriented to the east-northeast but lacking grave goods
were found in the vault. They were all set in contracted position on their right side with their right arms extended and
their left arms bent at the elbow; they faced the entrance.
Only the last burial was undisturbed; the other three exhibited
varying degrees of being moved further into the chamber. They
were all females of different ages.

   Chamber 17 was utilized on two separate occasions. Its
dimensions were 1.8 × 2.0 m, and the lower and upper vaults
had different entrances.

   The lower chamber (Figure 13) had its entrance on its
southern side before which lay the skeleton of a young boy
9-10 years old. It was placed facing the entrance on its left
side with its legs contracted, its arms bent at the elbows,
and its head oriented to the east. There were no grave goods,
but the shell of a steppe tortoise was placed near its legs.
The remains of fourteen additional individuals of both sexes

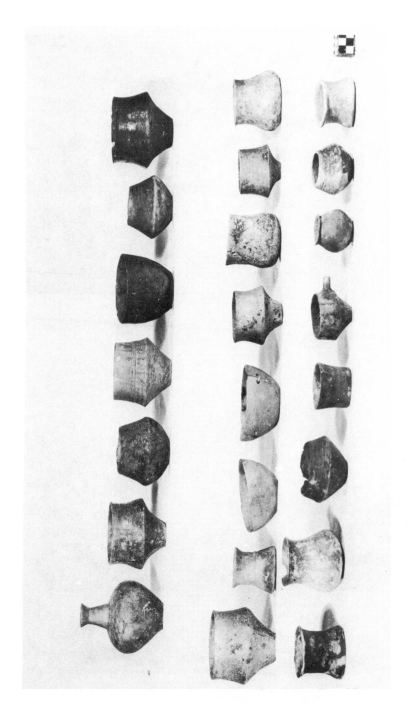

Figure 9. The Parkhai II Cemetery: chamber 8, upper vault, ceramics.

Figure 10. The Parkhai II Cemetery: chamber 10.

Figure 11. The Parkhai II Cemetery: chamber 10, ceramics.

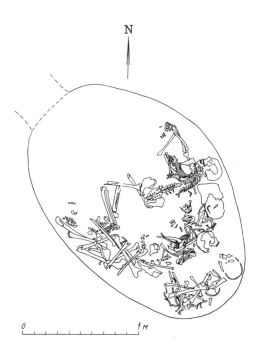

Figure 12. The Parkhai II Cemetery: chamber 16, plan.

Figure 13. The Parkhai II Cemetery: chamber 17, lower vault.

and varying ages were uncovered in the chamber; all these bones had been subjected to pressure insofar as the entrance to the upper vault came from the opposite side, and those who had buried the dead people of the upper vault had repeatedly walked across, sprinkling earth on the bones in the lower pit. Five vessels (Figure 14) were found among the bones: a goblet, a cup, a vase, two sphero-conical vessels, and many fragments.

Figure 14. The Parkhai Cemetery: chamber 17, lower vault, ceramics.

In the upper vault the bones were concentrated along the south-southeast wall of the chamber. Above them lay a female 20-22 years of age on her left side, facing the entrance with her head to the west. There were gifts near her. Six other individuals were preserved in this chamber: four men, a woman, and a child. Nine vessels were found among the bones: four goblets, four cups, and a pear-shaped vessel.

Chamber 19 also was used twice, but its upper chamber contained only the lower part of a female skeleton 25-30 years old, lying on its spine with its heel bones located beneath its pelvis. The skeleton lay with its head oriented to the east. In addition to this skeleton there was a pile of bones, representing seven individuals. Three vessels were found: two small goblets and a cup.

The lower vault (Figure 15) was separated from the upper by a layer of earth, and its chamber could be easily traced.

It had an oval plan (1.7 × 2.9 m), and its entrance came from the northwest. An undisturbed skeleton of a girl about 16 years old lay opposite and facing the entrance on its left side with its head oriented to the southwest. The legs were bent at the knees. The right arm was bent at the elbow with its hand set across its breast, while the left arm was similarly bent with its hand placed in front of its face. Above the woman's forearms lay a newly born infant in a contracted position

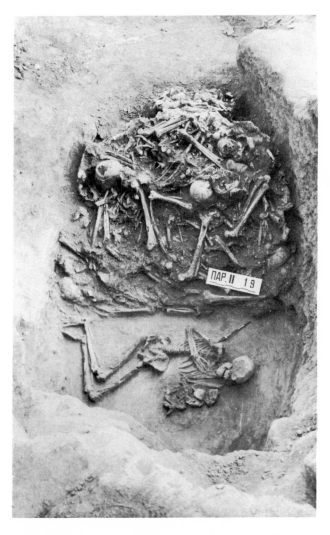

Figure 15. The Parkhai II Cemetery: chamber 19, lower vault.

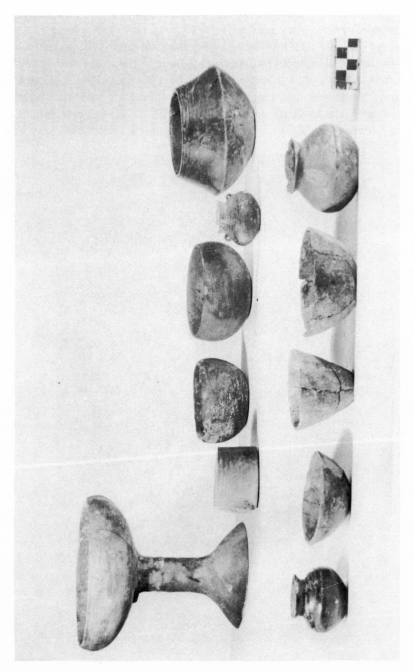

Figure 16. The Parkhai II Cemetery: chamber 19, lower vault, ceramics.

on its left side facing the entrance. Four vessels were placed near the head of the woman: a vase, a sphero-conical vessel, two spherical vessels, one of which had two handles, and a small marble vessel in the shape of a horn. Part of a double vessel lay near the child's head. A bronze ring lay under the woman's skull, and four bronze nails with large heads lay near her mouth.

A pile of bones containing 19 human skulls of both sexes and various ages, the bones of a ram, and a tortoise shell were located between the spine of the final burial and the back walls of the chamber. This pile contained six vessels: three cups, a conical drinking cup, a spherical vessel, and part of a double vessel, and three small bronze nails, a bronze pin with a button-shaped head, and three turquoise beads.

Chamber 24 (Figure 17) is interesting in that it is covered not only by a burial of the Late Bronze Age but by two chambers from the same period. This fact allows us to consider chamber 24 the earliest of the excavated burials. It has a circular plan (2.4 m diameter), and its entrance opens from the north. Four human skeletons, representing the final burials in the chamber, were placed opposite the entrance. The closest to the entrance was a woman about 23-25 years of age, who lay on her left side facing the entrance with her knees contracted and her head oriented to the west. Her right hand lay across her breast, and her left hand touched her pelvis. Two vessels and a bronze double spiral-headed pin (Figure 21, 2) were placed before her face. A child about 8-9 years old lay behind her back on its right side with its back to the entrance and its head pointed to the west. The knees were bent, the right arm extended, and the left bent at the elbow. Two bronze earrings were placed at the ears on the skull, and a steppe tortoise shell was set over the right hand. Two skeletons of newly born infants were placed on their left side in a contracted position in front of the face and above the lower right fibula and tibia of the second burial. The infants were buried without grave goods. A pile of bones was uncovered between these skeletons and the back wall of the chamber. This pile represented 13 skeletons of both sexes and different ages. Four vessels (Figure 18) were found among the bones: two cups, a spherical vessel, and a small painted two-handled pot. There were also three small bronze nails and a bead made from lapis lazuli.

19

Naturally, numerous questions are raised by the initial excavations at this site. Specifically, at this stage of the investigations one must consider most important the questions concerning how these chambers were built, the cultural affiliation or relation of this site to others, and its dating — at least in their general forms.

One can observe the following characteristics concerning the construction of these tombs:

1) The bottom of the burial chamber was situated at a depth of 0.9 to 2.0 m beneath the contemporary surface of the mound. In the deepest cases later burial chambers were constructed above the earlier ones, and these later constructions were then destroyed by natural erosion of the mound's surface.

2) Many observations attest to the fact that the contemporary surface of the mound is practically identical to the surface when the ancient cemetery was used.

3) When the cemetery was functioning, the burial chambers were not filled with earth, since they frequently were opened for subsequent burials.

Figure 17. The Parkhai II Cemetery: chamber 24.

Figure 18. The Parkhai II Cemetery: chamber 24, ceramics.

4) The chamber was reached through a side entrance, which was marked by mud bricks and stone slabs.

5) An entrance hole was set to the side of the funeral chamber, which was filled with earth and separated from the chamber either by a stone-brick foundation or by a vertically set stone slab.

6) In two cases, chambers 15 and 16, the remains of constructions were found that contained the upper parts of vertical columns.

On the basis of these traits one can reconstruct how the chambers were built in the form of a vault. First, they dug a pit about 2 m in diameter and beside it a rectangular hole (Figure 19). This hole, which was the entrance, was so positioned that its short side abutted the larger pit. They covered the vault by placing columns at the sides that supported a crossbeam; on this beam they spread twigs or reeds and covered it with earth. In order to bury someone in the vault, they had to remove the dirt from the side hole and take away the foundation stones between the hole and pit. They then set

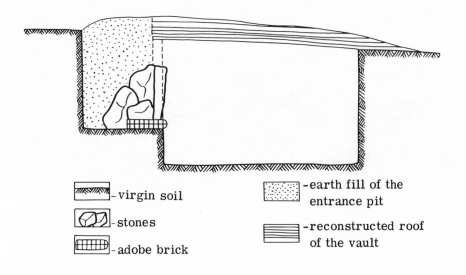

-virgin soil

-stones

-adobe brick

-earth fill of the entrance pit

-reconstructed roof of the vault

Figure 19. Reconstruction of a vault.

the deceased on its right or left side and put near it the funeral goods that custom required. They pushed the bones of the previous burial deeper into the chamber and set the newly deceased in the place vacated. When the burials were sufficiently numerous, the bones were thrown disrespectfully into a large pile. After the final burial, of a particular group of people who had to be buried together, the vault was closed. It was not used or opened again. When a new chamber was built over the abandoned vault, it bore no relation to the earlier tomb.

Ceramics, which were used exclusively by individuals, make up one of the basic classes of artifacts in the Parkhai II assemblage. Only rarely can one relate certain vessels to a

particular burial. The great majority of vessels are found among
the piles of bones; these vessels were shoved away along with the
bones at the times of subsequent burials. Although detailed analysis of the ceramics is still to be made, it is possible to note certain characteristics.

All the ceramics were produced without use of the potter's wheel,
but they still indicate a high level of perfection attained by the ancient craftsmen. One can already observe the basic shapes. The
overwhelming majority (about 50 percent) are biconical goblets,
which exhibit certain chronological distinctions. In the earliest
vaults these pots have incised, impressed, or burnished designs,
and the height of their lower section represents one quarter to one
third of the height of the entire vessel. In the later vaults the goblets lack these designs, and the lower part now forms roughly half
the height of the entire vessel. Different types of cups, which also
have significant chronological distinctions, are the second most
common shape (about 16 percent). Bell-shaped cups appear considerably later than conical and, particularly, sphero-conical vessels. Sphero-conical vessels of different sizes but identical proportions are the third most popular form (about 8 percent of the
corpus). Their relative dating is not completely clear, although they are older than the goblets without designs and the
bell-shaped cups. Then in roughly similar quantities (7-9 percent) appear pear-shaped vessels with suspension holes, decanters or carafes, small and regular-sized vases, conical
drinking glasses, and cylindrical and spherical vessels with
everted rims. All the remaining forms consist of a few examples, including unique rectangular vessels with four legs
(Figure 20).

The ceramic assemblage is interesting in that it helps us
establish chronological and, more importantly, cultural relationships with previously discovered sites. First, one must
note the striking correspondence to the ceramic assemblages
of the Late Neolithic and Early Bronze Age settlements in the
northern foothills of the Kopet Dagh: Kara-depe at Artykh and
Ak-depe near Ashkhabad. At the former site gray ceramics
were found in the upper building level as well as in graves
dug into that level.[4] At Ak-depe gray vessels made up a considerable percentage of the ceramic assemblage.[5] All these
grayware vessels clearly were imported into the sites of this

Figure 20. Rectangular footed vessels: 1. chamber 6;
2. chamber 15.

Figure 21. The Parkhai II Cemetery: objects: 1, 3, 9 — chamber 8, lower vault; 2 — chamber 24; 4 — chamber 15; 5 — chamber 11; 6 — chamber 6; 7 — chamber 16; 8 — chamber 10; 10 — chamber 19; 11, 13 — chamber 9; 12 — chamber 8, upper vault.

area and can always be considered to have been brought from northern Iran. In any case their appearance on these sites allows us preliminarily to date this recently discovered cemetery to the first half of the third millennium B.C.

Insofar as the Parkhai II ceramic assemblage forms a single unit while the grayware ceramics found on sites in the northern foothills of the Kopet Dagh are imported, one can consider that the grayware vessels came to southern Turkmenistan from the Sumbar Valley in the first half of the third millennium B.C., or during the time corresponding both to periods Namazga III and Namazga IV. In addition, the burials in the upper levels at Kara-depe exhibit a definite similarity in their ceremonial rites to those seen at several burials in the Parkhai II cemetery. This is especially true in the positioning of the deceased when placed on their sides or back with one arm bent and the other extended along the body. In light of what has been said, the upper levels at Kara-depe and Ak-depe were not so disturbed at this time, as was previously thought.[6] In the Early Bronze Age the Sumbar Valley and the northern foothills of the Kopet Dagh belonged to different cultural areas. On the other hand, the Parkhai II ceramics exhibit striking similarity to those from Shah-tepe levels III and IIB, which allows us to unite these sites into a single cultural sphere.

The collection of small finds is sufficiently large for such an early period. The bronze assemblage consists of double-edged knives, small fragments, and spiral-headed pins. These pins, which appeared in different sizes and were found both in the later and earlier burials, shared one particular feature: no spiral had fewer than four loops. Only six spiral-headed pins are known from the northern foothills of the Kopet Dagh. One came from Kyzyl Arvat and was dated to the Namazga IV period;[7] it is completely identical to the Parkhai examples and can be considered an import from the Sumbar Valley. The remainder — two from the southern mound at Anau, two from Namazga-depe, and one from Shor-depe — had small loops twisted only 1.5-2 times. They were found in Namazga V levels. In addition, identical objects were uncovered in Namazga V levels from cemeteries in northern Afghanistan[8] and Tadjikistan.[9] Slightly twisted spiral-headed pins from Mundigak (periods IV, 1 — IV, 3)[10] and multilooped spiral-headed pins from Tepe Hissar (period IIB),[11] which are identical to those from

Parkhai II, also are related to this period. Thus it follows that the spiral-headed pins can be grouped into two types divided according to the number of loops or spirals and the sharpness of their lower end; however, it is still not clear whether these distinctions signify chronological, cultural, spatial, or functional differences. In any case it is evident that they occur very infrequently. The number, different types, and chronological occurrence of these pins on one site, Parkhai II, allow us to propose that they were distributed throughout a great area of the Near East and Central Asia from the southeastern trans-Caspian region, specifically, the Sumbar Valley and southwestern Turkmenia.

Earrings in the form of unclosed rings with beautiful ends, pendant circles, massive bracelets with circular sections that extended 1.5-2 times around, and numerous small nails were also found. Beads were made from lapis lazuli, carnelian, turquoise, and limestone; they had not only the typical cylindrical shapes but also a trapezoidal form that has direct analogies with the burials from the upper level of Kara-depe at Artykh;[12] one must also mention the large lapis lazuli awl [pronizka] that is precisely paralleled in the IIIA graves at Tureng-tepe[13] and in the Royal Cemetery at Ur,[14] which are traditionally dated to the middle of the third millennium B.C. These objects help us push the date of the Parkhai II cemetery closer to the middle of the third millennium B.C.

Consequently, after just the first full field season, it is possible to date the Parkhai II cemetery to the middle of the third millennium B.C. and state that it belonged in a particular cultural area, distinct from that of the northern foothills of the Kopet Dagh. Specifically, it belonged in the cultural area that included the northern piedmont plains of the Elburz Mountains and the Atrek and Gurgan river valleys.

A gap of slightly more than a thousand years, which at present is not filled by any archeological sites, separates this newly discovered site from the Sumbar cemeteries of the Late Bronze Age. However, certain features appear in both cultures that help us bridge this gap. First, the tradition of preparing graywares is continued. Many traits of the later Sumbar ceramics already appear in the Parkhai II assemblage, e.g., spouts, tube-shaped feet, and button-shaped handles. Second, both complexes have similar stone mace heads or crooks. Third, they both share the custom of placing steppe tortoise shells in the burials.

Despite the formal differences in the construction of the burial
vaults in both cultures, it is possible to attempt to elucidate the
sources of the catacombs of the later Sumbar cemeteries with the
help of the materials of the Early Bronze Age. If there were known
sites of the developed or Middle Bronze Age, we might have a continuous series of burial constructions from the semisubterranean
vaults of Parkhai II to the catacombs of the Sumbar cemeteries. But
since such a series is still incomplete, we must attempt to clarify this
question on the basis of the presently available materials. The determination of the presence or absence of a genetic relationship in the
construction of the tombs allows us to raise a further question concerning the historical relationship (or lack of such a relationship) between
these sites that are separated by so long a period.

The catacomb burials of the Sumbar Culture have an oval chamber dug down about 4 m from the present surface. Their dimensions vary greatly: 1.4×0.9 m to 3.1×2.6 m along the axes.
There were two types of entrances: a vertical aperture set against
the middle or southern side of the chamber or a horizontal gallery
placed on the northern edge of the chamber; the chambers were
always dug out on their southern side. In general, those with vertical entrances were larger and filled with mud bricks; chambers
with horizontal galleries were smaller and filled with large stones.

Catacomb burials are well known in other areas, e.g., the lower
Don region and the Aegean world.[15] Much work has been devoted
to these cultures; its examination would take us far from our chosen theme and would not help us find a solution to our problem.
We believe that it is now impossible to discuss the connections of
our tombs with those of the so-called "hearths" or centers of the catacomb cultures, and for this reason we will only consider the Central
Asian "hearth" for the distribution of catacomb graves; more specifically, their distribution in this area's southern agricultural zone.

In terms of their construction catacombs appear to have gone
completely out of use in the Late Bronze Age. For this reason we
can propose two alternative explanations: either this construction
technique with its entire cultural assemblage was imported into
southwestern Turkmenia, or it developed independently on the basis of the construction of earlier burial types. It is currently impossible to evaluate the first alternative theory on the arrival of the
Sumbar Culture since similar sites are distributed along the northern slopes of the Elburz Mountains, northern Iran, and in the Atrek
and Gurgan valleys; the Sumbar Valley was attached to this cultural area, forming its northeasternmost extension. One can use

the results of the excavations at Parkhai II, consisting of the funeral vaults with collective burials described above, in responding
positively to the second possibility.

The funeral chambers from the Parkhai II cemetery are chronologically and developmentally similar to the chambers from Geoksyur, Chong-depe, Khapuz-depe, and Altyn-depe, which are situated in the southeastern zone of the northern foothills of the Kopet
Dagh and in the ancient delta of the Tedjen River. Originally these
latter sites were interpreted as burial grounds for members of
large family communes.[16] It now has been determined that the
graves can be seen as burial places for blood relations of a single
generation, i.e., children of the same father.[17] The funeral chambers of Geoksyur attest to the formation of patriarchal relations
in the society and were means for intentionally strengthening these
relations, i.e., it was necessary to make blood relations to the
father so important and so indissoluble that such related kinsmen
remained together after death, even though each had his own family
and lived separately. There is even reason to perceive similar
practices in the collective tombs at Parkhai II and attach to them
a similar significance.

Burial constructions of the developed or Middle Bronze Age in
southwestern Turkmenia — equivalent to Namazga V — are still
unknown. But one can definitely conclude that after a millennium,
or the time that separates the Parkhai II vaults from the Sumbar
catacombs, patriarchal relations had sunk into the consciousness
of the society, and that the need to maintain kin-related burial
vaults had passed. For the Sumbar Culture only individual burials
within the limits of a cemetery for a single village, which could
be considered kin-related, were characteristic. These latter cemeteries preserved members of different families who were related
to a common ancestor and, not surprisingly, possessed the same
unifying effect as that created by the earlier separate kin-related
vaults. The later custom also was similar in that all the burials
in a single cemetery were considered the children and descendants
of a single father or ancestor and simply could not be buried together in a vault.

Many cemeteries are now situated on the edge of Turkmen settlements, particularly at Kara Q'ala. Both special investigations[18]
and the long personal observations of the author have shown that
the local population continues to maintain its ancient funeral customs despite the fact that recollections about kin relations are only
preserved among the elderly. Not only are there separate Russian,

Armenian, and Turkmen cemeteries, but the last also are divided according to different ancestors or other groupings. Thus today only Gerkezi are interred in the cemetery situated on the burial grounds of Sumbar III regardless of where the people may have lived. A cemetery for the kin of the Vagi is situated a little further down the Sumbar. Before the war the kin of the Vagi used to live in this place, but then they moved. The kin relations, however, continue to use the old cemetery. Such kin-related cemeteries are distributed over a significantly broad zone that includes not only Turkmenia but other regions of Central Asia.[19]

Several changes in construction techniques accompanied the change from kin-related vaults to patriarchal-ancestral cemeteries with individual catacomb graves. First of all, the burial constructions were single and of the same type, and these features led to other essential changes. Thus, since it was no longer necessary to open the graves for repeated burials, each grave became smaller and deeper. Having dug the graves to a depth of about 3-4 m, it became necessary to strengthen the roofs of these constructions, since they now supported thick layers of loess soil. As a result of this, individual grave chambers or catacombs appeared in which the inhabitants of the Sumbar Valley of the Late Bronze Age were buried in kin-related cemeteries.

In order to build such catacombs it was necessary to use thick layers of undisturbed loess soil; correspondingly, the loose habitation levels could not have supported the vaults of the burial chambers. Exceptions would be possible only in those cases in which the chambers were sunk under walls whose masonry supported the vaults. This practice occurred at Sapalli-tepe.[20] For this reason it is obvious why separate cemeteries situated outside settlements are not found in the foothills of the Kopet Dagh. There are no natural mounds in this zone, and the frequency of numerous settlements in this area would have destroyed cemeteries that were not built on heights. Since the people wanted to preserve their cemeteries from destruction, they were compelled to bury their dead within their settlements in those areas, in particular, which were not occupied.

Separate cemeteries are situated only in the hilly terrain of intermontane valleys because the construction of the burial structures, like the structure of the cemetery in general, depended on the nature of the surrounding landscape. It is possible to observe two lines in the development of burial constructions, beginning with the essentially identical kin-related vaults of the Early Bronze

Age. In the intermontane valleys this line culminated in the development of ancestral cemeteries, consisting of individual catacomb graves. In the foothill plains the continuation of the tradition of collective burials in abandoned houses and an increase in the number of burials in each chamber (e.g., at Altyn-depe during Namazga V times) are observed.

If the Sumbar catacombs can be related genetically to the Parkhai vaults, then it is necessary to determine whether it is possible to establish the semantics or meaningful significance of these burial structures. Examining the building principles of the Parkhai vaults, one comes to the conclusion that their construction duplicates on a smaller scale their actual living quarters. Such residences were semisubterranean and consisted of two parts: the larger part was covered by a wooden and earthen roof and functioned as the living area; the smaller part was near the entrance pit where one began to descend and enter the living area. Such a residential dwelling is related to a very ancient tradition, but its reconstruction, it seems, is only hypothetical. One can tentatively propose that the older population of the mountainous regions of the Kopet Dagh lived not in mud-brick earthen houses but in semisubterranean and typologically more ancient structures that better fit local ecological conditions.

However paradoxically, support for the above hypothesis can be found in the ethnography of the Gokleni, a mountainous Turkmen tribe occupying the Sumbar Valley, particularly the settlement of Kara Q'ala around which are situated all the cemeteries I have mentioned. More importantly, there is no reason to consider that this tribe arrived recently in the Sumbar Valley. The isolated position of this valley meant that many conquests and other sanguinary events of history over the last 2,500 years did not heavily affect this area; it was only necessary for the local population to change their Iranian language to a Turkic language and their ancient faith to Islam. "In earlier times," wrote D. M. Ovezov, "the dwellings of the Gokleni were semisubterranean (kumė). They were usually built on the sides of hills (i.e., they were cut into the hill so that the hill formed their back and part of the side walls — I. Kh.). Above, the roof was pitched for water drainage. The door was always located to the south; to the right of it was an opening for light. A hearth for heating was in the middle, with a small opening in the roof above for smoke. In the kumė, as in the yurt, the right side was for the females and the left for males; the center was the place of honor for the guests. Only their turbulent life

31

forced the Gokleni to have a temporary dwelling — a yurt or hut."[21]

The semisubterranean dwellings of the Gokleni were perfectly suited to the ecological setting of the woody intermontane valleys where there was insufficient clay for building the traditional Central Asian mud-brick structures. Moreover, the absence of tepes [mounds], which are so common in the hilly plains, indirectly attests to the fact that semisubterranean structures were the residences of the mountain valley populations in the Early and Late Bronze Age. However, one cannot say that the local people were completely unfamiliar with mud bricks, since they used them to lay the foundation of the entrances of the vaults and catacombs. Different types of building materials were combined in the construction of the living quarters and burial chambers: stone, wood, and mud brick.

As opposed to this practice, mud brick was the only building material known on the piedmont plain of the Kopet Dagh or in the ancient delta of the Tedjen River. In these regions both wood and stone were scarce. As is well known, at Geoksyur and at other settlements both the houses and the dwellings for the dead, the burial chambers, were made of this material. In this respect it was felt that the Geoksyur vaults were surface structures, and the cemetery was reconstructed as a small city of the dead composed of small cupola-shaped houses on the edge of the settlement.[22] However, the obvious sunken nature of similar constructions in the Sumbar Valley allows us to question this opinion. The Geoksyur vaults were constructed so that the mud bricks formed a false arch covering the interior. The entrances into the vaults were covered with several bricks that were set flat. Thanks to circular masonry with an overlapping interior, the exterior surface of these vaults had broad wedge-shaped cracks that were dry inside and filled with earth. The exterior parts of the bricks, their corners and edges, were completely preserved. Such preservation could not be explained if the constructions had stood in the open, subject to the forces of nature; in such a case the corners and edges would have eroded. Such preservation could only occur when the constructions were protected from the natural elements. If the exterior had not been plastered, it would have fallen to the ground.

For the construction of the Geoksyur vaults it first was necessary to dig a foundation pit and construct a new building on its base that was made from the remains of earlier structures that had been knocked over. This work, in turn, depended on the number of the relations of the deceased for whom it was built.[23] Then all the constructions were covered with the earth that had been extracted from the pit. A trap door, set with mud bricks and placed lower than the surrounding dirt in the center of the cupola, acted as an entrance to the vault. The complete isolation of the body from external agents was achieved by such a construction, and the products of decomposition did not penetrate the exterior, which would have been inevitable if the chamber had been placed on the ground surface.

Thus the comparison of essentially identical, contemporaneous structures — the vaults of the Sumbar Valley and those of the Tedjen Delta — shows the reason for such significant external differences. The explanation relates to their different ecological circumstances. Consequently the broader conclusion can be drawn that the construction of burial chambers can change due to the effect of natural forces, and therefore that this attribute is unstable and cannot be considered one of the unchanging features that together form an archeological culture, i.e., before one designates any trait as an essential element of the culture, it is necessary to investigate carefully its origins and associations.

Thus we present partial publication and our initial thoughts on the extensive and new archeological material from the excavations of the Early Bronze Age Parkhai II cemetery. Just the questions raised in this article show the significance this work will acquire for the archeology of Iran and Central Asia. The investigations have only begun and yet already promise to yield many unexpected results.

Notes

1. I. N. Khlopin, "Raskopki Parkhai-tepe," Arkheologicheskie otkrytiia 1969 g., Moscow, 1970, pp. 420-21.

2. I. N. Khlopin, "Raskopki v doline Sumbara," Tezisy dokladov na Plenume Instituta Arkheologii AN SSSR, Tashkent, 1973, pp. 232-34; idem., "Drevnosti doliny Sumbara," Pamiatniki Turkmenistana, Ashkhabad, 1973, no. 1; idem., "Raskopki Sumbarskikh mogil'nikov," Tezisy, Kiev, 1974, pp. 113-14. I. N. Khlopin and L. I. Khlopina, Arkheologicheskie otkrytiia 1973 g., Moscow, 1974, pp. 511-12; idem., "Raboty Sumbarskogo otriada," Arkheologicheskie otkrytiia 1974 g., Moscow, 1975, pp. 531-32; idem., "Raskopki Sumbarskogo otriada," Arkheologicheskie otkrytiia 1975 g., Moscow, 1976, pp. 554-55; idem., "Mogil'nik Sumbar I (predvaritel'noe soobshchenie)," Izvestiia AN Turkm. SSR, SON, 1976, no. 2, pp. 83-86; idem., "Raskopki mogil'nika Sumbar I v 1972-73 gg.," KSIA, issue 147, Moscow, 1976, pp. 14-20; idem., "Raskopki Sumbarskogo mogil'nika," Arkheologicheskie otkrytiia 1976 g., Moscow, 1977, p. 555; I. N. Chlopin "Denkmaler der Bronzezeit im Tal des Flusses Sumbar (Sudturkmenien)," Iranica Antiqua, vol. 10, 1973; I. N. Khlopin, "Sumbarskie mogil'niki — kliuch dlia sin-

khronizatsii pamiatnikov epokhi bronzy iuga Srednei Azii i Irana," Le plateau Iranien et L'Asie Centrale des origines à la conquête islamique, Paris, 1977, pp. 143-54.

3. I. N. Khlopin and L. I. Khlopina, "Raskopki v doline Sumbara," Arkheologicheskie otkrytiia 1977 g.," Moscow, 1978, pp. 550-51; G. N. Kurochkin, L. I. Khlopina and I. N. Khlopin, "Raskopki v doline Sumbara," Arkheologicheskie otkrytiia 1978 g., Moscow, 1979; L. I. Khlopina and I. N. Khlopin, "Mogil'nik epokhi rannei bronzy Parkhai II," Sovetskaia arkheologiia, 1979; idem., "Mogil'-nik Parkhai II v doline Sumbara," Izvestiia AN Turkm. SSR, SON, 1979.

4. I. N. Khlopin, "Verkhnii sloi poseleniia Kara-depe," KSIIMK, no. 76, Moscow, 1959, pp. 42-49; V. M. Masson, "Kara-depe u Artykha," Trudy IuTAKE, vol. 10, Ashkhabad, 1961, pp. 319-463.

5. V. I. Sarianidi, "Iuzhnaia Turkmeniia v epokhu bronzy," Pervobytnyi Turkmenistan, Ashkhabad, 1975, pp. 82-111.

6. V. M. Masson, op. cit., p. 329.

7. E. E. Kuz'mina, "Metallicheskie izdeliia eneolita i bronzogo veka v Srednei Azii," SAI V4-9, Moscow, 1966, pl. XVI, 28.

8. V. I. Sarianidi, Drevnie zemledel'tsy Afganistana, Moscow, 1977, fig. 44, 4.

9. A. M. Mandel'stam, "Pamiatniki epokhi bronzy v Iuzhnom Tadzhikistane," MIA, no. 145, Leningrad, 1968, pl. VIII, 2.

10. J. M. Casal, Fouilles de Mundigak, M.D.A.F.A., XVII, Paris, 1960.

11. E. F. Schmidt, Excavations at Tepe Hissar, Damghan, Philadelphia, 1937, pl. XXIX.

12. V. M. Masson, op. cit., pl. XVI, 1.

13. J. Deshayes, "Rapport préliminaire sur les troiséme et quatriéme campagnes de fouille à Tureng tépé," Iranica Antiqua, vol. 5, 1965, p. 86.

14. J. Deshayes, "New Evidence for the Indo-Europeans from Tureng Tepe, Iran," Archaeology, vol. 22, no. 1, 1969, p. 14.

15. See L. S. Klein, "Proiskhozhdenie donetskoi katakombnoi kul'tury," candidate's dissertation abstract, Leningrad, 1968; S. N. Bratchenko, Nizhnee podon'e v epokhu srednei bronzy," Kiev, 1976.

16. For example, V. I. Sarianidi, "Eneoliticheskoe poselenie Geoksiur," Trudy IuTAKE, vol. 10, Ashkhabad, 1961, and other works.

17. J. N. Chlopin, "Kollektivgraber des 3./2. Jahrtausends v.u. Z. in Sudturkmenien," Ethnographische-Archäologische Zeitschrift, vol. 18, no. 3, 1977, pp. 385-98.

18. D. M. Ovezov, Naselenie doliny Chandyra i srednego techeniia Sumbara, Ashkhabad, 1976, pp. 175-79.

19. S. P. Poliakov, Etnicheskaia istoriia severo-zapadnoi Turkmenii v Srednie veka, Moscow, 1973.

20. A. Askarov, Sapalli-tepe, Tashkent, 1973.

21. D. M. Ovezov, op. cit., pp. 117-19.

22. V. I. Sarianidi, "Kollektivnye pogrebeniia i izuchenie obshchestvennogo stroia rannezemledel'cheskikh plemen," Uspekhi sredneaziatskoi arkheologii, no. 1, Leningrad, 1972, pp. 23-25.

23. J. N. Chlopin, "Kollektivgraber des 3./2 Jahrtausends v.u.Z. in Sudturkmenien," Ethnographische-Archäologische Zeitschrift, vol. 18, no. 3, 1977, pp. 385-98, Berlin.

CHAPTER 2

Namazga-depe and the Late Bronze Age of Southern Turkmenia

L. I. KHLOPINA

The problem of the Late Bronze Age in southern Turkmenia is one of the most important in the archeology of Central Asia. Materials from excavations of agricultural settlements of the Bronze and Early Iron ages of southern Turkmenia are of prime importance to solving fundamental questions (see Figure 1). The topic of my dissertation currently is significant in interpreting a very important historical period — the Late Bronze Age — not only in southern Turkmenia but in adjacent regions of Central Asia and Iran. In fact it is the first work of general synthesis for this period, one in which complex problems of the genesis of the culture of the Early Iron Age in southern Turkmenia and problems of the relative and absolute chronology of the Bronze Age in Central Asia are posed and given new answers, while important new archeological material is disseminated.

The purpose of my work has been:

(1) to make available to the learned community a set of archeological sources from the excavations at the "Tower" settlement at Namazga-depe dating to the Late Bronze Age (see Figures 2 and 3);

(2) to examine and investigate the interactions of the archeological, above all ceramic, assemblage of Namazga VI with the prior ce-

---

This dissertation abstract has been edited to omit references to structural and organizational features of the dissertation. Consult also L. I. Hlopina, "Southern Turkmenia in the Late Bronze Age," East and West, 1972, vol. 22, pp. 199-214. — P.L.K.

Figure 1. Namazga-depe: view from the south.

ramic assemblage of Namazga V and the subsequent one of Yaz-depe I, and consequently to determine whether these assemblages are isolated or represent genetic continuity; (3) to determine more precisely the relative and absolute chronological boundaries of the Late Bronze Age in southern Turkmenia and also in the southern agricultural zone of Central Asia.

The Namazga VI cultural assemblage was previously known only from scattered finds. Other, similar materials newly discovered include an assemblage of pottery from Tekkem-tepe, a Late Bronze Age site (excavated by A. Ia. Shchetenko), and materials from the Late Bronze Age from the Sumbar I and II cemeteries in southwestern Turkmenia (excavated by I. N. Khlopina).

A complex approach to the study of the ware allowed me not only to analyze precisely the archeological materials but also to reach specific conclusions, based on this analysis, with respect to the continuity of the evolution of ceramics. Careful observation permitted not only identification of previously unknown types of vessels and establishment of the absence of influences by the culture of the nomads to the north on the pottery assemblage from Namazga-depe, but the discovery of a fundamentally new type of tool among the archaic population of Central Asia — pottery scrapers for hides and leather and pottery planing knives for stakes.

Late Bronze Age Sites in Southern Turkmenia

Late Bronze Age materials came from the following sites: (1) the south hill at Anau (Pumpelly, excavations of 1904); (2) Elken-Tepe (Marushchenko, excavations of 1953, 1955, and 1956); (3) Namazga-depe (Kuftin, excavations of 1952); (4) Tekkem-depe (Ganialin, excavations of 1952-53; Shchetenko, excavations of 1970-76); (5) Ulug-depe (Sarianidi, excavations of 1967, 1968, 1970); (6) Ovadan-depe (author's reconnaissance of 1974); (7) Yangi-Kala (Ganialin, excavations of 1951); (8) Takhirbai 3 (Masson, excavations of 1954-56); (9) Auchin-depe (Masson, excavations of 1954-

Figure 2. The "Tower" at Namazga-depe: view from the south.

56; Sarianidi, excavations of 1972). Stratigraphic soundings were dug on all these sites, and material on the surface was picked up. Exceptions to this were the excavations by B. A. Kuftin at the Namazga-depe "Tower" (excavation of an area of 100 square meters), by V. M. Masson at the Takhirbai 3 site — 100 square meters of excavations — and 140 square meters of excavation by A. F. Ganialin at Tekkem-depe. A. Ia. Shchetenko is now conducting large-scale digging at the last site. Thus the assemblage of Late Bronze Age material represented a set of archeological evidence from different sites that could not display the nature of the culture of the Namazga VI period in sufficient detail.

The "Tower" of Namazga-depe

I will focus on materials excavated from the Namazga-depe "Tower" settlement in 1964, 1965, 1967, and 1974. They were not only of the type and time of Namazga VI but specifically from Namazga VI itself, a fact that in itself defines their importance for characterizing the Late Bronze Age in southern Turkmenia.

The excavated portion of the community comes to 1,800 square meters and, in layout, consists of three assemblages separated by streets. The western assemblage is associated with the production of pottery, as is shown by the remains of two kilns that were two-story structures of which the furnaces and, in part, the firing chambers remained, making it possible to reconstruct the general outlines of the process of firing pottery.

The two other assemblages were residential, of which the central one is better preserved. It was enclosed on all sides and consisted of dwelling and work-related structures and courtyards. The dwellings have well-finished interiors. Those best preserved were found to have vessels dug into the floor and special protective barriers for a warming hearth. All this, together with the well-coated floors, the plastered walls, and the sharply defined doorways with thresholds and stepping stones, indicates ancient traditions of home construction. The work-associated structures were considerably smaller. They usually did not form part of the residential building and were erected in the yards. It is difficult to determine what their specific purpose was, but auxiliary structures for storage and the like were needed. Each dwelling block, consisting of from one to three rooms, had its individual yards — plots

38

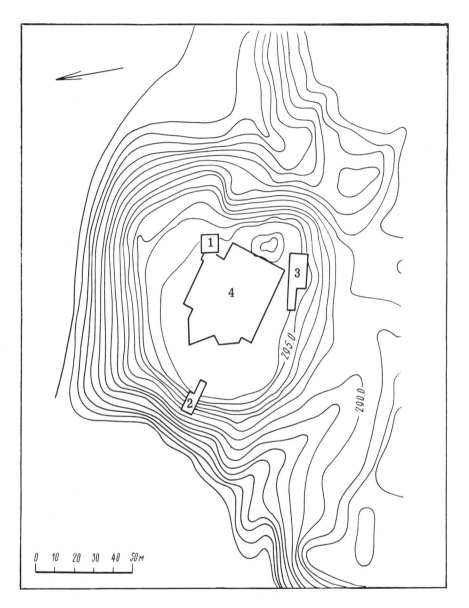

Figure 3. The "Tower" at Namazga-depe. Plan 1 — excavations of B. A. Kuftin, 1952; 2 — excavations of A. A. Marushchenko, 1956; 3 — excavations of A. F. Ganialin, 1959; 4 — excavations of I. N. Khlopin, 1964, 1965, and 1967, and excavations of L. I. Khlopina, 1974.

39

where there had been no construction, in which there were thick layers of garbage and hearths for cooking.

Pottery was the principal category of find at the Namazga-depe "Tower" as well as at all the agricultural communities. All the characteristics of a vessel (external appearance, size, shape, body, surface decoration) depended on the function assigned it by the craftsman when it was made. Proceeding from that primary criterion, the pottery is classifiable in three groups: tableware for the consumption of food, containers for storing products in the process of work, and kitchenware used in preparing food. Each of these groups consisted of a given number of specific forms that defined them and their attributes.

The tableware was almost all turned on the potter's wheel and made of well-levigated clay. Most often it showed in section a red or rose fabric and a red slip on the surface. Less often one finds ware that is gray both on the surface and in section. Five principal forms are known, with variations: I — bowls, with hemispherical and conical bodies, either of which may have everted or inverted rims; II — vases; III — cups; IV — small pots; and V — pitchers. The grayware includes a beaker with a sharp carination. The cups are particularly interesting. They were shaped by hand, had a black polished surface, and most important, contained crushed pottery inclusions worked into the body.

With few exceptions ware used in work had been thrown on the wheel. The shapes were those of large storage jars, smaller ones under 0.5 meter high, pots, basins, basins for straining, cauldrons, and ceramic pedestals and covers. The latter two forms are subsidiary parts.

The kitchenware is marked by a sooty black fracture and a distinctive heat-resistant body with a great amount of large and fine-grained sand and ground quartz temper. These admixtures resulted in a grainy surface and also made it difficult to use the potter's wheel in making this ware, for it was molded by hand and only in some cases was trimmed on the wheel. In shape the kitchenware can be divided into five types: 1 — pots; 2 — potlike vessels (no complete specimens remain); 3 — cauldrons; 4 — little pots; 5 — bowls. The most interesting admixture to the body was crushed pottery, which was found in the second and fifth types of kitchenware. Many vessels are decorated with incised ornamentation.

A diverse assemblage of tools for production is represented; they were made of various kinds of materials. There are 65 stone

Figure 4. Upper building level on the "Tower" settlement at Namazga-depe. Plan.

tools, including grain hullers, cow bells, mortars, pestles, scrapers, hammer stones, graters, grindstones, "shaft straighteners," ore grinders, a casting mold for pouring javelin tips with flanges, scale weights, stepping stones, flat covers, and stone vessels. There were only two finds of metal implements: a bronze knife with distinct handle and a round awl. Bone tools are represented by two fragments of polishers or spatulae.

Pottery tools constitute a distinct class. They were first identified by the author in processing the Tekkem-depe materials in 1973. In 1974 they were found by the author everywhere in Bronze

L. I. Khlopina

Age sites in southern Turkmenia: at the Namazga-depe "Tower," in material lying on the ground at Namazga-depe sites of the Namazga V period, Altyn-depe, Ulug-depe, Ovadan-depe, and even at the Sumbar site in the vicinity of the Kara Q'ala settlement. Study of some of these tools at the Laboratory of Archeological Technology of the Leningrad Branch of the Institute of Archeology of the USSR Academy of Sciences confirmed their initial typological identification as scrapers.

All the tools were made of fragments of table and, primarily, work-associated thrown pottery and can be divided visually by functions into scrapers, planing knives, and querns.

The scrapers divide into four groups according to the way the working edge is finished: finished on one side only, finished on both sides, with two bilaterally finished working edges, and flat disklike scrapers. The ideal scraper shape, to which each such tool tends, is trapezoidal with elongated sides or an elongated subequilateral triangle. The width of the working edge of the scraper varies from 4 to 11 centimeters. One scraper is unique. It was made of a special flat slab of pottery and not of a sherd. By analogy to stone implements of this type, the pottery scrapers should be regarded as specialized tools for the initial and secondary working of hides and raw material for leather. The pottery planing knives are made from the bottoms of vessels, their working edges are worked from within with small chips, and they are concave. Such tools might have been intended, for example, to remove bark from poles. There was a single quern, made from the handle of a vessel, with traces of wear visible to the naked eye.

Farming and herding were the principal activities in the ancient economy. The finds display techniques for processing products of agriculture and stockfarming. In addition, household crafts are evident, particularly metallurgical and ceramic. The available materials permit not only understanding the process of firing the ware but also the conclusion that there may have been different kinds of kilns to fit the dimensions and functions of the products. The structure of society in the Late Bronze Age, reconstructed in other writings, does not contradict the layout of the settlement excavated. Thus we can say that the "Tower" settlement at Namazga-depe was populated by a patriarchal group of kinfolk. It was divided into large patriarchal families. Each such family (judging by the layout of the settlement) consisted of several generations of blood kin and was divided into several nuclear families. The nuclear families lived separately from each other and prepared their food separately, but the agricultural work and some of the forms of household production were still probably carried out jointly by the entire population of the settlement.

Southern Turkmenia in the Late Bronze Age

In order to compare different sites from the same period it is necessary to match the components of their archeological assemblages: (1) layout of settlements; (2) implements of production; (3) pottery.

1. Of the eight settlements of the Namazga VI period, excavations were conducted at five: two of them did not reveal any layout (Anau, Ulug-depe), and two yielded minimal information (Tekkem-depe, the excavations by Ganialin, and Takhirbai 3). Only the dig at the Namazga-depe "Tower," which was continued until it extended over 1,800 square meters, made it possible to judge the principles of layout.

2. The implements of production divide into stone, metallic, and ceramic artifacts. Stone tools (grain hullers, grindstones, mortars, etc.) are found at all Bronze Age settlements. Perhaps when they are subjected to specialized investigation one will be able to elucidate chronological or local differences, but so far it has not been possible to do so. Intact metal tools of the period of Namazga VI are extremely rare. Comparing them by sites within the period of Namazga VI yields no results. Pottery tools have been found in the cultural layers of only two settlements, the "Tower" at Namazga-depe and at Tekkem-depe, and thus far they reveal no local features.

3. As we know, pottery is the basic and abundant archeological material, one of the fundamental indices of an archeological culture; it is a source and marker for continuity and contacts with other cultures. Therefore comprehensive study of pottery is the key to solving our problems here.

Statistical processing of the assemblages of pottery from the different settlements requires that the following be established: (1) a unified terminology; (2) a single technique for characterization; (3) categories and groups of indices characterizing each assemblage of ware; (4) the relative and absolute values for the indices. I use chiefly published materials, most of which have been lost. Such materials cannot be subjected to further study. Therefore we are compelled to rely on a typology of shapes of vessels, with maximal use of all supplemental information.

Since our focus is primarily the period of Namazga VI, it is the shapes of ware specifically from that period that are taken as our point of departure. Another circumstance in favor of this choice is the fact that the "Tower" settlement presently is the best studied of all sites of the Late Bronze Age in southern Turkmenia.

A more detailed comparison of assemblages of pottery, both horizontally (within the Namazga VI period) and vertically (between the Namazga V, Namazga VI, and Yaz-depe I periods) cannot presently be carried out for the further reason that pottery of the periods of Namazga V and Yaz-depe I was not subjected to special study (with the exception of the work of E. V. Saiko) and is known only from publications. Thus there is nothing with which the petrographic analysis conducted on a group of ware from the Namazga-depe "Tower" can be compared. All this compels us to rely on the formal-typological technique for investigating wares of the Late Bronze Age and the Early Iron Age as the only method available.

Pottery from all settlements of the Namazga VI period can be divided into three major groups: tableware, that used in the economy, and kitchenware.

Tableware consists of 10 types (see Figure 5):

Type I — bowls. Two subtypes are known: 1a — the spherical bowl with inverted rim; 1b — spherical bowl with everted rim; 2 — a conical bowl with an everted or inverted rim or with a broad-edged rim. Type II — vase. Type III — cup. Type IV — beaker. Type V — a glass with a bell-shaped mouth. VI — drinking glass. VII — teapot. VIII — small pot. IX — flask. X — pitcher.

We managed to divide the total ware used for daily economic and special auxiliary purposes into 9 types (see Figure 6): Type I — jars. Type II — jars under 0.5 meter high. Type III — pot. Type IV — kettle with tubular spout. Type V — basin. Type VI — basin for straining. Type VII — cauldron. Type VIII — pedestal. There are two subtypes of such supports: truncated-conical and hourglass. Type IX — lids.

The ceramic assemblages from sites of the Namazga VI period are virtually identical in all sites of that period, both in the zone at the base of the Kopet Dagh Mountains and in the Murghab Oasis. It is true that in the former area the tableware is red-slipped with vertical burnishing, but its absence in the Murghab Delta does not influence the forms of the ware.

The comparison of the types of ware of the three stratigraphically consecutive periods, Namazga V, Namazga VI, and Yaz-depe I, has been done in a generalized way here, without details, but it runs on the same principle as the comparison of the ceramic material of the Namazga VI period sites to each other.

Since the genetic continuity between the Namazga V and Namazga VI assemblages is universally accepted, we place no emphasis on proving that proposition. But several points of view exist with respect to the origin of the Yaz-depe I pottery assemblage, and this diversity compels us to give special consideration to this question. Some investigators (Ganialin, Marushchenko, and others) hold that pastoralists who penetrated from northern into southern Turkmenia played a significant role in the shaping of the assemblage. Others (Masson) hold that the Yaz-depe I assemblage is genetically connected to that of Namazga VI, but that there was a break of 100 to 150 years between them. A third group (Sarianidi) advances the point of view that the Yaz-depe I assemblage made its appearance in southern Turkmenia as the result of infiltration of population from eastern Khorassan. One of my objectives is an attempt to examine the available materials and determine which of these views corresponds most closely to them.

The appearance of painted ware of the Yaz-depe I type helps to disclose the materials of settlements at which layers of the Yaz-depe I period overlie those of Namazga VI. On the basis of the study of pottery assemblages from the settlements of Ulug-depe and Elken-depe, investigators came to the conclusion that painted ware of the Yaz-depe I Early Iron Age type appears in layers of the Namazga VI period, becomes the predominant type in the Yaz-depe I period, and is displaced by wheel-thrown ware in the Achaemenid period (Sarianidi, Gutlyev).

Another characteristic feature of the Yaz-depe I pottery assemblage is the admixture of crushed ceramics into the body of vessels of several forms. In the materials from the "Tower" at Namazga-depe it already proved possible to identify three groups of ware molded by hand; in shape, color of sherd, and admixture of crushed ceramics in the body, these groups do not differ from vessels of the Yaz-depe I type. One group is identifiable in the tableware category (type III — cups), and two other groups fall into the kitchenware category.

The discovery of attributes in the Yaz-depe I period ware such as painting of the surface (Ulug-depe) and admixture of crushed pottery in the body (Namazga-depe "Tower") in cultural layers of settlements of the Namazga VI period makes it possible to draw an unmistakeable conclusion: the assemblage of pottery of the Yaz-depe I type does not arise unexpectedly at settlements in the foothill

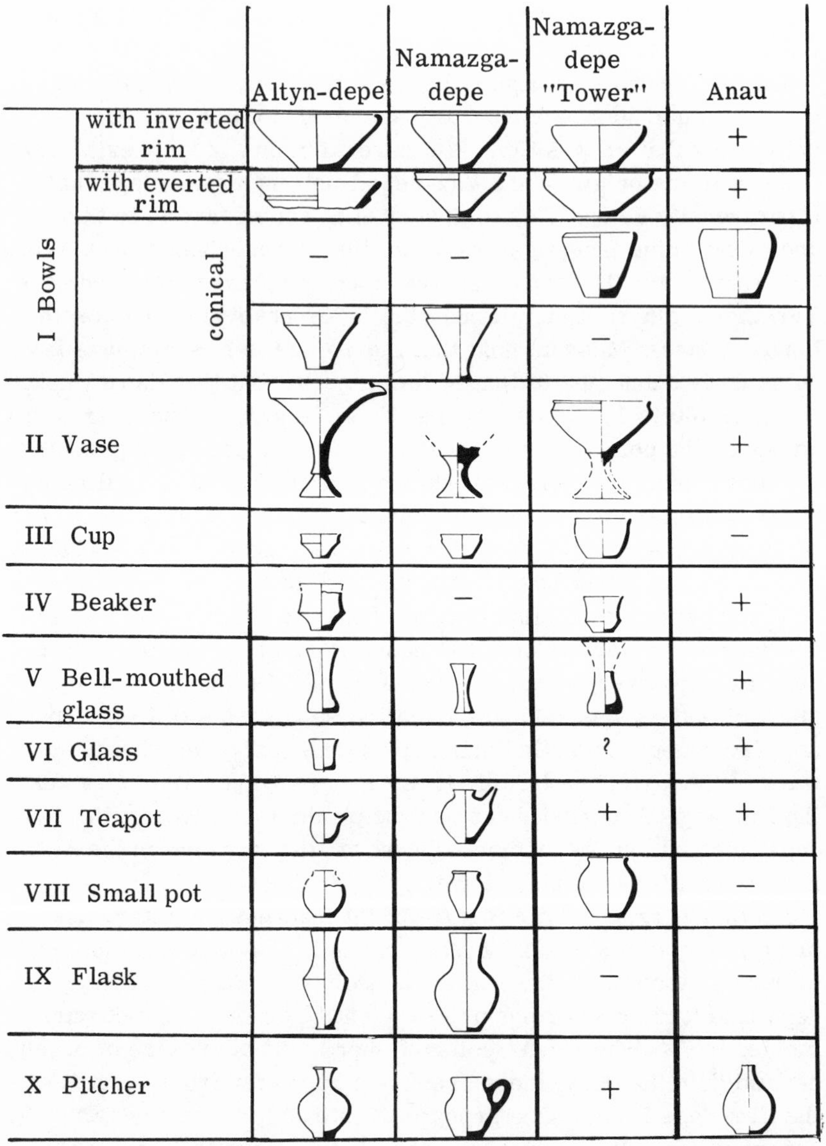

			Altyn-depe	Namazga-depe	Namazga-depe "Tower"	Anau
I Bowls	with inverted rim					+
	with everted rim					+
	conical		−	−		
					−	−
II Vase						+
III Cup						−
IV Beaker				−		+
V Bell-mouthed glass						+
VI Glass				−	?	+
VII Teapot					+	+
VIII Small pot						−
IX Flask					−	−
X Pitcher					+	

Figure 5. Forms of tableware of the Bronze and Early Iron Age.

46

Elken-depe	Tekkem-depe	Auchin-depe	Takhir-bai 3	Yaz I	Yaz II
+	+	−			
+	+				
−	−	−	−	−	−
−	−		−	−	−
+	+			+	
−	−	−			−
	+				
−	−	−	−	+	
−	−	−		−	−
−	−			−	−
−	+	−			
−	−			−	+
+	+	+	−		

47

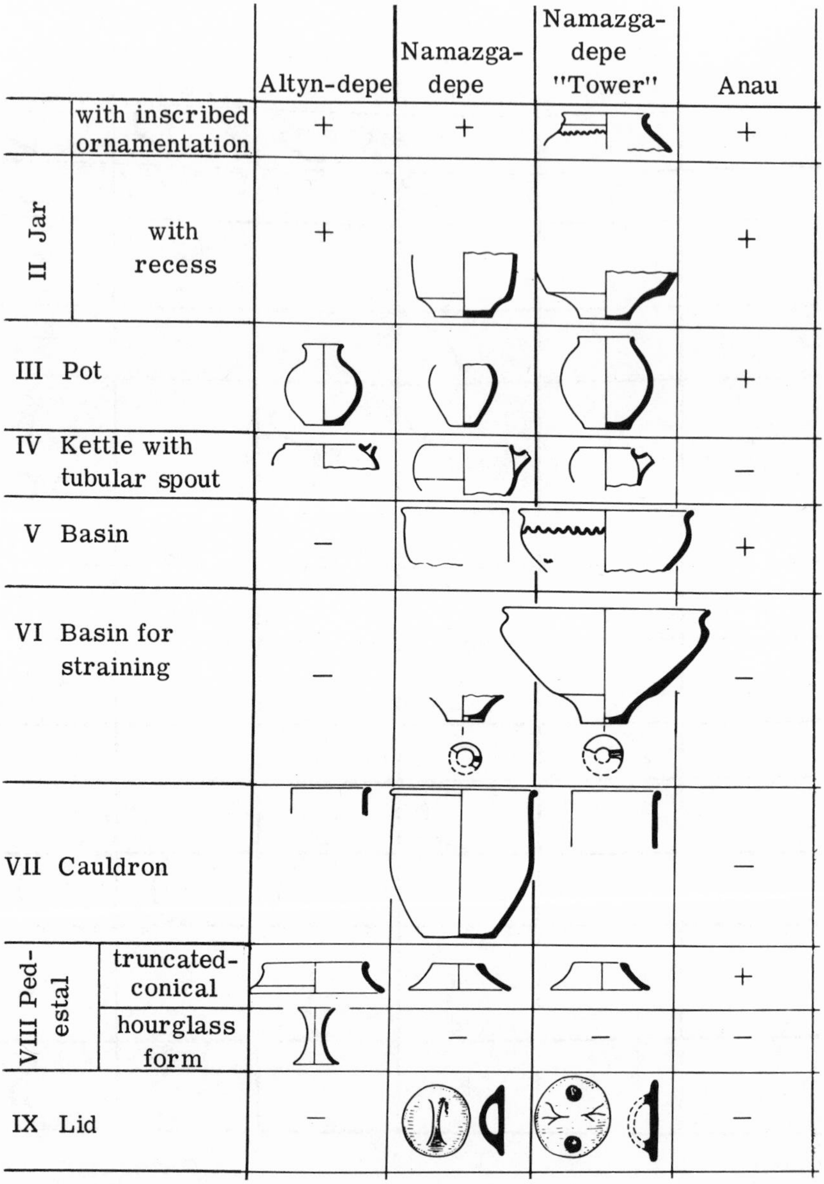

		Altyn-depe	Namazga-depe	Namazga-depe "Tower"	Anau
II Jar	with inscribed ornamentation	+	+		+
	with recess	+			+
III Pot					+
IV Kettle with tubular spout					−
V Basin		−			+
VI Basin for straining		−			−
VII Cauldron					−
VIII Pedestal	truncated-conical				+
	hourglass form		−	−	
IX Lid		−			−

Figure 6. Forms of household ware of the Bronze and Early Iron

Elken-depe	Tekkem-depe	Auchin-depe	Takhir-bai 3	Yaz I	Yaz II
+	+	+		+	−
+	+	+		+	+
+	+	+	+	+	
−	+	−	−	−	−
−	−				
		−	−		−
−	−	−	−	−	−
−	+	+			−
−	−	−	−	+	+
+	+	−	--		+

Age.

49

zone of the Kopet Dagh Mountains but as a consequence of the natural and regular development of the ceramic assemblage of the Late Bronze Age in southern Turkmenia.

Thus, after carrying out a comparative description and analysis of the three consecutive assemblages of pottery, it became possible to arrive at the following conclusions.

1. The pottery assemblage of the Namazga VI period differs in three features from that of the Namazga V period at sites in the foothills zone of the mountains of southern Turkmenia:

a) the absence of the elegant and in some cases even pretentious vessels that characterize and define the Namazga V period (for example, vessels of various shapes on thin legs);

b) the presence of red-slipped and burnished tableware;

c) the presence of a small group of grayware.

2. The pottery assemblage of the Yaz-depe I period differs from that of Namazga VI in two features:

a) the vast bulk of the vessels were made by hand with no use of the potter's wheel;

b) decoration of handmade table and, in part, of livelihood-associated ware, with painted patterns.

3. Continuity and genetic kinship of the pottery assemblages of Namazga V–Namazga VI–Yaz-depe I can be derived from such objective indicators as:

a) transfer of the principal forms of table and livelihood ware, i.e., the basic component of the ceramic assemblage, from the Namazga V period through the Namazga VI to the Yaz-depe I, in its natural evolution;

b) the presence in the Namazga V assemblage of the technological device of mixing crushed pottery in the body of ceramics and the further development of this technique in the Namazga VI period, while in the Yaz-depe I period this technique became an identifying sign of the ware of that time;

c) the appearance of pottery painting of the Yaz-depe I type within the ceramic assemblage of Namazga VI;

d) the coexistence in strata of early stages of the Yaz-depe I period of ware with the painting characteristic of that period and of red-slipped vessels more typical of the Namazga VI period;

e) grayware of the Namazga VI period continues to exist in the Yaz-depe I period as well;

f) the presence of incised cylinders among kitchenware in the periods of Namazga VI and Yaz-depe I;

g) special studies of the technology of wheel-thrown ware in the

Namazga V, Namazga VI, Yaz-depe I, and Yaz-depe II periods demonstrated a continuous line of development of the technological devices of pottery making (Saiko).

All the foregoing shows the continuity and uninterruptedness of traditions of pottery production during the indicated periods and the continuity of cultural history development at that time.

4. The period of Namazga VI can now be seen as the natural cultural-historical foundation for the Early Iron Age period of Yaz-depe I, as V. M. Masson once defined it, but the analysis of pottery assemblages of those periods demonstrates that no period of time elapsed between them. The pottery assemblage of the Early Iron Age in the southern Turkmenian foothills zone most probably came into being as the result of the evolution of the ceramic ware of the Late Bronze Age and does not contain evidence that elements of an external culture had penetrated into this territory.

The pottery assemblages of all periods divide into two categories: an unchanging basic group of vessels, and a variable one that shows the evolution of the ware. The nonvariable basic group reflects the virtually stable economy of the farming groups of the zone at the foot of the Kopet Dagh. Habits of conducting their operations, acquired over centuries, created a distinctive set of vessels that passed on from one period to another with insignificant changes in shape. I have tried to trace the interconnection and interdependence of forms of tableware and the means of decorating it.

Namazga III period. All ware is hand-thrown. Wide development of zoomorphic designs was the defining characteristic of the period. Geometrical ornamentation existed. Grayware made its appearance.

Namazga IV period. The appearance of the potter's wheel immediately affected the shapes of the vessels, for they acquired sharp-ribbed contours. The zoomorphic ornamentation degenerated while geometric designs attained perfection and defined the assemblage.

Namazga V period. All the ware was thrown on the wheel; sharp-ribbed vessels are developed further. Geometrical ornamentation and grayware were absent. The shapes of the vessels themselves became ornamental. The potter's wheel called into existence the near full-time craft specialization of the potter, and this itself required the organization of an internal market for the sale of craft ware. Hence society was on the threshold of the founding of the state. However, most of the population abandoned the zone at the foot of the Kopet Dagh, and old traditions began to be resurrected among those remaining.

Namazga VI period. Sharp-ribbed vessels occurred only in individual instances. The ornamentation of the surfaces of vessels, particularly red slip with burnishing, became the defining characteristic, and grayware reappeared. Toward the end of the period geometric painted decoration appeared, but not the "carpet-type" painting of Namazga IV, which had died, never to return. The replacement was cruder.

Yaz-depe I period. Red-slipped and grayware, which defined the previous period, declined to nothing. The ware was chiefly handmade; wheel-thrown pottery was rare but continued the tradition of Namazga VI. Careless geometrical painting and handmade ware were the determining criteria. In the upper layers there was an increase in the amount of ware thrown on the wheel.

Yaz-depe II period. The potter's wheel comes to dominate once again, as though repeating the period of Namazga V. Once again the shape of the vessel becomes the identifying characteristic, but it is not as mannered as in the period of Namazga V. This too is sharp-ribbed, but much cruder. In the lower layers one still finds fragments of painted and red-slipped ware.

Thus development of pottery in the settlements of the foothills zone of the Kopet Dagh during the Bronze and Early Iron ages reveals the following major patterns in the process of its evolution:

1. The determining element in the pottery assemblage of each period of cultural history is born in the preceding and dies in the succeeding period.

2. The style and means of decorating the vessels are indissolubly connected with the development of the technology of pottery production of the period.

3. The continuity and genetic relationship in the development of ceramics and, consequently, the culture of the ancient agriculturalists of southern Turkmenia from the Aeneolithic to the Achaemenid period follows from all the foregoing.

Questions of Chronology

The present practice of placing the Namazga VI period in the middle or during the latter half of the second millennium is too general to be satisfactory any longer. Moreover, archeological finds of recent years make it possible not only to attain considerably greater precision with respect to the chronology of the Late Bronze Age in southern Turkmenia but to pose the question of the need to reach greater precision with respect to a number of accepted chronological identifications for Central Asia as a whole.

First, I look at the relationship among all sites of the Late Bronze Age in the foothills zone of the Kopet Dagh Mountains, and then I fix a relative chronology both of the monuments and of the period as a whole (see Figure 7). The archeological data show that the Namazga VI period followed immediately after Namazga V. The duration of the period did not exceed the period of existence of the consecutive construction levels identified at the "Tower" at Namazga-depe. It is customary to regard one construction level as having existed on the average for no more than 40-50 years, which allows us to propose the total duration of the Namazga VI period as 280-350 years, i.e., not over 350 years.

A number of artifacts from the Namazga VI period match monuments of the Late Bronze Age in southwestern Turkmenia, particularly the burial grounds of Sumbar I and II near the village of Kara Q'ala. The presence in these cemeteries of imported utensils from settlements in the northern portion of the plain at the foot of the Kopet Dagh merely indicated contacts between the two neighboring culture zones but did not define the time of the contacts.

Whereas pottery is characteristic of a comparatively narrow territory, since it was made chiefly for internal consumption, bronze ware was more widely prevalent. In the Sumbar cemeteries a correspondence was found in 1973-76 between the period of Namazga VI and the culture of ancient Dakhistan, while the finds from the sites in the strip at the base of the mountains come both from burials and from villages.

Circlets or rings in the form of a ring of wire, not entirely closed, flat diadems, and pins with crosslike heads inscribed in circles are known from the cemeteries of Yangi-Kala and Sumbar. Whereas the circlets are widely disseminated, the diadems are known to exist only in the two cemeteries named and in burials of the Namazga VI period at Namazga-depe. However, the pins with these original end shapes are particularly interesting, for objects of this type can now be organized into a single chronological series (moving from east to west): a stone casting mold for precisely such pins from the fourth construction level of the "Tower" community of Namazga-depe, two bronze pins from burial 7 at the Yangi-Kala cemetery, and two bronze pins from burial 6 at Sumbar II. The artifacts listed are so distinctive that there is no doubt that they are relatively synchronous; consequently the sites where they were found are also contemporaneous. The finding of a casting mold at the zone at the base of the Kopet Dagh Mountains may indicate that

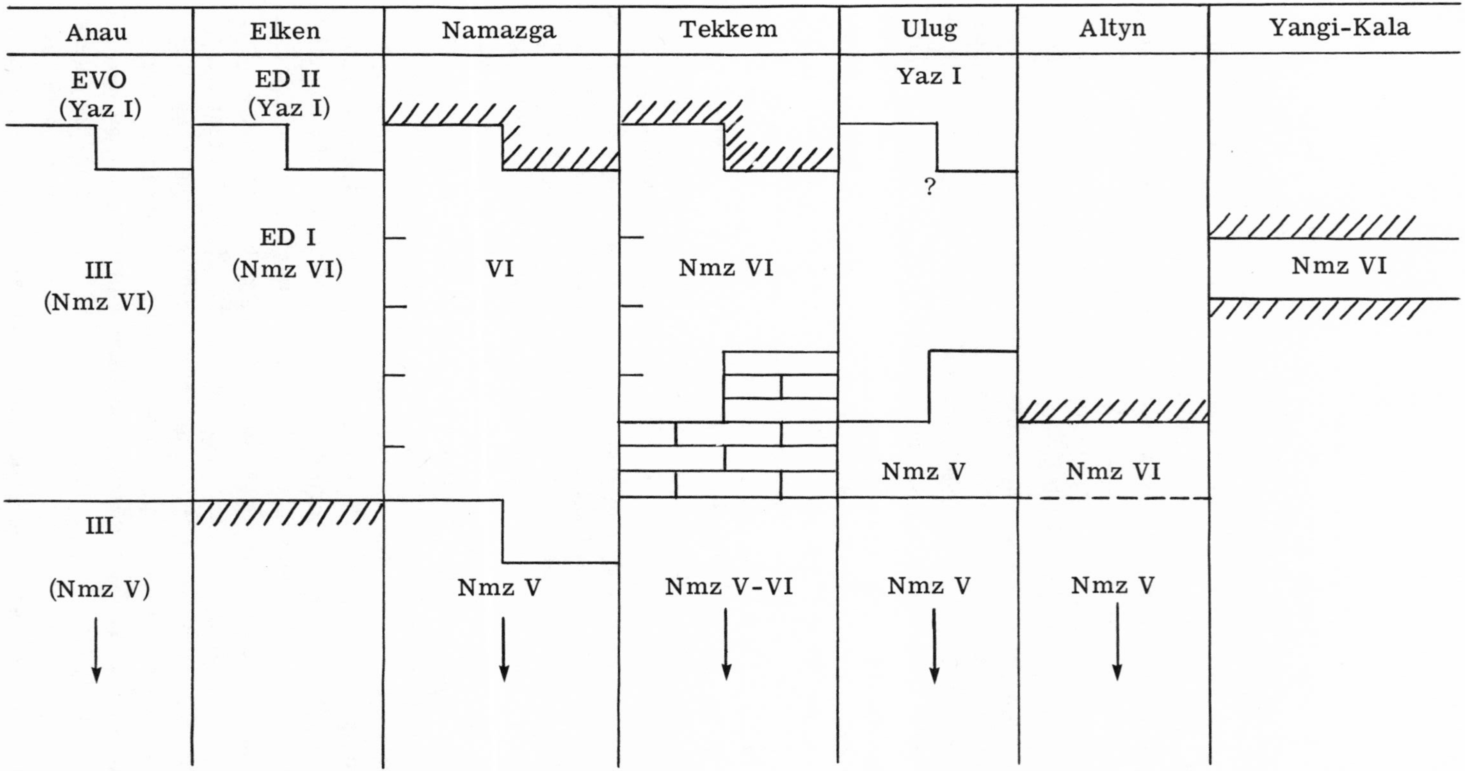

Figure 7. The synchronization of Namazga VI sites.

such pins were made in settlements in that zone. They may also have been made at sites in southwestern Turkmenia, although we have thus far not found casting molds for them. But it is hardly likely that utterly identical ornaments were made in such different cultural zones.

The artifacts confirming the contemporaneity of the Namazga VI period and the Sumbar cemeteries include arrowheads and dart tips with flanges at the transition to the haft. Such tips have been found both in the Sumbar cemeteries and at the "Tower" community. Most importantly, in the latter place a fragment of a casting mold for such tips was found. One can consider spherical stone maces as another group of related finds. They are known from the Tekkem-depe settlement of the Namazga VI period and from the Ulug-depe and Yaz-depe settlements of the Early Iron Age but are totally unknown in the Namazga V period. Eleven maces of this kind have been found so far in the cemetery at Sumbar I. The latest date of existence of such artifacts in southern Turkmenia can be identified quite accurately. At the southern mound of Anau, in the very lowest layers, dating from the Yaz-depe I period, fragments of an iron sickle were found permitting the dating of the early Yaz-depe I period to the beginning of the first millennium B.C. This is the most ancient iron implement in Central Asia, and it set the upper chronological limit of the Namazga VI period at approximately the beginning of the first millennium B.C.

Thus a number of metal and stone artifacts of the Namazga III period, coming from cultural layers of settlements in the piedmont strip, have direct correlates with sites of the Bronze Age of southwestern Turkmenia. Moreover, some artifacts can be regarded as imports from settlements of the zone at the base of the mountains in the southwest to the Sumbar Valley. All this indicates the archeologically documented contemporaneity of monuments of the Namazga VI period with the Sumbar cemeteries.

The pottery assemblage of the Sumbar cemeteries (611 vessels) consists of vessels made by hand (75 percent) and on the wheel (25 percent). Among the numerous forms one can identify teapots with long and complex spouts (half a tubular spout and half an open pouring channel); teapots with tubular spouts of elongated truncated-conical proportions with a sharp rib in the lower third of the body, sometimes on a low pedestal; conical vessels with open pourers; cups with vertical handles at their bases (less often at their rims); and others. These forms are absolutely not characteristic of the Late Bronze Age in the valley at the base of the Kopet Dagh but correspond totally to the pottery assemblage of the grayware culture embracing the southern trans-Caspian in a broad semicircle from the lower course of the Sumbar in the east to Lake Urmia in the west.

Sialk V, Khurvin, Marlik, Giyan I, Hasanlu V, and others fall into Iran's grayware culture. The cemeteries of Marlik and Khurvin do not contain iron artifacts. In the opinion of T. C. Young and R. Dyson, they fall into the Late Bronze Age. M. Tosi and L. Vanden Berghe date Khurvin (and Marlik) to 1300-1000 B.C., K. Schippmann offers the dating 1300-1000 B.C. for Hasanlu V and regards that period as pertaining to the Early Iron Age. In accordance with the generally accepted terminology of Young, these Iranian sites fall into the early grayware level, which is dated within the period of 1300-1000 B.C.

There were local differences within the culture. Thus in the ware of the western sites (Hasanlu V, Giyan I), mugs (or beakers) with extended proportions, handles, and raised small pedestals are widely found, while the teapots with the long, complex spouts are not encountered. At Khurvin the opposite is the case: these teapots are found in virtually all the cemeteries. The pottery assemblage of the Sumbar cemeteries finds marked analogues in the sites of the eastern part of the Iranian early grayware levels, specifically, Khurvin. These cemeteries have many features in common. Specifically, the teapots with complex spouts, imitating the heads of predatory birds with long beaks (cormorants ?), are the distinguishing type. There are also differences: the teapots of Khurvin always have handles, while those of Sumbar always have a piece molded on in imitation of a handle. Other forms of utensils provide less expressive analogues.

Comparison of the metalware from the Sumbar cemeteries with those from Iranian sites yielded a very broad time span (from the beginning of the second millennium B.C. virtually to the middle of the first). This also indicates that the roots of the culture of ancient Dakhistan are in the Iranian cultures.

Grayware makes up 10-15 percent of the total found at the sites in the piedmont zone of the Kopet Dagh (the "Tower"). At Iranian sites (Khurvin) it makes up 80 percent of the assemblage, while in southwestern Turkmenia (Sumbar) it is 40 percent. To us this evident decline in the amount of grayware from West to East is not random: in the regions of origin of this culture, grayware predominates, while on its periphery its presence declines by half. The influence of the Iranian grayware culture outside its native region was so great that it was still 10-15 percent of the total ware even in the foothill belt of the Kopet Dagh. Proceed farther east and the trail of grayware becomes even fainter. At the settlement of Sapalli-tepe there was a small collection (amount not indicated). In the Tigrovaia Balka and Early Tulkhar cemeteries of southern Tadjikistan, there was one gray-clay vessel each. Thus the mere presence of grayware may serve as proof of the contemporaneity of the cultures listed. Finally, one more comparison: at eastern sites of the early grayware level in Iran, the leading form, as already noted above, is the teapot with complex spout. It is also one of the determining forms in the Sumbar cemeteries. Several fragments of such teapots were found in the strip at the base of the Kopet Dagh (the "Tower" at Namazga-depe and Tekkem-depe). Farther east this type of teapot has been found only at the settlement of Sapalli-tepe. This line of comparison also serves as proof of the contemporaneity of the listed cultures. In Iran this unique form of ware appears only in the early grayware level of Iron Age I, 1300-1000 B.C. (Medvedskaia).

V. M. Masson has proposed dating the culture of ancient Dakhistan from the second half of the second to the first third of the first millennium B.C. Proceeding from the dating of the Iranian sites, the Sumbar I and II cemeteries can be dated to the closing centuries of the second millennium B.C. or, more precisely, to within the thirteenth to tenth centuries B.C., since no iron artifacts were found there. The Sumbar cemeteries fall into the level of the early Iranian grayware and are synchronous with the period of Namazga VI in the northern plain at the foot of the Kopet Dagh. Consequently the period of Namazga VI can be dated, with good reason, between 1350 and 1000 B.C. The dates suggested are not in conflict either with the total duration of the period, the synchronization of sites, or their connections with the neighboring western and north Iranian culture provinces.

It would be interesting to trace how the established dates harmonize with the dating of the farming cultures of northern Afghanistan and southern Uzbekistan, which it is common to periodize without citing absolute dates for the time of the late Namazga V and early Namazga VI cultures. Since there is, without question, an overwhelming southern Turkmenian component in the material culture of these places (a fact best explained as the result of the migration of a considerable number of people from southern Turkmenia via the Murghab Delta and the northern piedmont plain of the Hindu Kush — northern Afghanistan — to the right bank of the Amu

Darya), the appearance of settled farming communities in the easternmost part of the area of the distribution of this culture has to be dated to about 1200 B.C.

The date proposed is in conflict with the dates generally accepted for this culture. It is about 500 years younger than that already established in the literature. However, the previously accepted dates also rest on archeological facts, and therefore I have examined these facts and the reliability of the conclusions based on them.

The group of Dashly settlements in northern Afghanistan is now dated to the middle and second half of the second millennium B.C. by analogy to materials of the Namazga VI type. Since we date the Namazga VI period to the final centuries of the second millennium B.C., while the metal artifacts on which the earlier dating relies (sickles and razors) cannot be regarded as older than 1200-1000 B.C., we can therefore hypothesize that the settlements of the Dashly group arose no earlier than the final quarter of the second millennium B.C., which corresponds totally with the just published radiocarbon date of the second floor of a building at the Dashly 3 site of 1110±70 B.C. (Sarianidi).

All the bronze artifacts used to arrive at the chronology of Sapalli-tepe (ceramic correspondences with sites outside the piedmont zone of southern Turkmenia are purely theoretical and cannot be considered) come from graves of the lower building level of the site and help define only the starting date of Sapalli-tepe, i.e., the beginning of the agricultural exploitation of the Central Asian lowland plains.

Our work considers bronze artifacts that may have significance for establishing the dates of the site: bronze flagons, a shaft-hole axe, a mirror with anthropomorphic handle, double-edged knives with distinct handles, maces, and seals. On this basis the conclusion is drawn that not one of the bronze artifacts listed can be dated to earlier than the middle of the second millennium B.C., or the time when researchers date the end of habitation at Sapalli-tepe. All the artifacts, however, come from the bottom building level and consequently define the time not of the end but the beginning of habitation at the site. The bronze flagon requires separate discussion. This artifact, found in 1975 in the Sumbar cemetery, establishes contemporaneity of that burial ground and the lower construction level of the Sapalli-tepe settlement. This established a closed triadic connection among the principal sites of the Bronze Age in the south of Central Asia: (1) the bottom layer of Sapalli-

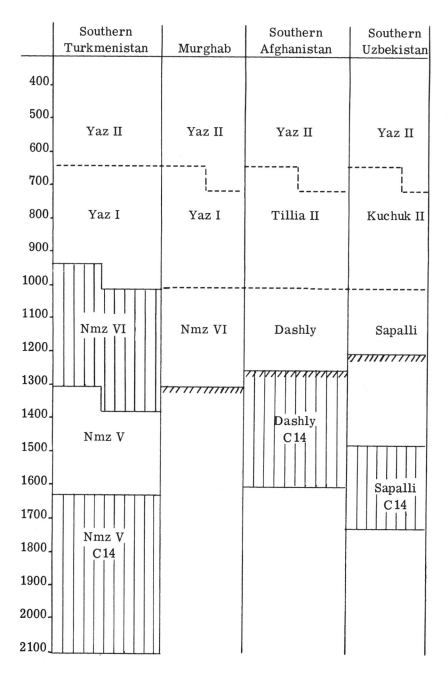

Figure 8. The Bronze Age chronology of southern Central Asia (areas with vertical striations represent periods determined by C14 dates).

tepe is synchronous with the beginning of the Namazga VI period; (2) the bottom level of Sapalli-tepe is synchronous with the Sumbar cemeteries; and (3) the Sumbar cemeteries are synchronous with the middle of the Namazga VI period.

Thus the artifacts on which was based the synchronization of sites of the Sapalli type with early stages of the Namazga VI period proved (in absolute dates) to be considerably younger than previously considered. They have to be placed in the final quarter of the second millennium B.C. (also see the comparison of grayware and teapots with complex spouts from Sapalli-tepe through the piedmont zone of the Kopet Dagh with Iran).

New dates have recently been suggested for agricultural sites of southern Uzbekistan (Askarov): early Sapalli dates 1700-1500 B.C., and late Sapalli 1500-1300 B.C. Without commenting on the change in earlier dating, it should be noted that Askarov had already raised the upper chronological boundary of the Sapalli-tepe settlement to the lower boundary of the Namazga VI period suggested by us, i.e., to 1350 B.C.

The radiocarbon dates obtained for sites of the Namazga VI type in southern Turkmenia, northern Afghanistan (except Dashly 3), and southern Uzbekistan demonstrate an absolutely opposite tendency: the farther to the east of southern Turkmenia the site is, the more ancient it is, according to those determinations. Since the spread of the culture from west to east is an objective conclusion from an entire series of archeological studies, we can conclude that the radiocarbon dates conflict with archeological facts in this specific instance (see Figure 8).

Conclusions

First, the Late Bronze Age in southern Turkmenia can be identified by the following major criteria: the presence of red-slipped and gray polished tableware and the decline in the areas of settlements.

Second, the continuity of the ceramic tradition of the Namazga V, Namazga VI, and Yaz-depe I periods confirms the continuity of these periods in terms of cultural history.

Third, the Namazga VI period has been tied into the chronological scale of the Iranian sites, which made it possible to define the chronological framework of the Namazga VI period as 1350-1000 B.C. In this connection we can theorize that sites of the Dashly and Sapalli type could not have arisen earlier than the thirteenth century B.C.

PART TWO

Excavations at Altyn-depe

CHAPTER 3

Altyn-depe during the Aeneolithic Period

V. M. MASSON

Systematic excavations at Altyn-depe in southern Turkmenistan
have already provided us with a graphic picture of the internal
structure and cultural form of an early urban settlement of the
Bronze Age.[1] It is now quite clear that this very ancient civilization of our country belonged within that extensive zone of ancient
civilizations between Mesopotamia and the Indus Valley. The
highly developed culture of the middle and second half of the second millennium B.C. that has been found within the past few years
along the middle course of the Amu Darya[2] was related to Altyn-
depe by a whole series of genetic links. Naturally the problems of
the genesis of this early urban culture and the forms and features
of its earlier sources are especially important for relating it to
the later Bactrian cultures. Most recently this problem has gone
beyond the territorial limits of Central Asian archeology. The discovery of a significant number of painted ceramics that are identical to the south Turkmenian Namazga III forms in the earliest
levels at Shahr-i Sokhta in Seistan naturally led to the hypothesis
that the formation of a settled agricultural way of life in Seistan
occurred as the result of the dispersion of south Turkmenian communities.[3] Not long ago the question was raised in a publication
concerning the presence on the Iranian plateau at the end of the
fourth and beginning of the third millennium B.C. of two primary
interaction spheres — a Mesopotamian- or Jemdet-Nasr-related
sphere and a south Turkmenian sphere.[4] All this work made especially relevant the study of the early stratigraphy at Altyn-depe,

which was done in 1970, 1971, and 1974 along with continuing excavations of the upper levels of the site.[5] By 1960 preliminary soundings at the site established the presence of a Late Aeneolithic culture with painted ceramics of the Geoksyur type.[6] Now it is possible to present a sufficiently complete stratigraphic column of this major site and, to a great extent, paint the picture of its development during the Aeneolithic period.

The most significant material defining the Aeneolithic stratigraphy at Altyn-depe was obtained in excavation 1, which is situated on the eastern edge of the "hill of the craftsmen." In 1965-66 three building levels, dating to the time of Namazga V, were uncovered here and were labeled respectively Altyn 1, 2, and 3. Then Altyn level 4 appeared, containing painted ceramics of the type belonging to late Namazga period IV.[7] In 1970 work on the study of the stratigraphy in this excavation was continued. In a trench four meters wide with steps extending down the slope of the mound, the cultural levels were excavated to virgin soil, and horizons Altyn 5-15 were defined (Figure 1). Finally, in 1974 this trench was extended at the level of horizons 9-10 for the purpose of obtaining material characterizing the Late Aeneolithic complex. The results of this excavation are presented in a short table (Figure 2).

The placement of this excavation on the edge of the settlement meant that the excavated building levels were preserved only partially; the outside wall of the excavated rooms usually was destroyed. The Aeneolithic levels in excavation 1 begin from building horizon 9. Here a rectangular furnace was found on the edge of the trench; its walls were covered by a layer of slag. Next to the furnace was a depression filled with a significant number of pebbles. Judging from the uncovered wall stubs, a multiroomed building was located near the furnace, but it was possible to uncover only part of one room of this building. In the middle of this room a circular hearth was excavated which contained a white, marblelike limestone vessel. A horn of an animal (Figure 4, 20) was placed next to the hearth on the floor alongside a greatly disturbed burial (no. 278). Apparently this room with the oval hearth functioned as a kind of domestic shrine, numerous examples of which are found in the multiroomed structures of the Late Aeneolithic settlements of Geoksyur 1 and Chong-depe.[8] It is noteworthy that the disturbed bones of three individuals were found on the floor of one such shrine at Geoksyur; it is true that these remains from Geoksyur 1 lay on top of burned wood, which V. I. Sarianidi related to a cultural rite of cremation,[9] while such traces of fire were

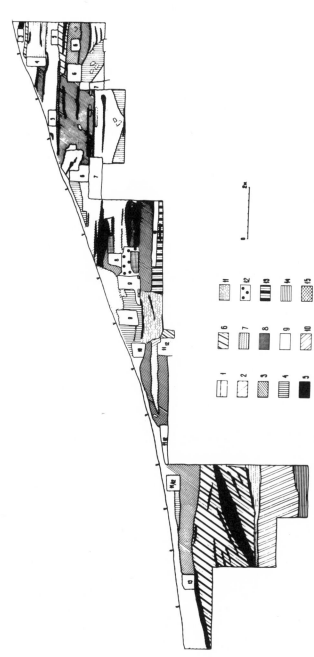

Figure 1. Profile of the stratigraphic trench of excavation 1: 1 — loose levels with small bits of unfired bricks; 2 — a dense obstruction of unfired bricks; 3 — rubbish levels with bits of unfired bricks; 4 — ash levels; 5 — rubbish levels with greenish streaks; 6 — accumulated levels with greenish streaks; 7 — scorified bricks; 8 — adobe walls in section; 9 — stratified and crumpled clay; 10 — loose brownish levels; 11 — scorified remains of a ceramic kiln; 12 — clay foundation; 13 — virgin soil; 14 — loose brownish levels with bits of unfired bricks.

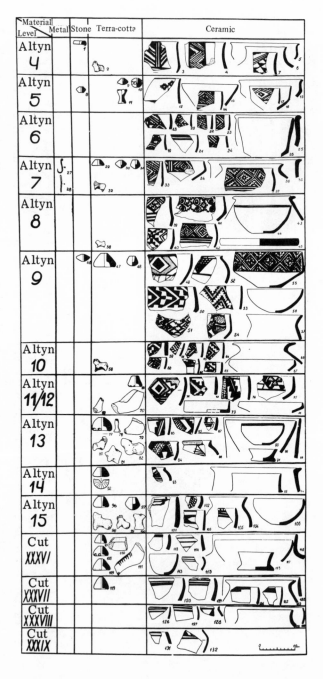

Figure 2. Archeological sequence from excavation 1.

absent in the shrine of Altyn level 9. Nevertheless the association of human remains in the shrines at Geoksyur and Altyn-depe is sufficiently clear.

The western wall of the room we examined was twice as thick as to the others and apparently functioned as the exterior face of the entire multiroomed complex. Indeed, we discovered here in an area not built up an oval-shaped collective grave that is characteristic both for settlements of the Geoksyur type and for shrines with oval hearths. Two burials were placed in this grave: the earlier, no. 282, was partially covered by the later, no. 281. Both skeletons lay on their right sides with their heads turned north. Mat impressions were found on the floor of the chamber; similar impressions could be traced in spots on the earth above the skeletons. Grave goods consisted of two ceramic vessels, including an earthen saucer painted in a style characteristic of Kara-depe, two terra-cotta whorls, one stone bead, and one small copper triangular point — possibly an arrowhead. Part of the western wall of the grave was destroyed by a third burial, no. 283, which related to a later horizon and not to Altyn level 9.

After two seasons' work (1970 and 1974) we obtained a sufficiently diverse assemblage for Altyn level 9, particularly a well-defined ceramic corpus (Figure 5). This corpus included a polychrome vessel of Geoksyur style and vessels with decorations representing a development of this style to one that utilized monochrome techniques and more intricate, almost fragmented designs. The discoveries in this level of imported ceramics of Kara-depe style, including one fragment depicting a snow leopard, and local wares that clearly imitated this group of painted ceramics are particularly significant.

In the next level, Altyn 10, parts of an adobe building, the plan of which was not clear, were uncovered. The discovery of an oval-shaped tomb almost directly under the chamber in Altyn 9 was especially interesting. The graves in this tomb were situated on two levels: an upper level (Figure 3), which contained the tightly packed remains of four people (tombs 291-94) whose skeletons were oriented partially to the north northwest and lacked any burial goods; and a lower level, separated from the upper level by 20 cm of clayey fill, which contained burial no. 296, located directly on the floor of the chamber. The corpse had been placed on its left side with its head pointed north. The left arm of the skeleton was bent at the elbow and supported the remains of an infant, no. 295, which had been placed in front of its skull. Its right hand was ex-

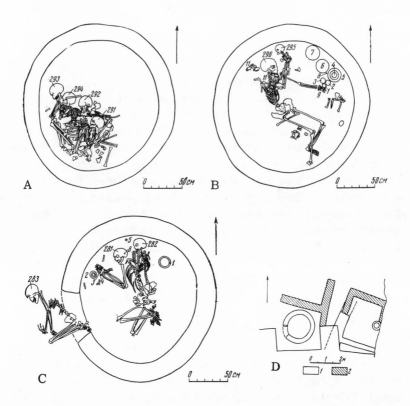

Figure 3. Plan of Aeneolithic burials in excavation 1: A — tholos of level 10 in the upper building horizon; B — tholos of level 10 in the second building horizon (1 — stone vessel of white limestone; 2 — vessel of a rosy limestone; 3 — an unpainted small ceramic pot; 4 — a painted small ceramic pot; 5-7 — painted cups; 8 — ceramic bead; 9 — copper pin; 10 — copper knife; 11 — turquoise necklace, 10 beads); C — tholos level 9 (1 — painted saucer; 2 — small pot made from red clay; 3 — stone spindle whorl (or bead?); 4 — fragment of a copper point or arrowhead; 5 — fragment of a terra-cotta spindle whorl; 6 — clay bead); D — structural plan of level 9 (1) and Altyn 10 (2).

tended to the east toward the burial goods occupying the eastern part of the chamber. These goods consisted of five ceramic vessels, two stone vessels — one of which was white, the other rose-colored (Figure 4, 18) — a copper shovel-shaped pin, ten turquoise pendants, and a small, flat copper cutting knife. This last object lay among the forelegs of a young ram that had been placed along the eastern wall of the chamber. The animal's mandible and some of its vertebrae had been placed in front of the skull of the primary burial.

The ceramic assemblage of Altyn level 10 (Figure 7) contains the same two groups of ceramics as Altyn 9, although the paintings on polychrome vessels are larger and reminiscent of the ceramics from the upper levels at Chong-depe.[10] Highly stylized sub-rectangular figures of goats, separate fragments of which imitate vessels from Kara-depe, are found together with vessels with geometric designs. Among other finds one must mention terra-cotta figurines of animals, including an expressively modeled goat, elegant figurines of seated women, and a fragment of a small terra-cotta box, the exterior of which is covered with deep geometric designs.

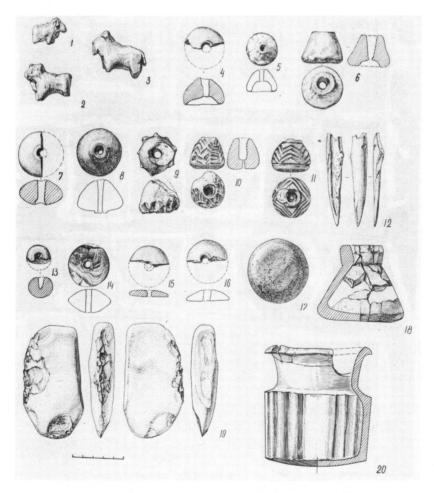

Figure 4. Stone, bone, and terra-cotta objects.

Figure 5. Ceramics from level 9.

The following level, Altyn 11/12, contains poorly preserved building remains. The painted ceramics of this level are executed in the fine traditions of the Geoksyur style. However, it is true that one spherically shaped vessel with a detailed net design can be considered a sort of replica of the Kara-depe painted ceramics.[11] Besides the anthropomorphic and zoomorphic figurines, terra-cotta conical-shaped whorls, fragments of stone vessels, and

Figure 6. Ceramics from level 9.

a flat, button-shaped object of unfired clay with a cross motif cut into one side were found in this level.

Altyn level 13 contains striking ceramics of the Geoksyur style,

71

Figure 7. Ceramics from level 10.

including fragments of red-slipped vessels that were painted red with unclear, almost trickled designs. This type of ceramic appears very early, characterizing the beginning stages of the formation of the Geoksyur ceramic assemblage.[12]

Massive female figurines, which were made of chaff-filled clay and sometimes decorated with painted designs (Figure 8, 8, 15, 16), are part of the zoomorphic and anthropomorphic finds of this horizon. This group of terra-cotta figurines is identical to those that appear in the earliest Geoksyur assemblages,[13] that is, they are closely linked with the modeling traditions of the Middle Aeneolithic period.[14]

Finally a thin level containing rubbish deposits with great quantities of ashy fill and encompassing arbitrary cut XXXIII was defined as horizon 14. It contained an unpainted red-burnished ce-

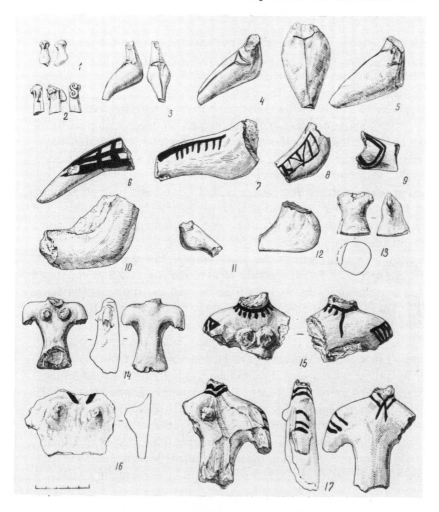

Figure 8. Terra-cotta figurines.

ramic with dark spots on its exterior surface that closely resembled a vessel from the third level at Geoksyur 1 that divides the stratum with ceramics of the Geoksyur style from the lower levels of the preceding Yalangach type.[15] The discovery of the lower half of a large female figurine with dark brown paint on red clay indicates the diffusion of figurines of the archaic type.

The absence in horizon 14 of architectural remains reflects the changing character of the cultural strata exposed by excavation 1. While previously this excavation had contained a relatively fully built up part of the settlement, it now had changed to rubbish levels on the edge of the settlement which sloped increasingly downward. It was very obvious in section how the rubbish levels, particularly those with an ashy fill, ran down the ancient edge of the mound. Essentially the relatively thick wall, discovered in arbitrary cuts XXXIV-XXXV but also found in horizon 15, was a sort of double fence behind which began the dump or refuse area.

Horizon 15 at Altyn-depe contained many ceramics with red exterior burnishing covered by black spots. Vessels with parallel lines painted along the rims were characteristic; there also was a fragment decorated with a triangle filled with a type of net design that was commonly found in the fifth level of Geoksyur 1.[16] Conical terra-cotta spindle whorls, both fired and unfired zoomorphic figurines, and the torso of a large female figurine with a necklace represented by black paint on red clay completed the material assemblage of this horizon.

Building remains were completely absent lower down in the examined section. Thus the strata of arbitrary cut XXXVI consisted of fill washing down from the mound beyond the limits of the sounding. This clayey fill contained sherds, charcoal, and bits of brick. Further down, the horizontal levels clearly showed that we had reached the bottom of the ancient mound; when it rained, currents trickling down from the tepe carried the material remains of human activity. These levels continued in arbitrary cuts XXXVII-XXXIX, where crumpled, flaky clay, frequently greenish in color, indicated the presence of standing water. However, sherds and bits of charcoal were found throughout these levels. In arbitrary cut XL the horizontal levels no longer contained traces of human activity. One must mention that the cultural levels ended 4.5 m below the contemporary surface of the plain surrounding Altyndepe.

Naturally the ceramic assemblage from cuts XXXVI-XXXIX was relatively poor. However, rims of very fine vessels with painted parallel lines running along them and fragments of thick, heavily chaff-tempered storage jars with dark-brown paint on a light background proved that these ceramics belonged to the Yalangach-type assemblage or to the Middle Aeneolithic period.

Thus the stratigraphic work in excavation 1 provided a sufficiently coherent column to observe the general changes in the cultural assemblages at Altyn-depe. Nevertheless this sondage, located along the edge of an exploratory trench, was outside the limits of the center of the ancient settlement. The fragmentary material obtained from the lower cuts in this sondage allowed us to conclude that in all probability, the "hill of the craftsmen" was not occupied on any significant scale during the Early Aeneolithic or Namazga 1 period. These early levels subsequently were sought in the central part of Altyn-depe, where a significantly higher summit led us to assume earlier levels than those present in the lower "hill of the craftsmen."

Work in sondage 11, which was situated on a small hollow on the southern slope of "tower hill," completely confirmed this assumption. This hollow was sufficiently deep so that we could hope to uncover immediately Aeneolithic levels without excavating Namazga IV and V horizons. This sondage was opened in 1960, but heavy rains permitted us to dig only to a depth of 2.5 meters.[17] In 1971 the sondage was moved slightly and dug to virgin soil, which was encountered at a depth of 13.5 meters, or 8.5 meters lower than the surrounding plain (Figure 9). Since the maximum height of "tower hill" was 22 meters, we could conclude that the maximum depth of cultural levels at Altyn-depe was at least 30 meters.

The first two cuts of this sondage consisted of mixed levels containing Namazga V and, less frequently, Namazga IV ceramics; these materials had washed down from the higher part of the settlement. Clear traces of substantial runoff that had brought numerous pebbles and large sherds were observed in the lower half of the second arbitrary cut. Immediately beneath this cut levels of the Aeneolithic period that contained remains of mud-brick architecture began. On the basis of the painted ceramics, these levels could be divided satisfactorily into three cultural assemblages: vessels of Geoksyur style (cuts III-XI); vessels of the Yalangach type (XII-XVI); and Namazga I vessels (XIX-XXVIII).

Mud-brick architecture with clearly defined floors was characteristic of the first assemblage; four building horizons were uncovered. However, judging by the fill of these buildings, we could postulate two additional horizons, although their walls were situated

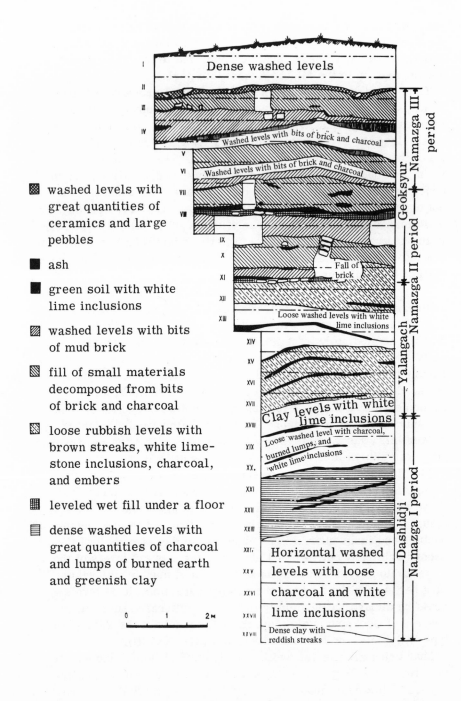

Figure 9. Profile of the trench of excavation 11.

beyond the limits of the sounding. From our point of view one of
these postulated building levels corresponded to the fill found at
the end of the third and in the fourth arbitrary cut, and the other
to the fifth and sixth cuts. In general, then, we can propose six
building levels, attaining a depth of 4.25 meters for the Geoksyur
cultural assemblage. The first of these building levels contained
ceramics of the late Geoksyur form and an imported vessel of the
Kara-depe type that allowed us to correlate this horizon with Altyn
horizon 9. We also mention here the find of a fragment of a terra-
cotta box with a cut design on its exterior surface; the number of
polychrome Geoksyur ceramics was very limited in these levels
as well as in arbitrary cut V. It is completely clear that this assemblage can be related to the finds from arbitrary cut V of the
1960 sondage, which contained imported Kara-depe ceramics, including a fragment depicting a leopard.[18] The following five horizons corresponded to the four building levels of excavation 1 (Altyn
horizons 10, 11/12, 13, and 14); occupation seemed more intense
on "tower hill," since the levels containing Geoksyur style ceramics were thicker than those of excavation 1. The general evolution
of painted ceramics observed in the horizons of the trench at excavation 2 were the same as those established at excavation 1.
The deeper one went the greater the number of polychrome vessels;
the painted motifs also became larger. Stylized depictions of goats
with rectangular bodies frequently were encountered. Fragments
of red-slipped bowls with a sort of trickled design, analogous to
ceramics from Altyn 13 in excavation number 1, were found in the
very lowest building horizon of the Geoksyur assemblage, which
consisted of arbitrary cuts X and the first half of XI.

Lower down the nature of the cultural levels abruptly changed.
Any building remains or fill was virtually absent. Soft rubbish
levels with ashes and charcoal appeared interspersed with soft
washy fill. The somewhat steep slope of these levels showed that
here, as in excavation 1, our trench had come on the refuse remains that had fallen down the slope of the ancient village. In
other words, the central part of the village lay outside our trench.
As already mentioned, levels containing Yalangach-like ceramics
with parallel painted lines running along the rim were found from
the second half of the eleventh through the seventeenth arbitrary
cut. Black-on-red ceramics decisively dominated the ceramic assemblage from the fourteenth cut downward. We must mention the
discovery in the twelfth cut of two polychrome sherds that were
clearly imports from the Kara-depe–Namazga-depe region;[19] in

the fifteenth and seventeenth cuts torsos of large, sumptuous female figurines covered with a red slip and decorated with black paint were found.

The same type of rubbish and washed levels interspersed with ash lenses that had a decidedly marked slope were preserved in cuts XVIII-XXIII. These cuts contained Namazga I painted ceramics in their late Dashlidji form (Figure 10). Although in general one could observe continuity with the Yalangach vessels, there was a slight increase in the number of vessels with painting on a white background, and basins appeared with paintings on their interior surfaces and conical bases. In the seventeenth cut a fragment of a small strainer with pierced holes in its base was discovered, and in cuts XXII-XXIII rims of fat open cups, decorated with wavy designs in relief on their exterior surfaces, were found. We also mention the discovery in the twenty-first cut of a bone piercer and in the nineteenth cut of a flat copper object, the function of which was unclear.

Finally, in cuts XXIV-XXVII, horizontal washed levels containing bits of charcoal and white limestone appeared. The ancient foot of the mound, which formed the earliest settlement at Altyn-depe, remained far beyond the limits of our trench. The quantity of sherds in these levels, naturally, was minimal, but they all related to the Namazga I type. Virgin soil in the sounding of excavation number 2 consisted of compact clay with soft, mildewy, or rusty streaks.

In 1974 exploratory trenches were excavated in the western and eastern parts of the mound in order to determine the limits of the settlement during the period of Geoksyur-style ceramics; two were dug with traditional shovels, but the third with a deep borer or drill UGB-50M.[20] This operation worked with a borer that was 65 cm in diameter and extracted samples every 50 cm; in other words, this method completely corresponded to the traditional arbitrary cut used in Central Asian archeology. Careful examination of the samples showed that even large ceramics were practically undamaged, and 12 meters of cultural levels were reached after three hours.

This experiment proved to be highly efficient and scientifically profitable for the application of a similar operation in a preliminary trench in a settlement that contains more than ten meters of cultural deposit.

Trench 3, which was excavated by such means, was located in the southern part of the "hill of the living quarters." Unfortunately,

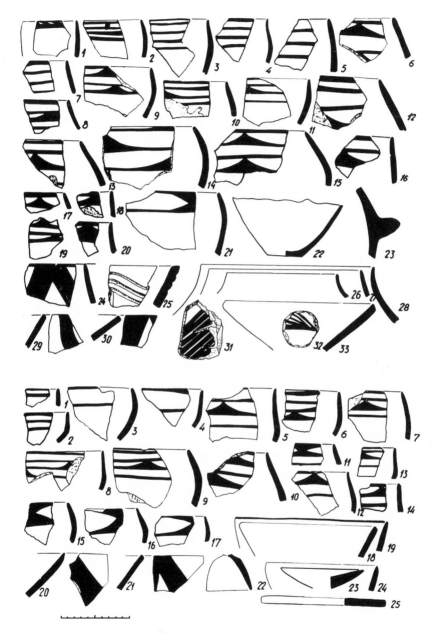

Figure 10. Namazga I ceramics from trench 1 in excavation 11.

the great quantities of ash in the upper levels made it impossible to draw the exposed section of this trench, which, in principle, is fully possible given its diameter. In general the classification of

the ceramics from trench 3 yielded the following picture: Namazga V ceramics were found in cuts I-V; Namazga IV ceramics appeared lower down in cuts VI-XI; and in the twelfth cut a fragment
of a vessel painted in the Kara-depe style allowed us to synchronize this level with Altyn horizon 9. Thick cultural levels with
Geoksyur ceramics were found beginning from the eleventh arbitrary cut. Fragments of mud bricks brought up by the borer attested to the existence here of building remains. Vessels with
polychrome designs disappear completely in cuts XXII and XXIII,
but numerous red-burnished ceramics with black spots were analogous to vessels from horizon Altyn 14. Virgin soil in this area
appeared as a yellowish clay. Thus it was established that this
area was occupied in the period when Geoksyur-style ceramics
began.

A second trench was placed at excavation 8 at the entrance to
the central square on the southern edge of Altyn-depe, where fragments of Aeneolithic ceramics were found as early as 1969.[21] Excavations in 1974 showed that Geoksyur-style vessels were found
in sufficiently great numbers in levels with Namazga IV ceramics
that, apparently, had been mixed with earlier or lower levels.
Finally, trench 2 was placed on the western edge of Altyn-depe;
five building levels were uncovered in this trench: the three upper
levels contained painted Namazga IV ceramics; the fourth — painted
ceramics of the type found in Altyn horizon 9; and the fifth — indisputable Geoksyur ceramics, including polychrome ware. In
addition to the ceramics, a copper awl, a clay goat, an elegant female figurine, and the head of a woman with a complicated S-shaped
curl (Figure 8, 2) were discovered; all of these frequently occur
in the Late Aeneolithic assemblages of southern Turkmenistan.[22]

Thus these excavations allow us to establish a comparative
stratigraphic column at Altyn-depe and to incorporate it into the
relative stratigraphy of early agricultural sites in southern Turkmenistan. The synchronization of these separate excavations and
trenches at Altyn-depe has been mentioned briefly and can be presented in tabular form (Figure 11).

The stratigraphic correspondences of the earliest levels, which
contain Namazga I ceramics, have been precisely determined; first
of all, they relate to the lower levels of the Geoksyur 1 settlement[23] and to the Dashlidji-depe complex in the Geoksyur Oasis.[24]
In both cases this is the last stage of the development of this type
of painted ceramic. The Yalangach-type ceramics found at Altyn-
depe have precise eastern parallels: again with the settlement of

Geoksyur 1 (levels 4-7) and numerous settlements in the Geoksyur
Oasis. Finds of fragments of ceramics with polychrome Namazga II
designs confirm the contemporaneity of these levels with Namazga II–Anau II assemblages in sites of the western group. The precise determination of the stratigraphic correspondences for the
Late Aeneolithic period of southern Turkmenistan relate to the
materials from the levels containing Geoksyur style ceramics at
Altyn-depe. As is well-known, at Geoksyur 1 itself this diagnostic
and elegant painted ceramic type is found together with imported
Kara 2 forms or the final stage of the Namazga II period.[25] At
Chong-depe the local ceramic assemblage has traits that show a
separate evolution and is accompanied by finds of imported Namazga III ceramics. Detailed familiarity with the relevant materials show that the upper levels at Chong-depe contain Kara 1B or
early Namazga III ceramics.[26] In this respect the Altyn 9 assemblage is stylistically later than the Chong-depe ceramics and the
accompanying Kara 1A wares (later Namazga III); above all, this
assemblage represents the last stage of the development of Geoksyur-
style ceramics. Apparently one must relate to this final stage the
levels of the eastern group sites, which contain imported ware together with diminished quantities of polychrome painted Geoksyur-
style ceramics. From our point of view the end of the Aeneolithic
period in this region in general and at Altyn-depe in particular has
been determined, and the division between the Namazga III (Late
Aeneolithic) and Namazga IV (Early Bronze) has been established.
All the data, including the results of statistical analyses,[27] indicate
that these two periods are closely linked with each other in terms
of their genetic or historical relationship. Thus the stratigraphy
of the Aeneolithic settlement at Altyn-depe presents a picture of
continuous cultural development that not only directly corresponds
with that obtained from other sites in southern Turkmenistan but
also helps us to precisely establish a general view that is significantly complex and detailed.

Until more thorough investigations are undertaken, the absolute
chronology of the Aeneolithic complexes of southern Turkmenistan
remain within limits traditionally dated from the fifth to the beginning of the third millennium B.C.[28] At Geoksyur 1 two radiocarbon determinations date respectively 2860 ± 100 B.C. and
2490 ± 100 B.C.; at Altyn-depe the levels of the late Yalangach
period are dated 3160 ± 50 B.C. If one applies the correction factors to these determinations, which are supported by a series of
investigators in Iran,[29] then the corresponding dates for the early

Figure 11
Stratigraphy of Altyn-depe

			Altyn-depe		
Namazga-depe	Geoksyur Oasis	type of ceramic complex	excavation 1 ("craftsmen's hill")	trench 3 (hill of "living quarters")	excavation 11 ("Tower" hill)
Namazga V	Khapuz-depe cuts I-II	Namazga V ceramics	Altyn 1, Altyn 2, Altyn 3	cuts I-V	cuts I
Namazga IV	Khapuz-depe cuts III-XII	Namazga IV ceramics	Altyn 4, Altyn 5, Altyn 6, Altyn 7, Altyn 8	cuts VI-X	
Namazga III	Chong-depe; Geoksyur 1, Geoksyur 2, Geoksyur 3	Geoksyur ceramics	Altyn 9, Altyn 10, Altyn 11/12, Altyn 13, Altyn 14	cuts XI-XXII	6 building horizons

Scale: 1m, 2, 3, 4, 5, 6, 7, 8, 9, 10

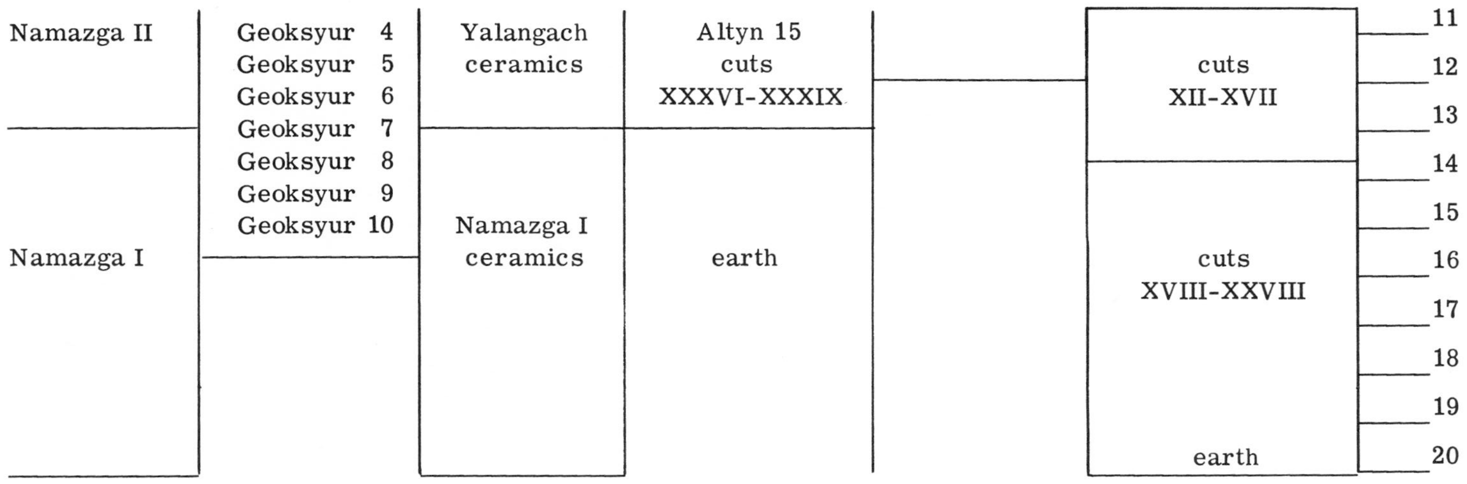

11
12
13
14
15
16
17
18
19
20

cuts
XII-XVII

cuts
XVIII-XXVIII

earth

Altyn 15
cuts
XXXVI-XXXIX

earth

Yalangach
ceramics

Namazga I
ceramics

Geoksyur 4
Geoksyur 5
Geoksyur 6
Geoksyur 7
Geoksyur 8
Geoksyur 9
Geoksyur 10

Namazga II

Namazga I

Geoksyur period would be 3240-3410 B.C. and for the late Yalangach 3810 B.C. These dates correspond well with those from
Shahr-i Sokhta 1, where southern Turkmenian type ceramics were
found.[30] For other dates we refer to finds at Tal-i Iblis in southeastern Iran of typical Kara 4 ceramics in a level with an uncorrected radiocarbon date of 3645 ± 59 B.C.[31]

To a great extent the excavations of the early levels at Altyn-
depe allow us to characterize the growth of this settlement (Figure 12). While the earliest materials from the site could be related to the last phase of the Namazga I period, it is not impossible
that somewhere in the depths of this huge site are buried the remains of still earlier periods. In any case the Meana-Chacha region was settled with a sedentary culture in the middle phase of
the Djeitun period; three sites have already been found that are
related to the last phase of the Djeitun culture: Chagylly-depe;
Mondjukly-depe; and Gadymi-depe.[32] The first two are situated
not far from Altyn-depe itself, and they all represent small hamlets not larger than 0.5 hectares. Two small Anau IA sites are
also present relating to the period preceding Namazga I.

At Altyn-depe itself ceramics of the late Namazga I type were
found in the sounding of excavation 2 and in mixed context in sounding 3. It is not impossible that Altyn-depe already occupied an
area of several hectares at this time and may have been a relatively large center. In any case, "tower hill" apparently was completely occupied and contained many meters of cultural deposit
that was uncovered in excavation 2. Painted ceramics, terra-cotta
spindle-whorls, and relatively few bone and copper objects make
up the usual assemblage of the material culture of sites occupied
at this time. On the basis of its painted ceramics, Altyn-depe is
related to the eastern group of settlements, which also includes
the sites of the Geoksyur Oasis. Levels of this period were recorded at the settlement of Ilginli-depe, which is situated 10 km
to the southeast of Altyn-depe.[33]

The following period is characterized by the spread of Yalangach-
type ceramics; the growth in the occupied area of Altyn-depe is
evident even in those materials that we have ordered. At this time
the area called "craftsmen's hill" was occupied, and life would
continue there until the destruction of the settlement. The sounding in excavation 11 yielded particularly representative cultural
levels from this period. Painted ceramics with circular lines
running along the rims clearly relate Altyn-depe to the range of
sites of the eastern group, a cultural-historical determination that

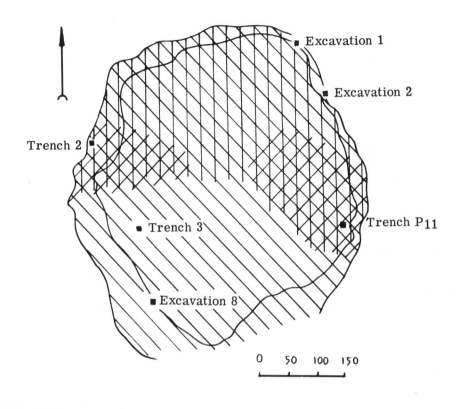

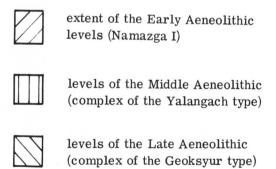

extent of the Early Aeneolithic
levels (Namazga I)

levels of the Middle Aeneolithic
(complex of the Yalangach type)

levels of the Late Aeneolithic
(complex of the Geoksyur type)

Figure 12. Schematic representation of the growth of Altyn-depe.

85

is completely confirmed by finds of polychrome imported vessels coming from western sites that are sharply distinguished from the local ware. Eastern analogies include the large terra-cotta figurines of sitting women. Covered with light or more frequently red slip, these figurines commonly have black paint representing necklaces or jewelry that form different shaded outlines on their shoulders and thighs. At Altyn-depe these figurines are found in levels dated to the post-Yalangach period, while in excavations at Geoksyur 1 these sculptures were found in early Geoksyur levels,[34] symbolizing, as it were, the genetic succession of these two assemblages. Animal figurines, anthropomorphic statuettes that are commonly very expressive, and conical clay spindle-whorls complete the characteristic objects of the material culture of this period. Ilginli-depe also yields clear materials of this type; at least during the late Yalangach period,[35] the settlement attained maximum dimensions of almost 12 hectares. The contemporaneous settlement at Altyn-depe probably was not smaller.

Finally, in the Geoksyur period the Aeneolithic settlement at Altyn-depe blossomed to its full extent. First of all, the territory of the settlement sharply increased; at this time Altyn-depe reached the limits that continued into the Bronze Age. Population movement into the southern part of the site where levels with Geoksyur ceramics lie directly on virgin soil, as if symbolizing the building expansion of the growing settlement, is especially notable. This indisputable growth is observed in other parts of Altyn-depe where late Aeneolithic levels have been revealed. Thus in excavations 1 and 2 Late Aeneolithic houses cover rubbish deposits that accumulated at the edge of the Yalangach settlement; the number of buildings occupying the former edge of the settlement indicates the growth of the site in Geoksyur times. Typical features of the settlements of the Geoksyur Oasis at this time are types of constructions with multiroomed houses with domestic shrines and circular mortuary tholoi located nearby. Qualitative structural changes of the settlement itself can scarcely be observed in the existing materials, but quantitative growth is present. Differences in funeral goods, observed in the burials of excavation 1, mainly indicate the complex social structure of Altyn-depe in this period. Notably, the neighboring settlement of Ilginli-depe decreases in size during the early Geoksyur period and is completely abandoned at the end of the Late Aeneolithic period. Most likely some of the inhabitants of this earlier large center were absorbed as a result of the growth of Altyn-depe, and this nucleation of the population was one of the most important indices of the future urbanization process of this society.

Painted ceramics of the Geoksyur style are characteristic features of the material culture of Altyn-depe during the Late Aeneolithic period; these ceramics undergo a gradual transformation of their original motifs to the tiny carpetlike designs that characterize the local Namazga IV wares. Also present are stone vessels ground from a white marblelike limestone; terra-cotta boxes with sides decorated with carved designs of figures, crosses, and half-crosses; and terra-cotta statuettes of sitting women, sometimes with nearly rectangular shoulders, which are characterized by elegant and flowing lines that distinguish them from the massive figurines of the late Yalangach period (Figure 8, 4). The heads of such statuettes are shown with large hooked noses, deep almond-shaped eyes, and S-shaped hair whirls or pendants (Figure 8, 2). This relatively standard selection is practically identical to the cultures of Geoksyur 1 and Chong-depe.

Insofar as there exists a division into two cultural provinces in southern Turkmenistan during the Late Aeneolithic period, one must acknowledge that in its basic traits Altyn-depe is related to the eastern region. Still one must observe that the differences between the two regions in terms of their material cultures are less significant than the signs of cultural uniformity that united southern Turkmenian sites of this date into a single whole. Multi-roomed houses, vessels ground from stone, the forms of copper objects, particularly the so-called small shovels, the style of terra-cotta sculptures and the details of their final decorations, the tradition of collective burials in single tombs — all are traits that are practically identical in both the east and the west. The differences lie primarily in the painted ceramics. In the western sites are distributed vessels of Kara-depe type, while in the eastern sites, including Altyn-depe, are found vessels in the Geoksyur style. Similarly, one also must observe that the separate design elements, such as crosses, half-crosses, stepped pyramids, and the like, are identical as separate composition solutions in both provinces and are distinguished only by their different combinations and scales of depiction. Thus at Kara-depe the painting is more divided and variegated, while at Geoksyur large geometric figures that are not reduced to small ornaments dominate. Since ceramics — no matter how expressive they were — constitute only one element of a complex,[36] one must speak in this case about two variants — Kara-depe and Geoksyur — within a single cultural community or culture area.

Thus as early as the Late Aeneolithic period Altyn-depe emerges
as a large population center with stable material culture elements
that repeat themselves throughout an entire territory. Inevitably
questions arise as to the ties of this Aeneolithic settlement with
the Bronze Age city that Altyn-depe became nearly a thousand
years later. Although we are not concerned with all the details of
this problem, we nevertheless mention the perceptible links of
continuity that include several important features of the material
culture. Thus the oval hearth of the Late Aeneolithic sanctuary
is analogous to a similar hearth in one of the houses of the "elite
quarter" in the Namazga V settlement; in both instances there are
internal domestic shrines. A link also is apparent in the burial
rites: in the Bronze Age at Altyn-depe as in the Aeneolithic period,
collective graves occur, although they change from having a circular to a rectangular plan. The later graves maintain the dominant pattern of the old Aeneolithic orientation of the burials, with
their heads turned north. We mention such a feature as the preservation of the tradition of making terra-cotta boxes with their sides
covered with carved designs.[37] Thus we have grounds to speak
about the preservation in the culture of the Bronze Age settlement
at Altyn-depe of the tradition of the Aeneolithic period. For a more
detailed examination of this question, we must analyze in greater
detail the Namazga IV complex, which is founded directly on the
Aeneolithic levels and contains obvious parallels in painted ceramics[38] and terra-cotta sculptures.[39] One can certainly talk about
a definite line of succession between the Aeneolithic settlement
and the urban city of the Bronze Age.

This circumstance is all the more evident since analogous elements of the local Aeneolithic levels can be traced in a series of
archeological Bronze Age assemblages in the Middle East that relate to the urban level of social development. The first question
of Turkmenian-Baluchistan parallels was formulated broadly on
the basis of materials from Quetta[40] and later from Mundigak.[41]
Now the number of sites reflecting contacts among the tribes of
Central Asia and the Middle East at the "dawn of urbanization" has
sharply increased.

Let us examine the question of these links and correspondences
in light of the detailed stratigraphy at Altyn-depe, a record that
allows us to define with great certainty in relative chronological
terms the position of the elements that exhibit parallels.

Exceptionally interesting in this respect are the remains from

Shahr-i Sokhta, where the earliest materials lie directly on virgin soil and can be divided into three horizons. These materials were brought together by M. Tosi as the Shahr-i Sokhta I assemblage. [42] Three Jemdet-Nasr cylinder seals that were found in this level confirm the general date of this assemblage to the end of the fourth and the first third of the third millennium B.C., insofar as cylinders in this style are commonly encountered in levels of the Early Dynastic period. From the very beginning of the excavations, the investigators directed their attention to the great similarity of the painted ceramics with south Turkmenian designs, which in some cases are so close that one can speak about almost complete identity. [43] It is true, however, that in some cases one speaks about the similarity of these ceramics with Kara-depe and in other cases with Geoksyur wares. On data established by M. Tosi, the painted ceramics of Shahr-i Sokhta I are subdivided in the following way: vessels of local type — 48.1 percent; Geoksyur type — 27 percent; and Kechi Beg type (a ceramic ware from northern Baluchistan) — 24.7 percent. The division by stratigraphic levels of the so-called Geoksyur type breaks down as follows: level 8 — 24.3 percent; level 9 — 31.9 percent; level 10 — 21 percent. There is one fragment among the published depictions of this ware that appears to continue the late Namazga II tradition as represented at Kara-depe 2; [44] some of the material has direct analogies to the ceramics of early Namazga III (Kara 1A), [45] and some — including ornaments with applied figures — can be associated with the ceramics of Altyn 9 and 10, representing the latest phase of the development of Geoksyur-type ceramics that do not appear at the Geoksyur settlement itself. [46] It is not excluded that a more detailed and layer-by-layer examination of the Shahr-i Sokhta I ceramic assemblage would allow us to establish that the designs on these wares originated in different stratigraphic horizons. Thus one can conclude that the south Turkmenian ceramics found in the lowest levels at Shahr-i Sokhta can be associated in general with Namazga III assemblages of both the western and eastern groups. Finds of female clay figurines in the upper levels of Shahr-i Sokhta, which clearly are related to the plastic tradition [47] of Geoksyur and Kara-depe and similar in this respect to terra-cotta figurines of the Namazga IV period, allow us to conclude that the corresponding cultural parallelism is by no means limited to painted ceramic wares alone.

It has already been noted in the literature [48] that in its geometric designs the ceramic assemblage from the Quetta Valley carries traces of unmistakeable interrelations with southern Turkmenian ware during Namazga III-IV. Roughly speaking, such resemblances can be observed in almost 25 percent of the design motifs, and parallels in female figurines and seals confirm the strong and non-accidental nature of the southern Turkmenian ties. Thus the sites in the Quetta Valley and Shahr-i Sokhta illustrate significant links with the cultural assemblages of the southern Turkmenian settlements.

Less numerous but still sufficiently clear parallels can be observed with sites from southern Afghanistan: Mundigak, Deh Morasi Ghundai, and Said Qala. Designs clearly linked with Kara 1A[49] and 1B[50] and Altyn levels 8 and 9 (i.e., Namazga III and part of Namazga IV) are found on the painted ceramics of Mundigak III. In Mundigak IV, 1, a sherd with a spotted leopard design (a typical motif of late Namazga III) was found together with vessels in the Quetta style that have the clearest analogies with early Namazga IV.[51] In general the carved stone vessels from Mundigak IV develop the same decorative tradition.[52] Particularly significant is the presence in Mundigak III of collective burials, a feature that is so typical for Late Aeneolithic Turkmenistan. The graves at Mundigak, however, are nearly square in plan, as at Kara-depe, and not circular, as at Geoksyur or Altyn-depe.

Judging by the preliminary report on the excavations at Said Qala, decorated ceramics are found that have analogies to the Altyn 8 and 9 assemblages; these parallels appear on two types: the Morasi type or a local ware, and the Quetta type, which is treated as an import.[53] Judging from the field account, Quetta ware ceramics are found throughout the cultural deposit at Said Qala, which reaches a depth of 7.5 m. Significantly, a large number of female figurines found in the lowest level have, in the words of J. Shaffer,[54] direct Central Asian parallels. The abundance of terracotta figurines at once distinguishes southern Turkmenian settlements from contemporaneous sites in Iran; the great quantity of these figurines in the lowest levels attests to the strong occurrence of a Central Asian tradition in its early stages. Later female figurines at Said Qala occur relatively rarely.

Figurines depicting sitting women, which are clearly made in the Central Asian (Geoksyur) style, have been found in the past few years at a series of pre-Harappan agricultural sites in the Indus Valley.[55] The concentration of these sites in the northern zone, i.e., in territorial proximity to the southern Afghanistan assemblages, demonstrates that real historical contacts are repre-

sented by these analogies. Especially noteworthy is the stratigraphy of Jalilpur, situated 50 km from Harappa. Here crude handmade ceramics, found in the lowest levels, gradually are replaced
by wheelmade ceramics, separate sherds of which have direct
parallels to Mundigak III.[56] These levels also contained terra-cotta
figurines of the Geoksyur type.

These parallels and analogies, the detailed analysis of which is
somewhat hindered by the preliminary character of many reports
and publications, primarily attest to the direction of these links.
J. M. Casal in his time actively proposed the hypothesis that the
consolidation of Quetta-style ceramics in Baluchistan was the result of the spread of Susa-inspired ware from there to southern
Turkmenia.[57] However, one can easily see that vessels decorated
in this style from sites of the Middle East are found in set percentages among the diverse local ceramic assemblages, percentages
that drop off the farther the settlement is from southern Turkmenia.
One must also refer to the terra-cotta figurines. Other types of
terra-cotta figurines, particularly the so-called Zhob figurines,
whose iconographic features are well recognized, are found in the
Quetta Valley and at Said Qala alongside the figurines of the
Geoksyur—Kara-depe type. On the Turkmenian sites ceramics
with geometric paintings of the so-called Quetta type and the local
clay figurines form a basic unit. Despite all the elements of cultural links with Mesopotamia and Iran,[58] the local populations at
Kara-depe, Geoksyur, and Altyn-depe continued in a whole series
of features the tradition of the preceding period. It would not be correct to refer to the influence of Susa and Tal-i Bakun styles on the
southern Turkmenian cultural assemblages.[59] As a ceramic assemblage the vessels of both the Geoksyur and the Kara-depe type
form a single legitimate unit in which separate design elements
or motifs, but not the style as a whole, can be linked with traditions
located beyond Turkmenia.

All this allows us to consider southern Turkmenia as one of the
centers of active cultural influences that first of all was linked
with the spread of tribes in the Middle East at the end of the fourth
and in the first half of the third millennium B.C. — a point of view
that is now shared by a significant number of investigators.[60] Since
these influences from a number of well-known sites are particularly strong at Shahr-i Sokhta and in the Quetta group of settlements, one can suggest a basic direction for this movement (Figure 13). This powerful current had reached Mundigak III in somewhat attenuated form, although related traditions continued to exist

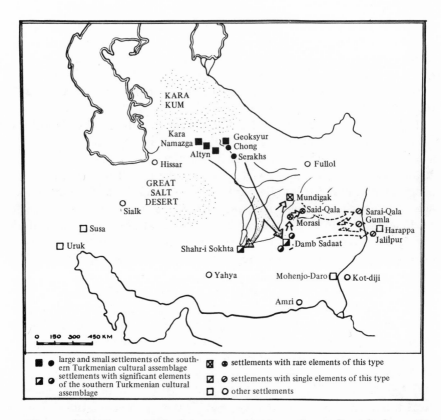

Figure 13. The spread of southern Turkmenian cultural elements throughout the Middle East.

in Mundigak IV that were partially stimulated by contacts with the Quetta group of early agricultural settlements. Finally, relating to terra-cotta figurines, separate impulses can be observed in the northern part of the Indus Valley. Thus one can consider that the Late Aeneolithic Turkmenian culture, represented by both its Kara-depe and Geoksyur variants, played an important role in that cultural substratum which underlay the early urban civilizations of Central Asia and the Middle East. In southern Central Asia it provided the basic foundation for the local processes of urbanization during the Bronze Age, while in Seistan and northern Baluchistan it formed one of the basic elements in the original cultural stratum of the early agricultural settlements out of which developed the large urban centers best documented by M. Tosi at Shahr-i Sokhta. A corresponding role was played by the Geoksyur–Kara-depe tradition in the formation of the cultures of southern Afghanistan. The find of the Fullol hoard with gold vessels decorated in Kara 1A style again demonstrates the force and significance of this tradition.[61] Finally, in the Indus Valley during the first half of the third millennium B.C., an early agricultural culture that developed from the original Harappan stratum flourished; but in the northern part of this region we find clear indications of southern Turkmenian influences. It would be inaccurate to propose that these links were somehow exceptionally significant for the creative and formative impulses in this region. However, it is sufficiently clear that the southern Turkmenian Aeneolithic culture occupied an important place on any detailed map of the cultural and economic development of early agricultural societies on the way to civilization. Its significance is once more confirmed by a series of new archeological discoveries in the Middle East.

Notes

1. V. M. Masson: "Protogorodskaia tsivilizatsiia iuga Srednei Azii," SA, 1967, no. 3; Raskopki na Altyn-depe v 1969 g., Ashkhabad, 1970; "Raskopki pogrebal'nogo kompleksa na Altyn-depe," SA, 1974, no. 4.
2. A. Askarov, Sapalli-tepe, Tashkent, 1973; V. I. Sarianidi, "Baktriia v epokhu bronzi," SA, 1974, no. 4.
3. M. Tosi, "Excavations at Shahr-i Sokhta. Preliminary Report on the Second Campaign," East and West, 1969, no. 3-4, pp. 287-88, fig. 37; R. Biscione, "Dynamics of an Early South Asian Urbanisation: the First Period of Shahr-i Sokhta and its Connection with Southern Turkmenia," South Asian Archaeology, London, 1973.
4. C. C. Lamberg-Karlovsky and M. Tosi, "Shahr-i Sokhta and Tepe Yahya: Tracks on the Earliest History of the Iranian Plateau," East and West, 1973, no. 1-2, p. 52.
5. A. Ia. Shchetenko, "Raboty artykskogo otriada Karakumskoi ekspeditsii," AO-1969, Moscow, 1970, p. 416; V. M. Masson, "Izuchenie stratigrafii i topografii Altyn-depe," AO-1970, Moscow, 1971, pp. 428-29; "Izuchenie obshchestvennoi struktury rannegorodskogo poseleniia Altyn-depe," AO-1971, Moscow, 1972, p. 529.
6. V. I. Sarianidi, Pamiatniki pozdnego eneolita Iugo-Vostochnoi Turkmenii, SAI, B 3-8, part IV, 1965, p. 27.
7. V. M. Masson "Protogorodskaia tsivilizatsiia," pp. 168-70; A. Ia. Shchetenko, "Raskopki na Altyn-depe v Iuzhnoi Turkmenii," KSIA AN SSSR, 1968, no. 114. Stratigraphic excavations at Altyn-depe were done by building levels, and in their absence by arbitrary levels 50 cm thick.
8. V. I. Sarianidi, "Eneoliticheskoe poselenie Geoksiur," IuTAKE, vol. 10, 1970, pp. 231-35; Pamiatniki pozdnego eneolita Iugo-Vostochnoi Turkmenii, pp. 10-14.
9. V. I. Sarianidi, "Kul'tovye zdaniia poselenii anauskoi kul'tury," SA, 1962, no. 1, p. 51.

10. V. I. Sarianidi, Pamiatniki pozdnego eneolita Iugo-Vostochnoi Turkmenii, plate XIII.

11. See at Kara-depe vessels with similar shapes and designs of this type (V. M. Masson, Kara-depe u Artykha, TIuTAKE, vol. 10, 1960, plates XXV, 18, XXXIV, 4, and XXXVI, 7).

12. I. N. Khlopin, Geoksiurskaia gruppa poselenii epokhi eneolita, Moscow-Leningrad, 1964, pp. 35-36, 122-23.

13. V. I. Sarianidi, Pamiatniki pozdnego eneolita, pp. 32-33.

14. V. M. Masson and V. I. Sarianidi, Sredneaziatskaia terrakota epokhi bronzy, Moscow, 1973, p. 16.

15. V. I. Sarianidi, "Eneoliticheskoe poselenie Geoksiur," pp. 271-72.

16. Ibid., table VIII, 14-25; I. N. Khlopin, "Pamiatniki razvitogo eneolita," p. 21, fig. 5.

17. V. I. Sarianidi, Pamiatniki pozdnego eneolita, pp. 8, 27.

18. Ibid., plate XVI, 1-26.

19. On these imports, see V. M. Masson, Eneolit iuzhnikh oblastei Srednei Azii, SAI — B 3-8, part 2, 1962, pp. 19-20.

20. This operation was conducted with the advice and kind assistance of the geologists I. N. Moment'ev and K. N. Iurgenson.

21. V. M. Masson, "Raskopki na Altyn-depe v 1969 g.," p. 10.

22. V. I. Sarianidi, Pamiatniki pozdnego eneolita, p. 33; V. M. Masson, "Novye raskopki na Dzheitune i Kara-tepe," SA, 1962, no. 3, p. 163.

23. V. I. Sarianidi, "Eneoliticheskoe poselenie Geoksiur," plate VIII.

24. I. N. Khlopin, Eneolit iuzhnykh oblastei Srednei Azii, SAI — B 3-8, part 1, 1963, plate XX.

25. V. I. Sarianidi, Pamiatniki pozdnego eneolita, plate VII; V. M. Masson, Pamiatniki razvitogo Eneolita, plate XIX.

26. V. I. Sarianidi, Pamiatniki pozdnego eneolita, plate XIV, 1-38.

27. L. B. Kircho, "Stratigrafiia Altyn-depe i kolichestvennyi metod opredeleniia otnositel'noi khronologii," Karakumskie drevnosti, vol. IV, 1972.

28. V. M. Masson, Kara-depe u Artykha, pp. 378-79.

29. G. F. Dales, "Archaeology and Radiocarbon Chronologies for Protohistoric South Asia," in South Asian Archaeology, London, 1973.

30. C. C. Lamberg-Karlovsky and M. Tosi, "Shahr-i Sokhta and Tepe Yahya," pp. 25-26.

31. J. R. Caldwell, Investigations at Tal-i Iblis, Illinois, 1967.

32. O. Berdyev, "Chagylly-depe — novyi pamiatnik neoliticheskoi dzheitunskoi kul'tury," in Material'naia kul'tura narodov Srednei Azii i Kazakhstana, Moscow, 1966; G. F. Korobkova and V. T. Volovik, "Gadymi-depe — novyi pamiatnik dzheitunskoi kul'tury," USA, 1972, no. 2.

33. A. F. Ganialin, Kholm Ilgynly-depe, Tr. IIAE Turkm. SSR, vol. V, 1959.

34. V. I. Sarianidi, Pamiatniki pozdnego eneolita, p. 32, plate XX, 8, 13; plate XXIII, 10.

35. In the northern part of the site corresponding levels were uncovered in a trench excavated by A. F. Ganialin. In 1966 during the cleaning of a section in the southern part of the mound, these levels were observed lower than building remains with Geoksyur ceramics.

36. V. M. Masson, "Kamennyi vek Srednei Azii i poniatie arkheologicheskoi kul'tury," IMKU, 1974, no. 11.

37. V. M. Masson, "Protogorodskaia tsivilizatsiia," p. 182, fig. 14; A. Ia. Shchetenko, "Raboty Artyksogo otriada," p. 416.

38. L. B. Kircho, "Stratigrafiia Altyn-depe."

Altyn-depe during the Aeneolithic

39. V. M. Masson and V. I. Sarianidi, Sredneaziatskaia terrakota epokhi bronzy, Moscow, 1973, pp. 20-21.

40. V. M. Masson, review of W. A. Fairservis, Excavations in the Quetta Valley, SA, 1960, no. 3; and Srednaia Azii i drevnii Vostok, vol. 6, Moscow-Leningrad, p. 437.

41. V. I. Sarianidi, Pamiatniki pozdnego Eneolita, pp. 49-50.

42. M. Tosi, "Excavations at Shahr-i Sokhta," 1968, pp. 287-88; C. C. Lamberg-Karlovsky and M. Tosi, op. cit., pp. 25-26.

43. R. Biscione, "Dynamics of an Early South Asian Urbanization," p. 114.

44. M. Tosi, op. cit., fig. 37, n; V. M. Masson, "Pamiatniki srednego eneolita," plate XII, 12.

45. M. Tosi, op. cit., fig. 37 c,d; V. M. Masson, "Novye raskopki na Dzheitune i Kara-depe," SA, 1962, no. 3, fig. 8, 7, 8.

46. M. Tosi, op. cit., fig. 37, k, and in the present article, Figure 8, 25-29.

47. Ibid., p. 360, fig. 37 (compare V. M. Masson and V. I. Sarianidi, Sredneaziatskaia terrakota, plate XXIV, 6).

48. V. M. Masson, review of W. A. Fairservis, Excavations in the Quetta Valley, SA, 1960, no. 3, pp. 350-52.

49. J. M. Casal, op. cit., fig. 54, 65; V. M. Masson, Kara-depe u Artyka, plate XXX, 1.

50. J. M. Casal, op. cit., fig. 54, 69; V. M. Masson, op. cit., plate XXII.

51. J. M. Casal, op. cit., fig. 77, 269.

52. Ibid., fig. 135, 11c, d.

53. J. G. Shaffer, "Preliminary Field Report on Excavations at Said Qala Tepe," Afghanistan, 1971, vol. XXIV, no. 2-3, p. 93.

54. Ibid., p. 102.

55. A. H. Dani, "Excavations in the Gomal Valley," Ancient Pakistan, no. 5, 1970-71; G. F. Dales, "Turkmenistan, Afghanistan, and Pakistan," in Propyläen Kunstgeschichte, Berlin, 1972, fig. 83, p. 174.

56. M. R. Mughal, "New Evidence of the Early Harappan Culture from Jalipur," Archaeology, 1974, vol. 27, no. 2, pp. 111-12.

57. J. M. Casal, Fouilles de Mundigak, vol. 1, pp. 100, 115.

58. V. M. Masson, Srednaia Aziia i drevnii Vostok, pp. 424-33; V. I. Sarianidi, Pamiatniki pozdnego eneolita, pp. 48-50.

59. J. M. Casal, La Civilisation de l'Indus et ses énigmes, Paris, 1969, p. 78.

60. Besides M. Tosi, C. Lamberg-Karlovsky, and R. Biscione, also see G. F. Dales, Archaeological and Radiocarbon Chronologies for Protohistoric South Asia, p. 166.

61. M. Tosi and R. Wardak, "The Fullol Hoard: A New Find from Bronze Age Afghanistan," East and West, 1974, vol. 22, no. 1-2.

CHAPTER 4

The Problem of the Origin of the Early Bronze Age Culture of Southern Turkmenia

L. B. KIRCHO

The stratigraphic study of Altyn-depe made in recent years and the results of surveys and excavations at certain other sites make it possible to examine the origin of the Early Bronze Age culture of southern Turkmenia on the basis of comparatively broad data.

The first information on it was obtained by the exploratory dig into the southern hill at Anau by R. Pumpelly's expedition in 1904 (Anau III assemblage) [29, pl. 34, 35]. The excavations made by A. A. Marushchenko at Ak-depe near Ashkhabad in the 1930s yielded materials of an assemblage of the Early Bronze Age, which acquired the designation Anau III A in the literature [24, p. 152].

The principal data for defining the chronological stages of development of the Anau cultures were obtained in excavations and exploratory soundings undertaken in 1949-52 at Namazga-depe near Kaakhka. In the system of the general stratigraphy of Namazga-depe, the Early Bronze Age culture came to be called the Namazga IV assemblage. The strata of that period, identified on the basis of a distinctive assemblage of painted ceramic ware, were found in sounding 1 (levels V-XII) [6, pp. 37-40, 42-46, fig. 4, 7-10], sounding 2 (levels VI-VII), and sounding 4 (levels V-VI). Pottery of the type of late Namazga IV has been obtained in excavation of a building at the third construction level, on the so-called square with hearths [1, pp. 58-63; 5, pp. 277-78; 10, pp. 302-6, pls. XXIX-XXXVI].

A special study of the layers of the Namazga IV period was undertaken in 1962 by the Geoksyur Division of the Kara Kum Expedition at the settlement of Khapuz-depe in the area of the ancient delta of the Tedjen River. Excavations of burial chambers and the finds in soundings 1 and 2 significantly increased our understanding of the Early Bronze Age in southwestern Turkmenia [20, pp. 58-63].

Study of the stratigraphy of sites in the Kaakhka area showed that at the base of small settlements of the developed Bronze Age lie the levels of late Namazga IV: Shor-depe, sounding 1, levels V-VIII; Taichanak-depe, sounding 1 [26, pp. 26, 27]; Kosha-depe, sounding 1, levels XI-XV [8, pp. 25-28]. Pottery of the Namazga IV type was also found at the Gara-depe site near Kaushut [26, pp. 19, 24].

Materials of assemblages of the Early Bronze Age were collected in 1969, 1972, and 1973 at two unnamed sites near Ashkhabad (near the village of Bagir and in the vicinity of Geok-tepe [7, pp. 507-9]).

The most extensive investigations of the culture of the Early Bronze Age were undertaken at two sites in the eastern area: Ulug-depe at Dushak and Altyn-depe at Meana. At Ulug-depe construction assemblages of the Namazga IV period were uncovered at excavation 1 (the Ulug 2-Ulug 4 layers), and a poorly preserved layout was identified at excavation 2. At excavation 3, layers of the Namazga IV type were found at a depth of 5 meters from the surface of the settlement [22, pp. 342-45; 23, pp. 434, 435].

Vestiges of a fortification wall and a considerable number of burials of the Namazga IV period were found at Altyn-depe in 1959-61 [2, pp. 207-13]. Stratigraphic investigations undertaken in 1965-66 at excavation 1 (the craftsmen's hill) revealed four construction levels, of which the lowest (Altyn 4) contained material of the type of late Namazga IV [12, p. 170]. Study of the early levels at the site in 1969, 1970, and 1974 made it possible to identify 11 construction levels, Altyn 5-15, which combine into three cultural-historical assemblages [4, p. 175; 14; 15, pp. 428, 429; 27, p. 417]. The Early Bronze Age culture consists of layers Altyn 4-8 and is about 4 meters thick.

Excavations of the upper construction levels of the settlement and special soundings sunk in 1974 in the "copper mound" and in the "residential neighborhood mound" showed that layers of the Namazga IV type can be traced over the entire area of the settlement. In a number of cases (in a trench at excavation 1, in sounding 2, "the living quarter mounds," and in a sounding at excavation 8, "the copper mound") it proved possible to demonstrate that layers of the Late Aeneolithic directly underlay layers of the type of early Namazga IV.

Thus 12 ancient agricultural settlements containing layers of the Early Bronze Age culture are now known in the piedmont strip at the base of the Kopet Dagh Mountains. By their dimensions these settlements can be divided into three major groups: small sites, ranging from 0.5 to 1.0 hectare (Ak-depe, the southern hill at Anau, Shor-depe, Taichanak-depe); medium-sized sites, from 6 to 10 ha (Khapuz-depe, Ulug-depe, Gara-depe); and large sites, over 20 ha (Altyn-depe, Namazga-depe). It is difficult to arrive at a complete idea of the nature of the layout of the settlements, since virtually no excavations covering large areas have been made. At Ak-depe an assemblage of 12 rooms was uncovered that apparently, based on their materials, served different functions. They include dwelling rooms, rooms for storing supplies, and apparently, a small shrine [24, p. 152]. At Namazga-depe's "square with hearths" a square building has been excavated consisting of five rooms [5, p. 277, Figure 4], two of which, 12 to 15 sq m in area, were probably dwellings, while three small ones (3-4 sq m) probably served auxiliary purposes. This building was apparently part of some larger architectural entity, for some of the rooms continue past the eastern end of the excavation.

In studying Khapuz-depe, construction assemblages of groups of rooms (15-30 sq m in area) were identified, connected by common passages [20, Figure 15, no. 23]. The large-scale work at Ulug-depe has not yet had detailed treatment in the press. According to preliminary communications, the layout of the Ulug 2 and Ulug 3 layers reveals the remains of two houses containing many rooms separated by an alley [23, p. 343]. At Altyn-depe a number of rooms of the ordinary type of multiroom houses, whose thickened outer wall formed the edge of the settlement, were found at excavation 1 in the Altyn 4 layer.

For a characterization of the architecture of the Namazga IV period, study of the fortification wall on the "mound of the wall" at Altyn-depe is important. The early fortification wall "B" was built atop layers of the Namazga III period during early Namazga IV and consisted of several sections stepped back from each other within the settlement. At a number of spots the wall was flanked by projecting pilasters [12, p. 170, figures 4, 5]. The presence of a strong fortification wall on the "mound of the wall" during late Namazga IV was confirmed by work in 1973. Massive masonry was found at excavation 5 on the outskirts of the settlement encircling this area and reinforced by two buttressing towers [16, p. 511].

Thus two basic traditions can be traced in the architecture of the Early Bronze Age: on the one hand, multiroom complexes were built that were divided by narrow alleys and had rooms differentiated into economic household and dwelling areas within the complex and had small courtyards (a tradition from the Aeneolithic period); and on the other, the first appearance of large fortification walls flanked by towers and projecting pilasters.

The limited nature of the available materials makes it possible to provide only the most general description of the economy of the Early Bronze Age Culture. Unquestionably the concentration of considerable populations in one place and, correspondingly, the appearance of settlements larger than 10 ha in size were possible only under conditions of a developed system of irrigation agriculture [24, p. 164]. Judging by osteological material, the composition of the stock of domesticated animals had not significantly changed in comparison with the Aeneolithic period. At excavation 1 in Altyn-depe, bones of cattle, sheep, and goats were found, while among the wild animals there were the bones of onagers and gazelles [3, pp. 177-78, pl. 2].

Various fields of production on the basis of which specialized crafts began to take shape during the developed Bronze Age attained high levels. During the Namazga IV period, particularly during the late phases of its development, hand-molded pottery was totally replaced by ware thrown on the wheel. Two-story, highly efficient kilns appeared for the first time. The earliest two-story kiln was found in Altyn layer 9 (end of the Namazga III period). No doubts exist as to the wide use of two-story kilns in the late phase of development of the Early Bronze Age: kilns 1 and 2 at Khapuz-depe [20, p. 61, figure 15, no. 24] , and kilns 6 and 7 at Ulug-depe [9, p. 38, figure 2].

By comparison to the Aeneolithic there was an increase in the number of metallic objects — punches, piercers, so-called pins with flattened oval or bispiral heads, needles with eyes, etc. The find of a copper (?) set fishhook in Altyn layer 7 is quite interesting.

Stoneworking also probably became a specialized skill. Thin, elegantly chiseled vessels, a variety of pendants, beads, and carved seals of polished marblelike limestone, turquoise, carnelian, and lapis lazuli testify to masterful understanding of both materials and the techniques for working them.

The thickness of the Early Bronze Age culture layers fluctuates from 4 to 5 m at various sites (Altyn-depe, Khapuz-depe, Ulug-depe, Namazga-depe, Ak-depe) for layers containing the remains

of ordinary dwellings, and about 9 m at Altyn-depe for layers containing the remains of fortification walls. At most sites four to six construction levels of assemblages of the Namazga IV type were found.
It goes without saying that the Early Bronze Age culture did not remain
unchanged during this entire period. Its chronological and local differences are thus far traceable chiefly in pottery. The early assemblages of Altyn-depe, Khapuz-depe, and Ulug-depe are characterized by a predominance of vessels molded by hand and finished
on the potters' wheel. The ornamentation was in dark-brown paint
on a greenish-white or reddish-pink slip. Two-color ornamentation,
repeating the principal motifs of the monochrome painted ware, is often
encountered in the assemblages of the eastern group of sites. The ornamentation is geometrical, intermittent, and close, in the so-called
carpet style. Unpainted ware repeats the major forms of the painted.

In the western area (Namazga-depe, Ak-depe) vegetative and zoomorphic ornamentation is encountered in addition to geometrical.
Burnished grayware of the Shah-tepe II type is widely encountered,
sometimes with scratch ornamentation. It is suggestive that the
farther west one goes, the less painted ware and the more gray
burnished ware is found. There is virtually no painted ware at all
at the Geok-tepe site [7, p. 507].

During the late stage of Namazga IV, virtually all the vessels
are made on the potter's wheel, the painting becomes more careless, and the formerly precise cross-shaped and pyramidal figures acquire the eroded contours of "spots with eyelashes," the
space between which is filled with networks of parallel continuous
or broken lines. Polychrome painting disappears at Altyn-depe,
and the quantity of gray burnished ware at Namazga-depe declines.
Minor differences in shapes, slip color, and painting details between the eastern and western districts are quite natural in so
large a territory. Thus it is possible to identify at least two
stages of development of the pottery assemblage of the Namazga
IV type. For the early stage, moreover, one can trace western
and eastern local variants of the culture.

In the stratigraphy of Namazga-depe the culture layers of the
Early Bronze Age are dated to the middle and latter half of the
third millennium B.C. Carbon from Altyn layer 4 (end of Namazga
IV period) is dated by radiocarbon analysis to 2120 B.C. (±50 years)
[13, p. 249], while that from the Ulug 3 layer is dated to 2190 B.C.
(±100 years), and from Ulug 2 to 2145 B.C. (±100 years) [19, p. 59].
Taking into consideration G. Dales's dating for the cultures of
South Asia [28, pp. 157-69, figure 11, 2] and data based on the

corrections proposed by American researchers for radiocarbon dates, the late stage of Namazga IV can be dated at 2620 B.C. (±50 years), 2690 B.C. (±100), and 2645 B.C. (±100). To date the Early Bronze Age culture at no later than the middle of the third millennium B.C. is not only in closer accord with a number of archeological parallels (Namazga IV–Mundigak IV–Quetta-type ware) but also brings the Early Bronze Age assemblages closer in time to the Upper Aeneolithic Culture.

The fact that the layers of the Namazga IV period lie directly above those of the Upper Aeneolithic period, as well as the stylistic ties of the early Namazga IV-type pottery painting with ware of the Geoksyur and Kara-depe styles, serve as the basis for the hypothesis that the Early Bronze Age Culture developed from the Geoksyur I and Kara I assemblages [10, p. 303; 20, pp. 64, 65].

Pottery is the most widely prevalent and characteristic material of the Early Bronze Age Culture. The major features of the pottery assemblage are shapes, design elements, and compositional patterns of decoration. Materials found at Altyn-depe in transition layers Altyn 8-10 (end of Namazga III and beginning of Namazga IV period) make possible a detailed tracing of the genesis of these characteristics of the Early Bronze Age ware.

The bulk of the ware in assemblages Altyn 8-9 (the earliest in the Early Bronze Age period) was made of dense clay without visible impurities. Shaping was by hand, but the concentrically precise circular diameters of the vessels suggest the use of a primitive potter's wheel or, more probably, of a support that could be turned. The painted and unpainted tableware is represented by at least seven principal forms: bowls with sharp or rounded rims, of two types: (1) conical open bowls, and (2) hemispherical bowls; basins with sides that are vertical or curved slightly inward, also of two types: (3) open, and (4) deep; rounded biconical vessels with smooth wall curvature in the midsection, of three types: (5) with sharp rims, (6) with markedly everted rims, and (7) small pots with clearly identifiable short necks and slightly everted rims. All these forms are known in the Geoksyur ware [21, pl. VI]. However, unlike the Geoksyur assemblages themselves, where the hemispherical bowl is the principal form, carinated forms predominate quantitatively in the Altyn 8-9 assemblages: basins and biconical vessels. It is on the basis of these forms that conical beakers appear in Altyn layer 7 with sharp carinated edges in their lower portions and having the upper third of the vessel turned smoothly outward.

Regrettably the pottery of the western region, which is synchronous with the Altyn 8 assemblage, has had little study and virtually no publication. One can only note a general correspondence between the shapes of the vessels of layers 8-9 at Altyn with those of Kara 1A. The presence at Kara-depe of beakers with carinated edges near their bottoms [11, pls. XXXV, 3, XXXVI, 13] is suggestive. Judging by the very small ornamentation, it is one of the very late forms of ware in the Namazga III period.

The richness and complexity of ornamentation of the ware of early Namazga IV is emphasized by all investigators: "extremely small ornamentation," "carpet style," "lavish painting" — this is the impression that the ancient craftsmen were able to achieve by skillful use of a very limited set of devices. The designs were formed on the basis of five leading compositional patterns by symmetrical rearrangements of four depictive elements [for further details on symmetry, see 25, chaps. 1-5, 7, 8].

The elements of ornamentation were: 1 — the straight line; 2 — a line combined with a slanting border of isosceles triangles (a stepped line); 3 — a background right triangle; 4 — a background right triangle with stepped sides that appears in paintings of the Geoksyur style and is gradually modified in the course of the Early Bronze Age (Figure 1).

In ornaments of Altyn layer 10, corresponding to the late phase of development of the Geoksyur style, elements 2 and 4 are made up of a slanting border consisting of two or three large right triangles. The principal motifs in the ornamentation are stepped pyramids, squares, diamonds, crosses, and bilaterally stepped squares. It is interesting to note the virtually complete absence of the slanting border of diamonds, although it is quite typical of the synchronous Kara 1A assemblage and served as the basis of one of the leading elements of ornamentation of the Namazga IV assemblage — a slanting border of ovals. The absence of such elements is probably to be explained by persistent traditions of Geoksyur polychrome in which certain ornamental motifs were separated by bands of a different color and had no tendency to merge.

In the ornamentation of pottery from Altyn layers 8 and 9, the stepped character of components remains, but the number of triangles in the slanting border increases (4-5), while the triangles themselves become smaller. In the strata of Altyn 6-7 the stepped elements of ornamentation are made up of small acute isosceles triangles.

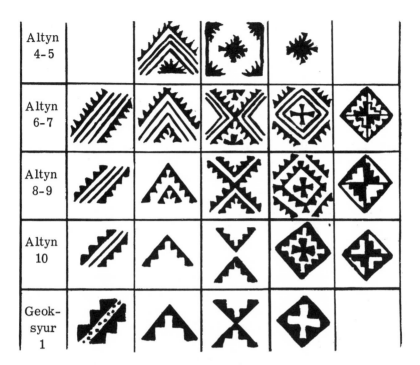

Altyn 4-5					
Altyn 6-7					
Altyn 8-9					
Altyn 10					
Geok-syur 1					

Figure 1. Origin and development of pottery ornamentation patterns in the Early Bronze Age Culture.

The leading compositional patterns also find direct analogies in ornamentation of the Geoksyur style. They are: 1 — horizontal border (a): two of slanting straight and stepped lines [21, pl. IV, type V, 1, 2, 4-7]; 2 — borders and network of (a) horizontal, (b) vertical zigzags (a:b) : 2 · a [21, pl. IV, type IV]; 3 — borders made up of alternating squares or diamonds and pyramids with facing apices (a) : 2 · m [21, pl. IV, type III, B, 9; C, 1-4]; 4 — borders representing part of bilateral network ornamentation (a : a) : ab : 4Ob [21, pl. IV, type III, B, 10]; 5 — (a) network or (b) bordered symmetrical ornaments (a : a) : 4 · m [21, pl. IV, type III, D, 2] (Figure 2).

The development of composition is achieved primarily by increasing complication of the unit of division of the ornamentation. In pottery of the Altyn layer 10, the decorations are usually made by simple repetition or alternation of one or two motifs. In the ornaments of the Altyn 8-9 assemblage, the unit of repetition consists of several motifs one inscribed within the other, each of which is repeated concentrically two or three times. Sometimes

103

the units of the pattern are separated by vertical lines, so that the ornament seems to consist of repeated panels. In Altyn layers 6 and 7 the ornamentation becomes even more fragmented. The complexity of applying stepped motifs repeated many times results in only the junctions of the ornamentation remaining stepped while being surrounded by concentric motifs of straight lines.

In the western area the painting of pottery of the Namazga IV assemblage generally continued the local Kara-depe traditions. As before, zoomorphic and vegetative ornamentation was widely prevalent, although the depictions of spotted animals entirely disappeared [24, p. 160, figure 36, 1, 2]. The ornamentation was strictly monochrome. The earliest here, apparently synchronous with layers 6-7 of the Altyn assemblage, comes from levels X-XII of sounding 1 at Namazga-depe [6, figures 8-9]. The ornaments were made up of straight lines and slanting borders of ovals. The principal compositional device, in which each unit of the repeated pattern is a complex network panel and the ornamentation is constructed of a number of such panels, is widely represented in the Kara 1A assemblage [11, pls. XXXV, 2, 3, XXXVI, 8, 10, 13].

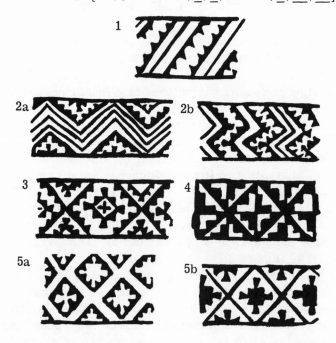

Figure 2. Principal compositional patterns of the ornamentation.

The Origin of the Bronze Age in Southern Turkmenia

A specialized study of terracottas by V. M. Masson and V. I. Sarianidi showed that the iconography of the small number of figurines known from the Early Bronze Age is also very closely related (particularly types I and II) to the preceding period [18, chap. 2]. The rectangular burial chambers at Khapuz-depe and the round tholos chamber in Altyn layers 9-10 are analogous to the burial structures of Geoksyur and Kara-depe. We have already spoken above of the connections in the traditions of house building. The available materials and their analysis permit the conclusion that on the basis of a substratum of Aeneolithic cultures, an Early Bronze Age culture came into being during the first half of the third millennium B.C. and served in turn as the basis for the protourban civilization of southern Turkmenistan.

References

1. Ganialin, A. F., K stratigrafii Namazga-depe. Trudy IIAE AN TSSR, vol. 2, Ashkhabad, 1956.
2. Ganialin, A. F., "Raskopki v 1959-1961 gg. na Altyn-Depe," Sovetskaia arkheologiia, 1967, no. 4.
3. Ermolova, N. M., "Ostatki mlekopitaiushchikh iz drevnikh pamiatnikov Iuzhnoi Turkmenii po raskopam 1970 g.," in Karakumskie drevnosti, issue 4, Ashkhabad, 1972.
4. Kircho, L. B., "Stratigrafiia Altyn-Depe i kolichestvennyi metod opredeleniia otnositel'noi khronologii," in Karakumskie drevnosti, issue 4, Ashkhabad, 1972.
5. Kuftin, B. A., "Polevoi otchet o rabote XIV otriada IuTAKE po izucheniiu kul'tury pervobytnoobshchinnykh osedlozemledel'cheskikh poselenii epokhi medi i bronzy v 1952 g.," Trudy IuTAKE, vol. 7, Ashkhabad, 1956.
6. Litvinskii, B. A., "Namazga-depe. Po dannym raskopok 1949-1950 gg.," Sovetskaia arkheologiia, 1952, no. 4.
7. Liapin, A. A., and I. S. Masimov, "Obsledovanie pamiatnikov rannei bronzy," in Arkheologicheskie otkrytiia 1973 g., Moscow, 1974.
8. Masimov, I. S., "Izuchenie pamiatnikov epokhi bronzy i rannego zheleza v raione stantsii Baba-Durmaz," in Karakumskie drevnosti, issue 2, Ashkhabad, 1968.
9. Masimov, I. S., "Izuchenie keramicheskikh pechei epokhi bronzy na Ulugdepe," in Karakumskie drevnosti, issue 4, Ashkhabad, 1972.
10. Masson, V. M., "Raspisnaia keramika Iuzhnoi Turkmenii po raskopkam B. A. Kuftina," Trudy IuTAKE, vol. 7, Ashkhabad, 1956.
11. Masson, V. M., "Kara-depe u Artyka," Trudy IuTAKE, vol. 10, Ashkhabad, 1960.
12. Masson, V. M., "Protogorodskaia tsivilizatsiia iuga Srednei Azii," Sovetskaia arkheologiia, 1967, no. 3.
13. Masson, V. M., "Otkrytie monumental'noi arkhitektury epokhi bronzy v Iuzhnom Turkmenistane," Sovetskaia arkheologiia, 1968, part 2.
14. Masson, V. M., Raskopki na Altyn-depe v 1969 g., Ashkhabad, 1970.

L. B. Kircho

15. Masson, V. M., "Izuchenie stratigrafii i topografii Altyn-depe," in Arkheologicheskie otkrytiia 1970 g., Moscow, 1971.

16. Masson, V. M., "Prodolzhenie raskopok na Altyn-depe," in Arkheologicheskie otkrytiia 1973 g., Moscow, 1974.

17. Masson, V. M., "Raskopki pogrebal'nogo kompleksa na Altyn-depe," Sovetskaia arkheologiia, 1974, no. 4.

18. Masson, V. M. and V. I. Sarianidi, Sredneaziatskaia terrakota epokhi bronzy, Moscow, 1973.

19. Romanova, E. N., A. A. Sementsov, and V. I. Timofeev, "Radiouglerodnye daty obraztsov iz Srednei Azii i Kazakhstana laboratorii LOIA AN SSSR," in Uspekhi sredneaziatskoi arkheologii, issue 2, Leningrad, 1972.

20. Sarianidi, V. I., "Khapuz-depe kak pamiatnik epokhi bronzy," in Kratkie soobshcheniia Instituta arkheologii AN SSSR, issue 98, Moscow, 1964.

21. Sarianidi, V. I., "Pamiatniki pozdnego eneolita Iugo-Vostochnoi Turkmenii," in Svod arkheologicheskikh istochnikov, B 3-8, part 4, Moscow 1965.

22. Sarianidi, V. I.,"Prodolzhenie rabot na Ulug-depe," in Arkheologicheskie otkrytiia 1968 g., Moscow, 1969.

23. Sarianidi, V. I., and K. A. Kachuris, "Raskopki na Ulug-depe," in Arkheologicheskie otkrytiia 1968 g., Moscow, 1969.

24. Sredniaia Aziia v epokhu kamnia i bronzy, Moscow and Leningrad, 1966.

25. Shubnikov, V. A., and A. V. Koptsik, Simmetriia v nauke i iskusstve, Moscow, 1972.

26. Shchetenko, A. Ia., "Raskopki pamiatnikov epokhi eneolita i bronzovogo veka v Kaakhkinskom raione," in Karakumskie drevnosti, issue 1, Ashkhabad, 1968.

27. Shchetenko, A. Ia., "Raboty Artykskogo otriada Karakumskoi ekspeditsii," in Arkheologicheskie otkrytiia 1969 g., Moscow, 1970.

28. Dales, G. F., "Archaeological and Radiocarbon Chronologies for Protohistoric South Asia," in South Asian Archaeology, London, 1973.

29. Pumpelly, R., Explorations in Turkestan, vol. 1, Washington, 1908.

CHAPTER 5

Man at the Dawn of Civilization

V. M. MASSON and T. P. KIIATKINA

The mound of Altyn-depe, which is situated near the village of Meana to the south of the town of Tedjen in the Turkmen Republic of the Soviet Union, at first gives the impression of an unassailable giant. Spreading over an area of 46 hectares and rising to a height of 22 meters,* the site is strewn with fragments of broken pottery and other traces of intensive human activities; its very size forces one to reflect on the limited abilities of the archeologist who labors only with a simple shovel and small knife. The dimensions of this ancient site alone show that before us stands a monument of unusual significance; and even a cursory familiarity with the objects that cover the site's surface, which were washed out by melting waters and eroded by the wind, bespeaks their considerable antiquity: nearly 4,000 years old. These purely external features led us to believe that before us lay the ruins of a city that is perhaps the most ancient in the Soviet Union (Figure 1).

Ten years of excavations — during which time various devices were used to remove earth besides the traditional spade and knife — have completely verified this proposition. The mound of Altyn-depe preserved excellent and, in many respects, unique materials that characterized the state of society and man himself in

---

*The site was remapped in 1978 and was discovered to extend for fewer than 30 hectares. The cultural levels at Altyn-depe continue for eight meters beneath the present level of the plain, creating a total cultural deposit of about 30 meters. — P.L.K.

that distant age when urbanization took its first steps.

Civilization in the Desert

At present, Altyn-depe is located in a desert steppe that is enlivened with fresh, green, but short-lived vegetation in the spring. During the summer only occasional mirages, rising above the burning takyr,* bring variety to the monotonous landscape. However, the palaeogeographic investigations of G. N. Lisitsina have shown that 4,000 years ago this landscape was more comfortable and agreeable.

The analysis of ancient charcoal from levels dated between the sixth and second millennia demonstrates that throughout this region tugai, or an open woods vegetation, dominated that was composed of poplars, maples, elms (or locally karagach), and ash trees. Judging from the samples, it is interesting to note that in the sixth

---

*A takyr is an alkaline soil formation consisting of clays with algae and lichens. — P.L.K.

Figure 1. Altyn-depe: aerial view. The excavation of the "elite quarter" is in the foreground; the excavation of residential units for single separate families (the second type) appears in the upper left background.

to fifth millennia, or during the Neolithic period, the elms (karagach) dominated, while in the fourth millennium, or during the
Aeneolithic period, poplars occurred more frequently. From then
until the end of the third or beginning of the second millennium B.C.,
karagach, in general, was absent. This perennial had probably
been subjected during the earlier periods to the destructive activities of man. Thus the occurrence of these species demonstrates
the incomparably greater availability of water in this region in
more ancient times when streams, now almost dessicated, irrigated the land and ensured the growth of dense tugai vegetation.

The indisputable decrease in water resources in connection
with the clearing of mountain forests is evident almost everywhere
throughout the pre-Kopet Dagh piedmont plain. At the same time,
the faunal evidence clearly attests to the proximity of this tugai
zone to the broad steppe and desert regions. The bones found at
Altyn-depe demonstrate that the game hunted by ancient man included not only those animals inhabiting the mountains (e.g., the
mouflon, argali, and bezoar goat) but also animals frequenting the
steppe and desert, such as the onager, djeiran (gazelle), and saiga
antelope. The numerous shattered bones of the onager and the
djeiran indicate the constant use of the meat of these animals.

Woody tugai thickets stretched along the primary and lateral
channels of the Akmazara River as far as its cone-shaped delta
fan adjoining parts of the desert steppe. Such was the immediate
environment during that epoch when the oldest civilization in the
Soviet Union was in the process of formation.

By the term "civilization" one must understand a system of social and cultural phenomena achieved by a society located at a
specific level of development. For ancient times this level is inevitably linked with the existence of early class society. The following traits have primary significance in analyzing archeological
materials that indicate the attainment of civilization: 1. the appearance of a city as a new type of inhabited locality qualitatively
distinct from previously existing settlements; 2. a high degree of
property differentiation; 3. the appearance of monumental architecture (religious or secular); 4. the discovery of signs of a
written language, indicating the transition to a qualitatively new
level of information storage and transfer.

At Altyn-depe we clearly observe the presence of the first
three features but are uncertain of the fourth, a written language
(a trait we still expect to find). However, the absence of one of
the features is a sufficiently understood phenomenon. It is the

case because civilization does not take shape immediately, and
not all the elements are present during its formation. The complete composition of a civilization occurs at a higher stage of development.

The systematic excavations at Altyn-depe clearly demonstrate
that this site was formed by a society which had attained a very
high level of development. And they clarify the spatial and temporal limits of this society. The site occupied an upper piedmont
valley of the Kopet Dagh where the availability of water flowing
down from the mountain streams and rivulets permitted the development of a sufficiently effective system of irrigation agriculture. In addition to Altyn-depe, another large settlement, Namazga-
depe, the ruins of which are situated west of Kaakhka, occupied
this same piedmont zone. A series of radiocarbon determinations
conducted by laboratories in Leningrad and Berlin (German Democratic Republic) agree with well-dated archeological complexes in
Iraq, Iran, and India and allow us to date the existence of this society to 2100-1750 B.C.[1]

According to archeological terminology, this period is known
as the Bronze Age. Among the metal objects found at Altyn-depe,
alloys of copper with arsenic (As from 1.5 to 8 percent) are widely
distributed; alloys with lead (Pb from 7 to 12 percent) appear less
frequently. Tin-bronze or classical bronze has yet to be found, a
fact best explained by the distance of the ore sources of this metal.* The preparation of metal objects — ranging from vessels and
adzes to figured seals (Figure 2) and different sorts of ornaments
— was one of the forms of ancient craft production; together with
irrigation agriculture and cattle herding, this production formed
the economic base of the society.

The potters' art was a very specialized craft which, for its
time, possessed substantial technical equipment. A swiftly rotating potters' wheel and two-chambered kilns of a sufficiently complex construction to attain a stable firing temperature of 1000-
1200° C permitted the large-scale production of elegant vessels
of standardized forms and high quality. Calculations made by

*Apparently Soviet geologists have recently discovered huge deposits of tin in western Afghanistan along the Iranian border north
of the Helmand Basin in association with numerous archeological
sites (I. M. Diakonov, personal communication). Their discovery,
still unpublished, could solve the vexing problem of the location of
tin sources for the Ancient Near East. — P.L.K.

E. V. Saiko demonstrate that in one kiln at Altyn-depe, 16,000-20,000 vessels and in another no fewer than 50,000 vessels could have been fired in a single year. It is clear that such large production was intended not only nor primarily for internal use (such a quantity of vessels is simply not needed for 5,000 inhabitants at Altyn-depe) but for exchange with neighboring communities. Such production is obvious evidence of the division of labor and the major role of exchange in this society.

Altyn-depe, the ruins of which cover 46 hectares, was a large population center for this period. For comparison we note that the area of so well-known a Sumerian city as Ur had reached only 20 hectares at the beginning of the third millennium.

Monumental architecture is present at Altyn-depe. During the course of excavations,[2] a large cult center was discovered with a four-tiered pyramid, built along the lines of a Mesopotamian ziggurat,[3] a structure which in the Biblical tradition is referred to as a Babylonian tower (Figure 3). A priestly sepulcher or tomb was found near this structure which contained a series of cult objects,

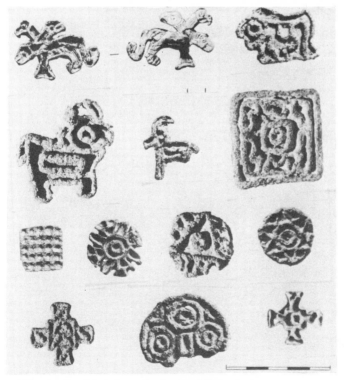

Figure 2. Metal seals from Altyn-depe.

111

including the gold head of a bull symbolizing a moon god (Figure 4). The situation is more complicated regarding one of the most important markers of ancient civilization, writing. A system of frequently occurring signs on terracotta statuettes that represent various female deities has a series of analogies with proto-Elamite and proto-Sumerian script. During the excavations of 1975 a seal with a pictographic inscription closely resembling the writing of the ancient Indian civilization of Harappa was discovered. For these reasons one can suggest that the inhabitants of Altyn-depe already knew some system of writing, utilizing in this field the achievements of neighboring peoples.

In any case, the accumulated data allow no doubt that the society that left us sites such as Altyn-depe and Namazga-depe can be studied as a civilization, at least as one at a formative stage. The main element in this civilization, its basic and characteristic feature, was the presence of large settlements, which can quite justifiably be considered the first cities.

The City of the Living and the City of the Dead

One must not only consider the size of the ancient settlements (although in itself this attribute is essentially significant) but also

Figure 3. Part of surviving cult complex and tower at Altyn-depe.

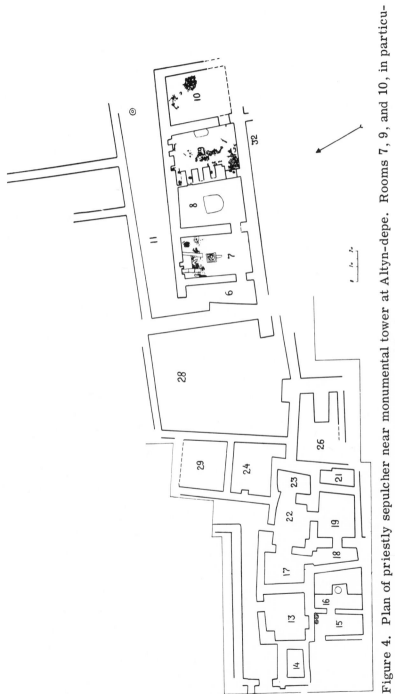

Figure 4. Plan of priestly sepulcher near monumental tower at Altyn-depe. Rooms 7, 9, and 10, in particular, contained skeletal materials and numerous rich objects.

take account of their structure, which reflects their corresponding
level of social development and forms one of their major and distinctive characteristics. Excavations have shown that at the beginning of the second millennium B.C., Altyn-depe was a settlement characterized by densely congested building and the incipient
utilization of vertical or multistoried structures. The following
areas can be defined within the city: 1. a monumental cult center
with a multistepped tower and graves of priests; 2. a production
center consisting primarily of an area for the mass production of
ceramics; 3. domestic quarters composed of three distinct types
of structures. More complicated than the Neolithic and Aeneolithic
settlements, this city reflects the more complex structure of its
society: the three types of domestic structures indicate the existence of at least three social groups that had graphically expressed
features of property differentiation.

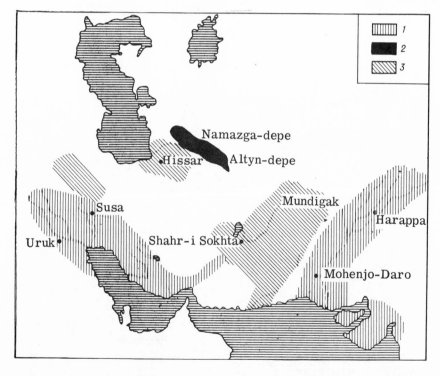

Altyn-depe in the system of ancient eastern civilizations from the
second half of the third to the beginning of the second millennium
B.C.: 1 — large urban civilizations; 2 — Altyn-depe civilization; 3 —
other civilizations of the second rank between Mesopotamia and India.

The first type of domestic structure consists of multiroom houses found near the production center; the quarters of the craftsmen were situated in proximity to their workshops. Each of these structures contains a general household courtyard, kitchen, and living quarters intended for a small separate family. These structures form the typical homes of large family communes, which were supported by a more general household economy. Their standard of living was not high, as is apparent from the comparatively poor quality of these buildings, which were not distinguished by proper planning or careful decoration. This low standard also is indicated by the composition of their diet. Approximately half of the osteological remains consist of the bones of wild animals: onagers, gazelles, and bezoar goats. Possibly the ancient craftsmen did not possess large flocks, and it was necessary to supplement their diet by hunting.

Houses of the second type were distinguished by a better quality of finishings and more accurate planning. But their most characteristic feature is that they were designed for a single separate family with its own personal kitchen, personal courtyard, and personal hearth for baking bread. The meat consumed by the inhabitants of these houses was principally that of domestic animals, chiefly sheep and goats. We see before us the quarters of self-sufficient citizens, set apart by a higher level of comfort.

Finally, the third type consists of very spacious homes, laid out, as a rule, on a square or rectangular plan, occupying an area from 43 to 102 m^2 (Figures 5-6). All the evidence suggests that one such house was the residence of a high priest; it is described as a cult complex. In one of the residential sections of Altyn-depe an entire "elite quarter" consisting completely of similar houses was uncovered. The streets separating the houses were built of potsherds that formed a very convenient road, particularly during heavy rains. Along such streets harnessed camel carts could easily move; models of such carts (Figure 8) have frequently been found during excavations. In this quarter the largest and most elegant terra-cotta figurines of female deities, numerous bronze and silver seals, some of which depicted imaginary animals, and various bronze and silver ornaments were found. The bones of young sheep completely dominated the faunal remains.

Thus the excavations at Altyn-depe clearly show that this was not simply a settlement of non-nomadic agriculturalists containing a certain number of houses with few differences in their decoration or plans. The monumental cult complex, the large production center, and the different types of constructions all reflect the high level of social and property differentiation that is representative of a new type of settlement at Altyn-depe, a city.

Figure 5. Part of the "elite quarter" at Altyn-depe.

Figure 6. Spacious residential units in the "elite quarter."

The above-mentioned features were shaped by functions which, at that time, were performed by urban settlements. In fact, one of the oldest of such functions was the role of organizational center for an agricultural region. The trading and craft functions of Altyn-depe are most clearly observed in those crafts the superior products of which are represented by numerous archeological finds. Finally, the function of ideological leadership is clearly reflected in the available materials. Its presence was reinforced, according to the norms of that epoch, by the construction of a cult complex dedicated to an astral deity (at that time small settlements in the same area of Turkmenia contained no such complexes). All these functions were characteristic features of the initial phase of urbanization, when the intensive accumulation of economic and cultural potential took place in the major centers.[4]

Although they did not constitute a basic structural unit, places of burial were an essential part of the city organism. In this world of the dead one finds a striking reflection of the world of the living.

At Altyn-depe two types of burials were distributed: in individual graves situated on the edge of the city and usually dug up in the collapsed ruins of older houses, and in collective graves — a sort of family sepulcher located right in the living quarters beside houses where the prosperous relatives continued to live (Figure 8). In these collective tombs burials occurred over a protracted period of time, and the bodies of those who had died earlier were simply pushed to one side, sometimes with careless lack of ceremony, for the new internments. Personal ornaments — rings, beads, bracelets, and even funerary gifts in the form of vessels with some type of food, including a ram's carcass whose bones were preserved in proper anatomical order — were placed alongside the deceased. Sometimes terra-cotta figurines of female deities, and along with them miniature vessels for libations, were placed inside the graves or just outside their walls.

To a certain degree the similarity of rites reflects the ethnic unity of the society; but the inequality which is also obvious in them necessarily balances one's initial sense of monotonous repitition. A tomb of priests stood by itself; it formed its own place of successive burials, not in a single crowded building, but in an entire funerary complex (Figure 9). The deceased were interred with a complex ritual in which some of their skulls were deliberately detached and placed in niches in the walls (Figure 10).

The distribution of funerary goods by graves in different parts of the ancient city paints an even clearer picture of social differ-

Figure 7. Model of cart drawn by camel from Altyn-depe. Several two-humped or Bactrian camel figurines have been discovered during the course of the excavations.

entiation. In the craftsmen's quarter the graves were situated in close proximity to the houses; neither ornaments nor figurines and only a few clay vessels accompanied these artisans to the afterworld. Another picture emerges in the quarter of the well-to-do citizens. Here more vessels and a sufficiently diverse collection of ornaments, including beads made of bronze and semiprecious stones and bronze rings and seals, were found. In the elite quarter the variety and, to a significant degree, the value of these objects increased. The funerary inventory of the multi-room tombs of the priests were distinguished by their unique wealth; here were found artistic creations of gold (Figure 11), silver, and semiprecious stones (Figures 12-13), including the golden head of a bull encrusted with turquoise (Figure 14).

Thus a sufficiently complex picture of the social structure of this urban settlement is reflected in their burial customs.

The age ranks separating children from adults and grown youths

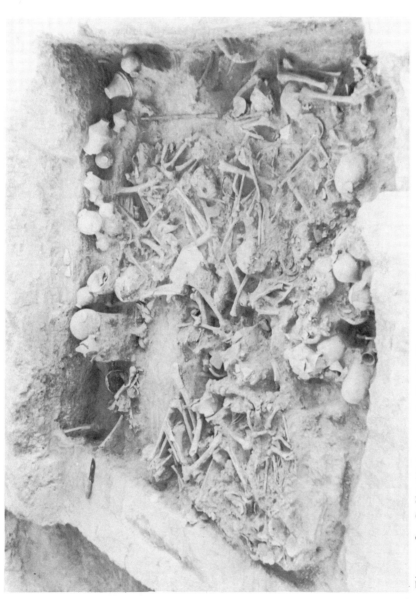

Figure 8. Collective grave in the "elite quarter."

from those members of the society having full and equal rights are shown rather precisely by the materials in the burials. In collective tombs children were placed with adults only after they had reached the age of six or seven; before this they were buried separately in small pits or in large vessels. Sometimes two children were placed in a single pit or in a single vessel. Tiny infants (i.e., newborn to the age of one or two) were buried inside the houses under the floor or threshold or in the corners. The rights and privileges of the parents were bequeathed to the children. In the craftsmen's quarter the burials of children contained only bones, while in the quarter of the prosperous burghers the children frequently were buried wearing rich necklaces.

The ancient tombs and burials at Altyn-depe contain information not only about the property and social relations or the customs and laws which regulated this society but also about the people themselves, the creators of this urban culture. Careful study of the osteological remains — in all more than 200 burials were discovered — permits us to form a series of interesting conclusions.

The People of the Bronze Age

What was the population at Altyn-depe like? The extant osteological materials allow us the possibility — utilizing a series of formulas proposed by the Soviet anthropologists V. V. Bunak and G. F. Debets and the English biologist and mathematician K. Pearson — of determining the stature and weight of the people at that time.

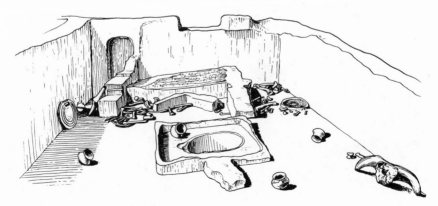

Figure 9. Plan of room 7 in funerary complex, showing osteological materials and artifacts.

Figure 10. Room 10 in funerary complex with pile of human remains and offerings.

Six complete skeletons were found at Altyn-depe; three men and three women. The height of the men ranged from 166 to 177 cm (according to the formulae of Bunak and Debets); where the skeletons were incomplete, the height of the men was calculated by measuring separate bones. Using Pearson's formula their stature varied within very broad limits: 161 to 185 cm. Thus one can confidently state that the majority of men living in this ancient city were taller than average (compared to the stature of all mankind), though a significant minority were medium-sized.

The height of the three complete female skeletons ranged from 154 to 168 cm, while that determined from the separate bones of partial skeletons varied from 151 to 164 cm. Thus the women — according to the categories cited — must be considered medium-sized.

Figure 11. Gold beads from room 7 of funerary complex.

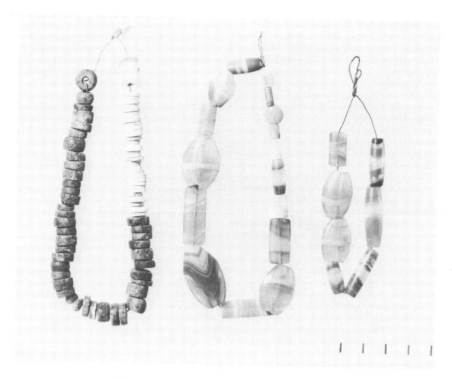

Figure 12. Agate, lapis lazuli, and ivory beads from room 7.

In order to present more graphically how the people of Altyn-depe looked in terms of height, we will provide some data about the stature of our contemporaries. The height of average Russian men from Moscow and the surrounding area is 165 to 168 cm. The population of the pre-Baltic states is taller — more than 169 cm — and this difference is quite distinct. (One must remember that when speaking about stature, one is referring to an average value characterizing the height of this or that group; the range of individual variation from this figure, of course, is highly significant.) And what are the figures for the population of present-day Turkmenia? According to data from the Soviet anthropologist L. V. Oshanin, the Turkmen (males) are 166.6 to 170.5 cm tall, i.e., they form a group of tall to medium-sized individuals. In general, one can say that the stature of contemporary Turkmen is very close to that of the people living 4,000 years ago at Altyn-depe.

We should discuss the weight of the men and women of this ancient city, although less is known about it than about their height. The weight of the three males is calculated at 70, 76, and 78 kg;

Figure 13. Lapis lazuli pendant or seal from room 7.

the weight of the three women at 60, 64, and 70 kg. Despite all the possible variations in these calculations, it is clear that the food rations of the ancient city-dwellers were by no means insufficient.

There is no doubt that the inhabitants of Altyn-depe — as was true, incidentally, for the whole population of Central Asia in antiquity — belonged to the great European race. They were people with long, narrow faces, large, dark (judging from the figurines) eyes, and sharply projecting, narrow noses with clearly outlined nostrils; they had comparatively small, well-formed heads with projecting occipital bones and pronounced ridges above the nose and eyebrows. That is how — in a rather masculine form — we conceive these people.

Figure 14. Golden bull with turquoise inlay from room 7.

The women's features were rather muted, but the nose was big, straight, and, as with the men, quite prominent.

If we compare the appearance of the inhabitants of Altyn-depe with our contemporaries, we can say that these people were much more narrow-faced and "sharp-nosed" than Russians living today in the central belt of the Soviet Union; the large projecting nose of the Russians would seem very small, "flat," and quite plain to the inhabitants of Altyn-depe. In comparison with contemporary Turkmen, it is clear that the people were very similar in the shape of their heads, the outline of their faces, and in the notorious trait of having large noses.

The ornaments found in the graves and the hair styles depicted on the clay figurines (Figures 15a and b), which the ancient people clearly modeled in imitation of themselves, allow us to augment somewhat our understanding of the characteristic external appearance of these first urban dwellers in our country. The women typically arranged their hair in thick, heavy plaits that fell down their backs; with various cosmetic aids they emphasized the arches of their thick eyebrows. They wore multistringed necklaces;

strings of red carnelian or milk-white agate, lightly marked with
a yellowish film, were especially fashionable. Silver, gold, and
bronze rings were worn on their fingers. Belts, frequently composed of several rows of beads which covered their thighs, also
were in vogue among the class of wealthy women; such belts are
depicted in the form of incised lines on the terracotta figurines.
In general, the women devoted great attention to their physical appearance; in one of the rich graves, a whole cosmetic set consisting of a double vessel made of marble, every conceivable type of
silver hairpin, and even a silver mirror was placed on a small
platform near the head of the buried individual. Gazing into this
mirror, the former beauty from Altyn-depe could have persuaded
herself of the success of her ingenious tricks.

The strong, tall, well-proportioned men and the smartly dressed
women with their splendid tresses[5] filled the streets and squares
of Altyn-depe. (As already mentioned, according to our estimates
this ancient city contained nearly 5,000 people.) But the burdens
and adversities of life at that time were concealed by these signs
of purely external prosperity. To a significant extent such difficulties are also reflected in the burials.

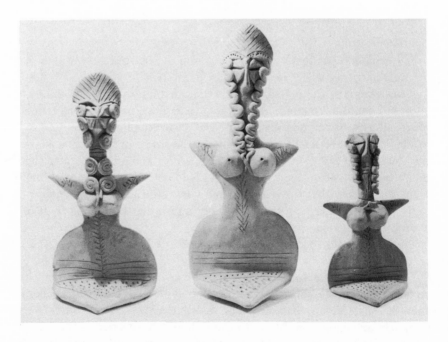

Figure 15a. Three female figurines from Altyn-depe: frontal view.

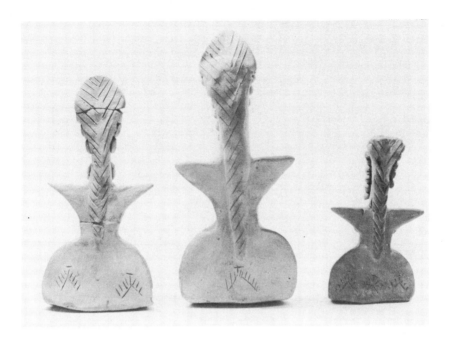

Figure 15b. Incised marks on lower backs of figurines. Such signs and isolated seals are the only indication of a possible writing system in southern Turkmenistan.

The Short Life of the First City-Dwellers

It is possible to divide the people buried in the graves and collective tombs into different age categories (see Table 1).

What is striking in Table 1? First of all, the great number of children not reaching the age of 13. This group represents almost one quarter of the total; more precisely, of every 100 dead, 22 are children. An even more painful picture emerges when one is able to determine which subgroup of the children's burials is the highest: of the 22 children dying before the age of 7, nine (more than 40 percent) were newborn, consisting either of stillborn or infants buried in the first days of life.

Among the individuals in the juvenile group (ages 13 to 20), there is an extremely significant division by sex: of 14 individuals (sex could be determined for only 14 of the 17 individuals in this category), 11, i.e., almost 80 percent, were female. What explains such early mortality? One can definitely associate this high incidence of juvenile female burials with their entry into child-bearing

Table 1

Age groups	Children* (0–13)		Juveniles (13–20)	Young adults (20–35)	Middle-aged (35–55)	Elders (over 55)	Total
	(0–7)	(7–13)					
Number of people	22	9	17	56	25	3	132
(in %)	16.7	6.8	12.9	42.4	19.0	2.2	100

*The divisions of the groups into age categories was done in accordance with the gradations or ranks ac-
cepted by the Soviet anthropological school.

age, the various complications caused by pregnancy, the process
of giving birth, and the postnatal period. The great number of infants who perished in the first hours or days of their lives could
be linked with the young age of the mother, since stillbirths, as
is well-known, are more common among young than middle-aged
women. In any case, a high death rate for children, particularly
infants, and for young women is observed among the people of
Altyn-depe. We suggest that these two facts are related.

Table 2 shows the division of the adult population of the city
by sex: among 84 individuals who reached the age of 20, only
three (two women and one man) lived to the age of 60; 81 (or
97 percent) did not attain the age of 55. Death was highest
among young adults; two thirds of the adults did not reach the

Table 2

Age groups	Young adults (20-35)	Middle-aged (35-55)	Elders (over 55)	Total
Number of people	56	25	3	84
(in %)	66.7	29.7	3.6	100
Males	28	16	1	45
Females	28	9	2	39

age of 35. Death was less frequent in the following age group
for the simple reason that a lower percentage of the population
ever attained this category. Very few people lived to an old age.

Table 3

Age groups	Juveniles	Young adults	Middle-aged	Elders	Total
Males	3	28	16	1	48
(in %)	6.2	58.3	33.3	2.2	100
Females	11	28	9	2	50
(in %)	22	56	18	4	100

Even a cursory glance at Table 3 is sufficient to show the lack
of similarity among the death rates of men and women. If one
mentally divides the table in half, then the left half, which contains
the young people (13-35) shows a great number of women (78 percent) and a smaller number of men (64 percent); on the other hand,
the right half contains a greater number of men (36 percent) and
a smaller number of women (22 percent). In other words, life expectancy for women was considerably lower than for men. Our
calculations show that the average life expectancy at Altyn-depe
was 22.6 years. Many sites dated to this period provide a similar
figure. For example, at the site of Sapalli-tepe, which is located
further east in southern Uzbekistan, the average life expectancy
was 22.9 years (according to the data of T. Khodzhaiov).

Since many sites only record the adult population (due to the
fact that the bones of children frequently are poorly preserved in
the ground), we also calculated the life expectancy of the adults at
Altyn-depe; the figure is 35.7 years.

Table 4 presents data on the average life expectancy of adults
from different archeological sites dated to the third and second
millennia B.C. (the information is taken from works related to
various sites).

Table 4

Archeological sites	Average age of the adult population	Number of people
Cemeteries at Khriashchevka and Iagodnoe (Lower Povolzhe)	30.2	36
Vykhvatinskii Cemetery (Moldavia)	44.3	21
Balanovskii Cemetery (Middle Povolzhe)	31.7	31
Altyn-depe (southern Central Asia)	35.7	84
Kokcha 3 Cemetery (Aral Region)	35.4	24

Table 5 presents interesting data concerning the differences in
life expectancy between men and women. In general, the death
rate among women was higher than among men and the life
expectancy, obviously, shorter (excluding the data from the
Kokcha 3 and Balanovskii cemeteries).

130

Table 5

Sex	Central Asia			Eastern Europe		Moldavia
	Altyn-depe	Sapalli-tepe*	Kokcha 3	Balanovskii Cemetery	Cemeteries at Khriashchevka and Iagodnoe	Vykhvatinskii Cemetery
Male**	36.1 (45)	35.1 (47)	33.6 (14)	31.4 (15)	32.7 (20)	48.2 (12)
Female**	35.2 (39)	33.4 (49)	37.5 (10)	32.0 (16)	27.0 (16)	39.2 (9)

*The data from Sapalli-tepe were kindly provided by T. Khodzhaiov. His figures include juveniles where their sex was determined.

**The numbers of individuals examined are shown in parentheses.

One reason for such a low percentage of people reaching middle age might be the great number of diseases that existed in the congested living conditions of cities in the Bronze Age. While the anthropological material from Altyn-depe was not subjected to detailed analysis for the study of osteological pathology, separate observations were made in the form of a preliminary analysis. There were many traces, for example, of tooth caries; sometimes after the complete destruction of the crown, the caries led to the further destruction of the pulp and, finally, of the maxillary bone itself. Numerous bone fractures occurred, particularly of thigh bones, which healed during the individual's lifetime; this fact is shown by the presence of large osteocallosities. Cranial afflictions also are recorded, including in one case the trepanning of the skull of a possibly still living individual.

In the System of Ancient Civilizations

Archeological and anthropological materials allow us not only to reconstruct a general picture of the civilization at Altyn-depe but also to define its place relative to a series of other ancient cultures.

The excavations have shown that the base of Altyn-depe contained the ruins of a small village of early agriculturalists that can be dated to the end of the fifth and beginning of the fourth millennia B.C. These agriculturalists fashioned handmade, relatively coarse ceramic vessels that were decorated with simple geometric designs. One should remember that the remains of small villages of early agricultural societies lay at the base of such well-known Sumerian cities as Eridu, Uruk, Nippur, and Lagash.

A period of substantial growth at Altyn-depe occurred at the beginning of the third millennium B.C. The site already occupied an area of not less than 20 hectares and had become one of the largest centers for the early agricultural tribes of southern Turkmenia. As we have seen, the archeological materials from this time on do not show any kind of important break or discontinuity suggesting a change of population. The anthropological data confirm this picture: dolichocephalic Caucasians, very similar in physical appearance to contemporary Turkmen, lived here in the fourth and third millennia B.C.

Altyn-depe was by no means a separate or isolated entity. According to the available data, it is quite obvious and clear that the site enjoyed constant relations with its neighbors and made use of the cultural achievements of other centers. Ivory was imported to

Altyn-depe from the Indus Valley; ivory objects frequently are found in houses of the elite quarter or in rich tombs. Isolated ceramic and metal objects might also have been imported from the Indus Valley, since several things made by the Altyn craftsmen clearly reflect Indian models.

Close ties also existed with Mesopotamia. They are evident in architecture (primarily in the very principle of erecting a multistepped tower), in art (particularly in the style of the execution of the golden-headed bull that was found in the priests' tomb), in the inscribed signs on the clay figurines of female deities, and in a series of other traits from the material culture.

The civilization of Altyn-depe was situated on the very edge of the northeastern periphery of the cultural world of the ancient Near Eastern civilizations; nevertheless, it maintained close contacts with the main centers of this world. New investigations have shown that in the second half of the third and the beginning of the second millennia B.C., a series of local urban civilizations developed that were situated in the broad region between Mesopotamia, on the one hand, and the Harappan civilization of the Indus Valley on the other. One of these was the southern Turkmenistan civilization of the Bronze Age.

Recent excavations in Iranian Seistan permit us to speak about the existence there at this time of a large cultural nexus, the center of which was a city whose ruins are known as Shahr-i Sokhta. Analogous centers are beginning to be recognized in northwestern and northeastern Iran. The characteristic traits of these cultures appear everywhere: the formation of large population centers of an urban type, the intense development of crafts, and the appearance of monumental architecture. All these centers developed from a local basis but actively utilized the cultural achievements, laws, and canons developed by the high or first-order civilizations, such as Sumer or Elam.

Thus, ever expanding, the process of primary urbanization in the Near and Middle East left its clear imprint on all aspects of the development of society and of mankind itself.

Notes

1. Altyn-depe no longer existed in the seventeenth century B.C.; at the same time, Namazga-depe also was abandoned. We do not actually know what occasioned the abandonment of these then large centers of early agriculture in southern Turkmenia.

V. M. Masson and T. P. Kiiatkina

2. Concerning the excavations of Altyn-depe, also see Priroda, 1973, no. 3, p. 114; 1975, no. 3, pp. 107-10.

3. A ziggurat is a cult building made of mud-brick that is found on many sites in ancient Mesopotamia; it forms a tower of parallel-sided structures placed one on top of the other, resembling a truncated pyramid.

4. See L. B. Kogan and F. M. Listengurt, "Urbanizatsiia i priroda," Priroda, 1975, no. 3.

5. See Priroda, 1975, no. 3, p. 2, cover.

CHAPTER **6**

Urban Centers of Early Class Society

V. M. MASSON

The great attention that the Tashkent school of archeology de-
votes to the study of ancient cities — their topography and internal structure as reflected in specific traits of urban organization
and the individual features of their historical development — is
one of its characteristic features. Courses on the historical topography of the large urban centers of Central Asia — Samarkand,
Bukhara, Tashkent, and several others — were taught systemati-
cally by M. E. Masson in the Department of Archeology, Tashkent
State University. Specific methods for the study of Central Asian
cities were devised with the aim of the maximum utilization of
preserved information for the purposes of historical reconstruction. One of the most important features of this school was the
creative approach to the study of the microrelief of large sites,
not just through the formal establishment of a horizontal topographic plan but also through a study of the specific archeological remains that reflected, in particular, elements of the city organism,
such as walls, streets, squares, large buildings, and the like, that
existed beneath the surface. According to this approach observations even on the nature of the soil itself, which nourished different
types of vegetation, offered considerable assistance. On the basis
of such methods a general plan for the study of the abandoned cities
was established by M. E. Masson which reflected the structure of
the largest urban settlements in southern Turkmenistan. The utilization of this method seemed the most effective approach for
studying urban centers, particularly those of great antiquity.

135

V. M. Masson

Such a study became all the more relevant because in recent
years there has been a sharp increase in interest in seeing ancient
city organisms as a sort of nuclear kernel of the most ancient
class formations, frequently called city-states. Large centers
that were the loci of dense populations developed from conditions
based on a settled agricultural economy that had populations concentrated in rural regions or oases; these centers became the
storehouses for various products, the centers of craft activities
and community temples, and the organs of power. To a large extent these functions were concerned with an organization of rural
agricultural activities that had a tremendous impact on both the
irrigation agriculture of the Near East and the slash-and-burn
cultivation practiced in pre-Aztec Mesoamerica. The necessity
of organizing the life of society by entire districts led to the formation of a complicated system of managing the economy and society which, in turn, brought about the appearance of a qualitatively
new system for the preservation and transmission of information:
writing. The complexity of early systems of writing promoted the
formation of a special stratum of professional scribes that became
part of the new administrative apparatus that gradually transformed
the organs of primitive self-rule. In this way such urban centers
were the bearers of the social progress of that epoch. Nevertheless elements of the primitive social formation continued to play
a significant role in these most ancient class societies or, as they
have recently been referred to by investigators, early class societies. The study of the character and structure of the first urban centers thus plays a decisive role in the analysis of early class
societies.

A sufficiently extensive literature has been devoted to these
problems. I. M. D'iakonov and his school have ascribed great significance to the internal structure of the ancient Near Eastern city,
which they elucidate on the basis of written sources.[1] Robert McC.
Adams's group has completed extensive studies on the typology of
early urban settlements in Mesopotamia and the dynamics of their
development on the basis of archeological maps and the calculations
of the areal dimensions of specific sites.[2] An entire series of
general questions concerning the problems of early urban centers
was discussed at a conference in London specifically devoted to
problems of settlement, man, and urbanism.[3] In the final analysis
the tendency at this conference was to examine the city as a specific abstract phenomenon removed from its concrete historical
setting, as if set in a peculiarly external and indigenously formed

vacuum. As opposed to this, Soviet investigators examine both
the city itself and the accompanying processes of urban development as one of the aspects of the development of society.

Particular importance is attached to the practical analysis of
the specific sites of the first cities or protourban settlements in
applying the principles of a concrete historical approach. Such
sites were formed by a natural development from still earlier social structures; these cities emerged from early agricultural
settlements that suffered a corresponding functional and structural
deformation.[4] With such an approach the range of possible sources
proves quite limited. Dozens of Mesopotamian sites, which have
been convincingly divided into several groups by R. McC. Adams,
have not been investigated at all in terms of their internal structure. For the most ancient stages of development, the basic concern of archeologists was directed at excavations of cult centers
and not at the emerging structures of the urban organism. Referring to the studies of Old Babylonian cities, I. M. D'iakonov directly observes that in this case, we are not dealing with the formation of a pristine urban organism but "with the establishment
of a special type of city that formed as a result of the breakdown
of the almost completely despotic monopoly of the king's economy
that was characteristic of the preceding period, particularly in the
cities."[5] Granting this perspective, one can attach considerable
significance to the study of the structures of large, stable agricultural settlements that became cities in other parts of the ancient
Near Eastern historical and cultural region. Of course, typologically such settlements can help us reconstruct the specific features
of development by studying problems of the forms of the most ancient cities on the basis of archeological materials.

Before we turn to one such example that represents an archeological investigation for the science of history, let us consider two
general questions: the problem of defining the concept of a city,
and the question of the typology of ancient urban settlements.
From a socioeconomic perspective ancient cities can be defined
as large nodes or places for the concentration of population, tools
of production, and cultural potential that performed basic regula-
tory, craft, and trading activities. The role of the city as a locus
for the concentration of activities is directly reflected in morphological features that are characterized, first of all, by the compact
construction and development of monumental architecture. It is
well known that at the beginning of the earliest stages of the development of early class societies, special canons were devised

for the construction of elite or prestigious buildings; palaces and temples were usually situated in the centers of the cities. The quantitative determination of population density should be associated with its calculation for societies with different economic structures, particularly different agricultural systems. It is also well known that V. Gordon Childe proposed that one could distinguish cities from villages by calculating the number of inhabitants, with cities consisting minimally of about 5,000 people. That is, if we take the generally accepted figure for the density of the population of ancient Near Eastern cities as about 400-500 inhabitants per hectare, a city should minimally cover roughly 10-12 hectares. However, the area of the well-known site of Knossos, which clearly performed a range of urban functions, was not more than 3.5 hectares, as is true for the small urban settlements of Asia Minor. Along with these external quantitative indicators, internal qualitative structural changes that allowed a special class of the population to be characterized as urban were especially important.

One should determine the different types of urban settlements that already existed in the earliest periods of their development. The functions performed in the urban centers can serve as the basis for a typology. Thus cities can be divided into centers for managing rural districts, craft and trading districts, and loci for military-administrative and cultural-ideological activities. In each specific case various functions are combined. Ancient cities not only performed definite functions but also were complex socioeconomic organisms that formed an essential part of a whole socioeconomic system. They usually were the concrete embodiment in very clear and representative forms of the system's characteristic features. Just as the polarization of class forces leads to a typology of ways of life based on social classes, so one can reconstruct a map of the class and prestige groupings of an urban area by analyzing building types and other signs in the archeological record.

One must mention that the method for the analysis of cities devised by the Tashkent archeological school lends itself to the reconstruction of their infrastructures. This type of analysis was performed for the urban site of Altyn-depe, located near the village of Meana, where materials from its surface and upper levels presented us with a picture of the life of a large population center that could be dated to the end of the third and the beginning of the second millennium B.C. (Figure 1), or to the Namazga V period according to the accepted archeological terminology. Systematic work conducted at the site by the Fourteenth Division of the Southern Turkmenian Complex Archeological Expedition (IuTAKE) and the Kara Kum Expedition of the Leningrad Sector of the Institute of Archeology, USSR Academy of Sciences, was directed toward this task.[6]

Detailed analysis of the microtopography of this urban center in conjunction with large-scale excavations, the locations of which were determined by such topographic analyses, allowed us to record several basic features of the internal structure of this settlement. Thus on the basis of the topography, the large sunken area in the southern part of the site that was filled with eroded clay and covered with grass in seasons when there had been abundant pre-

Figure 1. Altyn-depe: original plan of settlement and excavated areas in 1967.

cipitation was carefully noted. A small gulley that ran along the center of this sunken area and stripped the levels to a depth of one meter permitted us to speak about the absence at this level of any cultural strata. The drop from the surrounding part of the mound on which two ancient houses were excavated was 5 meters. This sunken area was thus designated a central square which, apparently, was structurally significant, at least in the last stage of the city's existence.

Further to the south the entire depression, designated an ancient square, ends in a hollow that cuts through the edge of the mound and probably indicates the position of an ancient entrance or gate. However, the verification of this identification by means of excavations was a very complicated affair; the very selection of a place to excavate was made only after rigorous analysis of the particular microtopography and nature of the destruction of the ancient cultural levels. The slopes at Altyn-depe have been so thoroughly washed away that the topmost building level has usually been completely destroyed; this is particularly the case if the slope is very steep. The area of the proposed entrance or gate from the east was cut off both by a mound with very steep sides and by unmistakable indications of severe erosion; here one could not expect to find any preserved fortification wall. However, to the west the short and stubby slopes of the mound gave us hope for more fruitful results. Excavations conducted on this western slope in 1969 revealed the remains of a fortification wall of the late period and a corner tower that flanked its entrance. All these constructions had somewhat amorphous, unclear plans[7] and were situated not on the summit of the mound but lower down the slope, a feature that again can be explained by the severe erosion. During the continuation of this work in the following seasons, a still earlier entrance complex that dated to the time of Namazga IV and continued to exist until the early Namazga V period was uncovered. In turn this complex was replaced only in the period of the gradual decline of the city by the construction that was uncovered in 1969. It seemed that the entrance was enclosed by two monumental tower-pylons, each having dimensions of 6.2×3 meters, which were decorated with projecting rectangular pilasters. These towers flanked the monumental parade entrance to the city. The entrance itself had a breadth of 15 meters, along which were walls that divided a sort of main thoroughfare, which was 4-5 meters wide and apparently designed for wheeled transport, from two narrower streets with a width of 1.5-2 meters.

The third important element of the planned structure at Altyn-depe appeared as a result of the detailed analysis of the surface of the ruins. Large ovals marked by the edges of burned earth clearly appeared on the surface, particularly after rains, and represented, as excavations determined, ancient ceramic kilns. The slope of the northern part of the mound was found by such analysis to be the place of the greatest concentration of such kilns and received the appellation "craftsmen's quarter." The remains of nearly 60 such kilns were seen on the surface, and during the course of excavations new kilns were uncovered that previously had not been detected. The excavations (excavation 10) conducted by I. S. Masimov completely confirmed our hypothesis that this part of the settlement represented a special structural unit of the city: a large, powerful production center.[8]

During the first seasons of work the presence and location of the cultural center of the city remained unresolved. The basic fact of the existence of such a center with monumental architecture seemed logical from the general nature of the site and from the character of ancient Near Eastern cities in general, but it was impossible to find. At first the hypothesis was proposed that it was located on a very high and isolated part of the mound, which was called "the hill of walls" since large Namazga IV fortification walls were discovered at its base. Excavation 5 was opened in this area to study this fascinating subject; however, by the second season of excavations it was already clear that this section of the mound contained only typical living quarters. The complete study of the topography of the ruins continued. During this time our attention was drawn to a separately located small mound that was situated on the eastern face of Altyn-depe and connected with the major remains of the city by a saddle; the grassy vegetation on this saddle outlined the remains of a small side street. The nature of the cultural levels on the slope of this hill seemed unusual; although the summit was filled with broken sherds, the eastern slope completely lacked them and was characterized by a loose fill that took on a brownish coloration after it had been moistened. Excavations revealed the presence of a large pile of unbaked bricks that — unlike in domestic areas — contained very few fragments of pottery. In the course of excavations from 1967 to 1969 in this area (excavation 7), a monumental construction, stretching from front to back a length of 55 meters, was exposed. Part of this complex consisted of a twice reconstructed four-stepped tower that clearly represented a type of Mesopotamian ziggurat (Figure 2). In 1972,

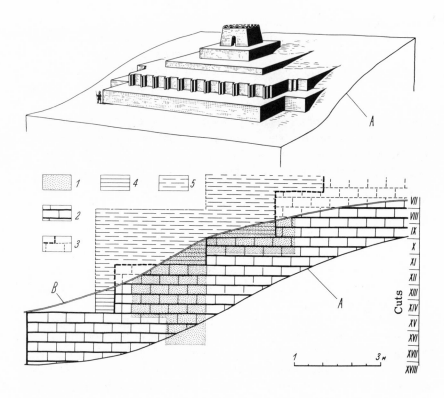

Figure 2. Reconstruction of monumental tower at Altyn-depe.

after this complex already had been excavated to its third construction level, a tomb of priests was uncovered who had been buried in a complicated ritual and laid to rest with rich gifts, including the golden head of a bull that had a lunate-shaped turquoise inlay set in its forehead (Figure 3). The analysis of the finds allowed us to define this whole ensemble as a cult complex devoted to the moon god, a deity who, like the Mesopotamian Nanna-Sina, was symbolized in the form of a heavenly bull. Thus was revealed one characteristic element of the settlement, an ideological center formed by a monumental structure.

All these data demonstrated that at Altyn-depe we were dealing not simply with an unusually large village that contained extensive

Figure 3. Plan depicting stone objects and golden head of a bull from the tomb of priests in the cult area (excavation 7).

remains of multiroomed houses but with a site that had a complicated internal structure, permitting us to characterize it as a protourban or early urban center. The question naturally arose about
the structure of the society that left this site, about the class and
prestige rankings that divided its urban territory. Excavations 5
and 10 had already revealed two types of domestic structures. The
first was represented by multiroom houses, almost Aeneolithic
in character; the second consisted of houses that obviously were
designed for individual families (Figure 4).[9] The ongoing annual
study of the topography of the ruins, which was aided by observations on the vegetation cover, led to the discovery in 1969 of a
large subrectangular building that had been carefully planned; we
called it "the house of the priest" (Figure 5). Grass, which grew
abundantly along the line of contact between the unbaked adobe
walls and the cultural levels that filled the interiors of the rooms,
allowed us to reconstruct the plan of this building prior to its excavation. In the course of uncovering the building, this plan was
partially verified. As a result of a new excavation (number 9), a
new, third type of domestic structure for the city was revealed.
Continuing work at this excavation from 1973 to 1975 showed that

Figure 4. Plan of domestic structures for individual families (excavation 5, first building horizon).

this entire section was filled with large domestic dwellings, which gave this area the name "the elite quarter." The three types of houses were correlated with the three levels of "the distribution of wealth" that could be traced through the inventory of grave goods that lay in the immediate proximity of each type of dwelling.[10] All these materials allowed us to state that the plan of Altyn-depe reflected a division of the society into groups possessing differing amounts of property and having different social standing; these groups resided in separate compact quarters.

One must note that the selection of places to excavate would have led to unsuccessful results had not we carefully considered in a series of cases the microtopography, the character of the soil cover, and the nature of the surface archeological materials. Thus

144

Figure 5. Well-preserved "house of the priest" in the "elite quarter" (excavation 9).

at the very beginning of the work at Altyn-depe, excavation 2 was
laid out in the western part of the settlement, where it was hoped
that we would find evidence of domestic architecture. However,
it proved that the adobe walls were very poorly preserved in this
area, and the excavations were discontinued. It seemed that rodent
holes frequently were located in those areas where there had been
courtyards or rubbish heaps or, in other words, where the ground
was soft in comparison with sections filled by living areas that
contained numerous adobe walls and partitions.

The analysis of the internal structure at Altyn-depe and the materials found during the course of the excavations permits us to
reach certain conclusions about the functions of ancient urban centers that have been discovered in the USSR. Altyn-depe clearly
emerges as a large center for the consumption of the products of
an agricultural economy. Grinding stones and baking ovens (tandyrs) were found in each of the living complexes. At the same
time, however, there was no substantial area for grain storage in
any of the houses. A peculiar "warehouse complex" consisting of
small rooms grouped around a large rectangular courtyard was
uncovered in excavation 9. It represented a kind of general gra-
nary, possibly under the control of the urban leaders. The products of animal husbandry were strewn throughout separate activity
areas. The zoologist N. M. Ermolova has determined that the remains of these animals were butchered in such a fashion as to destroy the large bones and to suggest that the people may not have
been familiar with the anatomy of the animals. Apparently, professional shepherds whose skills had been forgotten by the urban
consumers managed the herds themselves — although it is also
possible that the citizens took part to some degree in these activities. In any case, a bronze sickle was found in one of the houses.
Given this data, Altyn-depe functioned as the consumer of the products of a sufficiently broad agricultural region, as the storehouse
of these products, and most particularly, as the organizer of the
production of the area taken as a whole. The development of
wheeled transport in the form of large four-wheeled carts drawn
by one or two camels facilitated this sort of activity and, possibly,
often was determined by it. Models of such vehicles were sometimes found during the excavations at Altyn-depe.

Craft activities at Altyn-depe appear with exceptional clarity.
Potters made up to thirty types of standardized vessels; the large
area where the craftsmen worked was a sort of industrial suburb
that was overcast with the smoke of dozens of pottery kilns. In-

vestigations by N. N. Terekhova[11] have shown that during Namazga V times the flourishing metallurgical industry was characterized by the utilization of very different alloys and by a sort of internal specialization in which master craftsmen were assigned special, narrowly defined functions, such as in the preparation of seals cast according to the lost wax method, which must have been made from a permanent master-copy of the seal in the form of the figures of animals. To a lesser extent one can speak about the development of trade, although at Altyn-depe ivory objects, procured from the ancient Harappan civilization (Figure 6), were common decorations or ornaments for the privileged strata of the society. Characteristically, fortifications were poorly developed, corresponding in general to the low development of military affairs among the societies peacefully developing on the edge of the then civilized world, an area apart from the political antagonisms and military confrontations that beset the Middle East. In fact, at Altyn-depe weapons are found very rarely, and hundreds of skeletons, analyzed by T. P. Kiiatkina, display no evidence of wounds suffered in battle.

Figure 6. Ivory sticks and gaming pieces (?) from Altyn-depe similar to objects from Mohenjo-Daro.

Thus Altyn-depe stands before us as an early urban organism with a specific internal structure and a class-affiliated division of territory, as a city fulfilling the functions of the center of the surrounding agricultural economy, craft activities, and ideology, as indicated by the monumental cult complex. Although Altyn-depe utilized a series of features that were developed in the earliest urban centers of the ancient Near East, it naturally evolved from its local agricultural base. Detailed results were obtained due to the combination of planned excavations of the site and methods for the analysis of the infrastructure of large cities and settlements that were devised by the Tashkent archeological school.

Notes

1. I. M. D'iakonov, "Problema vavilonskogo goroda II tysiacheletiia do n.e.," Drevnii Vostok. Goroda i torgovlia, Erevan, 1973; N. V. Kozyreva, Starovavilonskii gorod Larsa, Leningrad, 1974.

2. R. McC. Adams and H. J. Nissen, The Uruk Countryside: The Natural Setting of Urban Societies, Chicago, 1972.

3. R. Tringham, P. Ucko, and G. W. Dimbleby, Man, Settlement, and Urbanism, London, 1972.

4. V. M. Masson, "Pervye goroda (k probleme formirovaniia gorodov v srede rannezemledel'cheskikh kul'tur)," Noveishie otkrytiia sovetskikh arkheologov, Kiev, 1975.

5. I. M. D'iakonov, op. cit., p. 36.

6. V. M. Masson, "Protogorodskaia tsivilizatsiia iuga Srednei Azii," Sovetskaia arkheologiia, 1967, no. 4; "Raskopki na Altyn-depe v 1969 g.," Materialy IuTAKE, 1970, no. 3; "Tsivilizatsiia drevnevostochnogo tipa na iuge Srednei Azii," Pamiatniki kul'tury. Novye otkrytiia, Moscow, 1976; "Tsivilizatsiia Altyn-depe," Pamiatniki Turkmenistana, 1974, no. 2 (18).

7. V. M. Masson, "Raskopki na Altyn-depe v 1969 g.," Materialy IuTAKE, 1970, no. 3, fig. 5.

8. I. S. Masimov, Keramicheskoe proizvodstvo epokhi bronzy v Iuzhnom Turkmenistane, Ashkhabad, 1976.

9. V. I. Knyshov, "Raskopki zhilykh kompleksov epokhi bronzy na Altyn-depe," KSIA, 1971, no. 127.

10. V. M. Masson, "Tsivilizatsiia drevnevostochnogo tipa," op. cit., pp. 432-33.

11. N. N. Terekhova, "Istoriia metalloobrabativaiushchego proizvodstva u drevnikh zemledel'tsev Iuzhnoi Turkmenii," candidate's dissertation abstract, Moscow, 1975.

CHAPTER 7

Seals of a Proto-Indian Type from Altyn-depe

V. M. MASSON

Archeological research of recent years in southern Turkmenistan has led to the discovery of protourban centers existing there
at the end of the third and beginning of the second millennia B.C.,
whose establishment was the logical culmination of the socioeconomic evolution of the local communities of settled agriculturalists
from the sixth to the fourth millennia B.C. Two such centers are
known: Namazga-depe at Kaakhka and Altyn-depe at Meana, where
systematic excavations have been conducted since 1965 through the
joint efforts of the Kara Kum Expedition of the Leningrad Branch
of the Archeology Institute, USSR Academy of Sciences, and the
Southern Turkmenistan Complex Archeological Expedition of the
Turkmenian Academy of Sciences (IuTAKE).[1] This work established that Altyn-depe had a complex internal structure with a separate quarter for craftsmen, a religious center with a monumental
ziggurat and a tomb for priests alongside it, quarters for ordinary
citizens, and an area occupied by the spacious homes of the local
elite. From the size of the dwellings, the composition of the meat
foods of the inhabitants of the houses, and the grave goods of the
associated tombs, it is possible to identify three social groups in
the population of Altyn-depe. The materials obtained made it possible to propose that in this instance we are dealing with the most
ancient civilization that existed on the territory of the USSR, and
one that clearly belonged to the cultural world of the ancient East.[2]
The culture of Altyn-depe was not a self-contained and isolated
phenomenon but was part of the system of early urban civilizations

of the Bronze Age, which archeological research during the past decade[3] has documented in the broad zone between Mesopotamia and India.

Among the numerous finds at Altyn-depe, particular interest attaches to two seals, the images on which are sufficiently characteristic for them to be confidently assigned to the category of artifacts of the Harappan type (Figure 1). Let us describe them.

1. A seal, approximately square, carved with a metal tool in a soft white stone resembling alabaster. On the face side two signs of the proto-Indian script, carved with a triangular instrument. On the back a square projection measuring 9 × 9 millimeters, 3 mm high, with a drilled hole for hanging. The seal measures 14 × 15 mm and is 4 mm thick. It was found in 1975 at excavation 9, in room 105.

2. A seal, approximately square, carved with a metal implement in a soft white stone resembling alabaster. On the face a swastika depicted with double lines within a square frame. On the back an oval projection 3 mm long and 2 mm high, pierced by a hole for hanging. The seal is somewhat worn, apparently indicating that it had been used repeatedly in antiquity. The seal measures 11.5 × 13 mm and is 3 mm thick. It was found in 1972 at excavation 7, in room 7.[4]

Especially important are the contexts of these discoveries. Excavation 7 uncovered the ritual center at Altyn-depe, already referred to above, and room 7 was part of a large ensemble including a tomb for priests. In the group of rooms room 7 functioned as a shrine where various valuable artifacts were found near the altar, including the golden head of a bull and the seal (2) described. Stratigraphically the burial ensemble falls into the earliest stage of existence of the center of worship, corresponding in the classification adopted in southern Turkmenia to the transition between the Namazga IV and V assemblages.

In layout, dimensions, and quality of finish, the structures uncovered at excavation 9 were homes of the prosperous elite, and the entire section was given the tentative designation "elite quarter." It was specifically here that the rectangular "house of the leader"[5] was found, as well as the richest group of tombs,[6] and the artifacts are distinguished by their careful manufacture.[7] The seal was found in a cultural layer not associated with the burial assemblage. In stratigraphic position the structures uncovered here represent the third construction level of the Namazga V period and are thus later by two levels than the burial ensemble of excavation 7.

Proto-Indian Seals from Altyn-depe

Figure 1. Altyn-depe: 1 — seal from excavation 9; 2 —
seal from excavation 7: face side.

Figure 2. Altyn-depe: 1 — seal from excavation 9; 2 —
seal from excavation 7: back side.

Thus the contexts of the seals permit two important conclusions
to be drawn: seals of this type belonged to the category of particularly valued artifacts (found in the shrine and in the "elite quarter")

151

and existed over a long period.

As already noted, the figures on the seals leave no doubt that they belong to the class of seals of proto-Indian type. Thus seals depicting a swastika filling the entire field are quite common for finds at Mohenjo-Daro.[8] As for the second seal, the signs incised in it are typical of proto-Indian script and are listed in the catalogue of signs compiled on the basis of the Mohenjo-Daro materials under nos. 15 and 96.[9] It is true that no inscription consisting specifically of these two signs is recorded in materials from Hindustan, but in general, two-sign inscriptions were common enough there. If we accept the deciphering proposed by N. V. Gurov,[10] the signs on the seal from Altyn can be read as belonging to the class of sacrificial inscriptions, in which Y means "hand," "handful,"

"sacrificial tribute," while $\mathsf{\sqcup\!\sqcup\!\sqcup}$ is the name of the divinity. Naturally, since there is still no generally accepted interpretation of the proto-Indian texts, this is just one possible interpretation of our inscription.[11] The shape of the Altyn seals, with a perforated boss on the back, and their dimensions are common in Harappan glyptics, where they vary in size from 15 to 25 mm. Somewhat unusual for Harappan glyptics is the absence on the seal of an image accompanying the signs, but seals (including square examples) that only have inscriptions are also known in materials from India, although they are comparatively rare.[12]

The overwhelming majority of Harappan seals were made of steatite, less often of faience, and still more rarely of ceramic.[13] The technique of making steatite seals on which figures and signs were incised with a small chisel or triangular cutter has been adequately elucidated.[14] After grinding with an abrasive, the finished seals were covered with alkali and fired.

One of the most recent concordances records 2,469 artifacts bearing proto-Indian inscriptions, most of them seals.[15] Their distribution is quite suggestive. They are most numerous in the two ancient capitals — 1,390 in Mohenjo-Daro and 891 in Harappa. Second-rank cities follow, the capitals of ancient provinces — Chanhu-daro (67), Lothal (54), and Kalibangan (37). Finally, from one to three were found at six minor sites in India and Pakistan, while twelve were found in various Mesopotamian centers (Ur, Kish, and Tell Asmar). In this respect, Altyn-depe is particularly interesting as a new site with inscriptions of the proto-Indian type.

At the same time, it must be stated that in a certain sense these discoveries are not particularly unexpected, since the Altyn-depe materials had long been found to have clear-cut connections with sites of the Harappa Culture, and therefore the question had been raised of the existence not only of an ocean or coastal route connecting Harappa and Mesopotamia but also a northern, overland route, passing through Mundigak to southern Turkmenistan.[16] New finds and further research have confirmed the accuracy of this postulate.[17]

In this respect finds that were unquestionably imports, such as elephant ivory artifacts, are particularly suggestive. In the priestly tomb already mentioned, which belongs to the earliest phase of the Namazga V complex, ivory beads have been found.[18] An entire group of decorated artifacts made of the same material, indubitably of Harappan origin, comes from a cache sealed into the wall of one of the houses at the "tower excavation,"[19] which in stratigraphic position was two construction periods later than the tomb of the priests. Finally, in 1973 a rich burial of a woman was cleared not far from this excavation, and its grave goods also include a small staff of decorated ivory of Harappan origin.[20] Thus we can say that the arrival at Altyn-depe of ivory or objects made of it occurred over a considerable period of time and is one of the vivid proofs of ancient commercial ties between southern Turkmenia and Hindustan. It is these ties that explain the influence of specimens from Harappa on a whole list of categories of objects found at Altyn-depe, from a seal with a three-headed design to types of metal artifacts and pottery vessels. Naturally these influences were less significant and perceptible than in the districts directly neighboring the great civilization of the Indus Valley, but the fact of their presence is beyond doubt.[21]

In light of these data the discovery at Altyn-depe of seals of proto-Indian type at first glance merely confirms the thesis regarding such stable contacts and expands the list of artifacts in which these contacts are materially expressed. However, another aspect of this problem deserves attention in connection with the discoveries of these seals.

A seal of proto-Indian type bearing an impressive depiction of an animal accompanied by pictographic text might have played a cult role in countries neighboring Hindustan merely by virtue of the presence of this image. But in the case of a seal bearing only an inscription, a question arises about the possible use of the information contained in it, i.e., about the ability to read the inscription. In themselves seals with projecting bosses on their backs and with

various figures on their faces are quite common for the Bronze Age
culture of southern Turkmenia. Among them square seals do exist,
but until now none had borne inscriptions.[22] It seems to us that the
discovery of seals of the proto-Indian type at Altyn-depe, including
seals with proto-Indian inscriptions, compels us to address ourselves to the problem of the ethnic affiliation of the local population
during the Aeneolithic and Bronze Age.

Although there is still no generally accepted system for deciphering proto-Indian texts, the view that the language depicted on
them belonged to the proto-Dravidian group is the most credible.
First expressed a comparatively long time ago,[23] this view has
been confirmed as texts have been studied by various methods, including statistical positional analysis.[24] The data of historical
linguistics also support this point of view. Such data include the
fact, established with certainty, of the role of the Dravidian substratum in the Indo-Aryan languages, where the corresponding influence can be traced in lexicon, phonetics, morphology, and syn-
tax.[25] A long list of data permits the conclusion that in antiquity
the Dravidian languages were spread over a comparatively broad
territory, evidence of which is provided, in particular, by the existence in Baluchistan of the tribe of Brahui, or Braui, who speak a
language of the Dravidian group. Most of the Brahui live in Pakistan, but they are also known in Afghanistan, Iran, and even, according to I. I. Zarubin, among the Baluchi in Turkmenia.[26] The
Brahui of the most ancient origin inhabit northern Baluchistan in
the area of Kelat,[27] and their very name is best interpreted se-
mantically as "northern mountaineers" or "people of the northern
mountains."[28] Today the Brahui live together with the Baluchis,
and the culture and everyday practices of these groups are very
closely related. On the whole the Brahui represent a kind of ethno-
linguistic relic, disappearing as they assimilate the influences of
Iranian-speaking and Indian-speaking populations. There is evidence that part of the population of Seistan spoke just a few centuries ago a Dravidian language related to Brahui. This language
was later lost.[29]

The long-established fact of the tie between the Dravidian languages and those of the Finno-Ugrian group is important for identifying the territory over which the former languages were disseminated in antiquity. It was also proposed that this was based on
genetic kinship, but a majority of researchers incline to the conclusion that the evidence suggests more remote connections.[30] In
any case, it was on this basis that S. P. Tolstov quite justifiably

suggested that in the pre—Indo-Iranian period (at least in the fourth and third millennia), Dravidian or Dravidian-related tribes existed "immediately adjacent to Central Asia under conditions broadly permitting cultural contact with the peoples of the Aral Basin."[31] The Neolithic Kelteminari Culture then widespread there was marked specifically by strong mutual ties with the cultures of the Urals and western Siberia. The literature even raises the possibility that in the fourth and third millennia, an immense cultural community existed that embraced the Cis-Aral region, the Urals, and the southern part of western Siberia. Such a community was formed by groups of related tribes that were most likely the ancestors of the Ugrian population.[32]

The treatment of the glottochronology of the Dravidian languages by M. S. Andronov is exceptionally interesting.[33] Lexicostatistical analysis led him to the conclusion that the breakup of the proto-Dravidian language occurred at the beginning of the fourth millennium, when the Brahui language split off in northwestern Hindustan; the differentiation of other linguistic groups proceeded with further movement into the depths of the subcontinent. The Finno-Ugrian ties of the Dravidian languages permit one to speak of the latter having spread specifically from north to south in Hindustan, which is taken as the basis of the map drawn by Andronov.

One's attention is drawn by some coincidence between this model and the stages of propagation in Hindustan of the cultures of the early agricultural type that widely used painted ware.[34] In the mountain areas of northern Baluchistan, settlements of sedentary farmers were widely present in the fourth millennium. (Is it not possible that the ethnonym of the Brahui — "people of the northern mountains" — dates to them?) In the first half of the third millennium, early agricultural tribes were already mastering the valley of the Indus on a large scale, and Harappan civilization took shape there in the second half of that millennium. Along with local elements and the formation of clearly distinctive Hindustani cultures (W. Fairservis calls this process "Indianization"), the Iranian-Central Asian contacts in these complexes are indisputable. Their appearance most probably was associated with the movement of tribal groups from the regions of Sialk-Hissar in central northern Iran and Kara-depe and Geoksyur in southern Turkmenia, which is particularly noticeable at the end of the fourth and the beginning of the third millennia. In the middle of the second millennium, a number of assemblages of sedentary farmers with painted ware arose in central India. Their culture combined the tradition of the local stratum of Neolithic hunters and gatherers with innovations, such as agriculture, metallurgy, and painted ware thrown on the wheel, which were clearly associated with the influences of the Harappan civilization.[35] The mechanism of these influences has been insufficiently studied,[36] but they certainly can be associated with moves by ethnic groups. In turn these central Indian assemblages of sedentary agriculturalists influenced the formation of the so-called Megalithic Culture in southern India during the first millennium.[37] Despite certain chronological difficulties, the coincidence of the general tendency of the spread of sedentary agricultural assemblages from north to south, as established by archeological data, and the pattern of settlement of the Dravidian-language tribes, determined by lexicostatistical analysis, must be noted.

We know about a long series of attempts to compare various archeological complexes and cultures with the Dravidian-speaking population of the ancient period. In one case they are identified with the creators of the Megalithic Culture of southern Hindustan during the first millennium, and it is postulated that they had migrated from areas of central Iran or from Elam;[38] or they are compared to the pastoralist Neolithic of the same southern area, as worked out in detail by F. R. Allchin.[39] There is a prevailing view that the Harappan population belonged to the proto-Dravidians,[40] and the same is true, but on a more hypothetical basis, of several Aeneolithic tribes of more southerly regions. Attempts are sometimes made to produce a more precise identification of the position of the proto-Dravidians in the extensive population of northwestern Hindustan in the Bronze Age.[41]

The intricate problem of studying ancient ethnic processes demands special care in using methods and a clear-cut initial methodological concept. In this respect Soviet ethnographers have performed major and fruitful work, summed up in the book by Iu. V. Bromlei.[42] He notes that the principal bearers of ethnic qualities are ordinary consciousness, the language of daily use, and traditional-everyday culture.[43] Archeological materials usually make it possible to identify specifically a traditional-everyday culture, with a stable set of types of objects characterizing it, and also, to a certain degree, some elements of ordinary consciousness on the basis of types of artifacts associated in some way with the ideological realm. Since they do not carry ethnic information as such, the physical anthropological characteristics of a population that has left specific archeological assemblages should be used in this situation only as indirect evidence that can provide some part of the description of an ethnic situation. Thus in the case of interest to us, notions like "Dravidian languages" and "Dravidian anthropological type" are homonymous concepts in different disciplines and, as far at least as ancient periods are concerned, do not have the rigorous connection that is often ascribed to them consciously or otherwise.

Furthermore, it must be borne in mind that at the present level of our knowledge, questions of reconstruction of the ethnic history of the Middle East during the Paleolithic can only be answered at the level of the most general comparisons. Thus it seems that a considerable number of tribal groups and, perhaps, even peoples[44] of the proto-Dravidian or archaic Dravidian language family appeared that have today totally disappeared in the process of assimilation, just as the Dravidian language had already in the Middle Ages lost one of its ethnic groups in Seistan. However, at the level of general comparisons, the particularly important and marked resemblance and connection between the Dravidian and the Elamite languages, which V. S. Vorob'ev-Desiatov had once noted,[45] permit the hypothesis, according to I. M. D'iakonov's conclusion, "that tribes related by language to the Elamites and Dravidians were spread widely throughout Iran, or at least in its southern portion, in the fourth and third millennia."[46] The evidence of Finno-Ugrian contacts with the Dravidian languages specifically permits the hypothesis of an even broader variant of D'iakonov's formulation.

In that case the broad zone populated by the early agricultural tribes that made painted ware and existed from the Zagros Mountains to the Indus River in the fourth and third millennia can be regarded as the territory inhabited by tribes with languages similar to those of the Elamites and Dravidians. On the basis of numerous archeological materials describing a stable everyday culture, as early as 1942 D. McCown identified assemblages of two types on the Iranian plateau: the northern, in which he placed Sialk, Hissar, and Anau, and which he tentatively named the "red ware region"; and the southern, represented most vividly by Susa and Tal-i Bakun and characterized by a so-called buff or cream ware.[47] Today, as a result of the discovery of an enormous number of new sites on this territory, this division retains significance only at the most general level and describes neither archeological cultures nor cultural communities adhering to the structural subdivision of the grouping of sites. Most likely it signifies an even larger entity approximating the idea of "a territorial or cultural zone."[48]

It is significant that it was precisely within the bounds of the southern zone that the Elamite language prevailed to the degree to which we know of it from the earliest sites with writing (Figure 3). Today one can add to the sites with Elamite script in Susa and Malamir the materials from Haft-tepe[49] and from a point so remote from Susiana as Tepe Yahya in Kerman.[50]

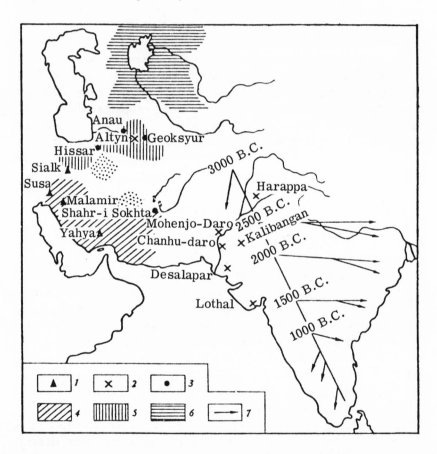

Figure 3. Cultural zones and distribution of sites of Elamite and proto-Indian script in the Middle East: 1 — sites with Elamite script (third and second millennia); 2 — sites with proto-Indian script (third and second millennia); 3 — other sites; 4 — southern cultural zone of early farmers (fifth and fourth millennia); 5 — northern cultural zone of early farmers (fifth and fourth millennia); 6 — Kelteminari cultural community (fifth to third millennia); 7 — distribution of Dravidian tribes according to M. S. Andronov.

The significant differences between the northern and southern cultural zones emerge quite clearly in the materials from Shahr-i Sokhta in Iranian Seistan, which is a region of contact between two cultural zones. Here in its earliest levels we see a combination of two traditions: one, the southern, originating in the final analysis in the Tal-i Bakun ware, and another, the northern, associated with ware of the Geoksyur style, i.e., with Central Asia.[51] When tablets with proto-Elamite script appear in Sialk IV, in the heart of the northern cultural zone, the entire assemblage of the traditional culture is sharply distinguished from the local, earlier culture, as represented by Sialk I-III. Sialk IV essentially can be regarded as foreign, Elamite-Mesopotamian, if not purely Elamite.[52] Therefore it appears quite legitimate to compare the southern cultural zone, whose distinctive features as a region took shape at least in the fourth millennia, with a region of dissemination of the Elamite language or, in other words, with the Elamite ethnic community.

In that case, naturally, the hypothesis arises as to whether the northern cultural zone of painted ware farmers had a connection with the tribes of the proto-Dravidian linguistic community, whose gradual dissemination, through the northern route across Afghanistan and Baluchistan, was reflected in the pattern of propagation of the Dravidian languages established by lexicostatistical analysis. Note that this localization also explains well the Ugro-Dravidian linguistic matchings, which thus find an archeological parallel in the cultural ties between the Kelteminari Neolithic of the Cis-Aral region and the painted ware culture of southern Turkmenistan.[53] When the question is put this way, the finding at Altyn-depe of a seal with an inscription of the proto-Indian type might be regarded as evidence of the utilization by the local society, which had attained the level of civilization, of a preexisting system of writing adapted to a language related to what this local population spoke. In other words, one could see the creators of the Altyn-depe civilization, like their contemporaries at Harappa, as tribes of the proto-Dravidian ethnic group.

Naturally such a hypothesis can be offered only on the most general level, but evidence favoring it, in our opinion, is presented by the discovery at Altyn-depe of a specifically epigraphic seal lacking any image, whose cult magic might have been valued by illiterate barbarians on the periphery of Harappan civilization. It is clear that further study of questions pertaining to the Paleoethnic situation in the Middle East in the period when the early farming painted ware cultures prevailed there will in many ways be associated with

159

the identification by means of detailed analysis of the archeological materials of stable cultural groupings (cultures and variants of cultures) reflecting the traditional-everyday culture of the tribes that once lived there. In his superb analysis of Dravidian-Elamite correspondences, I. M. D'iakonov observed that "one can regard as plausible the hypothesis that Elamite represented perhaps a very early and rather remote branch from the common Dravidian base language; or that the latter and Elamite came from a common prototype."[54] From the standpoint of cultural genesis, we note that the Zagros cultural community of the seventh and sixth millennia (sites such as Jarmo and Tepe-Guran) was of great importance to the earliest settled farming tribes both in the northern and, to a certain degree, the southern zone. The distribution pattern of the Zagros farmers in two streams — a northern route and a southern route that bypassed the immense deserts of the Dasht-i-Lut and Dasht-i-Kavir — has already been dealt with in the specialized literature.[55]

Linguistic similarity facilitated assimilation in the tribal group migrations that are repeatedly observed in the fifth to third millennia within the great mass of early farming tribes east of Mesopotamia. However the questions we have raised are solved, the very fact of the discovery at Altyn-depe of seals of the proto-Indian type has significance for the ancient history of the Middle East.

Notes

1. V. M. Masson, "Protogorodskaia tsivilizatsiia na iuge Srednei Azii," SA, 1967, no. 3; idem., Raskopki na Altyn-depe v 1969 g., Ashkhabad, 1970; idem., "Raskopki pogrebal'nogo kompleksa na Altyn-depe," SA, 1974, no. 4; V. M. Masson and T. P. Kiiatkina, "Chelovek na zare urbanizatsii," Priroda, 1976, no. 4.

2. V. M. Masson, "Tsivilizatsiia Altyn-depe," Pamiatniki Turkmenistana, 1974, no. 2 (18); idem., "Novaia tsivilizatsiia drevnevostochnogo tipa na iuge Srednei Azii," in Pamiatniki kul'tury. Novye otkrytiia. Ezhegodnik 1975, Moscow, 1976.

3. V. M. Masson, "Zona rannegorodskikh tsivilizatsii mezhdu Shumerom i Indiei," Tezisy dokladov na sessii, posv. itogam polevykh issl. 1969 g., Moscow, 1970; C. C. Lamberg-Karlovsky and M. Tosi, "Shahr-i Sokhta and Tepe Yahya: Tracks on the Earliest History of the Iranian Plateau," East and West, 1973, no. 1-2.

4. See Masson, "Raskopki pogrebal'nogo kompleksa," fig. 7, 1.

5. Masson, Raskopki na Altyn-depe, pp. 10 ff.

6. V. M. Masson, "Izuchenie obshchestvennoi struktury rannegorodskogo poseleniia Altyn-depe," AO 1971 g., Moscow, 1972, pp. 526 ff.

Proto-Indian Seals from Altyn-depe

7. V. M. Masson, "Izuchenie sloev eneolita i bronzy na Altyn-depe," AO 1974 g., Moscow, 1975, p. 527.

8. J. Marshall, Mohendjo-daro and the Indus Civilization, vol. 3, London, 1931, p. 374, plate CXIV, 500-15.

9. Ibid., pp. 434, 439.

10. N. V. Gurov, "Nekotorye problemy lingvisticheskoi interpretatsii proto-indiiskikh tekstov," author's abstract of candidate dissertation, Leningrad, 1971, pp. 19-21. Gurov has graciously provided the information that he is currently deciphering this combination of signs as "great god" or "great divinity."

11. For a different reading of the same signs, see, for example, M. V. N. Krishnarao, "Foreign Rulers in the Indus Seals," in Radiocarbon and Indian Archaeology, Bombay, 1973 (cited below as RIA); S. R. Rao, "The Indus Script — Methodology and Language," RIA.

12. Marshall, op. cit., 3, plate CXIV, 471-77, 479-82.

13. E. Mackay, Chanhu-Daro Excavations, 1935-1936, New Haven, 1943, plate LI, 9, 11, 12; XLIII, 11.

14. E. Mackay, Drevneishaia kul'tura doliny Inda, Moscow, 1951, pp. 113 ff.

15. J. Mahadevan and K. Visvanathan, "Computer Concordance of Proto-Indian Signs," RIA, p. 292.

16. Masson, "Protogorodskaia tsivilizatsiia," pp. 188 ff.

17. A. Ia. Shchetenko, "Raboty na stratigraficheskom raskope Altyn-depe v Iuzhnoi Turkmenii," KSIA, 91, 1958; same author, "O torgovykh putiakh epokhi bronzy po materialam turkmenistano-kharappskikh parallelei," KSIA, 122, 1970; D. Gul'muradov, "Novye dannye o torgovykh sviaziakh Turkmenii i Indostana v bronzovom veke," USA, issue 3, Leningrad, 1975, pp. 73-74.

18. Masson, "Raskopki pogrebal'nogo kompleksa," p. 5.

19. A. F. Ganialin, "Raskopki v 1961-62 gg. na Altyn-depe," SA, 1967, no. 4, p. 216, fig. 6; Masson, "Protogorodskaia tsivilizatsiia," p. 188.

20. V. M. Masson, "Prodolzhenie raskopok na Altyn-depe," AO 1973 g., Moscow, 1974.

21. For analysis of the corresponding data, see Masson, "Protogorodskaia tsivilizatsiia," pp. 188 ff.; Shchetenko, O torgovykh putiakh, pp. 60-62; E. E. Kuz'mina, Metallicheskie izdeliia eneolita i bronzovogo veka v Srednei Azii, Moscow, 1966, pp. 88-89.

22. V. M. Masson, "K semantike znakov sobstvennosti epokhi bronzy," in Sibir' i ee sosedi v drevnosti, Novosibirsk, 1970.

23. See, for example, H. Heras, Studies in Proto-Indo-Mediterranean Culture, Bombay, 1953.

24. Predvaritel'noe soobshchenie ob issledovanii protoindiiskikh tekstov, Moscow, 1965; "Soobshchenie ob issledovanii protoindiiskikh tekstov," Proto-Indica, 1972, Moscow, 1972; "Soobshchenie ob issledovanii protoindiiskikh tekstov," Proto-Indica, 1973, Moscow, 1973; A. Parpalo, S. Koshniemi, S. Parpalo, and P. Aalto, Decipherment of the Proto-Dravidian Inscriptions of the Indus Civilization, Copenhagen, 1969.

25. V. S. Vorob'ev-Desiatovskii, "K voprosu o roli substrata v razvitii indo-ariiskikh iazykov," SV, 1956, no. 1.

26. Narody Iuzhnoi Azii, Moscow, 1973, pp. 754 ff.; M. S. Andronov, Iazyk braui, Moscow, 1971, pp. 9-10.

27. Narody Iuzhnoi Azii, p. 755.

28. Andronov, Iazyk braui, p. 11.

29. Vorob'ev-Desiatovskii, "K voprosu o roli substrata," p. 101.

30. M. S. Andronov, "O kharaktere dekkano-ural'skikh analogii," in Iazykovye

V. M. Masson

universalii i lingvisticheskaia tipologiia, Moscow, 1969, pp. 312-20.

31. S. P. Tolstov, Drevnii Khorezm, Moscow, 1968, p. 350.

32. Istoriia Sibiri, vol. 1, Leningrad, 1968, p. 104.

33. M. S. Andronov, "Leksikostaticheskii analiz i fakty istorii o khronologii raspada protodravidskogo iazyka," in Indiiskaia i iranskaia filologiia, Moscow, 1964; idem., Dravidskie iazyki, Moscow, 1965, pp. 13, 99-101.

34. On the spread of settled farming cultures in Hindustan, see V. M. Masson, Sredniaia Aziia i drevnii Vostok, Moscow and Leningrad, 1964, pp. 246 ff.; W. A. Fairservis, The Roots of Ancient India, New York, 1971, pp. 111 ff.; H. D. Sankalia, The Prehistory and Protohistory of India and Pakistan, Poona, 1974, pp. 317 ff.

35. The corresponding materials are systematized best in the book by A. Ia. Shchetenko, Drevneishie zemledel'cheskie kul'tury Dekkana, Leningrad, 1968, pp. 108 ff.

36. See, for example, Shchetenko's hypothesis on the distribution of settlements of master craftsmen (op. cit., p. 135).

37. S. B. Deo, "The Dating of Megaliths in Maharashtra: Evaluation of Some New Evidence," RIA, p. 135.

38. G. M. Bongard-Levin and G. F. Il'in, Drevniaia Indiia, Moscow, 1969, p. 296.

39. F. R. Allchin, Piklihal Excavations, Hyderabad, 1960.

40. Iu. V. Gankovskii, Narody Pakistana, Moscow, 1964; pp. 28-32; Bongard-Levin and Il'ian, op. cit., p. 297.

41. K. Zvelehil, "Harappa and the Dravidians — an Old Mystery in a New Light," New Orient, 1965, vol. 4, no. 3.

42. Iu. V. Bromlei, Etnos i etnografiia, Moscow, 1973.

43. Ibid., p. 175.

44. Compare, for example, Gankovskii's amply supported conclusion regarding the "proto-Indian people" of the Harappa period (Gankovskii, Narody Pakistana, p. 27).

45. Vorob'ev-Desiatovskii, "K voprosu o roli substrata," pp. 100-101; idem., "Drevniaia Indiia," in Ocherki istorii drevnego Vostoka, Leningrad, 1956, p. 76.

46. I. M. D'iakonov, Iazyki drevnei Perednei Azii, Moscow, 1967, p. 87.

47. D. McCown, Comparative Stratigraphy of Early Iran, Chicago, 1942, pp. 48-50.

48. On the notion of "territorial zone" in the Paleolithic, see G. P. Grigor'ev, "K metodike ustanovlenii lokal'nykh razlichii v paleolite," USA, issue 2, Leningrad, 1972, p. 18.

49. S. A. Matheson, Persia: An Archaeological Guide, London, 1972, p. 142.

50. C. C. Lamberg-Karlovsky, "The Proto-Elamite Settlement at Tepe-Yahya," Iran, 9, 1971; idem., "An Early City in Iran," Scientific American, 1971, vol. 224, no. 6, p. 104; A. A. Vaiman, "O sviazi protoelamskoi pis'mennosti s protoshumerskoi," VDI, 1972, no. 3, p. 132.

51. Lamberg-Karlovsky and Tosi, "Shahr-i Sokhta and Tepe Yahya," pp. 25-26.

52. Masson, Sredniaia Aziia i drevnii Vostok, p. 231.

53. A. V. Vinogradov, "K voprosu o iuzhnykh sviaziakh kel'teminarskoi kultury," SE, 1957 no. 1, pp. 38-42; idem., Neoliticheskie pamiatniki Khorezma, Moscow, 1968, pp. 82-83; Masson, Sredniaia Aziia i drevnii Vostok, pp. 177 ff.

54. D'iakonov, Iazyki drevnei Perednei Azii, p. 112.

55. Masson, Sredniaia Aziia i drevnii Vostok, p. 202.

PART THREE

Margiana and Settlements
in Southeastern Central Asia

CHAPTER 8

Margiana in the Bronze Age

V. I. SARIANIDI

Although the early history of oases began to attract the attention of
specialists at the beginning of this century,[1] and subsequently, investigations and partial excavations were conducted in this region,[2]
detailed investigations of Bronze Age sites began only with the
work of IuTAKE,[3] parts of which were published in the form of a
monograph.[4] Nevertheless, until 1972 no more than five or six
settlements of the Bronze Age were known to be situated in the
ancient deltaic basin of the Murghab River; for this reason a special Archeological Expedition to Margiana was created to conduct
a complete investigation of the entire region. Beginning its work
in 1974, a special section of the Institute of History, Academy of
Sciences, Turkmenistan SSR, was initiated to investigate the lower
Murghab and elucidate the earlier unknown Kelleli, Taip, Adam
Basan, and Adzhi-kui oases.[5]

The efforts of the current five-year project, which consisted
primarily of survey work, resulted in the discovery of more than
100 Bronze Age sites in the lower Murghab region, an area of
roughly 300 square kilometers. Settlements of the Early Iron Age,
the Achaemenian period, and classical times were also found here,
but these materials are not examined in the present article. In
general, the sites are situated deep in the southeastern part of the
Kara Kum Desert. Frequently they are hidden by barkhan (dune)
ridges and partially covered by windblown sands, so that there is
considerable evidence to suggest that no fewer than 25-30 percent
of the unexposed sites are today covered by sands and dunes.

The present publication is primarily based on materials obtained from surface surveys, and the map of sites (Figure 1) is only a rough outline that needs to be made precise through an instrument survey. Nevertheless, the cartography of the sites to be described

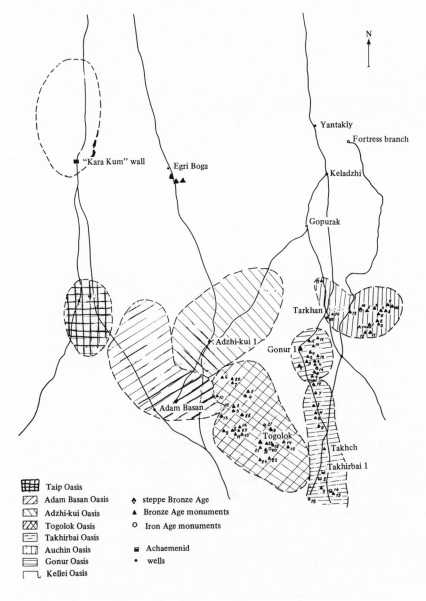

Figure 1. Schematic map showing location of oases.

allows us to define preliminarily several groups or microooases that in antiquity were situated along the basic major channels of the former deltaic fan of the Murghab River. The following micro-oases are defined in preliminary fashion: (1) Kelleli; (2) Auchin; (3) Adzhi-kui; (4) Adam Basan; (5) Gonur; (6) Taip; (7) Togolok; and (8) Takhirbai. Each microoasis has received its name from the nearest well, and each such area includes a principal settle-ment which surpasses the remaining sites in size. It is possible to define preliminarily three chronological stages for these sites during the Bronze Age: early — represented by material from the Kelleli Oasis (Figure 2); middle — represented by material from Gonur (Figure 3); and late — represented at Togolok (Figure 4). This outline, of course, will be refined on the basis of new arche-ological materials. We also mention that the first attempts at settling the lower Murghab occurred during the Aeneolithic period. As proof of this, two partially destroyed sites with polychrome pottery and anthropormorphic figurines in the Geoksyur style were found in the Kelleli Oasis. [6] In addition, the takyr or clayey deposit of Kelleli, which is situated 120 km northwest of Mari, was the area of the initial inhabitation and first agricultural settlements in the region during the Bronze Age. The Kelleli sites are not only those situated furthest north but also are the earliest in rela-tion to other mounds of the Bronze Age. The largest of them, Kelleli 1, consists of two mounds occupying an area larger than five hectares. Their surface is densely covered with potsherds; and numerous fragments of metal artifacts, terra-cotta sculptures of people and animals, and stone and clay objects also were en-countered. Several ceramic kilns are concentrated on the surface of the northern mound. Excavations have shown that the depth of cultural deposit at Kelleli 1 is about three meters, while at Kel-leli 3 and 4 it does not exceed one meter. Moreover, part of a multiroomed house and a large ten-meter-long wall, made of un-fired bricks (dimensions: 50-54 ×24 × 9-12 cm), were revealed. The other settlements of the oasis are situated 4-6 km northwest of Kelleli 1; although smaller than the principal settlement, these sites are not distinguished from it either by their surface remains or by external signs.

Excavations at the settlement Kelleli 4 have uncovered part of a multiroom house consisting of a courtyard and a series of inter-connected rooms built of unbaked bricks and carefully coated with plaster on their interior. Except for the cooking ware, the ceram-ics were all made on the potter's wheel with a very fine quality of

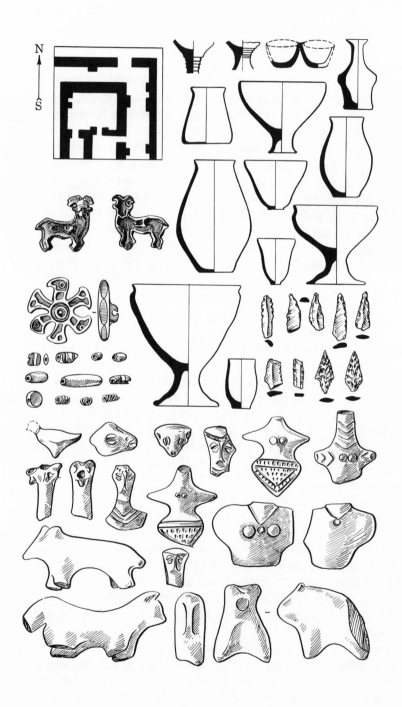

Figure 2. Kelleli stage (early).

clay; the slip was usually light-yellow or, more rarely, reddish color. The ceramic forms include vases on hollow feet; tiny bottles with high narrow throats; tall, well-proportioned goblets; and open cups. The cooking ware was all handmade and tempered; in general this ware consists of pots that occasionally have spouts. Along with the ceramics were found spindle-whorls, fragments of toy carts, bronze pins with biconical heads, twisted bracelets, and polyspherical fragments of knives or spears. A complete metal seal cast in the form of a ram or goat was found on the surface of the site.

Very high quality ceramics include: goblets with flat bases and profiles that swell to their tops; deep cups with broad, straight rims; pots with small necks; and basins. Drinking-glass-shaped vessels, small jars, and vases on high, conical feet, including those that are crimped or goffered (particularly characteristic of Namazga V forms), also are encountered. Among the rarer forms one must mention double vessels and even strainers; cooking ware includes jars, spherical pots that occasionally have small spouts, and frying pans.

Terra-cotta figurines of people and animals made up an interesting group of remains. The female figurines are fashioned in the same way as those from the piedmont belt of the Kopet Dagh Mountains. Especially common are zoomorphic figurines in the form of rams, cattle, goats, and pigs.

The metal objects consist of fragments of tiny pins, punches, sewing needles, toggle pins with shovel-shaped heads, and circular mirrors, sometimes with a small handle. Fragments of metal seals with geometric or cross-shaped designs, including one with a depiction of a whirling rosette that consists of three birds with bent beaks and large circular eyes, also were found.

Several flint arrowheads and spearpoints and fragments of cereal hullers, mortars, pestles, rollers, and graters were found. Beads and spindle-whorls, including one with circular designs, were fashioned from stone.

The available material testifies to the close and nearly identical similarity to the cultures of the piedmont belt of the Kopet Dagh Mountains. The absence in the ceramic assemblage from the Kelleli Oasis of biconical and sharp-ribbed vessels, which are characteristic of other Middle Bronze Age assemblages, suggests that we can relate the Kelleli ceramics to the last stages of the Namazga V period.[7]

The following Gonur stage (Figure 3) is marked by the fluores-

Settlement   Metal   Flint

Stone

Ceramics   Signs on ceramics

Seals   Terra-cotta   Amulets

Hearth

Figure 3. Gonur stage (middle).

cence of the local culture which, apparently, is associated with the advent of new tribes, a fact supported by the appearance of numerous, heavily populated oases. Thus the Taip Oasis includes the central Taip 1 settlement, which consists of two large mounds occupying about twelve hectares and rising to a height of about four meters. The northern mound is the more interesting; a rectangular fortress (135 × 125 m), strengthened by semicircular towers at its corners, abuts this mound's eastern side. A fragment of a thick-walled vessel that had unique impressions of two cylinder seals depicting a battle between a bull and a bird of prey came from this site.

The Adam Basan Oasis includes more than fifteen settlements, the largest of which is Adam Basan 4, occupying about ten hectares. Preliminary soundings demonstrated that the thickness of the cultural levels of settlements in this oasis did not exceed 1.5 meters.

The following Adzhi-kui Oasis contains eight mounds, the central one of which, Adzhi-kui 1, spreads over five hectares and rises to a height of about 3.5 meters. One poorly preserved burial of a person interred in a contracted position with head oriented to the north was excavated at this site; the funeral goods consisted of nine vessels, a stone spindle-whorl, tiny paste beads, and a bronze bracelet and earrings.

An isolated building complex (30 × 27 m) was revealed on Adzhi-kui 8; it was delimited by a series of long blank walls. The fortification walls preserved on their interior numerous rectangular pilasters; two passages, one of which was a foundation, were uncovered in the southern corner of the complex. A broad courtyard was cleared in the inside of the southwestern part of the complex, and east of this a series of interconnected rooms were found. Room 1 was defined as a small rectangular structure with niches and fireplaces set into its walls. One characteristic feature of this uncovered complex was the fact that nearly all the rooms failed to preserve any cultural levels and were covered from their floors to the contemporary surface of the mound with windblown sands. The materials, particularly the ceramics, from the Adam Basan and Adzhi-kui oases were very similar to each other. One characteristic feature was the presence of a significant quantity of plain handmade wares and, more rarely, graywares and steppe ceramics with inscribed designs along with finely made wheel-turned forms. New types, such as footed beakers and vases on pedestals with inverted rims, occur together with Kelleli-like forms.[8]

Stone seal-amulets, which are still unknown in the Kelleli Oasis, are characteristic. Thus, for example, a fragment of a green steatite seal depicting the head of a bird on one side and a bull on the other was found. Another seal preserved an illustration of a snake with its jaws agape on one side and the drawing of a fantastic creature on the other. One must consider a seal-amulet with nearly identical representations of predatory winged beasts, possibly lions, with snakes as the most interesting of this series of objects. Seal-amulets were found with other drawings, such as antelope, trees, geometric designs, and crosses.

The next oasis, Auchin, is situated along the northeastern edge of the lower Murghab River. The largest main settlement, Auchin 1, consists of a fortress and an unfortified settlement attached to it. The nearly square fortress with three-meter-thick defensive walls was reinforced with circular towers. Most of the architecture is situated along the fortification walls, leaving an open central section in the fortress; this feature recalls the plan of such Bactrian sites as Dashly 1 and Sapalli-tepe.

Small, generally unfortified settlements with thin cultural levels (0.3 to 0.8 meters) were stretched out in a chain from Auchin 1, apparently along an ancient water course. Wheel-made, light vessels — in a few cases covered with red paint — were clearly dominant among the ceramic types; only a limited number of graywares were known. The most common forms include: vases and goblets on high feet, tea pots, sauceboats, and decanters. Almost all the vessels are plain; a small quantity is inscribed with simple wavy lines, and in a very few cases, depictions of goats appear. Rare bridged spouts and attached handles also were made. A few ceramics similar to those from the steppes were found on both settlements and surface scatters. Stone arrowheads along with metal objects, such as bracelets, pins, and beads, were widely distributed. Biconical beads with circular designs, bottles, and footed goblets were made from white and red alabaster and black steatite.* A few button-shaped stone seals and amulets are decorated not only with geometric designs but also with engraved pictures of snakes and trees. Beads, pendants, and awls were fashioned primarily from lapis lazuli, turquoise, and carnelian. A characteristic feature of the Auchin Oasis is the complete absence of anthropomorphic figurines; only figurines of animals as part of sculptured

---

*Although not analyzed, this material is better identified as chlorite, not steatite. — P.L.K.

friezes on cult vessels are encountered. Tubular-shaped animal bones are decorated with inscribed external designs. A burial was discovered at Auchin; fourteen vessels, a bronze bracelet, lapis lazuli, gypsum, and turquoise beads, and a stone amulet with the representation of a snake were found within it.

A small necropolis was excavated on the edge of Auchin 1; it contained contracted skeletons that were mainly oriented to the north. Several graves were covered by bricks; the funeral goods included ceramics; metal bracelets; gypsum, paste, and lapis lazuli pins; alabaster bottles; biconical beads with circular designs; and stone amulets.

The Gonur Oasis provided the most significant materials of the middle stage of the Bronze Age occupations in the lower Murghab (Figure 4). This oasis contained the central Gonur-depe settlement, which occupied more than 28 hectares and was perhaps the principal site in the entire Margiana region. The site consists of a small rectangular fortress with defensive towers and a very large unfortified settlement with an amorphous configuration. A ceramic craftsmen's "quarter" is situated on the edge of the settlement; it contains several rectangular, two-chambered pottery kilns with strong structural pillars in their centers. A trench dug on the site revealed three meters of cultural deposit and uncovered several burials. The skeletons were contracted and primarily oriented to the north. The funeral goods consisted of vessels, steatite biconical beads with circular designs, metal bracelets, and rings with unclosed ends placed near the temporal bones on the skulls. The remaining sites of this oasis are almost all unfortified, ranging from 1-2 to 8-10 hectares in area, and contain similar materials.

Excluding kitchen ware and Andronovo-like steppe ware, all the ceramics are wheel-made and are light or, more rarely, red colored and occasionally burnished. Graywares form a small distinct group. The basic shapes are the same as in the other oases; separate vessels and ceramic supports preserve signs that were scratched on them before firing and, more rarely, illustrations of goats standing near trees. Vases and footed goblets were fashioned, as well as spouts in the shape of horned bulls (Figure 5, 3-4) and, in one case, of a camel; bridged spouts (Figure 6, 4-5) also occur.

A ceramic sequence was obtained by materials from trench 1, which was placed on the highest point of Gonur 1. The trench cut through three basic building levels. The first or latest level (arbitrary cuts 1-3) revealed brick walls and floors of former rooms; charcoal from this level provided a date of 1610±70 B.C. (5568 half-

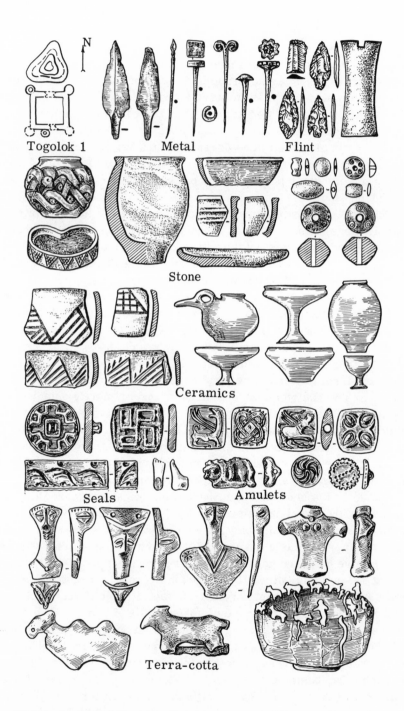

Togolok 1   Metal   Flint

Stone

Ceramics

Seals   Amulets

Terra-cotta

Figure 4. Togolok stage (late).

174

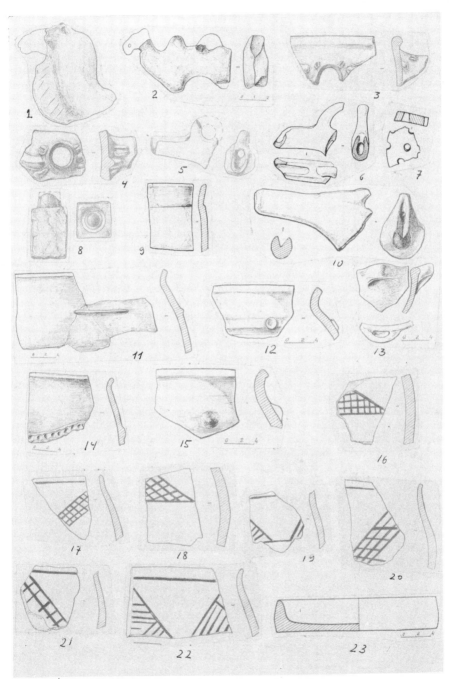

Figure 5. Ceramics and terra-cotta objects (3-10 wheel-made pottery; 11-23 handmade pottery from the Togolok Oasis).

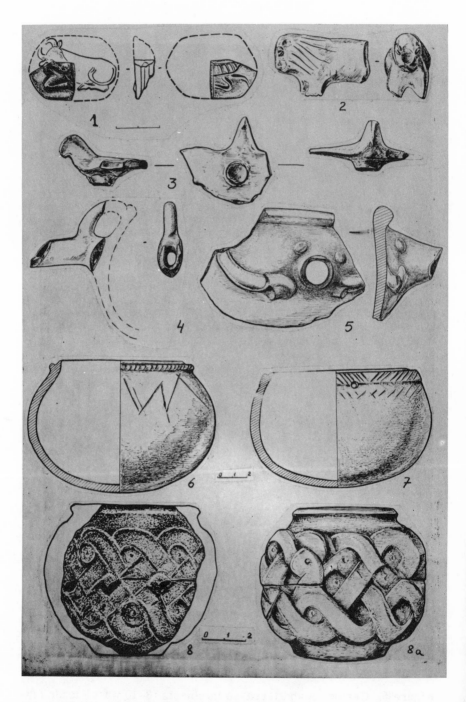

Figure 6. Stone (1, 8-8a) and ceramic objects.

life, uncorrected). Except for the handmade cooking ware, all the pottery was wheel-thrown and light-slipped.

The second building level (arbitrary cuts 4-5) also yielded brick walls and floors, while the third (cuts 6-7), only floors, the lowest of which rested on virgin soil. The ceramics of all three levels were only slightly differentiated. We mention the most typical forms: deep basins, earthenware pots, jars, vases, and footed goblets, decanters, and storage jars.

A significant collection of stone seal-amulets of the Murghab style with depictions of people, birds, and animals comes from the Gonur Oasis.[9] The depiction of a person with inverted animals and accompanying snakes is particularly interesting, since it recalls, to a great extent, the illustration on an archaic seal from Luristan.[10] Among the new finds we mention a fragment of a prismatic-shaped steatite amulet with a representation on one side of a bird holding in its sharp talons what appears to be a tortoise shell (Figure 7, 7-7a). One of the many works of art cut from stone is a thin steatite slab with a representation in high relief on one side of a recumbent cow with its head turned back and on the other apparently of a running antelope, only the hastily thrust forward feet of which are preserved (Figure 6, 1; Figure 11, 31). The beads and perforated objects of different shapes were made of steatite, lapis lazuli, turquoise, and chalcedony (Figure 11). Miniature columns, such as those from Hissar, were made from alabaster.

In general the anthropomorphic figurines consist of sitting women (and in a few cases men) with their arms placed along their sides. Sometimes they have complicated crownlike headdresses and primitively modeled faces with large noses and eyes. Some of them were marked with scratched signs; basically they are completely analogous to the figurines from the piedmont zone.

Two types of zoomorphic figurines are documented: sculpted friezes on cult vessels, and separate individual figures of boars, resting rams, roaring animals, and fish.

Copper-bronze objects primarily consist of types of jewelry: long pins with shovel-shaped, polyspherical, and biconical ends. Knife blades, daggers, and, possibly, spearheads are encountered less frequently. Compartmented copper seals (Figure 8, 5, 6, and 8) usually had simple, geometric, primarily cross-shaped designs; in one case the representation of a running hare was preserved (Figure 8, 5).

As is apparent, the material culture of the Gonur Oasis in general is identical to that of the Taip, Adam Basan, Adzhi-kui, and Auchin oases. This identity demonstrates the fluorescence of the local Bronze Age culture in its middle phase. One must mention

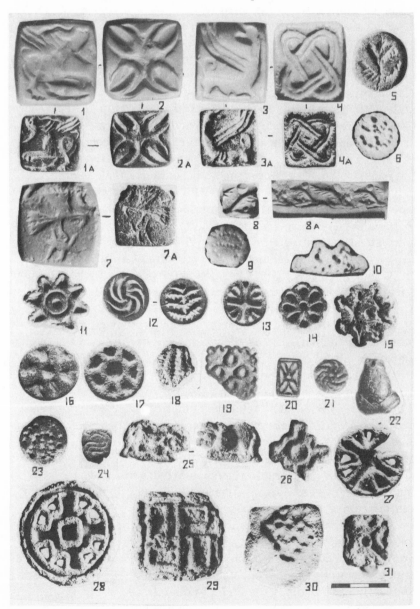

Figure 7. Stone amulets (1-24) and copper-bronze seals (25-29); seal impression (30); head of a pin (31).

that isolated sites with Yaz 1 materials are found in these oases; however, they are not characteristic markers for this time in this area. The Gonur stage was the time of the largest concentration of people in the lower Murghab, when the entire population, regardless of their locality, defined a single cultural community in the second half of the second millennium B.C.

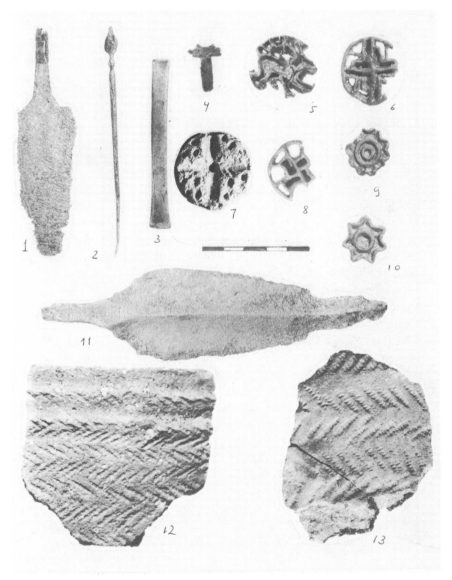

Figure 8. Copper-bronze (1-11) and ceramic (12-13) objects.

A different picture is observed during the following Togolok phase, when Bronze Age settlements and sites with painted Yaz 1 ceramics occur together, signifying the advent of the Early Iron Age.

The Togolok Oasis includes about thirty settlements, with its capital, Togolok 1, consisting of a high mound abutted by a lower settlement. Togolok 21 represents a typical fortified site, with its fortress, defensive towers, and adjacent, amorphously planned settlement (Figure 9). Not only ceramic but metallurgical production can be defined by the appearance of kilns and furnaces beyond the limits of the settlement.

In general the ceramic assemblage of the Togolok Oasis is almost the same as that for the previously mentioned oases, although we might eventually define chronological differences, such as those suggested by the appearance of funnel-shaped vessels. Almost all the vessels are light-colored — only rare examples are covered by a thick, red paint — and are sometimes decorated with incised wavy or broken lines on their shoulders. A few isolated examples contain series of hatched triangles, and scratched, sometimes attached designs of the traditional goats near trees are observed. Fragments of handmade Andronovo-like wares are found, as well as heavily grit-tempered handmade vessels that were covered by continuous toothed herringbone designs (Figure 8, 12-13).

Handmade and painted Yaz 1 ceramics (Figure 5, 11-23) are found in the upper levels on many, if not all, the sites in this oasis, a fact which shows that life continued in this area until the first centuries of the first millennium B.C. While the evidence allows us to define a late or Togolok phase, there are sites in this oasis that can be related to the Achaemenian period in their upper levels. Copper-bronze artifacts include daggers (Figure 8, 1-2), knives (and possibly spearheads), bracelets, temporal rings, and pins, including some examples with square heads that are similar only to types from Bactria (Figure 7, 31).

Anthropomorphic objects are documented by a large and significant collection of female figurines typical for southern Turkmenistan (Figure 10). Along with them more primitive figures from sculpted figures on cult vessels appear. One complete vessel had set on its rim an entire procession of people, birds, animals, and reptiles that formed a complicated mythological composition. Five miniature pots found inside this vessel most likely were associated with ritual libations. Similar vessels are known only from Bactria. Stone amulets include a circular mace head (Figure 6, 8, 8a; Fig-

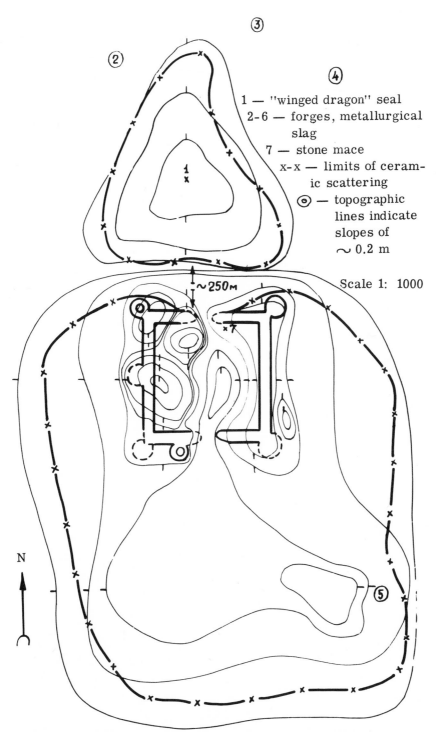

1 — "winged dragon" seal
2-6 — forges, metallurgical
slag
7 — stone mace
x-x — limits of ceram-
ic scattering
⊙ — topographic
lines indicate
slopes of
∼ 0.2 m

Scale 1: 1000

Figure 9. Togolok 21: plan of the settlement and fortress.

ure 11, 32) decorated with coiling bands that possibly imitate snakes
and a tiny kidney-shaped vessel that again finds direct parallels
only in Bactria (Figure 11, 27). Stone amulets in the Murghab style
with engraved representations of animals and reptiles are also

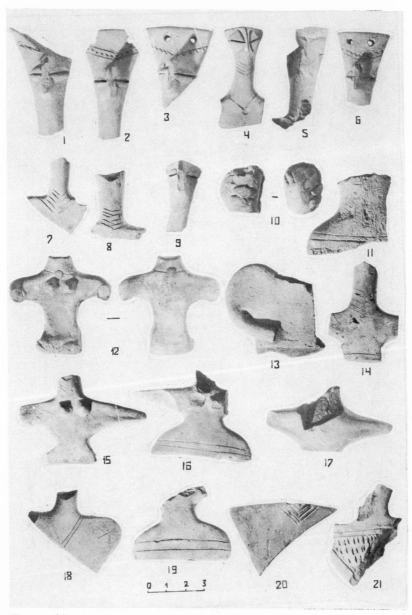

Figure 10. Anthropomorphic figurines.

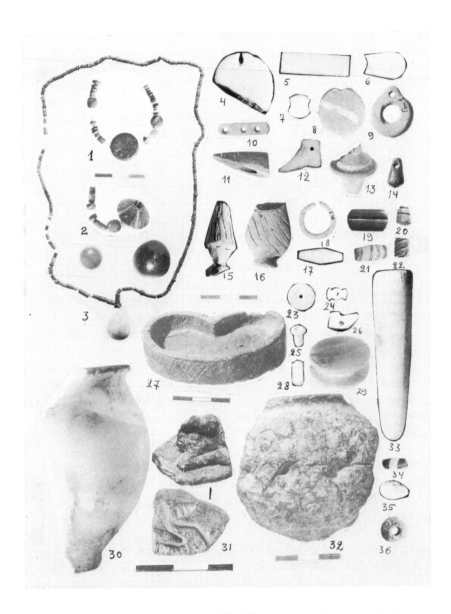

Figure 11. Stone and ceramic (15-16) objects: 1 — Auchin 1,
burial 4, lapis lazuli and carnelian beads, dark red amulet; 2 —
Auchin 1, burial 3, paste and lapis lazuli beads, steatite biconical
bead or whorl; 3 — Takhirbai 3, disturbed burial, lapis lazuli bead,
two small gold beads, pear-shaped pendant of a white stone, two
small balls of a black stone and carnelian; 4 — Gonur 1, white
stone pendant; [see footnote on p. 184 for continuation of Figure 11]

known from the Togolok Oasis. Among the new finds one must
mention a steatite amulet that has a four-petaled rosette on one
side and a winged lion, shown in profile with mouth agape and reptiles under its stomach and possibly above its back (Figure 7, 1-2),
on the other. Another steatite amulet (Figure 7, 3-4) is decorated
on one of its flat sides with a stylized depiction of fantastically
intertwined horned dragons devouring each other; on its other side
a winged griffin is depicted in a sitting position with its head turned
back. In addition to these amulets, button-shaped seals and amulets, which were decorated with swastikas, trees (Figure 7, 12),
whirling rosettes, and crosses, were found both on the surface
and in excavated graves. Finally, a cylinder seal of the Elamo-
Mesopotamian type (Figure 7, 8-8a) was found here as at Taip 1.
Fragments of steatite vessels are known from the Gonur and Togolok oases; they have both incised designs (Figure 12, 1, 5, 6, 13,
and 14) and high relief decorations (Figure 12, 4, 8, and 12). Steatite biconical beads with circular designs (Figure 12, 16-23) and
flint arrowheads (Figure 12, 25-41) also were fashioned.

   Copper-bronze compartmented seals primarily retain decorations of crosses (Figure 7, 26-28); in one case a seal was cast in
the form of some predatory animal (Figure 7, 25). Besides seals,
an impression on a fragment of fired clay, apparently from a bulla,
was encountered; traces of its cord (or string) are preserved (Figure 7, 30).

   Cenotaphs and grave pits, some of which are filled with funeral
vessels, were found along with customary burials. Beads, pendants, and awls were made from turquoise and lapis lazuli, and
vessels were even fashioned from marblelike alabaster. A steatite
amulet in the form of a frog with a perforation for a string also
was noted (Figure 7, 22).

5-6 — Gonur 1, stone inlays; 7 — Gonur 1, white stone bead; 8 —
Togolok 25, flat stone bead; 9, 13, 15, 16 — Gonur 1, ceramics;
10-11 — Togolok 10, schist; 12 — Togolok 1, step-shaped amulet,
cut from marblelike alabaster; 14 — Togolok 1, dark stone pendant; 18 — Gonur 1, bronze earring; 19 — Gonur 1, slate pendant
with two holes; 22 — Gonur 1, lapis lazuli, piercer; 23 — Togolok 24, polyspherical object with cut circles; 25 — Togolok 1,
mushroom-shaped stone object with a corrugated head; 27 — Togolok 13, cult vessel; 30 — marblelike stone vessel; 31 — steatite
plaque with representations on two sides; 32 — Togolok 21, head
of a pin or scepter.

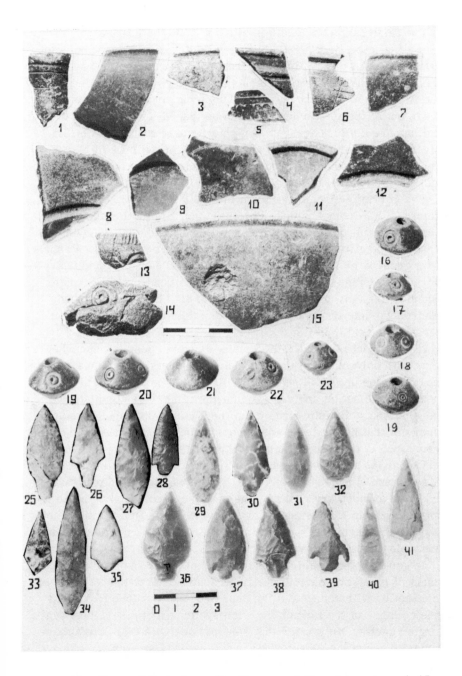

Figure 12. Stone objects from the Gonur and Togolok oases: 1-15
— fragments of steatite vessels (8, 12 — lower parts of vases;
9, 10 — flat bases).

The final Takhirbai Oasis is situated south of Togolok and relates to a later stage. Only Takhirbai 4 and 11 are fortified among
all the sites in this oasis. The largest, possibly central, settlement is Takhirbai 3, the eastern part of which was inhabited from
the Early Iron Age through the Achaemenian period. A bank extends out of this settlement and can be traced for more than three
km; apparently it represents a former course or channel of the
river, which had attained a width of 20-25 m. It is likely that this
represents a blocked section of the Murghab River out of which began its deltaic fan.

The ceramic assemblage from the Takhirbai Oasis closely resembles that from Togolok, with the minor distinction that the
ceramic forms are coarser and that there is a higher percent of
vessels decorated with scratched lines (Figure 13, 1-12). Vessels
with grooved rims (Figure 6, 6-7), the lower part of which bears
scratched designs closely reminiscent of vessels from Rahman
Dheri (Pakistan), are among the new forms. Besides handmade
Andronovo-like fragments, handmade painted sherds are encountered (Figure 13, 13-18).

Metal objects include knife points, daggers, possibly spearheads,
pins with polyspherical ends, temporal ringlets, and compartmented
seals. Stone biconical beads with circular designs, flint arrowheads, stone seals, and rare zoomorphic figurines complete the
general characteristic finds from the Takhirbai Oasis. It is no
accident that not a single anthropomorphic figurine has been encountered at this oasis, as at the Auchin Oasis.

Cenotaphs are found along with the customary burials of contracted skeletons; the latter usually are oriented to the north. In
addition to mortuary vessels, one of these cenotaphs contained a
tiny broken faience vessel, a small carnelian ball, a polished pebble, a lapis lazuli pear-shaped pendant, a small lapis bead, and
two gold beads (Figure 11, 3).

In general, the Takhirbai Oasis demonstrates the furthest movement of irrigation agriculture from south to north that occurred in
connection with changes in the course of the Murghab River and
the collapse of the former riverine systems into a series of separate runoffs. No wonder that ceramic deposits from the Achaemenid through the classical Hyarukal periods stretch for many
kilometers even further to the southwest.

Concluding our review of sites of the lower Murghab, we mention
that the earliest sites must be those of the Kelleli Oasis, the material culture of which has close analogies with cultures of the pied-

mont belt. These connections can be traced in an entire series of objects, particularly ceramics, terra-cotta figurines, and metal objects.

Figure 13. Takhirbai Oasis: wheel-made ceramics with incised designs (1-12) and painted handmade ceramics (13-18); 5 — from the upper level of Takhirbai 3; 13, 15 — from Takhirbai 13; 6, 18 — from trench at Takhirbai 3.

187

Table 1

Early stage (Kelleli) middle of the second millennium B.C.	Middle stage (Gonur) second half of the second millennium B.C.	Late stage (Togolok) end of the second/ beginning of the first millennium B.C.
Kelleli Oasis	Gonur Oasis Auchin Oasis Adam Basan Oasis Adzhi-kui Oasis Taip Oasis	Togolok Oasis Takhirbai Oasis

As mentioned above, the settlements from the remaining oases share several distinct material cultural traits in comparison with sites from Kelleli. The differences with Kelleli are clearly evident in the presence in the remaining oases of sites with fortresses, cult vessels with sculpted friezes, and seal amulets; all these features are absent both at Kelleli and in the piedmont belt of the Kopet Dagh. A series of ceramic forms, such as goblets and vases, is broadly distributed throughout the remaining settlements but is missing at Kelleli.

Although the available materials are still far from complete, they nevertheless give us a chance to trace the general outline of events that occurred in this region during the second millennium B.C. Despite the fact that occasional inhabitation of the lower Murghab had occurred even in the late Aeneolithic and apparently continued into the Early Bronze Age (Namazga IV), it is only during the time of the late Namazga V period that large settlements and groups of settlements, such as those located in the Kelleli Oasis, appear in the lower Murghab due to emigration from the piedmont belt of the Kopet Dagh. However, the cultural fluorescence and maximum inhabitation of the area occurred during the Togolok period primarily on account of the arrival of large groups of tribes from the west through Iranian Khorassan. The most probable original homeland of these foreign tribes was located along the southern edge of the Caspian Sea. Several large tribal movements in an easterly direction might have begun from this area around 1500 B.C. One wave traveled across the Gurgan Plain, passed through the piedmont zone of southern Turkmenistan, and settled in large numbers in the lower Murghab. A second wave from this same center rolled east as far as the Bactrian plain, a migration that explains the striking resemblance in all the basic aspects of material culture between Margiana and Bactria in the Bronze Age (Figure 14). Finally, the new painted ceramic culture of the Early Iron Age was distributed in both these regions at the end of the second and the beginning of the first millennium B.C. and took part in the already existing interaction that joined them; however, these later relations go beyond the limits of the present study. [11] All our material not only does not exclude but, on the contrary, supports the cultural and historical similarity of the material culture of southern Turkmenistan with that of Gilan-Mazanderan [Iran] in the preceding periods. At the same time, northern Iran belongs to an area dominated by graywares, and Bactria-Margiana, like southern Turkmenia, to a zone characterized by light-colored wares, a fact that points to the existence of several local variants within a single ceramic area. In general, the Iranian parallels clearly demonstrate that the primary correspondences to the Bactria-Margiana complex are found in the Gurgan Valley and, in particular, in the assemblage from Hissar III. Consistent with this interpretation, tubular-spouted vessels in the shape of bulls' heads and bridge-spouted forms find remarkable parallels in the Bronze Age ceramics of Iran as far as Luristan. [12]

We emphasize that miniature columns of the Hissar type, biconical beads with circular designs, shaft-hole axe-adzes, and in part, cylinder seals occur practically at the same time in northern Iran, Turkmenia, and Afghanistan, suggesting tribal movements west to east along the lower Murghab. Having arrived in southern Turkmenistan, some of these alien tribes occupied older settlements, such as Ulug-depe, while others founded new sites, such as Tekkem-depe. The vast majority, however, settled in the fertile oases of the Murghab. The decline of former urban settlements, such as Altyn-depe and Namazga-depe, was not linked to these movements; on account of insufficient water their inhabitants already had moved to new places, including the lower Murghab. The foreign tribes settled along the main runoffs of the deltaic fan and thus formed groups of settlements or microooases similar to those described above. The agriculturalists and pastoralists with similar forms of material culture had immigrated from northern Iran and had already intermingled with the local tribes of the lower Murghab. Together they formed a powerful tribal union called the lands of Margush. This very fact itself demonstrates that this politically and economically developed union or confederation,

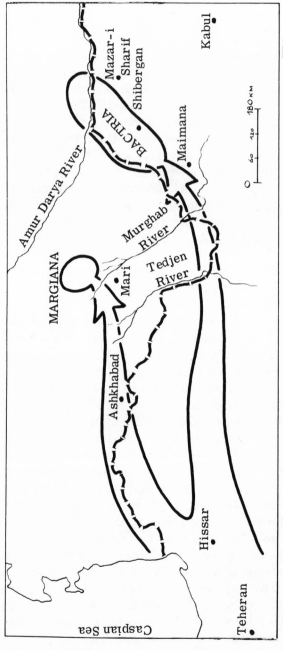

Figure 14. Schematic map showing distribution of Bactria-Margiana archeological complex.

190

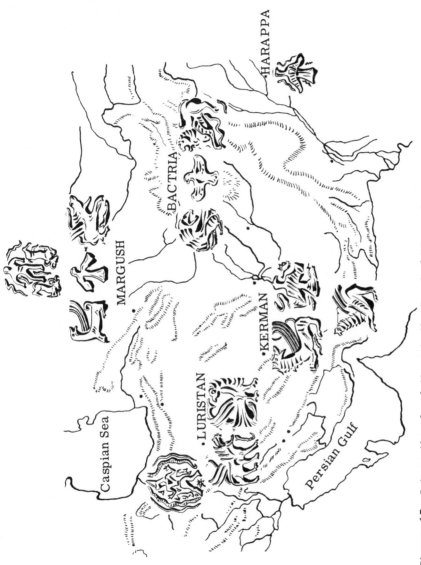

Figure 15. International relations to the Land of Margush.

191

which was mentioned in the writings of the most advanced centers of the Near East (Figure 15), already was located in the lower Murghab during the Bronze Age. One can propose that the central administration of this large union or federation of tribes during the Bronze Age was situated at the largest settlement, Gonur 1. Nevertheless there is no evidence to suggest the presence of regal power or a state; the local society was only at the threshold of such a historical process, which culminated in the incorporation of the lands of Margush into the Achaemenian Empire.

One can conclude with certainty that the Bronze Age culture of Margiana and Bactria formed one of the largest and most original centers of the ancient Near East.[13] Although uncertainty persists without written sources, it is highly probable that Margush and Bactria were closely related ethnolinguistically and cultural-historically; during the Achaemenian period this common origin received its political formulation. The boundaries of the political unit were not constant but shifted depending on internal (largely economic) and external political reasons. Single sites in northern Bactria, such as Sapalli and Mulali, developed on account of the spread of tribes from the left bank of the Amu Darya. Despite special surveys, no more than fifteen or twenty settlements have been found in southern Uzbekistan that date to the same period as the more than 100 sites known from Bactria. Apparently the ecological conditions of the right bank of the Amu Darya were less favorable and attractive for settlement; it formed the northern peripheral boundary of Bactria proper. Concerning the further penetration of agricultural settlements, one can mention the sites of the Zamanbaba Culture and, further east, those with the type of material remains relating to the second level at Shortugai, Badakhshan.

In conclusion we mention that the culture of the Bactrian and Margiana centers was characterized by its great distinctiveness and originality, which were reflected in its objects of ancient applied art. Thus the general theme of the abduction by reptiles, or possibly dragons, of the "life-giving seed" from animals, including bulls, which shares points in common with the later cult of Mithraism, is clearly detected on the stone amulets. Equally apparent is another theme, represented by fights between animals and dragons, that reflects the idea of the battle between good and evil, i.e., a dualistic concept that receives its ultimate expression in the teachings of Zoroaster. These two themes are not accidentally represented but, on the contrary, form the basic idea that stone

engravers repeated persistently on countless dozens of amulets.
Obviously, substantial reasons allow us to propose that the ethno-
religious conceptions and mythological representations of the
Bactria-Margiana centers to some extent influenced the formation
of the subsequent doctrines of Zoroaster. In this respect it is not
out of place to recall that in the Avesta, the land of Margab or Margush is characterized as "the powerful country believing in Asha,"
i.e., in the basic teachings of Zoroaster, a fact that perhaps testifies to the birth of a new religion in this and neighboring regions.

Notes

1. E. Huntington, "Description of the Kurgans of the Merv Oasis," R. Pumpelly, ed., Explorations in Turkestan, vol. 1, Washington, 1908.
2. D. D. Bukinich, "Istoriia pervobytnogo oroshaemogo zemledeliia Zakaspiiskoi oblasti," Khlopkovoe delo, Tashkent, 1924, no. 5; S. A. Ershov, "Arke-
ologiia v Turkmenskoi SSR za 20 let," Izvestiia Turkmenskogo filiala AN SSSR,
Ashkhabad, 1944, no. 2-3; S. A. Viazigin, "Stena Antiokha Sotera vokrug drevnei
Margiany," TIuTAKE, Ashkhabad, vol. 1, 1949.
3. M. E. Masson, "Kratkaia khronika polevykh rabot IuTAKE za 1948-1952
gody," TIuTAKE, Ashkhabad, vol. 5, 1955.
4. V. M. Masson, Drevnezemledel'cheskaia kul'tura Margiany, MIA SSSR,
Moscow-Leningrad, 1959, no. 73.
5. I. S. Masimov, "Izuchenie pamiatnikov epokhi bronzy nizovii Murghaba,"
Sovetskaia arkheologiia, 1979, no. 1.
6. Ibid., p. 113.
7. Ibid., p. 130.
8. Ibid., p. 119.
9. V. I. Sarianidi, "Pechati-amulety Murgabskogo stilia," Sovetskaia arkheologiia, 1976, no. 1, pp. 42-68.
10. P. Amiet, Les Antiquites du Luristan, Paris, 1976, fig. 1.
11. This subject is treated in greater detail in V. I. Sarianidi, Drevnie zemledel'tsy Afganistana, Moscow, 1977.
12. See G. Contenau and R. Ghirshman, Fouilles du Tepe Giyan, Paris, 1933,
pl. 18, no. 52, 2.
13. For more detail see V. I. Sarianidi, "Baktriia v epokhu bronzy," Sovetskaia
arkheologiia, 1974, no. 4, p. 70; P. Amiet "Bactriane Proto-Historique," Syria,
vol. 54, 1977, part 2, pp. 89-121.
14. V. V. Struve, "Vosstanie v Margiane pri Darii I," MIuTAKE, issue 1,
Ashkhabad, 1949, pp. 15, 27.

CHAPTER 9

The Study of Bronze Age Sites
in the Lower Murghab

I. S. MASIMOV

The archeological study of Bronze Age sites in the Kopet Dagh foothills that has been conducted during the past twenty years has led, as is well known, to remarkable scientific discoveries. The results of excavations of small settlements and large urban centers, such as Namazga-depe and Altyn-depe, are significant far beyond the immediately surrounding region. A whole range of thorny problems for the study of Bronze Age cultures has been worked out in a sufficiently complete and specific manner that undoubtedly represents a model for the analysis of ancient cultures not only in the southern part of our country but also for the ancient east.[1]

Based on this work, investigations of other regions of southern Turkmenia, including the lower course of the ancient Murghab River, were initiated. The study of the archeology of this area has always elicited great scientific interest on the part of specialists, and recent discoveries in northern Afghanistan and southern Uzbekistan have further attracted the attention of investigators to the area.

The first reports about the agricultural monuments of the lower Murghab are found in a few publications from the first half of this century.[2] Basic work in this region really began with the formation of IuTAKE (the Southern Turkmenian Complex Archeological Expedition) in 1946,[3] and large-scale systematic excavations were conducted in 1954-56 by the Fourteenth Division of this expedition, directed by V. M. Masson.[4] In addition to the excavations by this division, surveys were made, and the stratigraphy of the settlements, the history of irrigation works, and the chronology of the sites were determined.[5] After a long interval work in this area was renewed in 1972, when V. I. Sarianidi conducted minor excavations at the settlements of Auchin-depe and Takhirbai. That year a new large Bronze Age oasis was discovered with its center at Gonur-depe,[6] and in 1974 a second similar oasis was found with a central settlement at Togolok-depe.[7] Since 1974 a special division of the Sh. Batirov Institute of History, Academy of Sciences, Turkmen SSR, directed by the author,[8] has taken part in the investigation of sites in the lower Murghab. In 1975 and 1976 a large group of new settlements was found and investigated. Extraordinarily rich and interesting materials, which allow us to incorporate much new information into the study of the ancient Murghab Delta, were obtained during this work. The present article represents only a preliminary statement that attempts to introduce into scientific circulation this new material.

Investigations have been conducted in the triangle between the takyr deposits of Kelleli to the north (north-northwest of Mari), Adzhi-kui, 25-28 kilometers to the eastsoutheast of Kelleli, and Adam Basan, located 16 km southwest of Adzhi-kui or 38-40 km south of Kelleli (Figure 1). At present this expanse is covered by semistable sands with sparse vegetation cover. Both the small takyr areas and the occasional mounds with ceramics scattered across their surfaces attest to the fact that this area was once a locus of intensive settlement and that water from the now dry course of the Murghab flowed abundantly through it.

The settlements at Kelleli are situated farthest to the north.[9] Six mounds and a series of small surface scatters with ceramic materials were found here. None of the settlements is high, and all have amorphous contours or shapes. The largest of them, Kelleli 1, consists of two mounds occupying a total area of more than five hectares. The surface of the mound was covered with sherds; the remains of several ceramic kilns were discovered, and fragments of metal objects, including seals, points, punches, and fine flat objects that were probably mirrors were frequently encountered. Fragments of terra-cotta human figurines, wheels for model carts, biconical whorls, and other objects also were found. The other settlements, Kelleli 2-6, are situated 4-6 km northwest of the first settlement and are somewhat smaller in size, the tiniest being Kelleli 6, which occupies an area of no more than 0.2 hectares.

The majority of Bronze Age mounds in the investigated region are situated south of the group described above. The largest of

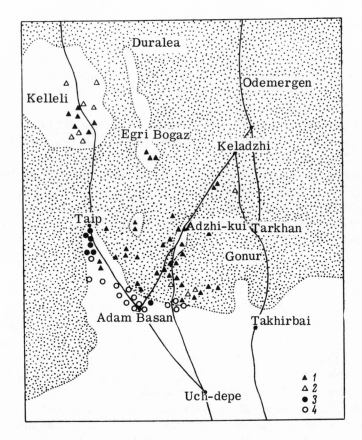

Figure 1. Map of the distribution of Bronze Age
sites: 1 — settlements of the Bronze Age; 2 — disturbed settlements; 3 — Yaz settlements; and 4 —
Yaz II and III settlements.

them, Taip-depe 1, is located 3 km east of a well bearing the same
name. It is 12 hectares in size and reaches a height of about 4 meters in different places. It occupies a smaller area than Gonur-
depe, which, based on the latest information, is no less than 28 ha
in size. Taip-depe 1 consists of two hills that are nearly the same
size and stretch in a line running north-south. The northern hill
is noteworthy, for it possibly has a fortification wall. Along its
southeastern side an area with rectangular planning that is possibly
surrounded by towers can be distinguished; a similar "construction"
cannot be seen on the second hill of Taip 1. Remains of several
groups of ceramic kilns and even great quantities of slag and ceramic wasters can be traced on a small eminence abutting the

second hill from the southeast. Apparently a center for the production of pottery was located here.

The second settlement of this group is located 8 km north of the well of Adam Basan and has been called Adam Basan 4. As opposed to Taip 1, this mound is extremely spread out in shape, occupying an area of 9.6 ha and rising to a height about 1.6 m above the plain; in other words, a large part of the settlement rises only slightly above the surrounding surface of the takyr. Traces of some kind of rampart and canal, which are attached to the main settlement by a small mound, are especially interesting; this area contained ceramic kilns. Traces of a canal that in some places is 4 m wide can be followed for 200 m.

Another series of mounds (Adam Basan 5-12) is situated to the north-northeast of this settlement. Among them, the largest is Adam Basan 7 (nearly 6 ha), and the smallest is Adam Basan 6 (no more than 0.4 ha). Another series of settlements was found east-northeast of the well, but they were distinguished neither by their shape (their height varies from 0.5 to 4 m), nor by the materials found on their surfaces. Unfortunately, the majority of them now are in a dispersed state or half-covered by sand dunes; thus it is impossible to determine their original area. Finally, eight other Bronze Age sites were concentrated around the well of Adzhi-kui, 16 km to the north-northeast of Adam Basan. The largest, Adzhi-kui 1, is situated at the well site and has an extended shape, stretching in a line northeast to southwest for approximately 330 m; its width is about 200 m, and its height about 3.5 m. A single grave with a poorly preserved skeleton, lying in a contracted position with its head to the north, was excavated on the northern part of this mound. Nine vessels were placed in the grave (four were complete: two pots and two small jars), a stone spindle whorl, several paste beads, a bronze bracelet, and near the head of the deceased, an earring. The remains of a potter's kiln of the two-chambered type with a stretched out oval shape and a furnace aperture in its southeastern side were cleared away on another settlement of this group, Adzhi-kui 4 (6.8 ha). The length of the kiln was 3.2 m; the diameter of the firing chamber 2.1 m, and 17 air vents were preserved. The lower furnace chamber of the kiln had two parts with a special hole on the side of the mouth of the kiln for filling it with fuel; its upper half had a column in the middle that supported the bottom of the firing chamber. The great amount of slag in the furnace attests to its long use. In terms of its construction the kiln is analogous to those excavated in the craftsmen's quarter at Altyn-depe and at the settlement of Ulug-depe.[10]

A group of three small sites was found near the Egri Bogaz Well halfway between Adzhi-kui and Kelleli.

Thus the Bronze Age sites in the investigated region cover a rather broad territory. In any case the discovery of two more Bronze Age mounds 10 km northeast of Adzhi-kui leaves open the question of their distribution in the ancient Murghab Delta. The archeological-topographic investigations that have been conducted allow us to define preliminarily three types of Bronze Age settlements in this area. The first type consists of mounds reaching 5 ha in area and 1 m in height; they are usually single mounds or the remains of extensive settlements in the form of ceramic surface scatters on the takyr. The second type unites those settlements ranging from 5-10 ha in size and more than 1 m in height; they often contain two or more hills on which there is a spot set aside for craft production, most frequently of ceramics. The third type includes those settlements larger than 10 ha in size with a separate production area and, possibly, fortification walls. The mounds of Taip-depe 1, Gonur-depe, and Auchin-depe,[11] situated east of the well of Tarkhan, can be put in this category.

The first stratigraphic sections for Bronze Age settlements in the Murghab area were made by V. M. Masson at Auchin and Takhirbai 3.[12] Several stratigraphic cuts were also made by us on several of the newly discovered sites. In the Kelleli group the three largest mounds — Kelleli 1, 3, and 4 — were subjected to stratigraphic study. Sounding 1 (4 × 1 m) was placed in the northeastern corner of the first of these sites.[13] The first arbitrary level contained loose fill with bits of building debris, ash lenses, and occasional sherds and animal bones. In the second arbitrary level a pit filled with embers was encountered that contained sands corresponding to virgin soil. All the remaining levels of this trench, which was excavated to a depth of 3 m, had alternating lenses of white sandy loam and a dense clay-filled brownish mass, a tuiun. Soundings 2 and 3, situated respectively in the middle and southeastern part of the settlement, also were carried to a depth of 3 m (Figure 2, A). The nature of these levels was almost identical to that of the first trench, and virgin soil was reached at a depth of 1 m. The levels of cultural deposit were even smaller at the Kelleli 3 and 4 settlements. In general the stratigraphic investigations showed that the settlements of the Kelleli Oasis contained no more than 1 m of cultural remains. Such a deposit means that the investigated settlements are single-period sites relating to one historical horizon, a conclusion also supported by the complete identity of the ceramics from the trenches with those lying on the surface.

At two sites stratigraphic investigations were also made of the large number of mounds situated south of Kelleli. At Adam Basan 4 a trench (2.5 × 2 m) was opened on the highest western portion of the mound. Arbitrary cuts 1 and 2 were filled with loose cultural debris and ash lenses. A level of sand that had blown in containing separate lumps of clay mixed with floral remains (straw?) was found throughout the trench in arbitrary cut 3. At the beginning of the fourth cut a floor of some type of room was discovered under which lay virgin soil in the form of a tuiun. The fifth, sixth, and part of the seventh cuts were filled with sands. Clearly the cultural levels of the mound only reached a depth of 1.5 m or slightly more than the deposits of the settlements in the Kelleli Oasis.

The sounding at Adzhi-kui 3 exposed levels that were thicker than 2 m (Figure 2, B). A wall was found in the second and third arbitrary cuts that was made of rectangular unfired bricks (35 × 9 × ? or 42 × 11 × ? cm) and was preserved to a height of 85 cm and a breadth of 65 cm. The fill on both sides of the wall consisted of the remains of a ruined building. A floor with a sharply defined ledge [vykruzhka] could be traced at the base of the wall. Slightly burned levels with small rubbish pits lay under the second floor, which was located in the middle of the fourth arbitrary level, and continued until the end of the fifth level. Lower down a compact level of deposited sandy loam began, which in the middle of the seventh cut became mixed with a level of windblown sand.

The study of the stratigraphy of these two settlements, situated to the south of the Kelleli Oasis, supports in general the data obtained from Kelleli 1, 3, and 4, i.e., all the sites contain only one cultural level. We also observe that the levels of Auchin and Takhirbai were not deep and did not continue beneath the level of the surrounding surface.

In addition to the stratigraphic studies at Kelleli 1, small excavations were made. A large wall running north to south for 10 m was partially exposed. It was 1.65 m wide and was preserved to a height of 80 cm; its rectangular bricks measured 50-54 × 24 × 9-12 cm. It was externally reinforced by a facing of these bricks at the base of the mound, a fact that allows us to speculate that the wall had a different function than that of a simple construction attached to a house. However, we must keep in mind that many similar examples can be seen in the architecture from Altyn-depe. Several rooms with narrow twisted walls, preserved to a height of 1 or 2 bricks, were attached to the wall on its northwestern side. A group of rooms, cleared from the southwestern side, were the best preserved. One of these rooms was completely covered by two floors, apparently relating

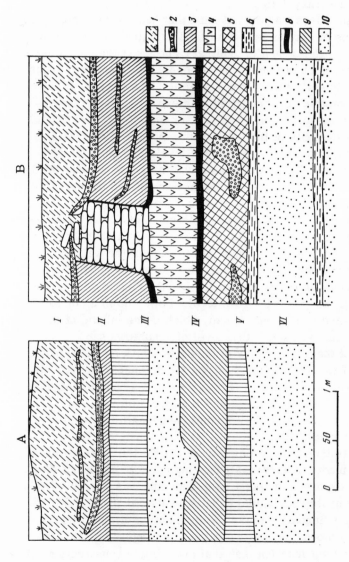

Figure 2. A — trench 2 at the settlement of Kelleli 1; B — trench at the settlement of Adzhi-kui 3: 1 — loose windblown level; 2 — ash lenses; 3 — levels with remains building debris; 4 — level of medium texture with bits of charcoal and bricks; 5 — level with a rubbish pit; 6 — densely accumulated levels; 7 — dense clayey levels; 8 — floor; 9 — level of white clayey sand; 10 — sand.

to two periods of occupation. The room measured 2.75 × 2.60 m, with its first floor 30 cm beneath the top of the walls and its second floor 50 cm lower. The fill on the floor of the second period was loose and contained many sherds and animal bones. N. M. Ermolova's preliminary determination of the osteological material has shown that they are the bones of domestic animals: cattle, sheep, camels, horses, dogs, and domestic pigs.[14]

The ceramics from the settlement can be divided into two assemblages that show chronological differences.

The first ceramics from the settlements at the Kelleli Oasis (Figures 3, 4) were made only on the potter's wheel. The clay is very well levigated, finely fired, and except for small bits of sand in some fragments, is not tempered. The sherds have a reddish-rose, light-rose, or more rarely, reddish color as their base. The so-called "Namazga" ceramics dominate the assemblage, usually showing a light-greenish coloring on their exterior surface. Excluding the traditional cooking ware, part of which was also made on the potter's wheel, handmade vessels were almost never found, and gray ceramics were completely absent.

The shapes of the vessels varied greatly. Bowls (Figure 3, 1-3, 11, 12, 16, 18, 21, 22, 33, 42, 45) were the dominant form and had two types of rims: a broken line or shoulder on the exterior surface (Figure 3, 1, 3, 16, 18, 21, 22); some also had deep thickened sections beneath the rim (Figure 3, 4, 12). Their bases usually were flat, with a concave section just above the base. Deep conical cups with straight, almost sharp rims and flat bases are also encountered (Figure 3, 10, 13, 35). These cups have slightly everted rims (Figure 3, 24), and smaller cups have thick sides and flat bases (Figure 3, 29, 30). There are many goblet-shaped vessels (Figure 3, 28, 38), small pots with flat bases (Figure 3, 19, 20) and with everted rims and short necks (Figure 3, 25, 27, 36) and also large, thick basins with slightly everted rims and cut bases (Figure 4, 1, 2, 9, 10). Vases on high conical stands, frequently decorated with incised lines, are also characteristic of ceramics from this first complex (Figure 3, 6; Figure 4, 6, 7, 21, 22). Jars with straight rims ending with a slight thickening (Figure 4, 5) and pots with everted rims and small necks (Figure 4, 16-20) are among the largest forms most frequently encountered. Large pithos-shaped pots with high necks and spouts are found much more rarely. A similar, almost complete pot had an inward-slanting profile above its base (Figure 4, 8). Jars have thick, egg-shaped bodies and inward-slanting sections above their bases (Figure 4, 14, 15). Storage jars have heavy walls more than 1 cm thick and everted rims that end either in a sharp point or in a half-rolled form. Sometimes on their shoulders there is a slight border or edge (Figure 4, 26, 29-32).

Besides these there are some rare forms, such as, for example, a double vessel (Figure 3, 26), a vessel with perforations on its exterior (Figure 4, 26), and also a fragment with a high neck and

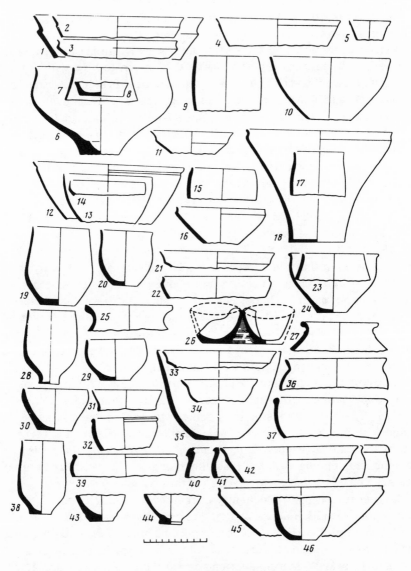

Figure 3. Ceramics of the Kelleli Oasis, first complex.

everted rim with an aperture in the middle, possibly relating to part of a pitcher (Figure 4, 11).

Very few kitchen ceramics were found. They were finished on a potter's wheel, probably to correct and complete the forms already made by hand. Besides small grains of sand, particles of limestone, quartz, or alabaster were used as temper. The sherds were brittle, and their basic forms were the following: kettle-

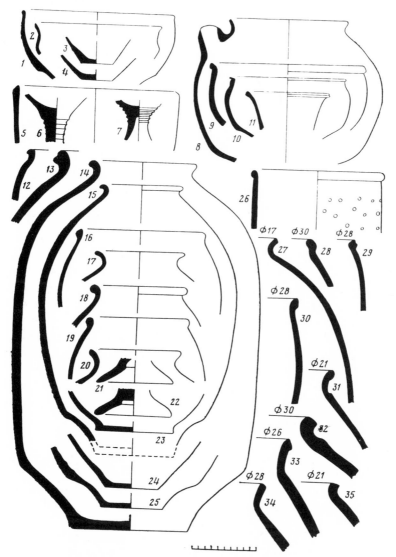

Figure 4. Ceramics of the Kelleli Oasis, first complex.

shaped pots and fragments of frying pans with small sides that were blackened on their exterior surface and, infrequently, on their interior surface as well. We also mention numerous ceramic stands or supports in this assemblage.

The second ceramic assemblage comes from settlements located to the south of the Kelleli Oasis. The color on their exterior surface is light-rose, light-yellow, and also light-green. The clay is well levigated, finely fired, and bits of sand were usually used as temper.

The forms of the vessels vary. As well as forms analogous to those from the first assemblage, completely new types of vessels, still not found at the Kelleli Oasis, appear.

Bowls of different sizes — from miniature examples to very large ones — occur more frequently (Figure 5, 6-16). Other frequently encountered forms include: cups with semispherical bodies and flat bases (Figure 5, 23, 49, 51); basins with slightly everted rims (Figure 5, 1-4, 24); and cups with thick walls and flat bases that also are often found in the first assemblage (Figure 5, 25). Among the forms not present in the first assemblage are goblets on high conical feet, fragments of vases with inverted rims and a small shoulder or edge on their exterior surface (Figure 5, 21, 22, 29, 30), and semispherical cups. Short squat pots (Figure 5, 37, 38) and pots with high necks and slightly everted rims (Figure 5, 34, 35) are very rarely encountered in the first assemblage. Characteristic shapes of the second assemblage also include: tall egg-shaped pots with flat bases (Figure 5, 33, 36); carinated pots with their sides curving inward to slightly everted rims (Figure 6, 4); and even spouted vessels (Figure 6, 7) and vessels with trough-shaped spouts at the rim (Figure 6, 6). Among the larger vessels we mention bowls of semispherical shape or with thick vertical sides (Figure 5, 47, 48, 50) and rims of large pots and small jars (Figure 5, 32, 39-46). Two complete jars, found in a burial at the Adzhi-kui settlement, had squat, spherical bodies, broad necks, and flat bases (Figure 6, 1, 2). It is interesting that both vessels had broad red bands on the upper sections of their bodies; the smaller jar had three bands.

In addition to these jars an entire sequence of rims of storage jars with different profiles and fragments of large ceramic stands of different sizes were found.

The second group of ceramics which were handmade can be divided into three subgroups on the basis of technological factors and design elements. The first subgroup contains admixtures of sand, quartz, limestone, and small bits of pottery. Vessels with such attributes frequently were used for cooking. The sherds are very brittle and easily broken. These are pot-shaped vessels with everted rims (Figure 6, 25-26), pots with spouts (Figure 6, 27), and a box-shaped vessel with straight sides and a flat base (Fig-

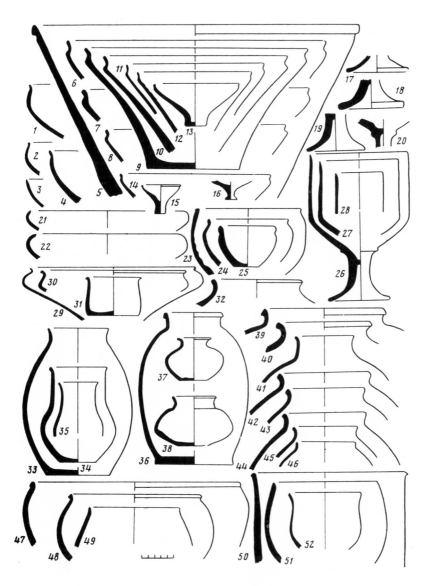

Figure 5. Ceramics of the Murghab settlements, second complex.

ure 6, <u>28</u>). Large semispherical jars with slightly everted rims (Figure 6, <u>29</u>) have circular lines in their interior indicating that they were finished on a potter's wheel. Vessels of the second subgroup are similar to the first but can be distinguished by designs impressed by simple marks or points. The characteristic designs are triangles beneath the rims that are filled in with obliquely slanting lines or tear-shaped impressions. A complete vessel of this subgroup, which was found at the Taip 1 Settlement, was completely covered with designs from its rim to its base (Figure 6, <u>31-36</u>).

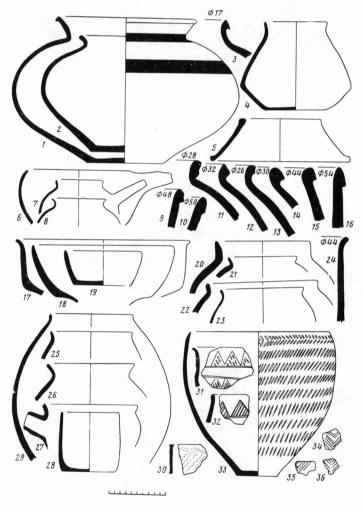

Figure 6. Ceramics of the Murghab settlements, second complex.

Finally, the most numerous subgroup consists of rough hand-made ware that is heavily chaff-tempered. The color of the sherds varies, but most frequently they have a rose, red, or white hue. The exterior surface of these vessels frequently is spotted with the same range of colors. As opposed to the two preceding subgroups, ceramics of this subgroup — with rare exceptions — are very solid and well fired. The most common shapes are large bowls with carinated bases, cups with thick sides and flat bases (Figure 6, 17-19), pot-shaped vessels with short but wide throats and everted rims (Figure 6, 20-23), and fragments of straight-sided everted rim vessels that were probably bowls.

One must observe that while the ceramics of the two preceding groups were known from earlier studied sites, those of the third group were first defined by V. M. Masson, who commented on the distinctive character of this ceramic assemblage,[15] at the settlement of Auchin-tepe. Now they are met at nearly all the settlements south of the Kelleli Oasis and constitute roughly one third of the surface materials. Single examples of this type of ceramic were found in the upper levels of test trenches at Adam Basan 4 and Adzhi-kui 3. One gets the impression that ceramics of this type are associated with the eroded levels of the majority of Murghab settlements. It is interesting that in comparison with the unpainted handmade ware of the Yaz 1 culture, one finds in general coarser handmade ware that is heavily chaff-tempered at these settlements. Similarity also is evident in terms of their shapes.[16] Thus forms of large bowls with carinated bases, which are analogous to those wheel-turned vessels from the first ceramic assemblage of the Kelleli Oasis, are encountered quite frequently (Figure 3, 1, 9, 10). Such similarity probably attests to the succession of separate forms that preserved their proportions during a considerable length of time. For this reason one can preliminarily relate this group of ceramics to a time preceding the Yaz 1 culture or to the earliest stages of that culture.

The human and animal figurines are especially interesting among the other finds. Figurines from the Kelleli Oasis are made in the same conventional flat style as those from Namazga and Altyn-depe (Figure 7, 1-9). Lines are incised on the figurines that represent decorations and belts and sometimes also symbols of trees. One can say that in this respect the terra-cotta figurines from Kelleli are the same type as those found on settlements in the Kopet Dagh piedmont area.

Figurines from settlements situated to the south of the Kelleli

Oasis are made in the same way but are heavier and lack representations of showy headdresses or hairdos. The majority of the figurines have heads that almost are triangular in shape with vertical holes on the back of their heads (Figure 7, 12-14, 19, 20). This group includes figurines that are very generalized, which are made from coarse clay, and examples that exhibit very fine, care-

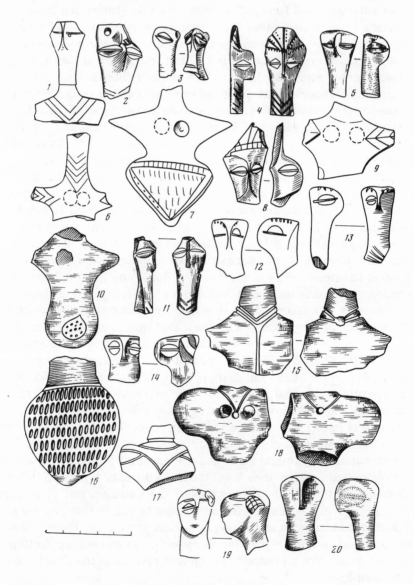

Figure 7. Terra-cotta human figurines.

fully executed details. Figurines with decorations on their necks (on one of them there is a "medallion") that hang down in front and in back as if tied by a string are especially noteworthy. We also mention a fragment of a torso, apparently male, in an elaborate attire (Figure 7, 17).

Animal figurines include representations of a camel, a dog (or ram), a bull, a pig, birds, and a goat whose head adorns the spout of a vessel (Figure 8). One must particularly point out a sherd that contains a fairly realistic applied head of a goat or gazelle that is eating the branches of a young tree (Figure 8, 1).

Seals made from stone, metal, and clay are an important group of finds. In addition to the well-known depictions of crosses, the metal seals include representations of animals. A large seal de-

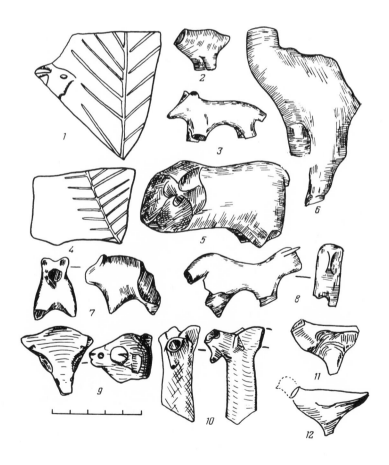

Figure 8. Terra-cotta animal figurines.

picting predatory birds (eagles?) revolving around a small circle (Figure 9, 1) is especially noteworthy. On their reverse sides all the metal seals have a raised, perforated boss or handle.

The stone seal-amulets, made of green steatite, usually have representations on both sides. A fragment of such a seal has the head of a bird on one side and a bull in an attacking pose with its tail flexed, head lowered, and horns set forward on the other (Figure 9, 5). Another seal depicts a snake with its mouth agape on one side and a fantastic creature, reminiscent of a peacock with long, barely raised wings, on its reverse. Especially curious is one seal in this series that has a similar depiction on both sides of a battle between a predatory beast and snakes (Figure 10). It is interesting that in the first representation the creature has a crocodile-shaped head with an open mouth and wings, and in the second it more closely resembles a lion-shaped predator with a bristling mane and a prominent protuberance above its head. The trunk and feet with grasping claws are depicted in a similar fashion. Noting the sufficiently complicated semantic subject matter of these seals, which undoubtedly is linked to mythological themes, we suggest that they belong to that circle of seal-amulets which

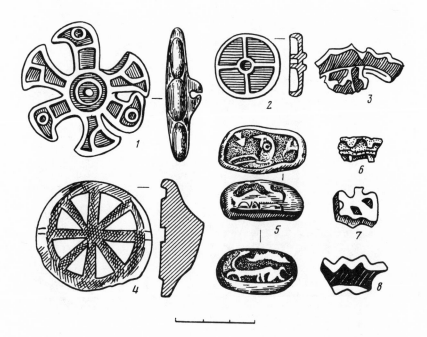

Figure 9. Seals: 1-3, 6-8 — metal; 4 — clay; and 5 — stone.

already has received a definitive interpretation in the literature.[17] A unique discovery was a clay sherd with impressions of two cylinder seals that was found at Taip-depe 1. Both impressions show the same struggle between a hump-backed bull with its head lowered and its large horns set forward and a lion with its paws lowered to the ground and its body ready to charge. A tree stands between them. One must say that this is a rare find for southern Turkmenia, and it does not have any close analogies. Nevertheless it is noteworthy that the figure of the bull on these impressions, especially on the second, totally duplicates the figure of the same animal on one of the seals already discussed (Figure 9, 5).

A great quantity of other objects of material culture was collected at the settlements. In this respect we must mention the significant number of metal artifacts that were found at almost every settlement (Figure 11). A metal object was found at Adzhi-kui 1 which, according to the preliminary determination of the geologists, was part of a copper blank. We also mention the discovery of a complete bronze skimmer with a handle, fragments of tools and military weapons, mirrors, and decorative objects. The discovery

Figure 10. Stone seal made of green steatite.

of a well-preserved fish hook is interesting (Figure 11, 20).
Moreover, stone tools and weapons were discovered that attest to

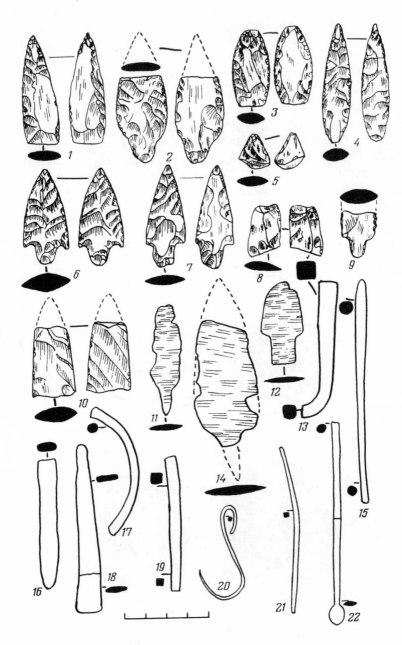

Figure 11. Various finds.

the broad utilization of this cheap resource. Among the weapons we mention arrow and lance heads (Figure 11, 1-10), and among objects utilized in daily life, fragments of all sorts of flint blades, pestles, burnishers, mortars, whetstones, and others. Fragments of mortars and stone vessels were found that were made both from a marblelike stone and from green steatite. A complete vessel of this latter material in the form of a small food dish was decorated with incised inverted triangles that were filled in with a slanting net design. Beads and spindle whorls, the majority of which were decorated with three dot-in-circle designs on each half, were finished on a lathe. Beads were made of semiprecious stones that were selected according to their different colors or shades, lending an attractive appearance to the ornament (Figure 12, 7, 8).

Clay objects include biconical and conical spindle whorls, sometimes with incised designs, and fragments of cart wheels with hubs from model carts. In one case the cart itself was found in the form of a fragment of a long, fired object with short borders and an opening underneath. It is also interesting that a clay model of a "boot tree" with an upturned end or snout was found; analogous

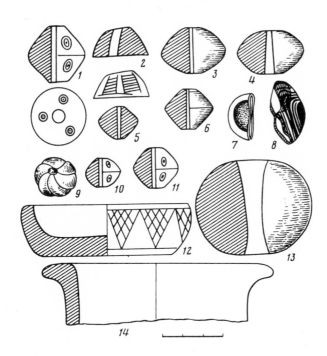

Figure 12. Various finds.

213

objects are encountered on settlements in northern Afghanistan[18] and at Shahr-i Sokhta.[19]

Turning now to an examination of analogies to our materials, we recall that the ceramics were divided into two assemblages. The first, as is known, comes from settlements in the Kelleli Oasis and consists of vessels turned on a potter's wheel with great professional skill. Except for kitchen ware, this assemblage lacks handmade vessels and graywares, which rarely occur among the vessels of the second assemblage. At the same time, in the Murghab area we still do not know the root from which this assemblage developed. It is clear that in the adjacent regions of northern Afghanistan and southern Uzbekistan, where sufficiently numerous sites with similar material cultures are located, there are no earlier lines of development. Moreover, on the basis of several facts these sites are somewhat later in comparison to the Kelleli ceramic assemblage. For this reason our basic comparisons are made with the Kopet Dagh piedmont zone, where settlements of the Bronze Age developed on the basis of a local culture that had existed for several millennia. The excavations that have been conducted for many years on settlements in this region, especially at Altyn-depe, allow the investigators to propose a preliminary chronology of the developed Bronze Age within the limits of the Namazga V period.[20] In the early stages of this period the dominant ceramics are biconical-shaped vessels with sharp edges,[21] which perceptive investigators associate with the craftsmen's still incomplete familiarity with the fast-turning potter's wheel. Later, after the accumulation of practice and experiments with this device, there appeared an assortment of clay vessels that were remarkably rich: different forms of vases, goblets, bowls, cups, plates, and an entire series of other vessels of elegant shapes and proportions. The potter's wheel at this time undoubtedly was capable of great speed, which permitted the gathering together and drawing up of the walls of the vessels.[22] Later less numerous sharp-ribbed vessels are observed, new forms appear, and they become less elegant. The forms include vessels such as pitchers, pots, deep cups, and others.[23] One can say that at this stage of the development of pottery production at Altyn-depe there is a close similarity with the materials from the Kelleli Oasis. Sharp-edged vessels have not yet been found in the ceramic assemblage from this oasis. However, we do find bowls with a characteristic broken profile at the rim that are similar to bowls found in great quantity at Altyn-depe.[24] Here one must mention as well deep cups with sharp rims and tumbler-shaped vessels.[25] Similarities are observed not only in vessels but in other objects of the material culture. Thus, for example, the terra-cotta plastic art at Kelleli depicts figures of women with the high headdresses or hairdos that are typical for the figurines from Altyn-depe;[26] however, one must also note that the applied braids characteristic of the terra-cotta figurines of the piedmont area still have not been found on the statuettes from the Kelleli settlements. Meanwhile, the flat style, which was always used in the preparation of these cult objects in ancient southern Turkmenia,[27] as we have seen, is completely preserved in the statuettes from the Kelleli Oasis. The list of analogies could continue for metal, stone, and clay objects that are typical for both regions. It would seem that even such a rare form as a double vessel that is more characteristic for regions south of Turkmenistan (Shah-tepe, Susa) is found both at Altyn-depe[28] and Kelleli.

A whole series of analogies also can be found with the other large settlement, Namazga-depe, particularly in relation to the Namazga V ceramic assemblage, which was first established by B. A. Kuftin[29] and then generalized by V. M. Masson.[30] The goffered feet of the vases found at Kelleli appear as characteristic attributes of such vessels, which have different variations and proportions,[31] at Namazga-depe. One must also mention the bowls, cups, jars, spouted vessels, and others typical for Namazga V.[32] The characteristic anthropomorphic and zoomorphic plastic art from Namazga-depe is similar to the materials from Kelleli.[33]

Beyond Turkmenistan we find basic similarities to the Kelleli material in northeastern Iran, where at this time — as opposed to southern Turkmenia — dark gray burnished ceramics are overwhelmingly the dominant type. Nevertheless there are obvious examples, such as types of deep vases on conical feet and cups with flat bases, that appear in the levels of Tepe Hissar III.[34] Shah-tepe also exhibits a series of analogies to the Kelleli material. They include, in particular, vases on pedestals and, even more significantly, double vessels,[35] which also are found in great quantity at Susa (necropolis, levels of period II),[36] in neighboring Mesopotamia (Khafajeh, hill C),[37] and at other sites. Definite and sufficiently clear links to the Kelleli assemblage can be found in the Seistan region and further east in the cities of the Harappan culture of the Indus Valley.

However, the closest analogies are found in the neighboring regions of northern Afghanistan and southern Uzbekistan. Thus vase-shaped vessels on high feet constitute about 80 percent of all the established dinnerware at the Dashly 1 Settlement.[38] Here one can find analogies in the bowls and other vessels. Nevertheless one must observe the absence of goffered feet on the vases and also deep cups with truncated conical shapes, flat bases, and slightly sharp rims, which are among the dominant forms in the ceramics from the Kelleli Oasis. We also mention the complete absence of terra-cotta plastic art at the northern Afghanistan settlements, although in other respects their culture is close to that of the settlements of southern Turkmenistan.

A similar picture can be drawn by comparing this material with the southern Uzbekistan settlement of Sapalli-tepe.[39] It is curious that the ceramics from this settlement are frequently burnished, while this is not characteristic for sites in Afghanistan or the lower Murghab.

A still greater similarity with the material cultures of southeastern regions can be discerned for the second Murghab ceramic assemblage. Thus numerous goblets on high conical stands, which are found at many settlements to the south of Kelleli, appear to be one of the major forms both at Sapalli[40] and at settlements of the Dashly type.[41] Cups with spheroconical bodies and trough-shaped spouts, teapots, various types of pots, and small storage jars also show close correspondences. We mention the complete identity of small, squat storage jars with convex bodies that are found at Dashly[42] with such vessels that are frequently found in the Murghab settlements, particularly in the graves at Adzhi-kui. At the same time, the goblets with high pedestals characteristic for the designated regions of the second Murghab assemblage have still not been found at Kelleli, and the deep cups with the truncated conical shapes, which appear in the ceramics of this latter region, have still not been encountered at settlements to the south of Kelleli nor in Bactria.[43]

The closeness of the material culture of the northern Afghanistan sites to those in the Murghab area is reflected not only in the ceramic assemblages. The similarity of the Murghab seals with those from northern Afghanistan has already been mentioned in the literature.[44] It is true that the impressions of cylinder seals, mentioned by us above, undoubtedly have Mesopotamian parallels.[45] We mention the finds at settlements of the Dashly type of a stone vessel, made of green steatite, with a short side and decorated on its exterior surface,[46] spindle-whorls or beads of biconical shape decorated with dot-in-circle designs,[47] metal ornaments,[48] and others. Finally, although it is absent at Sapalli-tepe, one can consider as a general feature for the two regions the presence of grayware.

The analysis of the finds, above all the ceramics, also allows us to differentiate preliminarily each region from the others. These differences apparently have a chronological significance. The earliest of the sites are those from the Kelleli Oasis; they are separated from the basic mass of sites in the Murghab Delta and in their material culture gravitate more closely to the sites in the Kopet Dagh foothills. This similarity is clearly evident in the ceramics, terra-cotta figurines, metal objects, and other remains of the material culture. The second assemblage, relating to the sites south of the Kelleli Oasis, is similar to the northern Afghanistan and southern Uzbekistan sites; in our opinion they are contemporaneous. A whole series of ceramic forms, particularly the goblets, attests to this, as do the seals and stone and clay objects. Nevertheless it seems to us that the basic roots of this assemblage go back to the material culture of the sites in the Kopet Dagh foothills and to the sites of the Kelleli Oasis. Following this reasoning and discounting an insignificant number of ceramic pedestals, the Kelleli sites of the first assemblage are related by us to the first and second quarter of the second millennium B.C., and those from the second assemblage are dated to the middle of the second millennium B.C.

Of course, this proposed dating still needs to be verified. Nevertheless the investigated sites — despite the lack of a significant cultural deposit — stand before us clearly with a complex economy and culture. The excellent ceramic vessels, splendid metal objects, stone artifacts, and clay objects were made with great skill and are more than ample evidence of the high levels of crafts on these sites. Agriculture undoubtedly played the leading role in the economy; large fields and sufficient quantities of water for irrigation that were drawn from channels and numerous runoffs from the Murghab aided this agriculture. Coming down onto the plain, the river dispersed, breaking into small branches and forming a sub-delta in its estuary.[49] In addition there is every reason to believe that in this region irrigation projects, which were extended in form and utilized by different communities, could have been built; such projects made possible different ways of watering the sown fields. A similar picture can be traced in the Aeneolithic settlements of the Geoksyur Oasis,[50] which is situated in the Tedjen Delta and which morphologically shares many features with the Murghab area. Animal husbandry also played a not insignificant role, as numerous osteological remains from the Kelleli settlement indicate. As opposed to Altyn-depe, bones of domestic pig dominated this assemblage. Judging by the discovery of beads made from semiprecious stones and the metal objects, the population of the lower Murghab maintained trading ties with neighboring territories. Very intensive trading links with the highly developed civilizations facilitated and accelerated the historical development of regions lying in the "barbarian" peripheral region between Mesopotamia and India.[51]

Since southern Turkmenia lacked natural resources, it was undoubtedly dependent on different metallurgical centers.[52] As is fully evident from the discovery of a metal blank, it is quite possible that semifinished objects were brought from separate regions and worked on the site.

Judging by the material culture, the Murghab population was founded after its migration from the Kopet Dagh foothills. This movement to new sites occurred in at least two stages. First, a small group of people settled in the Kelleli takyr; then, somewhat later, the bulk of the population occupied the large territory south of this already settled oasis.

Notes

1. V. M. Masson, "Uzlovye problemy arkheologii Srednei Azii," KSIA, AN USSR, 1970, no. 122; "Protogorodskaia tsivilizatsiia iuga Srednei Azii," SA, 1967, no. 3; "Stanovlenie klassovogo obshchestva na drevnem Vostoke," VI, 1967, no. 5; "Razvitie obmena i torgovli v drevnikh obshchestvakh," KSIA, AN USSR, no. 138; "Izuchenie obshchestvennoi struktury rannegorodskogo poseleniia Altyn-depe," AO-1971, Moscow, 1972; Ekonomika i sotsial'nyi stroi drevnikh obshchestv, Leningrad, 1976; V. M. Masson and V. I. Sarianidi, Sredneaziatskaia terrakota epokhi bronzy, Moscow, 1973; A. Ia. Shchetenko, "O torgovykh putiakh epokhi bronzy po materialam turkmenistano-kharappskikh parallelei," KSIA, AN USSR, 1970, no. 122; I. S. Masimov, Keramicheskoe proizvodstvo epokhi bronzy v Iuzhnom Turkmenistane, Ashkhabad, 1976.
2. E. Huntington, "Description of the Merv Oasis," in R. Pumpelly, ed., Excavations in Turkestan, vol. 1, Washington, 1908, pp. 219-31; D. D. Bukinich, "Istoriia pervobytnogo oroshaemogo zemledeliia Zakaspiiskoi oblasti," Khlopkovoe delo, 1924, no. 5, p. 98; S. A. Ershov, "Arkheologiia v Turkmenskoi SSR za 20 let," Izv. Turkm. FAN SSSR, 1944, no. 2-3, p. 32.
3. M. E. Masson, "Kratkaia khronika polevykh rabot IuTAKE za 1948-1952 gg.," TIuTAKE, vol. 5, 1955.
4. V. M. Masson, "Drevnemargianskoe poselenie Iaz-depe," Izv. AN Turkm-SSR, 1955, no. 3; "Poseleniia pozdnei bronzy i rannego zheleza v del'te Murgaba," KSIIMK, 1956, no. 64; "Izuchenie drevnezemledel'cheskikh poselenii v del'te Murgaba," Izv. AN TurkmSSR, 1956, no. 2; V. I. Sarianidi, "Keramicheskie pechi drevnei Margiany," KSIIMK, 1957, no. 69.

Bronze Age Sites in the Lower Murghab

5. V. M. Masson, "Drevnezemledel'cheskaia kul'tura Margiany," MIA, 1959, no. 23.

6. V. I. Sarianidi, "Drevnosti nizov'ev Murgaba," AO-1972, Moscow, 1973.

7. V. I. Sarianidi, "Novye otkrytiia v nizov'iakh Murgaba," AO-1974, Moscow, 1975.

8. The division was composed of the following members: I. S. Masimov, director; archaeologists A. A. Marushshenko, V. N. Pilipko, and G. Gutliev; and engineer-hydrotechnician A. A. Liapin.

9. The word "Kelleli" has geographical significance as a region that is most removed from a cultural zone.

10. I. S. Masimov, "Raskopki keramicheskikh pechei epokhi bronzy na poselenii Altyn-depe," AO-1972, Moscow, 1973; "Izuchenie keramicheskikh pechei epokhi bronzy na poselenii Ulug-depe," KD, 1972, no. 4.

11. The recent work of V. I. Sarianidi at this site has revealed the fortification walls, which were strengthened by semicircular towers. See V. I. Sarianidi, "Drevnosti nizovii Murgaba," AO-1972, Moscow, 1973.

12. V. M. Masson, Drevnezemledel'cheskaia kul'tura Margiany, pp. 12-17, 29.

13. All three soundings at Kelleli 1 utilized the remains of building trenches.

14. Having the opportunity, I express my gratitude to N. M. Ermolova.

15. V. M. Masson, Drevnezemledel'cheskaia kul'tura Margiany, p. 20.

16. Compare Figure 6, 20-23 with pl. XXVI, 1, 6; pl. XXVIII, 5, 7; pl. XXIX, 2, 10, and others, including the shapes of the painted vessels — see Masson, op. cit.

17. V. I. Sarianidi, "Pechati-amulety murgabskogo stilia," SA, 1976, no. 1.

18. V. I. Sarianidi, "Baktriia v epokhu bronzy," p. 65.

19. M. Tosi, "Excavations at Shahr-i Sokhta. Preliminary Report on the Second Campaign," East and West, 1969, no. 3-4, figs. 201-6.

20. V. M. Masson, Raskopki Altyn-depe 1969 g., Ashkhabad, 1970.

21. Ibid., p. 20.

22. E. V. Saiko, "K istorii goncharnogo kruga i razvitiia form keramiki," Dushanbe, 1971; "Tekhnologicheskaia kharakteristika keramiki ravitoi bronzy na Altyn-depe," KD, 1972, no. 4, p. 143.

23. I. S. Masimov, Keramicheskoe proizvodstvo epokhi bronzy, pp. 68-69.

24. Ibid., p. 59, fig. 8, 6, 10; fig. 10, 10; A. F. Ganialin, "Raskopki v 1959-1961 g. na Altyn-depe," SA, 1967, no. 4, p. 216, fig. 7.

25. I. S. Masimov, Keramicheskoe proizvodstvo epokhi bronzy, fig. 8, 4, 5, 7-9; fig. 10, 11, 18; V. M. Masson, "Raskopki Altyn-depe v 1969 g.," fig. 8, 9.

26. V. M. Masson, "Raskopki Altyn-depe v 1969 g.," p. 13, fig. 9, 10.

27. V. M. Masson and V. I. Sarianidi, Sredneaziatskaia terrakota epokhi bronzy, Moscow, 1973.

28. A. F. Ganialin, "Raskopki v 1959-1961 gg. na Altyn-depe," p. 216, fig. 7, 12; I. S. Masimov, Keramicheskoe proizvodstvo epokhi bronzy, p. 62, fig. 10, 15.

29. B. A. Kuftin, "Raboty IuTAKE v 1952 g. po izucheniiu kul'tur Anau," Izv. AN TSSR, ser. obshchestv. nauk, no. 1, Ashkhabad, 1954; "Polevoi otchet o rabote XIV otriada IuTAKE po izucheniiu kul'tury pervobytnoobshchinnikh, osedlozemledel'cheskikh poselenii epokhi medi i bronzy v 1952 g.," TIuTAKE, vol. 7, 1958.

30. V. M. Masson, "Raspisnaia keramika Iuzhnoi Turkmenii po raskopkam B. A. Kuftina," TIuTAKE, vol. 7, Ashkhabad, 1956.

31. I. S. Masimov, "Kompleks keramiki iz raskopa A-I poseleniia Namazga-depe," in Material'naia kul'tura Turkmenistana, no. 2, Ashkhabad, 1974, p. 41, fig. 1.

32. Ibid., pp. 42-52; also see Figures 3 and 4.

33. V. M. Masson and V. I. Sarianidi, Sredneaziatskaia terrakota epokhi bronzy, pp. 173-78.

34. E. Schmidt, Excavations at Tepe Hissar, Philadelphia, 1937, p. 178, pl. XXXVII, H. 5021; p. 182, pl. XLI, H. 3509; pl. XLII, H. 3506, H. 4115.

35. T. Arne, Excavations at Shah-Tepe, Stockholm, 1945, p. 156, no. 1430, 1431; p. 199, pl. LX, fig. 393.

36. R. Mecquenem, "Catalogue de la ceramique peinte Susienne," Memoires de la Mission Archeologique de Perse, vol. 13, Paris 1972, p. 45, pl. XXXII.

37. P. Delougaz, Pottery from the Diyala Region, Oriental Institute Publications, vol. 63, Chicago, 1952, p. 40, C. 634.253; p. 45, C. 634.373.

38. I. T. Kruglikova and V. I. Sarianidi, "Drevnaia Baktriia v svete novykh arkheologicheskikh otkrytii," SA, 1971, no. 4, p. 158; V. I. Sarianidi, "Baktriia v epokhu bronzy," SA, 1974, no. 4, pp. 59-60.

39. A. Askarov, Sapalli-tepe, Tashkent, 1973, pp. 73-81, pls. 15-18, 22.

40. Ibid., p. 75, fig. 3, type III, pls. 16, 2, 9, 10, 13, and others.

41. V. I. Sarianidi, "Baktriia v epokhu bronzy," p. 61, fig. 7, III, type 2B.

42. Ibid., p. 62, fig. 8, XIII, 4.

43. Unfortunately, the fragmentary condition of the ceramics from the Murghab sites — as opposed to the ceramics from Dashli and Sapalli-tepe — does not allow us to make a concrete comparative characterization of the described assemblages, and it also makes it difficult to show their correspondences with materials from other sites.

44. V. I. Sarianidi, "Pechati-amulety Murgabskogo stilia."

45. An impression of a cylinder seal from Tell al-Rimah in Iraq displays a striking similarity to these impressions from the Murghab area. Two pairs of figures are depicted in long garments with hands raised to the sun, which is placed between them in the sky. The space between them is filled with a scene of a battle between a hump-backed bull and a lion, above which is shown a torch-shaped decoration. See B. Parker, "Cylinder Seals from Tell al-Rimah," Iraq, vol. 37, part 1, London, 1975, p. 34, pl. XVII, 43.

46. V. I. Sarianidi, "Baktriia v epokhu bronzy," fig. 1.

47. Ibid.

48. Ibid., p. 67, fig. 12.

49. Ravniny i gory Srednei Azii i Kazakhstana. Geomorfologiia SSSR, Moscow, 1975, p. 37.

50. G. N. Lisitsina, "Istoriia oroshaemogo zemedelia v Iuzhnoi Turkmenii," USA, 1972, no. 1, p. 13; Istoriia oroshaemogo zemledeliia epokhi eneolita na iuge Turkmenii, Moscow, 1965.

51. V. M. Masson, "Obmen i torgovlia v pervobytnuiu epokhu," VI, 1973, no. 1.

52. E. E. Kuz'mina, Metallicheskie izdeliia eneolita i bronzy veka Srednei Azii, Moscow, 1966, p. 87.

CHAPTER **10**

Seal-Amulets of the Murghab Style

V. I. SARIANIDI

In the last few years surface investigations deep in the sands of
the southeastern Karakum Desert, where the ancient delta of the
Murghab River once was located, have led to the discovery of a
large number of previously unknown Bronze Age sites.[1] The settlements are located in several separate oases that are situated along
the branches of the former deltaic fan. Two such oases are particularly interesting: Gonur and Togolok, each of which consists
of a large capital city and several smaller associated centers.
The number of exposed sites, the general form of the culture, and
its broad areal distribution make it possible for us to suggest that
these sites in the lower Murghab represent that ancient land called
in later times, according to the Behistun inscription, "the land of
Margush."

In many respects these discoveries are of prime importance for
the ancient history and archeology of Central Asia. First, it has
been established that the opening up of the Murghab Delta relates
at least to the Middle Bronze Age, when such large sites as Gonur 1
and Togolok 1 were formed; the material culture of these sites
can be dated to the Namazga V period. There is reason to believe
that the first settlers came from the southeastern foothills of the
Kopet Dagh, possibly even from Altyn-depe.

The material culture of these colonies virtually cannot be distinguished from what prevailed in the large urban centers. Even
major settlements, which encompass more than 15 hectares, have
neither fortification walls nor citadels, yet inside them are large

squares that recall in their form the microrelief of such sites as Namazga-depe, Ulug-depe, and Altyn-depe. The ceramics were mostly made on a potter's wheel, and the ceramic kilns themselves were grouped together in a "potters' quarter" that lay beyond the limits of the site. There is a basis for assuming that some of the products of this quarter were prepared as goods for barter with the steppe cultures whose encampments were situated in the immediate environs. One can evaluate the complicated forms of the development of social life on the basis of the stone, ceramic, and compartmented metal seals, some of which depict zoomorphic designs. The continuation of the important local cult tradition (which had already begun in Aeneolithic times) is documented by the large collection of anthropomorphic plastic forms that are identical to those widely distributed in Namazga V settlements in the piedmont zone of the Kopet Dagh.

One can propose that — together with the exodus from the southern Turkmenian metropoli — new tribes from the west penetrated the region sometime in the middle of the second millennium B.C.; the material culture of these tribes corresponds to that known in the literature as Namazga VI. Though possessing a similar culture, these newcomers could be distinguished from the indigenous population in two respects. First, they constructed fortresses with large defensive walls strengthened by military towers. This type of rectangular fortress with towers at its corners had not existed earlier but appeared almost simultaneously in the Murghab Basin (Auchin and Gonur), southern Uzbekistan (Sapalli-tepe), and northern Afghanistan (Dashly 1); such coincidence excludes any possibility of chance. Rather it exhibits regular features that depended on the settling of tribes sharing the same general cultural features. Second, seal-amulets, which were completely unknown before, were discovered on a series of sites in ancient Margiana; these objects are especially interesting for the development of Central Asian glyptic art in the Late Bronze Age. One must mention that all these seal-amulets were found on the surface, although there is no compelling reason to doubt their corresponding antiquity. We note that in these oases there are no later settlements, a fact related to the natural retreat of the Murghab River. For this reason even the Achaemenian settlements are situated much farther to the south.

This fact, plus the indisputable parallels with the glyptic art of the Ancient East cited below, relates these Murghab seal-amulets to the Bronze Age. Strictly speaking, the very term "seal-amulet" is arbitrary; we have no compelling reason to view them as genuine seals. In this respect we express doubt about the accuracy of this designation for Harappan "seals," objects that could have been simple amulets.[2] However, the term "seal-amulets" is completely acceptable for the Murghab finds that interest us, since they were chiefly carved in the form of intaglio designs, a fact that in itself suggests that they were used to produce impressions.

These stone seal-amulets were first made from stone in the form of flat squares or rectangles and then ground with an abrasive, showing in section a flat, lentil shaped or three-edged profile. Next the engraving was cut with a sharp metal instrument; and finally, the last stage consisted of making an aperture through the seal for a cord by drilling holes from both sides, so that in some cases the opposed drill holes did not precisely coincide. Incidentally, we note that a similar technique is still practiced today among stone cutters in Afghanistan.

The Murghab amulets usually have a single aperture drilled along the long axis; in rare instances two holes were drilled in opposite corners of the seal. The engraving was made with deep carvings on both sides of the object in order to produce intaglio representations designed to make impressions; a relief representation or cameo was observed only once. Judging by the character of the engraving, drills, borers, chisels, and cutters could have been used to form the designs — as also was the case in Mesopotamia.[3] Dark or dark-green chlorite was the basic type of stone that was cut, although one amulet depicting a tiger was made from a red steatite or pyrophylite.[4] Anthropomorphic, zoomorphic, and floral designs were represented on the seals; a bird and a scorpion appeared on one example.

After these preliminary observations we turn to the seal-amulets themselves. One of the largest rectangular examples (4.5 × 3.5 × 1.2 cm) was found on the surface of Gonur 1 (Figure 1). The hole, drilled along the long axis, displays clearly observable horizontal grooves probably made by wear from a fine metal wire. The object has a lentil-shaped section; however, the edge of the amulet, which from long use had become jagged and broken, was rubbed and smoothed with an abrasive. As a result, some details of the design that adjoined the edge were partially effaced.

In the center of one side of the amulet (Figure 1, a-d), an apparently male figure with a belt falling across his hip is engraved with deep carvings. The head of the figure is so badly effaced that only the lower part of the face or, more probably, a beard was pre-

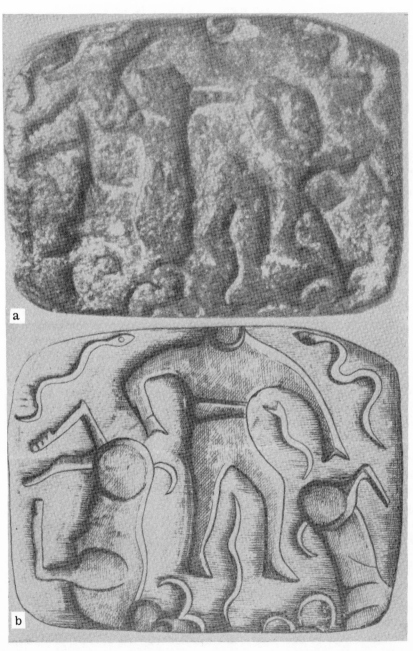

Figure 1. Gonur 1: Seal 1 with depiction of a fighting hero. In figures 1-14 the letters signify: a — photograph of the seal; b — tracing.

Figure 1. <u>c</u> — impression; <u>d</u> — tracing of impression.

served. Both arms of the figure hang down and seem to hold by
the legs two inverted bulls whose forelegs are tucked toward their
stomachs. The back legs are more clearly visible; they are bent
toward the spine and are separated at the end of the tail. The head
of one of the bulls is badly broken, and all that is left is one large
eye and a bent horn; in general the details of both animals repeat
each other. Single coiled snakes are depicted in the open field
above the shoulders of the human figure. A vertical wriggling line
between the legs of the man is not completely clear; but it also can
be considered a snake. In general the whole composition reflects
the theme of the battle and victory of a hero over animals; snakes
in the open field probably function as symbols of the all-conquering
strength and power of the hero.

A large depiction of a bull, which unquestionably occupies the
central position of the entire composition, covers practically the
entire surface of the reverse side of the seal (Figure 2). The carefully modeled, elegant head of the animal has a deeply worked large
eye, and a pair of horns that are widely divided but weakly turned
upward complete the profile of the animal's face. The body of the
bull is smoothly curved and worked with large puffs apparently
representing a woolly cover; the contour of the strong neck is emphasized by a series of small but deeply carved puffs. The long
tail turns energetically downward, and the thin straight legs end
in divided hooves above which appear the articulating joints of the
lower foot. A snake, which is curling into a circle and attaching
itself to the bull's stomach, is depicted between its legs; a vertical,
slightly bent band between the bull's forelegs is not completely
clear. A small figure of a feline, possibly a lion or leopard, is
carved in front of the bull as if attacking it. The feline's face has
a circular eye and open jaws that seem almost aimed against the
head of the bull. The aggressive pose of this predator is completed
by its raised mane and the clearly modeled musculature of its
strong body. It is shown in profile with two legs, the back paws of
which show extended claws. This last detail allows us to identify
the poorly preserved figure carved immediately above the bull's
spine. The upper part of this figure has been completely effaced,
so that all that is preserved is its lower stomach, part of the tail,
and legs, the back paws of which are rendered with extended claws.
This figure is probably another lion that either is shown with a
third leg or had a small snake placed between its legs by the ancient seal cutter.

The second seal (2.8 × 2.5 × 1 cm) with animal representations

Figure 2. Reverse side of seal 1 with depiction of bull and beasts attacking it.

Figure 2. Reverse side of seal 1 with depiction of bull and beasts attacking it.

comes from the settlement of Togolok 13 (Figures 3 and 4). It is made from a dark-green stone and has a rectangular form and a lentil-shaped cross section. On one side (Figure 3 a-d) the figure of a large horned animal, apparently a bull, is deeply cut. The bull's face is depicted with a partially open mouth, a large eye inside of which is carved with a small pupil, a petal-shaped ear, and crescent-shaped horns crowning its head. Its body is smoothly bent, so that its small hump and its croup are emphasized. The tail is not represented because there is no space for it on the seal; the feet have tiny hooves. An opening appears in the middle of the animal's body, which was formed by the incorrect drilling of the suspension hole; apparently such openings were drilled last, after the images had already been carved onto the seal. The same stylistic conventions produced this bull and the one described on the

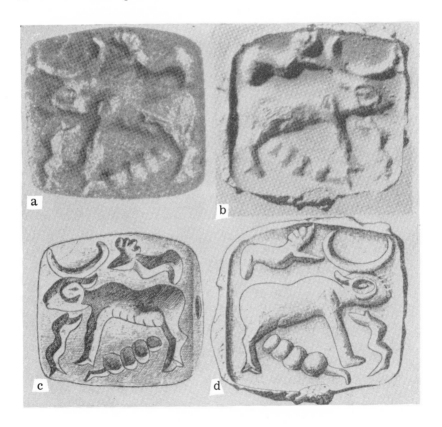

Figure 3. Togolok 13: Seal 2 with depiction of bull, snakes, and dragon.

previous seal. Although the bulls are shown in profile, the horns are twisted frontally. In both cases the bulls are attacked: one by predators and the other by dragons. A twisting dragon with open jaws and three "thorns" on its head in the form of a crown is carved above the bull's back. A second dragon with open jaws and a divided tail is placed vertically before the bull's face; traces of a crown or horns are preserved on its head. A snake twisting itself into a circle and, apparently, suckling the animal is set diagonally between its legs. In general this dramatic scene shows the bull standing peacefully, thoroughly confident, and unshaken in its strength and power before the predatory dragons attacking it.

An animal is also depicted on the back side of seal 2 (Figure 4, a-d), but now in a running pose. Its small head with long, slightly bent horns is thrown back, and its eyes, open mouth, and elongated downward-directed ear are weakly indicated. The body of the ani-

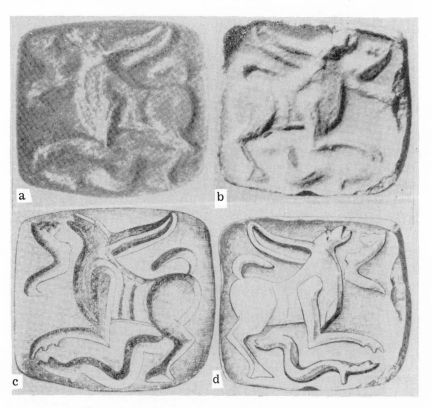

Figure 4. Reverse side of seal 2 with depiction of antelope, snakes, and dragon.

mal has been carved with marvelous mastery. The flexed muscles of the legs seem to play under soft, satiny skin; its small tail is energetically thrown up over its lower back. A dragon with a divided tail and a forcefully curled body is carved in front of its face; details of the dragon's face and legs are barely visible. A second dragon twists under the animal's stomach; the dragon's head is topped with a three-toothed crown, and it stretches toward the animal's back legs. Its strong body ends in a divided and, apparently, crested tail. In general the scene shows a frightened antelope (possibly a gazelle) chased by dragons.

Amulet 3 (1.7 × 1.5 × .5 cm) comes from Togolok 3; it is carved from red steatite and has a square form and a lentil shaped cross section. On one side (Figure 5, a-d) a tiger is shown in profile with a slightly bent striped body and a head with two pricked ears and a turned down muzzle. Extended claws can be seen clearly on only two of its paws, and its long tail is thrown back over its spine. The entire contour of the animal's body has been worked in small

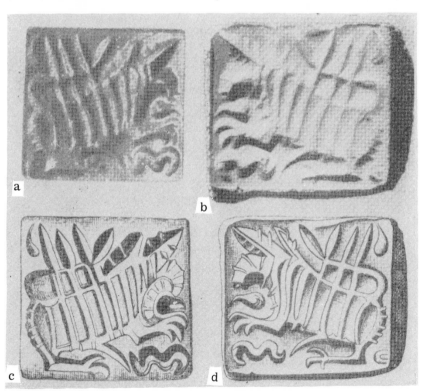

Figure 5. Togolok 3: Seal 3 with depiction of tiger and reeds.

chisel-shaped indentations. Two small depressions were drilled above the animal's tail and behind its back paw; they probably have decorative significance, while the vertical strokes represent reed thickets. Before us is a male tiger with a coiling snake at its belly.

A tiger also is depicted on the back side of the amulet (Figure 6, a-d); this time the tiger has open jaws and a drooping tail that is bent back at the end. Its legs are completed by grasping claws, and a snake is shown wriggling toward it beneath its stomach. Three branches with pointed leaves, possibly representing a sak-saul thicket, are carved in the open space above the animal's back. Also note that the perforated suspension hole was drilled perpendicular to the representation of the tiger.

The next amulet, 4 (2.2 × 2.2 × .6 cm), comes from the Gonur 1 settlement and is distinguished by its unusual rhomboidal shape and crenelated border. It was made from a dark-brown stone and has

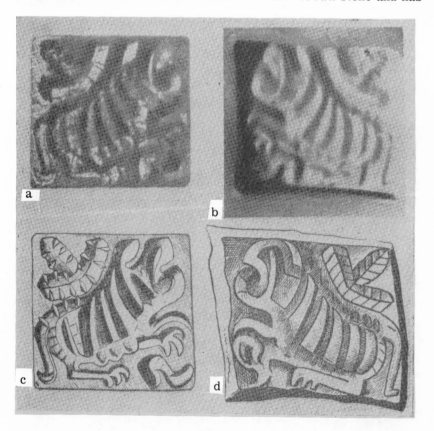

Figure 6. Reverse side of seal 3 with depiction of tiger in bushes.

two (not one) suspension holes drilled in opposite corners of the rhombus; the surface has been greatly effaced through use. A bird, possibly an eagle, is cut on one side (Figure 8, a-d). Its head, with its rapacious beak curved downward, is turned to the right, and its wings and tail are extended below; the bird's plumage is represented by thin fine strokes. On the reverse side (Figure 7, a-d) a "braid" is carved; the bodies of horned reptiles, apparently dragons, are intertwined, with their jaws agape, as if eating one another.

A unique cameo, carved from a dark-green stone that is rectangular in form and lentil-shaped in cross section, comes from the Gonur 1 fortress (Figures 9 and 10). A scorpion is depicted on one side (Figure 9, a-d); at the front of its head two eyes are represented by small circular beads. Four pairs of feet are set accu-

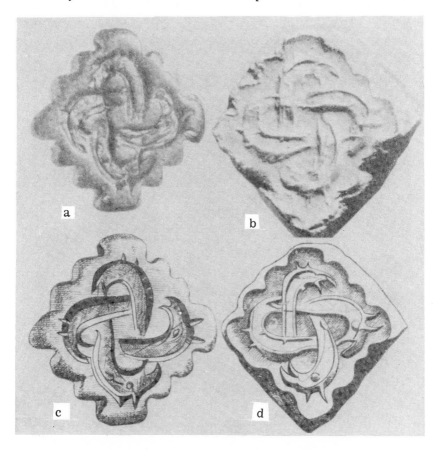

Figure 7. Gonur 1: Seal 4 with depiction of dragons.

rately along its back. Its forelegs are depicted with divided claws, and its small tail is bent to the side. A not altogether clear representation of four pairs of long arcs has been carved on the opposite side of the seal (Figure 10, a-d). The two outside arcs are finished with small but deep punches.

Two amulets from Gonur are decorated with floral motifs. One of them, 6 (Figures 11 and 12), was cut from a green stone; it is almost square in shape, flat in section, and has two holes in its opposed corners. These holes were drilled perpendicular to each other, a fact which perhaps explains why the brittle material was slightly broken precisely at the corner drilled. Branches, apparently representing saksaul, are carved on both sides of the amulet. On one side these branches are made with straight lines, on the

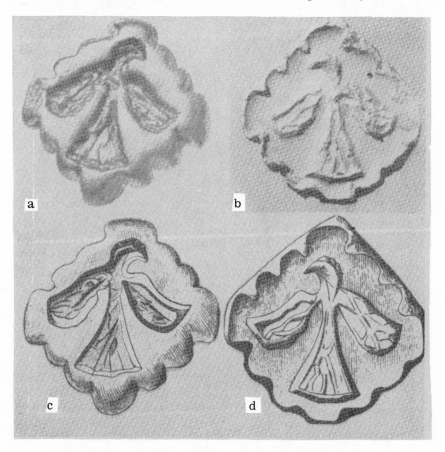

Figure 8. Reverse side of seal 4 with depiction of flying eagle.

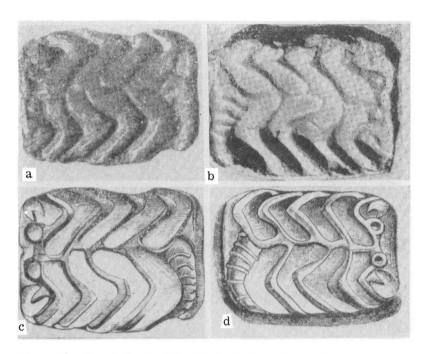

Figure 9. Gonur 1: Seal 5 with depiction of scorpion.

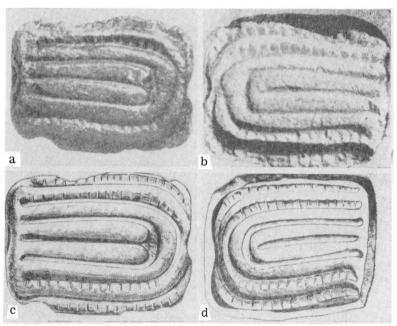

Figure 10. Reverse side of seal 5 with depiction of "ribbons."

235

other they are shown with curved needles. Thus different types of this typical desert plant from the Central Asian steppes are represented.

The second seal amulet, 7 (1.8 × 1.7 × .7 cm), is square with a lentil-shaped cross section and has a suspension hole; it is made from dark steatite. The images, which are carved on both sides, are not completely comprehensible. Not unexpectedly, some type of vegetation is shown on one side (Figure 13, a-d), while a toothed shell (Figure 14, a-d), an ancient symbol of fertility, is represented on the other.

A rectangular seal amulet (8), made from a dark-green stone, comes from Auchin 1. One side is decorated with intersecting lines that end in a border filled with small notches. On the other side triangular notches are inscribed between intersecting lines.

A single example (9), made from a dark-red stone, was found

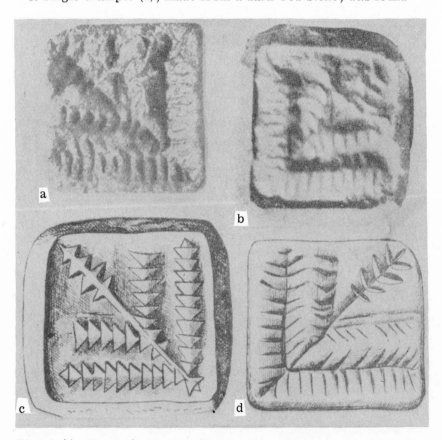

Figure 11. Gonur 1: Seal 6 with depiction of plant.

not on the surface but in a burial at Auchin 1, where it was placed
under the skeleton's mandible. It is so badly effaced that it is difficult to decipher the design. A person standing on a boat with
outspread arms is possibly depicted on the better-preserved side.
It is practically impossible to interpret the other side.

Finally, one circular and one rectangular seal with holes drilled
in their centers come from the surface of the same Auchin 1 settlement. Two mugs or glasses are shown on one side of the circular
seal, 10 (Figure 15, a-b), and a wriggling snake is shown on the
other (Figure 15, c-d). Representations of vegetation, possibly,
are shown on both sides of the rectangular seal (Figure 16, a-d).

These few but unquestionably original seal-amulets occupy a
special place in the corpus of the well-known glyptic artifacts from
southern Turkmenistan. It is true that almost all the representations have parallels in the local painted ceramics from Aeneolithic
times, and it is particularly important to emphasize that the best

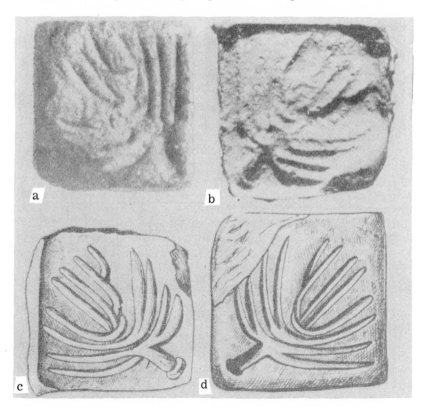

Figure 12. Reverse side of seal 6 with depiction of plant.

analogies are with those painted ceramics of the "Kara-depe style," which itself was formed under the indisputable influence of the ancient ceramic art of Iran. Although the basic representations on the seal-amulets are present on painted ceramics, the genetic connection between these two groups of objects in the south Turkmenian materials has not been established. In fact, geometric designs are most common in Namazga IV and replace the drawings of leopards, goats, birds (including eagles), people, bulls (or cows), and snakes that are typical for Namazga III vessels; these geometric designs, in turn, almost completely disappear in the Namazga V-VI ceramics. Thus a gap of more than 1,000 years separates the designs on the painted ceramics from those on the Murghab amulets; of course, during this period anthropomorphic, zoomorphic, and floral representations occur on nonceramic artifacts, particularly the metal seals of the Late Bronze Age. All this evidence forces us to direct our attention to the ancient Near East, where we can

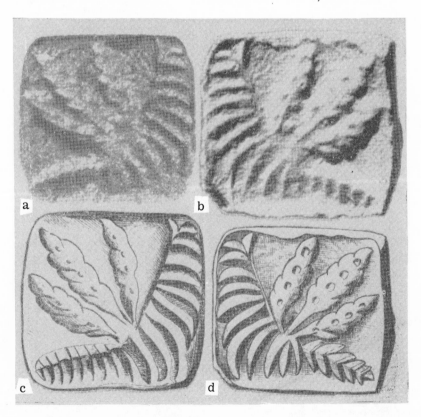

Figure 13. Gonur 1: Seal 7 with depiction of plant.

define several different zones in terms of the development of glyptic art. Thus in Mesopotamia cylinder seals[5] are the most broadly distributed form; on the Indian subcontinent seals of the Harappan civilization[6] are characteristic; and in a great part of Iran, Turkmenistan, and Afghanistan, compartmented stamp seals[7] are the dominant form. The intermediate position, as it were, between these three huge regions was filled with the glyptic art of Susa and southern Iran.[8] To a still greater extent this latter group is related to seals from the Persian Gulf;[9] the unique shapes and, especially, the drawings depicted on them reflect both local and foreign influences from Mesopotamia to the Indus Valley.[10]

A comparison of the Murghab seal-amulets with others from the Middle East shows in general an independent path of origin, but not without the influence of the glyptic art of neighboring lands. For example, the drawings of animals, birds, and reptiles to some ex-

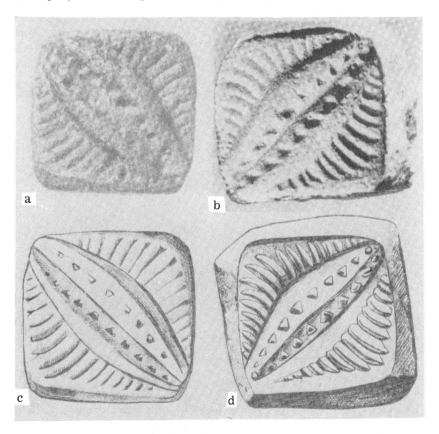

Figure 14. Reverse side of seal 7 with depiction of plant (?).

tent are well known practically throughout the ancient East, a fact ultimately based on the shared nature of the ancient economy and ecology.

In addition, separate stylistic and even iconographic motifs of the Murghab amulets are shared with those from separate zones; this sharing undoubtedly reflects cultural influences. The most important illustration of this is seen on the seal that depicts a battle between a hero and two animals. In itself this theme is a widely distributed subject of the heroic cycle, well known in the histories of religion; in antiquity it is best known from the Sumerian epic Gilgamesh and Enkidu. Both these figures are represented on numerous Mesopotamian cylinder seals where Gilgamesh frequently appears as a naked hero wearing a belt, the ends of which

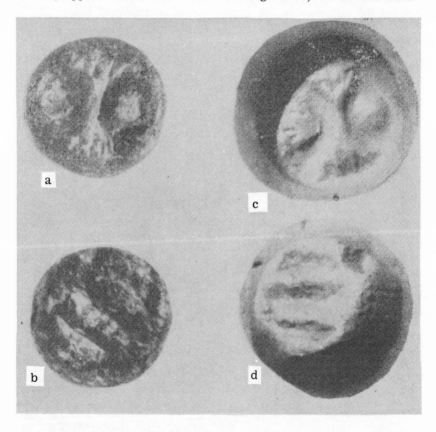

Figure 15. Auchin 1: a — seal 10 with zoomorphic depiction; b — impression; c — reverse side of seal 10 with depiction of snake; d — impression.

fall on his thighs; a horned head and beard complete this general representation.[11] Frequently the figure as well as the face are depicted frontally while the legs are turned in profile.[12] Commonly the hero fights with lions or horned animals standing on their back legs; in those cases when wild bulls are shown, the motif may depict the Elamite version of the epic.[13] As is apparent, the depiction on the Murghab amulet permits no doubt that it is the classic representation in Mesopotamian glyptic art of Gilgamesh. However, we believe it more accurate to speak not only of Mesopotamian but also Iranian iconographic elements in the depiction of this hero. Thus, although this iconographic representation of Gilgamesh can be related to Susiana and tribes of the Uruk culture, this divine figure is still fundamentally Iranian, particularly in those cases where he is shown with snakes. This last circumstance shows that this earliest anthropomorphic divinity was the lord of the animal world and possessed chthonic powers.[14] Moreover, as opposed to in Mesopotamia, in Susiana the motif of the hero-conqueror already existed in the protourban period[15] and continued

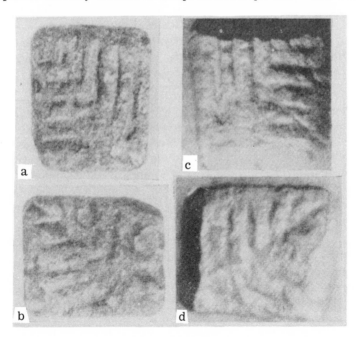

Figure 16. Auchin 1: a — seal 11 with depiction of plant; b — impression; c — reverse side of seal 11 with depiction of plant; d — impression.

until Achaemenian times.[16] All these data provide us a basis for relating the Murghab example to Elamite glyptic. The local treatment of the traditional Mesopotamian iconography is shown by the replacement of the lions with bulls whose heads are directed downward; similarly in the Indus Valley tigers are shown instead of lions.[17] It is true that there exists another opinion asserting the independent nature of this theme in both civilizations,[18] but E. During-Capsers has shown conclusively the movement of this theme, most likely from west to east.[19]

However, the image we have examined most closely relates to the period of Akkadian glyptic, when the motif of the hero, who is the protector of animals, is replaced by the theme of the battle of the powerful, anthropomorphic hero with these animals, i.e., the theme itself changes (A. Moortgat, H. D. Flittner, V. K. Afanas'-eva). Analyses of various scenes on the Akkadian seals show the possibility of relating them to the Gilgamesh epic; sometimes the description in textual sources very closely resembles the scenes depicted on the seals.[20]

Apparently the Murghab seal can be associated with numerous noteworthy examples in sphragistics that are linked with the cult of a hero or "lord of the animals," a theme developed independently among many peoples. However, the image we examined is indisputably linked to the glyptic art of Mesopotamia and Elam. It is perhaps not accidental that on the reverse side of the seal, a powerful figure of a bull is depicted in a peaceful pose despite its being attacked on all sides by predatory beasts. This subject also has sufficiently close analogies to a Sumerian poem, which, significantly, is related to the heroic cycle of tales. In such a case it is not simply a graphic illustration of a generally known poem but a creative elaboration of this theme that is clearly based on local traditional myths, evidence of which is the illustrations of snakes that continually appear on all our seals.

The seals with these heroic motifs presuppose the existence of a separate "heroic period" in the history of the tribes that made them; during such a period small kingdoms formed the basic political units headed by rulers who controlled military units and obedient popular assemblies. Historians of religion assert that it is in such situations that cults of anthropomorphic deities develop, which are attested in Sumer, Greece, and India. To a great extent a similar social formation existed in the Murghab Basin, where several irrigation oases with their own capital centers were clearly differentiated (Gonur 1, Togolok 1, etc.).

The rhomboid amulet (Figures 7 and 8) displays no less significant parallels. Well-known analogies both to its shape and to its design can be drawn in two cases.

One such rhomboidal seal with a drawing of an eagle and a cross comes from Harappa,[21] which presumably has a western, not local, origin.[22] The motif of the eagle is unique in the art of the Indus Valley, while at the same time, the design of the cross is much more broadly distributed, a fact that once again demonstrates its closeness to the southern Turkmenian images. On its reverse side the Murghab example preserves the drawing of an evil "foul knot" or braid consisting of ravenous dragons. This motif has direct parallels to the depiction of intertwined snakes on a cult slab from Elam.[23] A still closer similarity is found on interwoven but primarily horned dragons from Giyan[24] and, to a lesser extent, from Mesopotamia.[25] There is even depicted on one cylinder seal a braid of two snakes.[26] It seems that drawings of pairs of interwoven but extended snakes[27] were decidedly preferred in Mesopotamian art. This image could symbolize the ritual of the "sacred marriage" (Van Buren) or general fertility (Frankfort) and literally could be represented in given instances by the "foul knot." It is thought that this specific drawing is related more to Iranian rather than directly to Mesopotamian art; in this case the Murghab representation — basically showing two snakes with four heads — probably comes from Iran. One must consider that the drawing itself has magical significance; it has neither an end nor a beginning and, in the final analysis, symbolizes the concept of longevity (or immortality). The dragons devour each other — a motif that relates to the philosophical idea of an endless succession. In general the myth in which a god of horrors pursues and devours dragons is widely distributed among Indo-European peoples[28] and is evident on Assyrian cylinder seals.[29] The drawing on the Murghab amulet belongs to this group of similar representations. Accordingly, the theme of dragons devouring each other safeguards the owner of the seal from the vicissitudes of daily life.

In addition to the Harappan and Murghab seals there is another analogous rhomboidal amulet found accidentally at the Bronze Age Dashly Oasis in northern Afghanistan. Although the chronological and culture-historical relations of this find have not been determined, it is thought to relate to the same period as the two amulets described above. It is a flat, indented bronze rhomboid (1.8 × 1.8 × .2 cm) that has two holes in opposite corners (Figure 17, a-d). On one side a tree is depicted in the form of a straight trunk from which lower down sprout two branches with sharp-angled leaves. Above the branches a pair of birds with raised wings and extended legs are shown either landing or taking off. The top of the trunk, possibly a palm, is shaped in the form of a crown with short, fan-shaped branches which spread outward. One of the most difficult symbols to interpret in ancient Near Eastern art is the motif of a "sacred tree." However, on Kassite seals of the second millennium B.C., a tree with a pair of birds sitting on its branches on both sides is depicted very realistically and forms the central axis of the composition. In such cases this motif symbolizes a "sacred tree."[30]

W. Ward proposed that the drawing of the "sacred tree" did not simply represent fertility but a tree that yielded happiness or good

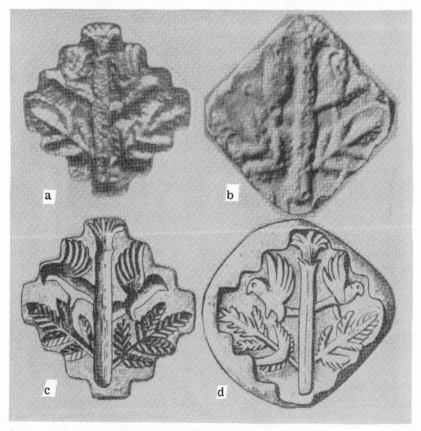

Figure 17. Northern Afghanistan, Dashly Oasis: Metal amulet 12 with depiction of tree and birds: a — amulet; b — tracing; c — impression; d — tracing.

fortune. It is perfectly appropriate to recall the passage in the Avesta that mentions a tree that contains all the collected seeds of vegetation of the world. A bird sitting on the tree peels away its branches while another bird gathers the fallen seeds and throws them to the skies, where they mix with rain, fall back to the earth, and produce new vegetation. One can compare this passage from the Avesta with the depiction on the amulet from northern Afghanistan. The scorpion, in turn, can be identified with the goddess Ishkar (and later Venus) in the Kassite pantheon and is mentioned in astrological texts.

A figure of a two-humped camel in profile occupies the central part of the reverse side of the amulet (Figure 18). It is difficult

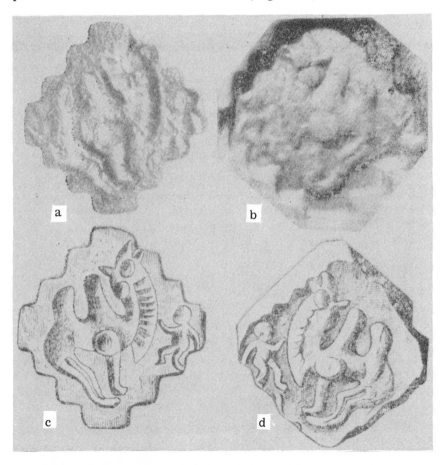

Figure 18. Reverse side of metal amulet 12 with depiction of camel and child: a — a seal; b — tracing; c — impression; d — tracing.

to interpret the small details shown on its head; they probably represent jewelry or, possibly, hair. Its smoothly curved neck has been carved with particular care, and a nude child is placed in front, holding the camel by its rein. The careful, precise modeling of the scene is evident in the tensed muscles of the animal caught in forward motion, it seems, by the tightly stretched rein. Apparently the motif of a camel is practically absent in the glyptic art of Mesopotamia and the Indus Valley, but it is known in Iran from its depiction on a Sialk III vessel, in Turkmenistan from numerous terra-cottas dated to the end of the third millennium, and now from this amulet from northern Afghanistan dated to the second millennium B.C. Moreover, during later periods this animal appears frequently in the Achaemenid art of Iran (e.g., on the reliefs at Persepolis) and in Bactria (on coins and on impressions on vessels).[31] These facts permit us to define an Afghan-Iranian-Turkmenian center in the system of the ancient East where the image of the camel occupied a special place in its cults and myths. In this connection we remember that in the Avesta the ancient cult assumed that the camel was the loftiest animal possessing the greatest strength and power.[32] As is clear, this amulet from northern Afghanistan combines the well-known ancient Near Eastern symbol of a "sacred tree" with the especially local image of the camel, an animal that played a unique role among the eastern Iranian tribes.

Returning to the three amulets mentioned above, we note their identical shape, two suspension holes, and presence of bird representations. Taken as a whole, these resemblances suggest the existence of a common center for their composition.

Indisputably, the Murghab amulet showing scenes of dragons assaulting animals is also quite interesting. The motif of the dragon is common in ancient Eastern art, where it assumes several iconographic forms, such as that having a slightly bent body, a snake's head, and short legs (or sometimes legless), frequently with horns or a crown on its head. A horned, legless dragon with a slightly bent body appears on a cylinder seal from Tell Asmar.[33] In several cases these fantastic beings stand vertically on their tails, resting on their short legs.[34]

We also mention a popular image of the dragon as a winged lion, which to a great extent resembles a creature on a seal amulet from Dashly 1 in northern Afghanistan (Figure 19, 2). In Van Buren's opinion the dragon symbolized fertility, created a sense of awe, and was not hostile to man. However, the Murghab amulets leave the impression that dragons — as opposed to snakes — symbolized

an intensely negative force. In fact, judging by our amulet, the
chief idea represented is a battle between good (animal) and evil
(dragon) principles. There are different variations on this theme.
The peaceful standing bull symbolizes absolute disregard for these
fantastic creatures, while the startled antelope in fear attempts to
free herself from her pursuer. In this respect we note that the
bull played a major role in the myths of the ancient Aryans. In
the Avesta it was the first creation of Ahura Mazda; in the Rigveda
it was the symbol of fire; and apparently, it was not accidental
that the god of war, Indra, is mentioned several times in connection
with a battle with a dragon. One hymn from the Rigveda in which
Indra, "infuriated like a bull," kills a dragon is especially interesting.[35] To a significant extent this theme is present on the Murghab
amulet, with its depiction of the bull and the attacking dragon. The
impression is left that on this seal the bull — as opposed to the
frightened antelope — symbolizes a positive principal that is not
subject to the evil the dragon represents.

In addition to the dragons, the theme of snakes is constantly repeated on the Murghab amulets. They either accompany the figure
of a man (Figure 1) or, more frequently, are attached to the hind
legs of animals (Figures 2-4). Without question this general idea
can be traced on all the amulets with animal representations, but
it is most clearly and unambiguously represented on the amulet
with the male tiger (Figure 5). Snakes, writhing between people or
animals, are a favorite and popular subject of ancient Near Eastern
art, at least in post-Ubaid times,[36] but are almost completely absent in the art of the Harappan civilization, where only single depictions of the cobra are known. Such subjects in ancient Near
Eastern art are distributed unequally. Snakes in scenes with animals are clearly dominant in Iran or, more precisely, the Susiana-
Giyan area, where the theme of an animal and a snake drawing its
body toward the animal is constantly repeated.[37] In connection
with this the opinion was expressed that the moufflon and snake
were sacred animals even for the first inhabitants of Iran and the
Susiana plain.[38] Moreover, in ancient Near Eastern glyptic from
Iran we find scenes similar to those on the Murghab seals. We
have in mind a depiction of a goat with a snake attached to its
stomach[39] from Sialk. The snake appears to be suckling milk
from the nanny.[40]

Similarly, we mention a drawing of snakes turning in a circle
that are attached to the hind legs of goats on a painted vessel from
Hissar that is contemporaneous with the Sialk drawing.[41] We think

that these Hissar-Sialk drawings not only are analogous in general
form but genetically precede the depictions of snakes and animals
on the Murghab seal-amulets. Moreover, the complicated nature
of the semantic themes of these compositions supports this interpretation. Dragons also appear alongside the snakes, and — when
decipherable — male animals are always depicted. Although the
relation to snakes always was two-sided,[42] it seems that on the
Murghab seals, snakes were opposed to dragons and symbolized
a positive principle. In fact, the communal villagers of the ancient
agricultural world instantly recognized the snake as a creature
that disappears, crawling into an underground hole or slipping into
water, and again reappears from either the ground or water. From
their observations the belief easily arises that snakes are linked
to the secret forces of water, which, in turn, flow from the underworld. In the final analysis the snakes become chthonic beings
that bless fertility in general and cultivated plants in particular
(Van Buren). The snake sheds its skin; for many peoples this fact
explains why the snake is a symbol of youth and the prolongation
of life (Frazer). Apparently, similar beliefs were held by North
American Indians who felt that the snake, a god of the sea and
underworld, sometimes appeared in the form of a canoe and brought
happiness to those who saw it.

Still another concept is related to the snake: sexuality. This aspect is seen on the early glyptic from Tepe Gawra[43] and, particularly, on an unambiguous representation on a vessel from Mari.[44]
The above-mentioned concept of the phallic symbolism of the snake
is again related to the idea of fertility.[45] It is thought that both the
Hissar-Sialk and Murghab representations of suckling animals are
equally related to this theme and that the chronological priority of
the Iranian drawings is not accidental; ultimately derived from
simple representations on painted ceramics, the subjects of the
Murghab glyptic took shape and became solidly established. We
also mention that a clearly ritual vessel from Togolok 1 contains
applied snakes that wriggle upward from the vessel's base and end
at the stomachs of sculpted animals moving along its rim. Such
are the firmly established ritual and mythological motifs that are
reflected in many kinds of cult objects of the local tribes.

At present there is still too little data to reveal the semantics
of these representations on Murghab amulets. Nevertheless one
can propose in a general fashion that the reptiles are trying to ab-
duct powerful, possibly supernatural forces that inhere in these
animals. One can recall the tradition in the Avesta in which it is

accepted that vegetation and animals arise out of the body and
semen of the bull. It is true that on our seals, tigers and ante-
lopes are represented as well; in all cases, however, there appears the theme of the acquisition (or kidnapping) of animal semen
as a symbol of supernatural power, linked ultimately to fertility in
its chthonic aspect.

The depiction of the scorpion (Figure 9) is apparently also related to the general concept of fertility. Scorpions appear in
erotic scenes on Mesopotamian seals,[46] suggesting a relationship
with human fertility. Scorpion representations are well known
both in northern[47] and southern[48] Iran and are completely absent
in the art of the Indus Valley;[49] their first depiction in Turkmenistan appears on the Murghab seals. Recently, a representation of
a scorpion, engraved on an amulet with a triangular profile (Figure 19, 1), was found at the Dashly 1 settlement; in this case the
specific shape of the triangular prism, which is also known at
Anau,[50] is especially interesting. It seems that seals of such a
shape were found neither in Elam nor in Mesopotamia and that
their current distribution is bounded within an Afghan-Turkmen
geographical area which, in all likelihood, will be extended in the
future to include regions of ancient Iran.

Finally, there are amulets with drawings presumably of the very
typical, if not identical, type of saksaul, the green branches of
which symbolize the continuity of life amid the dead, scorched surface of the desert. There is a saying among the Turkmen even
today when one addresses childless parents: "May you have as
many sons as there are saksaul in the sands." On the occasion of
the birth of a first born, they give the child one of the names of
the different types of saksaul (cherkez, gandim, adzhar, sazak,
suzen). In our case an aspect of fertility is present. If it is assumed that identical geographical conditions define similar ways
of life (producing similar beliefs), then one can suggest the close
semantic significance of these phytomorphic representations on
the Murghab amulets.

Such are our preliminary conclusions on these seal-amulets
that were used by local tribes in the Late Bronze Age. Having
described the definite stylistic and iconographic parallels in ancient Near Eastern glyptic, we must conclude in general that the
seal-amulets of the Murghab style have still found no direct analogies. The seals of the Jhukar Culture of the Indus Valley provide
a possible exception to this generalization. The origin of this
post-Harappan culture in many respects is still unclear: some

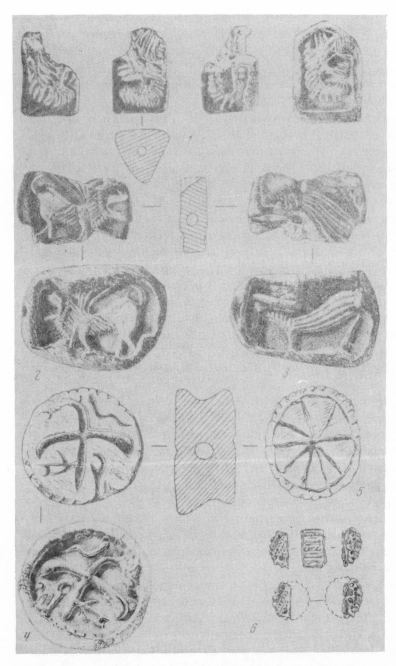

Figure 19. Dashly 1 and 6: 1 — stone prismatic seal 13 with depiction of scorpions and impression; 2 — stone seal 14 with depiction of winged lion and impression; 3 — re-

authors define it as a late, degenerate Harappan culture (W. Fair-servis, J. Casal), while others view it as a completely new, alien culture (S. Piggot, K. Dikshit). But regardless, all scholars concur that the seals of the Jhukar Culture differ sharply from those of the Harappan period and originate in the west.[51] The most complete collection of these seals comes from levels of the Jhukar Culture at Chanhu-daro II. These clay or stone seals have a circular or oval shape with a transverse hole or a raised handle on their reverse side. Representations, predominantly in the form of simple geometric designs and, more rarely, animals, are engraved on one or both surfaces.[52] According to E. Mackay, the seal-amulets of the Jhukar Culture most closely resemble archaic Elamite seals which, however, are at least 1,000 years older. On the other hand, both in their shapes and designs these seals share a great deal with the so-called Hittite seals. It is further suggested that there can occur in Elamite art a reappearance of ancient shapes and designs on seals which, most probably, have a western origin; the seals of the Jhukar Culture may come from such a source.[53]

When one compares the Murghab and Chanhu-daro seal-amulets, it is impossible to find direct analogies. However, indirect features point to a common origin. We note that among other finds from the Murghab delta there occur stone and ceramic seals with handles on the reverse side that are circular, square, or rectangular in shape and decorated with simple geometric designs; they provide sufficiently close analogies to the seal-amulets from Chanhu-daro.[54] On the other hand, amulets without handles but with holes for hanging are known at this time only from the Indus Valley, southern Turkmenistan, northern Afghanistan, and Susiana. We also note similar Indian representations, for example, a "braid" design; this motif was so rare that E. Mackay unhesitatingly asserted that an amulet with such a representation was an import from the Susiana plain.[55] One must particularly note an Indian amulet[56] with a drawing of a bird resembling an eagle,[57] a close analogue to which (both in shape and the fact that it has representations on both sides) exists in northern Afghanistan (Figure 19, 4). The drawings of birds on both these amulets are finished very schematically, so that it is difficult to interpret individual details,

---

verse side of seal 14 with zoomorphic depiction and impression; 4 — seal 15 with depiction of bird and impression; 5 — seal 15 from reverse side; 6 — seal 16 from Dashly 6 and impression.

such as their talons. A snake is drawn in the field on the Afghan
seal that is not duplicated on the Indian example. However, the
general treatment of this "eagle" was such that Mackay called it
a drawing of three snakes.[58] Snakes are shown under the wings of
an eagle on an amulet from Harappa.[59] It is very obvious that
there were iconographic parallels between the glyptic art of the
Indus Valley and that of Afghanistan and Turkmenistan at the end
of the second millennium B.C.

Thus one can consider established the fact that the Jhukar seals
and the seals of the Murghab style, including those from northern
Afghanistan, originated in the west, with a probable center in Susiana. Less clear are the parallels with the so-called Hittite
glyptic of northern Syria, where cylinder seals of a Mesopotamian
type were distributed in the third millennium and were replaced
in a later period by seal-amulets with local designs[60] that were
analogous to the Indian, Afghan, and Turkmen seal-amulets. We
believe that these parallels have a more formal character and
primarily reflect an identical but independent stage in the development of glyptic art, which throughout the ancient Near East began
with the so-called button seals. But as was shown above, both the
seal-amulets from the Indus Valley and those from the Murghab
Delta were sharply different from the local products of the preceding period and thus were connected with the spread of new
tribes (the Namazga VI archeological complex) from a general,
most probably ancient Iranian center.[61]

Not basing ourselves strictly on archeological sources, we note
that together with the distribution of new types of seals, the practice of making anthropomorphic figurines completely disappears
both in the Indus Valley[62] and in southern Turkmenia;[63] this disappearance undoubtedly reflects changes in the ideological beliefs
of the local population. We note that many authors see in the bearers of the Jhukar Culture the advent of new Indo-European tribes
on the Indian subcontinent and consider the seals from Chanhu-
daro one of the important indicators of this Aryan invasion.[64] In
the absence of new written sources, the question of an "Aryan invasion" will long remain a subject of great controversy, and of
course, the appearance of new types of seals, pins, or shaft-hole
axes in no way solves the entire problem.

We have attempted to show above that the Murghab seals in general are related to a fertility cult, and if that is so, there were
clear changes in cult practice while general concepts were preserved. In this respect it is interesting that a vast mound, com-

posed of a compact ash pit set on virgin soil, abutted the Gonur 1 fortress. It is not unlikely that this "sacrificial site" reflected the distribution of new types of cult practices and was associated with the appearance of the seal-amulets of the Murghab style. One must particularly note that stone and, more importantly, compartmented metal seals, which had a distinctly "secular" character and belonged basically to merchant traders, were distributed along with the seal-amulets.

Notes

1. V. I. Sarianidi, "Drevnosti nizovii Murgaba," AO-1972, Moscow, 1973; V. I. Sarianidi, "Novye otkrytiia v del'te r. Murgaba," AO-1974, Moscow, 1975.
2. J. Marshall, Mohenjo Daro and the Indus Civilization, London, 1931, p. 379.
3. H. Frankfort, Cylinder Seals, London, 1939, p. 5.
4. The determination was made in the Mineralogical Museum, USSR Academy of Sciences.
5. P. Amiet, La Glyptique Mesopotamienne Archaique, Paris, 1958; H. Frankfort, Cylinder Seals, London, 1939.
6. J. Marshall, Mohenjo-Daro and the Indus Civilization, London, 1931; Iren Gajjar, Ancient Indian Art and the West, Bombay, 1971.
7. S. Piggott, "Dating the Hissar Sequence — the Indian Evidence," Antiquity, XVII, 1943, p. 179.
8. P. Amiet, Elam, Paris, 1966; C. C. Lamberg-Karlovsky and M. Tosi, "Shahr-i Sokhta and Tepe Yahya: Tracks on the Earliest History of the Iranian Plateau," East and West, 21, 1973.
9. S. R. Rao, "A 'Persian Gulf' Seal from Lothal," Antiquity, XXXVII, 1963, p. 96; G. Bibby, "Arabian Gulf Archaeology," KUML, 1966, fig. 4.
10. E. Porada, "Remarks on Seals Found in the Gulf States," in Some Results of the Third International Conference on Asian Archaeology in Bahrain, Artibus Asiae, vol. XXXIII, 4, pp. 331-37.
11. H. Frankfort, Cylinder Seals, pp. X, XI, XIII, XIV.
12. E. During-Caspers, "Some Motifs as Evidence for Maritime Contact between Sumer and the Indus Valley," Persica, V, 1970-71, p. 111.
13. M. F. Williams, "The Collection of Western Asiatic Seals in the Haskell Oriental Museum," The American Journal of Semitic Languages and Literatures, XLIV, 4, Chicago, 1928, p. 233.
14. P. Amiet, La Glyptique Mesopotamienne Archaique, pp. 72-73.
15. P. Amiet, Elam, p. 58; E. During-Caspers, "Some Motifs," p. 111.
16. E. Porada, The Collection of the Pierpont Morgan Library, New York, 1948, pl. CXXIV, no. 824, 825.
17. E. Mackay, Early Indus Civilization, London, 1948, p. 67.
18. M. Wheeler, The Indus Civilization, Cambridge, 1968, p. 135.
19. E. During-Caspers, "Some Motifs," p. 112.
20. V. K. Afanas'eva, "Mifologiia i epos v sumero-akkadskoi gliptike," abstract of candidate's dissertation, Leningrad, 1965, p. 14.
21. M. C. Vats, Excavations at Harappa, Calcutta, 1940.

V. I. Sarianidi

22. M. Wheeler, The Indus Civilization, p. 103.

23. P. Amiet, Elam, p. 173, pl. 124.

24. P. Amiet, La Glyptique Mesopotamienne, pl. 7, no. 148.

25. L. Legrain, Ur Excavations, III, Oxford, 1963, pl. 29.

26. E. Douglas Van Buren, Symbols of the Gods in Mesopotamian Art, Rome, 1945, p. 40.

27. P. Amiet, La Glyptique, pp. 134-35.

28. V. V. Ivanov and V. N. Toporov, Issledovaniia v oblasti slavianskikh drevnostei, Moscow, 1974.

29. P. Amiet, "Un vase ritual Iranien," Syria, LXII, fasc. 3, 4, 1965, p. 243.

30. E. Van Buren, Symbols of the Gods, p. 25.

31. M. M. D'iakonov, "Arkeologicheskie raboty v nizhnem techenii reki Kafirnigan," MIA, 37, 1953.

32. For more detail see E. E. Kuz'mina, "Drevneishaia figurka verbliuda iz Orenburgskoi oblasti i problema domestikatsii baktriianov," SA, 1963, 2, p. 43.

33. E. Van Buren, "The Dragon in Ancient Mesopotamia," Orientalia, vol. 15, fasc. 1-2, Rome, 1946, pl. II, fig. 10.

34. Ibid., pl. I, fig. 4.

35. Rigveda, Selected Hymns, Moscow, 1972, p. 111.

36. P. Amiet, La Glyptique Mesopotamienne Archaique; H. Frankfort, Cylinder Seals; E. Douglas Van Buren, "Entwined Serpents," Archiv für Orientforschung, vol. 10, Berlin, 1935-36, pp. 54-56; Andre Parrot, Glyptique Mesopotamienne, Paris, 1954; G. Contenau, La Glyptique Syro-Hittite, Paris, 1922.

37. P. Amiet, La Glyptique, pl. 4, nos. 95, 98; P. Amiet, Elam, p. 270, fig. 200; compare also M. Tosi and R. Wardak, "The Fullol Hoard: A New Find from Bronze Age Afghanistan," East and West, 22, Rome, 1972, pp. 9-17.

38. P. Amiet, Elam, p. 28.

39. R. Ghirshman, Fouilles de Sialk, Paris, 1938, vol. I, pl. LXV, no. 121.

40. P. Amiet, La Glyptique, p. 134.

41. E. Schmidt, Excavations at Tepe Hissar, Philadelphia, 1937, pl. V.

42. P. M. Kozhin and V. I. Sarianidi, "Zmeia v kul'tovoi simbolike anauskikh plemen," in Istoriia, arkheologiia i etnografiia Srednei Azii," Moscow, 1968, pp. 35-40.

43. A. Toblet, Excavations at Tepe Gawra, vol. II, pl. CLXVIII, 87, pl. LVIII, 41.

44. A. Parrot, "Les Fouilles de Mari," Syria, vol. XXX, 1953, p. 203, fig. 4.

45. P. Amiet, La Glyptique, p. 134.

46. L. Legrain, Ur Excavations, vol. III, pl. 18, pp. 48-50.

47. E. Schmidt, Excavations at Tepe Hissar, fig. 118, H-2698.

48. C. C. Lamberg-Karlovsky and M. Tosi, "Shahr-i Sokhta and Tepe Yahya," figs. 1 and 121.

49. M. Wheeler, The Indus Civilization, p. 103.

50. R. Pumpelly, Explorations in Turkestan, Washington, 1908, p. 169, no. 400. A similar form is also found in the glyptic art of Crete among the socalled Hittite seals; however, this similarity is considered to be strictly formal. See E. Schmidt, "Archaeological Excavations in Anau and Old Merv," in R. Pumpelly, op. cit., p. 182. We also mention three ceramic and faience prisms identified as impressions that show, however, typical Indian motifs of the Harappan civilization. J. Marshall, Mohenjo Daro, pl. CXVIII, 9, 10, 12.

51. K. N. Dikshit, "Harappa Culture and Its Aftermath," Archeocivilization, 3, 4, Paris, 1967, pp. 28-29.

52. E. Mackay, Chanhu-Daro Excavations, New Haven, 1943, pp. 140-44, pl. XLIX, L.

53. Ibid., p. 144.
54. Ibid., pl. XLIX, 6, 14, 15.
55. Ibid., p. 144, pl. L, 4.
56. Ibid., pl. L, 15 and 15a.
57. M. Wheeler, The Indus Civilization, p. 103.
58. E. Mackay, Chanhu-Daro, p. 142.
59. M. Wheeler, The Indus Civilization, p. 103.
60. D. G. Hogarth, Hittite Seals, Oxford, 1930, p. 103.
61. V. I. Sarianidi, "Baktriia v epokhu bronzy," SA, 1974, 4.
62. E. Mackay, Chanhu-Daro, p. 151.
63. V. M. Masson and V. I. Sarianidi, Sredneaziatskaia terrakota epokhi bronzy, Moscow, 1973.
64. R. Heine-Geldern, "The Coming of the Aryans and the End of the Harappa Civilization," Man, October, 1956, vol. LVI, p. 138.

CHAPTER 11

Southern Uzbekistan in the Second Millennium B. C.

A. A. ASKAROV

One of the great successes of archeological investigations in southern Uzbekistan in the years of Soviet power has been the clear documentation of this area's extensive occupation and utilization in the Stone Age, the Kushan epoch, and later periods. However, the history of the entire period from the Stone Age to the appearance of early class societies in later times represented a major gap in the history of ancient Bactria, a lacuna that caused major difficulties in the study of the sources and genesis of archaic and classical cultures in general. The opinion was advanced that ancient Bactria was a mirage, that there were no earlier periods for the local development of the highly advanced urban culture of Bactria.[1] This view associated the later flowering with the activities of another civilization, specifically, the Persian conquest of the Achaemenian empire.

In the last ten years the remarkable discoveries of Uzbek archeologists in northern Bactria and their Moscow colleagues in association with Afghan archeologists in southern Bactria have disproved this earlier view and demonstrated — on the basis of substantial archeological materials — the formation in Bactria of highly developed societies of the ancient Near Eastern type in the Bronze Age.[2]

In the last few years excavations and surveys have revealed the existence of numerous settlements relating to two chronologically distinct archeological cultures: Sapalli and Kuchuk-tepe. The first culture was documented by large-scale investigations of such sites as Sapalli-tepe, Djarkutan, Bustan, and Molali and associated cemeteries, making a total of thirteen sites; the second was confirmed by excavations at the settlements of Kuchuk-tepe, Mirshade, and Bandykhan 1 (Figure 1).

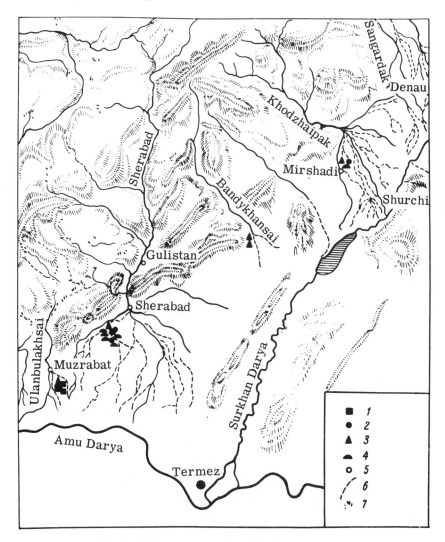

Figure 1. Schematic map of sites in southern Uzbekistan. Legend: 1 — sites of the Sapalli and Djarkutan stages; 2 — sites of the Molali stage; 3 — sites of painted ceramic cultures of the Late Bronze Age; 4 — cemeteries of the Sapalli Culture; 5 — contemporary settlements; 6 — dry river courses; 7 — salt marshes.

The systematic excavations of the settlement at Sapalli-tepe and its associated burials and the work on the cemetery at Djarkutan have allowed us to define the new Sapalli Culture, which on the basis of its archeological materials appears as a highly developed culture of the ancient Near Eastern type. This culture is related genetically to the early agricultural Namazga settlements located in the piedmont belt of southern Turkmenia.

The settlement at Sapalli-tepe occupies an area of about 4 hectares. Its center forms a square fortress 82 × 82 meters. Its fortification system is composed of rectangular walls around which are located eight corridor-shaped rooms. The spaces between the walls and the corridors form their own T-shaped corridors, which probably acted as false entrances to the fortress. The surrounding rooms behind the encircling wall are divided in two on each side of the square fortress, and the T-shaped corridors are formed by its corners and by the center of each of the sides (Figure 2).

The carefully recorded stratigraphy allows us to trace clearly the dynamics of construction within the fortifications and define three building periods. First, the entire fortification system was built along with a significant number of residential and utilitarian rooms that formed eight separate quarters. The living areas were divided by narrow streets and consisted of multiroomed economic and residential complexes that were square in shape. There were thirty domestic hearths in the first horizon.

During the second period open parts of the separate residential quarters and a series of other rooms and T-shaped corridors were developed intensively. According to the number of hearths, the living quarters during this period doubled, and the square layout of the settlement assumed its final complete architectural form.

A decline in occupation was observed during the third period. Some residential areas were abandoned — the number decreasing from sixty-one living rooms in the second phase to forty-seven in the third. This decline can be explained by the fact that a significant number of the inhabitants moved upstream along the middle course of the Bustansai in the vicinity of Djarkutan, where a large number of sites of this period, such as Djarkutan and Bustan, have been discovered. We will discuss these sites below.

The stratigraphic determinations made during the excavations at Sapalli-tepe show that the general plan of the fortress and its architectural design relate specifically to the first period, when the walls and surrounding rooms acted as a fortification system. The constructions of the residential quarters followed their own separate plans.

Each residential area had a fireplace and chimney built into the wall. Heating sandali-ovens in the living rooms and tandyrs, or

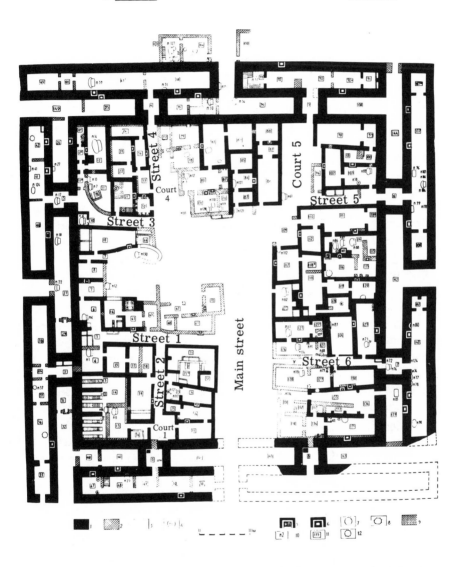

Figure 2. Plan of the remains of residential areas and fortification systems at Sapalli-tepe. Legend: 1 — walls of the first building period; 2 — walls of the second building period; 3 — internal partitions; 4 — storage jar; 5 — ceramic kiln; 6 — hearth of stones; 7 — bread oven; 8 — household pit; 9 — storage area of raw clay for pottery manufacture.

baking ovens, are also encountered. Pottery making was the most
common activity; for this type of production ceramic kilns were
the most important feature. Eighteen ceramic kilns, including two-
tiered, two-chambered, and one-chambered–combined types, were
excavated at Sapalli-tepe. The working area of the kiln was small,
not exceeding 1 sq m per section. Each quarter had its own kiln
for firing vessels and represented a single, large patriarchal
household consisting of several nuclear families. The number of
kilns in each quarter depended on the number of inhabitants. Finely
made vessels of different shapes, which attest to the professional
standards of ceramic production, were fired in these kilns.

It is noteworthy that 138 graves were uncovered during the excavations at Sapalli-tepe; they were situated under the floors of
the residential quarters and surrounding rooms and under the
streets and corridors. The majority of them contained numerous
clay and metal vessels, wooden plates, skins, straw, and matting.
The metal objects included jewelry, toilet articles, tools, weapons,
and objects of ritual significance, such as seal-emblems. Also
found were beads fashioned from semiprecious stones and the like.
It is worth noting that the remains of dried food were preserved
in many vessels from the graves.

Great significance is also attached to the excavations of the cemetery at Djarkutan, where over 700 graves have been uncovered.
Many of the Djarkutan burials have yielded rich materials: ceramics, metal objects, and stone beads. On the basis of the material
inventory of the graves, one can divide the remains at Djarkutan
into two chronological stages.*

In general, the excavations at the settlement of Sapalli-tepe and
the cemetery of Djarkutan have yielded both quantitatively and
qualitatively rich archeological materials that permit us to trace
the dynamics of cultural development for several centuries in the
second millennium B.C. In addition, supplementary materials
were recovered from the cemeteries of Molali and Bustan.

The analysis of all the archeological materials from this site
allows us to characterize precisely the Sapalli Culture and divide
it into the following three chronological periods. Materials from
the two lowest building horizons at Sapalli-tepe and corresponding
materials from the graves define the earliest stage, which we shall

---

*The chronological sequence at Djarkutan has been further sub-
divided into three stages by B. Abdullaev, who has recently completed his candidate's dissertation on this material. — P.L.K.

refer to as the Sapalli period. The remains from the upper building level at Sapalli-tepe and corresponding burial goods and materials from the cemetery and settlement at Djarkutan make up the subsequent Djarkutan period. And materials from the latest graves and final settlement at Djarkutan and from the cemeteries at Bustan and Molali characterize the final period.

Chronological distinctions are traced in the topography of the graves, the burial ceremony, and the orientation of the skeletons. During the Sapalli stage burials were placed inside the settlement under the floors of the living areas. At the end of the Sapalli period the burials began to be placed in the ruins of abandoned houses. The skeletons were put in the northwestern parts of the burial pits, and the goods were situated in the eastern and southeastern halfs of the graves. Burials also were found in storage jars and large pots. The dominant orientation of the burials was to the north (Figure 3).

A whole series of different practices was observed for the Djarkutan period. The cemetery was situated outside the settlement, and the burials most often had a northeastern or northwestern orientation; the skeletons typically occupied the northern half of the pit, and the grave goods, the southern portion. The custom of burying the dead in storage jars or pots, which was characteristic of the Sapalli period, disappeared during the subsequent Djarkutan period.

The changes in the Molali period are even more clearly delineated: the dominant orientation of the skeletons now shifted to the east and west, and the northern, northeastern, and northwestern orientation disappeared. Isolated instances of cremation now appeared for the first time. In the earlier periods the burial goods were numerous, sometimes consisting of over fifty objects, which included thirty ceramic vessels; such abundance was not observed for the Molali period. During this final period bronze objects had an exclusively votive character, while during the Sapalli and Djarkutan periods the graves contained household and utilitarian metal artifacts as well as weapons.

Handmade and wheel-thrown ceramics occur in all periods, but the number of the former was always limited, never exceeding 5 percent of the ceramic assemblage. Both in their preparation and firing, the wheel-thrown ceramics were distinguished by the high standards of craft production. Vases and goblets with long stems, conical vessels of different shapes, pots and earthenware jugs, small and large jars, teapots and cups with spouts, and cooking cauldrons and frying pans were typical forms in these assemblages.

The ceramics of the Sapalli Culture have no surface decorations; they are characterized by clinky, thin walls and beautiful shapes that attest to the professional competence of the artisans who made them (Figure 4). Most of the ceramics were made from red clays, although occasional graywares with similar shapes and technical characteristics also occur. During the Djarkutan period the ceramics became rougher; frequently their shapes were less stable or standardized. The sherds had a reddish-rose color and were fragile, and the vessels were large, heavy, and thick-walled. However, during the final period of the Sapalli Culture the glory of the

Figure 3. Burial 74 from Sapalli-tepe.

potters' art returned. In the Molali period the types of ceramics were somewhat reduced. All the conical-shaped vessels, pots, small jars, stemmed goblets, and flat food trays disappeared from use.

Figure 4. Ceramics from Burial 2 at Sapalli-tepe.

This chronological breakdown of sites of the Sapalli Culture also can be observed in the organization of ceramic production. Thus in the Sapalli period the making of ceramic vessels was still a household activity. Each large extended family had its own kilns for firing vessels, and these kilns were situated within each residential quarter. In the Djarkutan period we discern a completely new picture, with a concentration of ceramic kilns in one section of the settlement. Thus at the site of Bustan 3 six two-chambered kilns, unlike those at Sapalli-tepe, were excavated. All the furnaces and their heating vents were excellently preserved; in three cases firing chambers with a high-columned construction were also uncovered. All these kilns were large and circular in shape, with diameters from 1.5 to 3 m. The proximity of a large number of kilns in one area demonstrates the specialization of ceramic production, including the preparation of commodities or vessels for exchange (Figure 5).

The large-scale excavations of sites of the Sapalli Culture not only have yielded a large number of high-quality works of ceramic art but also have uncovered objects of metallurgical production

Figure 5a. Two-chambered ceramic kiln from Bustan 3.

Figure 5b. Two-chambered ceramic kiln from Bustan 3.

(Figure 6). Thus during the excavations of the settlement and the graves of Sapalli-tepe, more than 200 metal objects were found, including knives, axes, chisels, knitting hooks, needles, pins, awls, mirrors, surmadony, small shovels, toggle-pins, bracelets, earrings, arrowheads, spears, seals, and the like. A considerable number of stone and flint tools were also discovered. Wooden and bone objects, mat and straw baskets, and parts of woollen and silk dresses were also found in the graves (Figure 7).

The broad investigations that have been conducted over the past few years have also shed light on sites from southern Uzbekistan dating to the following periods: the Late Bronze and Early Iron Ages. Excavations at the settlements of Kuchuk-tepe, Mirshade, and Bandykhan 1 have yielded excellently preserved architectural plans of houses and hand-made ceramics with archaic shapes that are completely unlike those of the Sapalli Culture. These remains are assigned to the Kuchuk-tepe Culture, a name derived from the most thoroughly investigated site of this period. The Kuchuk-tepe peoples created their own distinctive culture with its own specific ethnic form; one cannot view this culture as a direct continuation of the Sapalli tradition (Figure 8). They did not continue the basic

Figure 6. Bronze pins from graves at Sapalli-tepe.

line of cultural and economic development from the preceding period, and their archaic handmade vessels seem to recall the an-

Figure 7. Objects of bronze, marble, wood, and straw from graves at Sapalli-tepe.

cient traditions of Neolithic times. However, agriculture in no way lost its leading role in the economy, as also was true for pastoralism.[3]

The data characterizing this culture show the combination of ancient local traditions with new elements brought by tribes from the steppes at the end of the second millennium B.C.

Excavations at Kuchuk-tepe have shown that the central fortified houses were erected on an artificial platform, a feature not present in the architecture of the Sapalli Culture. Four building periods were uncovered at Kuchuk-tepe in its Bronze Age levels; three of these can be dated to the Late Bronze Age, and the fourth, to the transition to the Early Iron Age. The construction of a fortified residential core area erected on a thick, 4 m high platform and surrounded by walls was utilized even during the first period. In the following period this platform was widened, and a second fortification wall was constructed parallel to the first; after some time had elapsed a third wall with semicircular towers was built beyond the double fortification wall. A broad corridor, which subsequently was used as a living area, was formed between the second and third fortification walls. After the third building period the settlement experienced a collapse, immediately followed by a

Figure 8. Objects of the Kuchuk-tepe Culture.

renewal. During the fourth period qualitatively new constructions appeared, and the settlement was surrounded by a fourth wall. The rooms became smaller, the walls narrower, and the sites for basic economic activities and the corridors, which were located between the circular walls, now functioned as residential areas. These qualitative changes in the domestic architecture were also reflected in the material culture of the inhabitants.

Thus our investigations have shown that southern Uzbekistan in the second millennium B.C. was one of the centers of the highly developed cultures of the ancient Near Eastern type that belonged to the level of socioeconomic development known as a formative civilization. Such a level of development was also characteristic for the ancient agricultural communities of the southern part of ancient Bactria in the second millennium B.C.

The great volume of archeological investigations in Bactria has forced us to correct our views on the genesis of early class societies in a significant part of Uzbekistan and Tadjikistan. This work has allowed us to define a new "Amu Darya" hearth for highly developed cultures of the ancient Near Eastern type that served as the basis for the formation and development of urban cultures of the archaic and classical periods in Bactria and Sogdia.

This hearth had two chronologically contemporaneous centers: southern Uzbekistan and northern Afghanistan. The inhabitants of the southern Uzbekistan center created a rich and distinctive material culture, including square fortresses and elegant high-quality vessels and seal-emblems.

The time of the formation of the ancient agricultural tribes of southern Uzbekistan coincided with great changes in the socioeconomic structure of the ancient Near Eastern civilizations that occurred over a vast territory in the first half and middle of the second millennium B.C. During this period the Harappan civilization of the Indus Valley collapsed; at the same time, similar declines were observed at Mundigak IV, Hissar IIIC, Shah-tepe IIA1, Namazga V, Shahr-i Sokhta IV, the Kulli Culture and so on.

The absolute radiccarbon dates for Sapalli and early Djarkutan coincide exactly with these events.* Standardized planned settle-

---

*In his monograph Drevnezemledel'cheskaia kul'tura epokhi Bronzy iuga Uzbekistana, Dr. Askarov equates Dashly 1 in northern Afghanistan with the Sapalli stage and cites dates of 1570 ± 45 to 1250 ± 45 B.C. (presumably 5568 half-life and uncorrected) for this settlement; similarly he equates Dashly 3, which has a radio-

ments with citadels and complicated fortifications, cemeteries outside the settlements, and the burial of animals as a substitute for missing males in the paternal line are some of the characteristic features distributed throughout the middle Amu Darya region at this time. It seems to us that the almost complete absence of zoomorphic and anthropomorphic figurines in sites of the Sapalli Culture can be explained by changes in ideological beliefs, which were shaped, in turn, by the evolution of socioeconomic relationships among the ancient agriculturalists. Apparently the wide distribution of glyptic art that functioned as symbols or totems of large kin-related groups or tribal communities was likewise associated with these changes.

The analysis of the archeological materials from a series of ancient agricultural centers, such as Murghab, Sherabad, Dashly, and Farukhabad, shows that the dominance of light-colored ceramics on these sites reflects their common origin, while the presence of a small number of gray ceramics reflects the influence of the cultural traditions of north Iranian communities on their material culture. One must note particularly that the different-shaped goblets on narrow, circular, concave, saucerlike bases with thin, well-fired walls, which were widespread in the Dashly Oasis, were characteristic forms of the southern Turkmenistan Namazga V ceramic assemblages; they were not found among the materials from the eastern Iranian sites. At Sapalli-tepe the typical vases on high stands and the conical vessels again show parallels with ceramics from southern Turkmenistan.

The genetic relationship linking the Sapalli Culture to Namazga-related sites is completely supported by the analysis of anthropological materials that characterize a specific type of dolichocephalic population with a low arch of the cranial vault.[4] Central Asia is the center of the distribution of this local variant of the eastern Mediterranean racial type. The sum total of similarities, even exact resemblances, in the materials of the Sapalli Culture with sites of the piedmont zone of southern Turkmenistan and in the physical anthropological materials allows us to postulate that the most probable origin of the Sapalli Culture is to be found among the ancient agricultural communities of Central Asia. The direct

---

carbon date of 1490 ± 50 B.C., with the Djarkutan stage. Later he mentions two dates from Sapalli, 1690 B.C. and 1560 B.C., and one from the lowest levels at Djarkutan, 1650 B.C. — P.L.K.

movement of tribes from eastern Iran to northern Afghanistan and thence their settling into southern Uzbekistan and the Murghab Oasis, which was proposed by V. I. Sarianidi,[5] is still not supported by actual data.

The period examined is noteworthy both for the strong influence of the economic advances of the southern agriculturalists on the northern regions of Central Asia and for the decline of the large agricultural centers, a process indicated by the sharp reduction in the size of earlier settlements and the formation of new agricultural oases. In linking this latter process with the spread of ancient agricultural tribes from the piedmont belt of southern Turkmenistan to the east, V. M. Masson correctly demonstrated the historical continuity of the assemblages of the Murghab Oasis with settlements of the Namazga Culture. Considering the abundance of similar and, at times, identical parallels between the Sapalli assemblages and those of the Namazga Culture and the Murghab Oasis, there can be no doubt that the southern Turkmenistan hearth of ancient Near Eastern civilization functioned as the initial source for the formation of the culture at Sapalli-tepe and of its neighbors from northern Afghanistan.

A still more appreciable change in the life of the primitive tribes of Central Asia occurred at the end of the second and the beginning of the first millennium B.C. During this period over a vast expanse of the steppes and valleys in the plains area of northern Central Asia, a transformation to a settled way of life occurred in those places where local conditions favored the development of agriculturally based cultures. These tribes from the steppes developed their new economy in the floodlands and lower small runoffs and streams that arose from local springs. Thus local ancient agricultural centers arose among the neighboring tribes of steppe pastoralists. These cultures include the Chust Culture,[6] the early Burgulyuk Culture of the Tashkent Oasis,[7] and the Sarazm Culture of the Zeravshan Valley.[8] Separate sites with handmade ceramics also are found in the Karshi Oasis.[9]

The archaic looking handmade ceramics of these cultures are found throughout a broad area occupied by ancient agricultural tribes distinct from the steppe pastoral and agricultural tribes of northern Central Asia. The surrounding natural conditions and ecological potential among some of these tribes, such as are represented by the Chust and Burgulyuk cultures, assured gradual sedentarization; among others — due to the instability and variability of water resources in the deltaic plains of rivers such as the Amu Darya, Syr Darya, Zeravshan, Kashka Darya, and the like — an agricultural way of life was not so widely distributed until the creation of the first large irrigation works, organized by state power, which were characteristic of the slave-holding socio-economic formation, e.g., among the Amurabad tribes. The appearance of cultures characterized by painted ceramics of the type found at Kuchuk-tepe, Yaz 1, and Anau IVA in southern Central Asia and at Tillya-tepe, Mundigak VI, and Sialk IVB, in those adjacent regions where there had earlier flourished highly developed agricultural societies of the second order, is somewhat unexpected.

Many specialists in Central Asian archeology have considered this appearance to be the result of a "barbarian occupation" of the zone of ancient agricultural oases.

The appearance of new tribes with handmade painted ceramics in regions formerly occupied by highly developed ancient Near Eastern cultures effectively slowed down the formation of early urban civilization in the Late Bronze Age. A few centuries later, sometime around the beginning of the eighth century B.C., the ancient cultural and economic tradition returned with great force over extensive areas of Central Asia. All this occurred due to the intensive development of agriculture and different sorts of highly advanced crafts. A similarly important factor was the accelerated accumulation of material wealth in the hands of tribal leaders and privileged sections of the community, the so-called azadi. In this situation centralized power was dictated by the actual circumstances; the ancient Bactrian kingdom and Great Khorezmia attest to this process.

Masses of material accumulated on both sides of the pre-Amu Darya hearth of highly developed cultures indisputably testify to the existence of an ancient Bactrian kingdom prior to the creation of the Achaemenian empire in Iran and to the local roots of the ancient urban cultures of Central Asia. This fact is one of the most important results of the archeological investigations in southern Uzbekistan for the second millennium B.C.

The analysis of archeological materials from sites of the Bronze Age of ancient Bactria does not allow us to speak with any certainty about the ethnic composition and language of the bearers of the Sapalli and Kuchuk-tepe cultures. The opinion that Iranian-speaking peoples inhabited broad areas of Central Asia, the Iranian plateau, and adjacent regions at the beginning of the first millennium B.C. does prevail, especially among linguists, in our national and in the foreign literature. Yet from this perspective it is impossible to relate the language of the peoples of the Sapalli Culture to the family of Iranian languages. However, it seems to us that the historical reality of the second millennium B.C. was somewhat different than what we have proposed, relying on the linguistic data, for the first millennium B.C. Not convinced by the linguistic arguments, we suggest that the center of the early formation of the Iranian languages can be considered to be Central Asia and the areas adjacent to it; until the advent of the pastoral tribes from more northerly regions (the "Aryans"), the language of the local people was Iranian. In our view the Hindu Kush mountains formed the southern and southwestern boundary for the distribution of Iranian-speaking tribes in the second millennium B.C. Apparently the bearers of the ancient agricultural cultures of southern and the pastoral tribes of northern Central Asia and, possibly, the south Russian steppes in the second millennium B.C. were linguistically related and spoke a language that could be called Iranian, at least in its different dialects. It seems to us that the bearers of the Sapalli Culture and the Kuchuk-tepe Culture understood each other and spoke a language that soon formed the ancient Bactrian language, one of the dialects of the eastern branch of Iranian languages.

Notes

1. See A. Foucher, La vieille route de l'Inde de Bactres à Taxila, in collaboration with Mme. E. Bazin-Foucher, 2 vols. (1942-47), Memoires de la Delegation Archeologique Française en Afghanistan (DAFA), I.

2. See V. I. Sarianidi, "Issledovanie pamiatnikov dashlinskogo oazisa," Drevnaia Baktriia, Moscow, 1976, and Drevnie zemledel'tsy Afganistana, Moscow, 1977; and A. A. Askarov, Sapallitepa, Tashkent, 1973, and Drevnezemledel'cheskaia kul'tura epokhi bronzy iuga Uzbekistana, Tashkent, 1977.

3. See A. A. Askarov and L. I. Al'baum, Poselenie Kuchuktepa, Tashkent, 1979.

4. See T. Khodzhaiov, Antropologicheskii sostav naseleniia epokhi bronzy Sapallitepa, Tashkent, 1977.

5. V. I. Sarianidi, "Baktriia v epokhu bronzy," Sovetskaia arkheologiia, 1974, no. 4, p. 69.

6. See Iu. A. Zadneprovskii, Drevnezemledel'cheskaia kul'tura Fergany, Materialy i issledovaniia po arkheologii SSSR, no. 118, Moscow, 1962.

7. See Kh. Duke, "Burguliukskaia kul'tura," Drevnosti Tuiabuguza, Tashkent, 1978, pp. 47-92.

8. See A. I. Isaakov and U. Eshonkulov, "Raboty kosataroshskogo otriada," Arkheologicheskie otkrytiia 1977 goda, Moscow, 1978, p. 558.

9. See Kh. Duke, "Iz arkheologicheskikh otkrytii 1972 g.," Uspekhi Sredneaziatskoi arkheologii, no. 2, Leningrad, 1972, and R. Kh. Suleimanov et. al., "Osnovnye itogi raskopok na Ierkurgane," Arkheologicheskie otkrytiia 1976 goda, Moscow, 1977, p. 545.

CHAPTER **12**

Excavations of the Bronze Age
Settlement of Sarazm

A. ISAKOV

The settlement of Sarazm is situated 15 kilometers west of
Pendjikent (Tadjik SSR) on the second flood terrace of the left
bank of the Zeravshan River. It appears as an elevation stretching
from west to east, about 1.5 kilometers in length and 400 to 900
meters in width.

The settlement consists of ten small mounds of different heights
and five depressions, the area of which fluctuates between 0.25
and 0.5 hectares.[1]

From its topography one can see that the settlement of Sarazm,
like many other Bronze Age sites, does not have a clearly defined
plan. A significant quantity of accidental finds, collected on different parts of the settlement, primarily from private plots, were
given to us by the local inhabitants. It appeared possible from
these finds to define preliminarily the area of the settlement,
which, apparently, during its most developed period exceeded 90
hectares. Today the village of Sokhibnazar lies on top of the northern and western parts of the settlement, and the village of Avazali,
on its northeastern section. The unobstructed or open part of the
ancient settlement is equal to 35 hectares.

Eight exploratory soundings, situated in different parts of the
settlement, and three excavation units were made at the settlement.
The soundings and excavations revealed that the site had four occupation horizons, three of which preserved building remains
(rooms with walls, hearths, heating and household pits).

The most interesting materials came from excavations I, II, and III.

273

Excavation II. This unit stretched from west to east more than
100 meters and from north to south for 30 meters; it was situated
on a relatively low prominence 100 meters south of the northern
edge of the settlement and 20 meters from private plots of the inhabitants of the village. The remains of 23 rooms, relating to
three building horizons, which preliminarily defined three periods,
Sarazm I, II, and III, corresponding to the lower, middle, and upper
levels, were found as a result of the excavations here in 1977-78
(Figure 1).

Sarazm I. The constructions of this earliest period were considerably disturbed as a result of subsequent building activity.
They were excavated in small areas in two sections. The first:
courtyard I; the second, considerably larger, in the northwestern
part of the excavation. In both sections the remains of walls 50-60
centimeters thick were found; they could easily be traced in the
northwestern part of the excavation. In this area it was possible
to determine the remains of three rooms (16, 17, and 18), two of
which (17 and 18) were connected by a doorway that was 55 cm
wide and had a clay threshold 20 cm high.

Sarazm II. The building remains of the second (middle) period
were found under the floors and walls of the upper level. The
rooms of this period were divided in terms of their function into
cult, residential, and economic-storage areas and were separated
into five living complexes. The first complex consisted of rooms
2, 3, 8, and 21; the second 4 and 19; the third 6, 7, and 16; the
fourth 11 and 12; and the fifth 1, 22, and 23. Rooms 13 and 14,
which also related to this period, are still not connected to these
complexes. All the complexes had a separate exit to a courtyard,
where hearths were situated and, apparently, bread ovens.

All the rooms of the complexes were connected by passages that
were 50-60 cm wide with the high (20-25 cm) adobe thresholds
characteristic of Bronze Age sites. The walls of all the rooms of
excavation II were built of adobe, and the walls and floors were
covered by two or three levels of plaster.

Sarazm III. The uppermost level related to the next period of
occupation. This level was 30-45 cm thick, and the surface of a
floor was found in its lower part, which preserved traces of plaster
in separate areas. Surfaces of floors that were burned red were
encountered in several areas; holes of hearths that were 18-25 cm
in diameter and 15-20 cm deep were found alongside these burned
floors. Burned hearths also were encountered that formed shallow
(15-20 cm) pits with diameters ranging from 70 to 100 cm; they

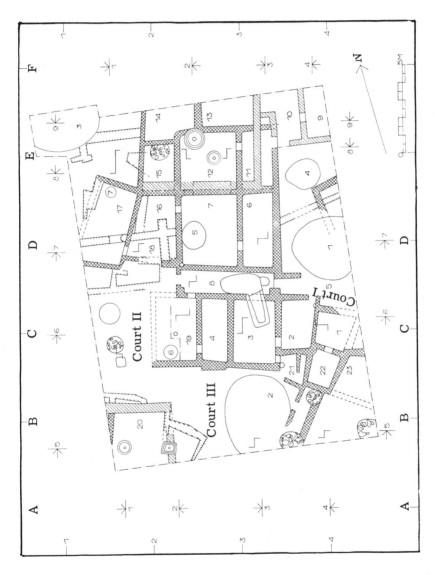

Figure 1. Plan of excavation II.

were filled with cracked river pebbles.

The remains of four rooms (9, 10, 11, and 20) were established; their dimensions ranged from 2.10 × 2.90 to 4.75 × 6.25 meters. The walls of these rooms, which were 35-50 cm thick and which were preserved to a height of 40-45 cm, were badly destroyed. Five burials (two children and three adults), which were all poorly preserved, also are related to the final period. The adults were in a contracted and the children in an extended position. Grave goods did not accompany the burials.

Circular hearths with borders on their edges and holes in their centers were found in only three of the excavated rooms (room 12, Sarazm II; and room 12a and 20, Sarazm III). In terms of their construction these hearths were similar to those from Aeneolithic sites in southern Turkmenia (Geoksyur and Aina-depe).[2] Having studied similar hearths with southern Turkmenian materials, I. N. Khlopin came to the conclusion that rooms containing such hearths functioned as cult areas.[3]

In addition to the residential and activity rooms, three open areas which, apparently, were small courtyards (in the plan, courts I, II, and III) were found during the excavations of the Sarazm II period in excavation 2. As opposed to the rooms, the courtyards were overloaded with ceramics, bones, and ash debris.

Excavation III. A third fixed excavation area was set up on top of the largest and highest mound in the center of the settlement. This mound stretched west to east for 50 meters and north to south for 25 meters. It rose more than 3 meters above the surrounding part of the settlement. As was true throughout the settlement, the surface of this mound has been plowed up as deep as 40 cm.

The remains of seven rooms (Figure 2) were found during these excavations. They were symmetrical and had a very original plan, suggesting the plan of a communal building. The location of a series of rooms (3, 4, 5, 6, and 7) connected with one another by passages speaks in favor of this hypothesis and resembles a suite of rooms. In turn, rooms 3, 4, and 5 have a single approach in their eastern wall from which one could enter the suite. The suite abuts from the south the small room 6 in the middle of which was placed a hearth. Its central hole was 20 cm in diameter and 16 cm deep. The sides of this hole were burned.

The unique dimensions of three rooms and their unique plan attract attention. Their walls were made of brick with dimensions of 58 × 26 × 11 cm and 59 × 27 × 12 cm, and their surfaces were carefully plastered.

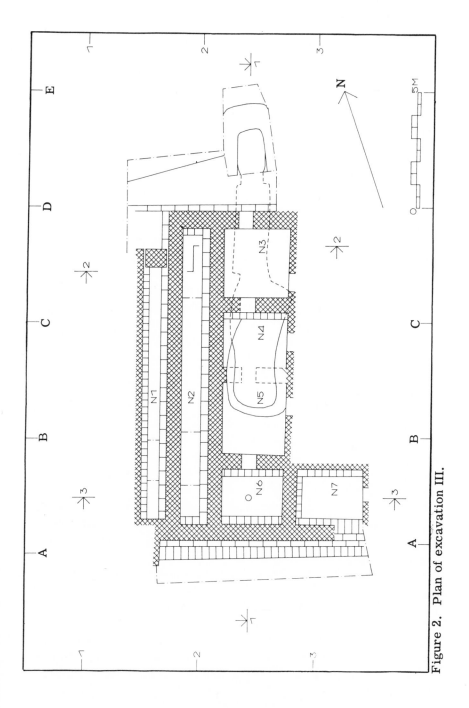

Figure 2. Plan of excavation III.

Two corridor-shaped rooms (1 and 2), which stretched south to north, apparently functioned as storage areas. There were no doorways, and it has been suggested that one entered through a hatch in the roof.

The complex of excavation II had north-south walls that functioned as a fortress. On their northern part these walls were excavated for four meters, and on their southern, for ten meters. Their insignificant thickness (1.10 × 1.15 m) indicates that the investigated building area was situated within the settlement and that these walls were the exterior walls of some multiroom building complex.

In terms of their construction the rooms of excavation III are markedly different from those of excavation II. The walls of the latter were adobe, while the walls of excavation III were made of brick. In addition, while the rooms of excavation II were constructed without a preliminary architectural plan, the symmetry of the rooms and the facade of the buildings of excavation III established that they were constructed according to a well-conceived plan.

While the buildings in excavation II were probably residential quarters, those in excavation III seem communal or cult areas; this hypothesis is supported both by the general plan of the building in excavation III and by the almost complete absence of material remains within it.

Significant interest attaches to the discovery of fragments of painted ceramics, which previously had not been found in the Zeravshan Valley of Central Asia; these ceramics can be divided by their features into two groups.

Polychrome ceramics form the first group; dark-brown and dark-rose designs are placed on red and light-yellow slipped wares (Figure 3).

The second group consist of monochrome wares with dark-brown designs on a light background (Figure 4). All the painted ceramic fragments from Sarazm share broad analogies with wares from southern Turkmenia, particularly those of the Namazga IV period.[4] Separate fragments with triangles and sawed designs inside rectangles are similar to ceramics from the upper levels of Geoksyur[5] and Kara-depe.[6]

Most of the ceramics are unpainted. They are distinguished not only by their technology and color but also by their wide variety of shapes (Figure 5). Different cooking and tablewares, including miniature examples, are found along with jars. In a series of cases bits of fired clay and lime-rolled pebbles had been added to the paste of the cooking vessels. Nearly all the cooking and tablewares were burnished. The majority of grayware cups were burnished on both sides. Separate examples were covered with a red-flint or dark paint, resembling a heavy varnish.

Among other finds we mention a spindle-whorl, the head of a pin, and a small stamp (a unique find). This stamp had a square shape (4 × 4 cm) and was 0.9 cm thick. Diagonally stretched grooves divided the stamp into four triangles in which were placed complicated rhomboid-shaped designs.

Not only ceramics but other stone objects from Sarazm are analogous to stone artifacts from Anau, Kara-depe, and non-Central Asian sites. Different articles relating to the local customs of the Sarazm peoples are the most interesting stone objects. This group includes plummets with diagonal and longitudinal grooves, cups, mortars, grinding stones, pestles, spindle-whorls, beads (lapis lazuli), jambs, whetstones, and the like.

Three stone weights assume a basic value for determining eco-

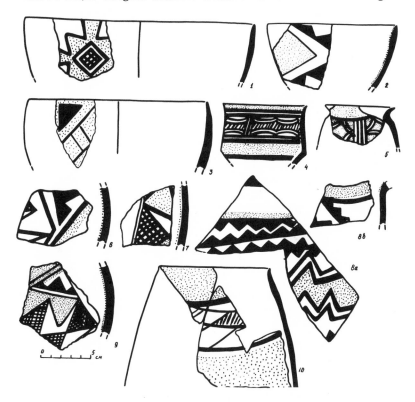

Figure 3. Polychrome ceramics: 1-3 — cups; 4-5 beaker-goblets; 6-10 fragments; 11 — vessel with cylindrical sides.

nomic conditions for the inhabitants of the settlement. Two of them
are disc-shaped with clearly defined handles. Both in form and
in weight, these objects appear analogous to weights from Anau,[7]
Kara-depe,[8] and a series of other sites in Iran and Afghanistan.[9]
One of the weights was found near a hearth in a courtyard of excavation II. Fragments of rims and sides of cups with polychrome
painting were found together with the weight in the fill of the hearth.
  The third weight also had a handle and was made from a riverine

Figure 4. Monochrome ceramics: cups and fragments of cups.

stone with an oval shape. In form and in weight this object is absolutely unlike the others and has no direct analogies.

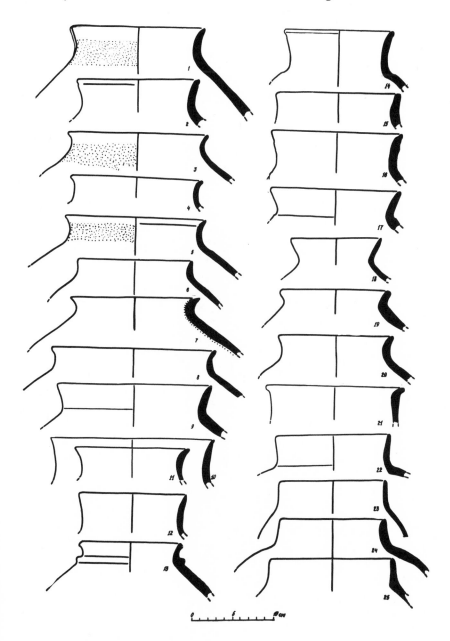

Figure 5. Unpainted ceramics: pots.

Two other unique stone objects were found. The first was complete; it was 14 cm long, and the diameter of its smooth, blunt end was 5.5 cm. Its upper part was shaped like a "bill" or "beak"

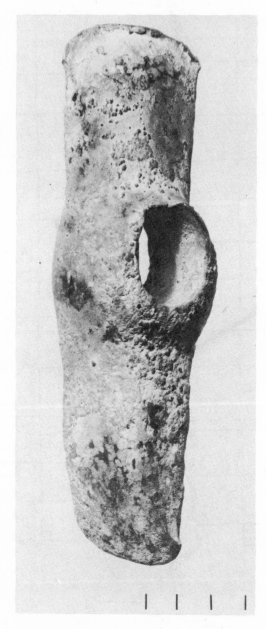

Figure 6. Bronze axe-adze.

under which, at its throat as it were, was an opening apparently intended as a metal handle. The second object was broken. The fracture occurred at the place where the opening should have been

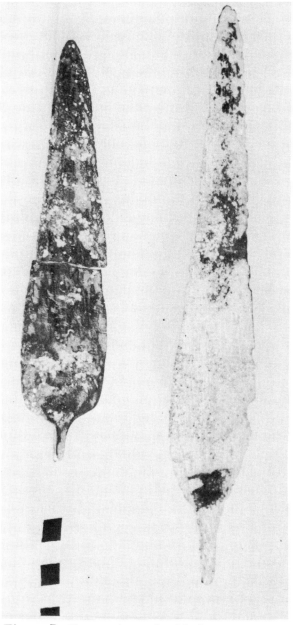

Figure 7. Bronze two-edged knives.

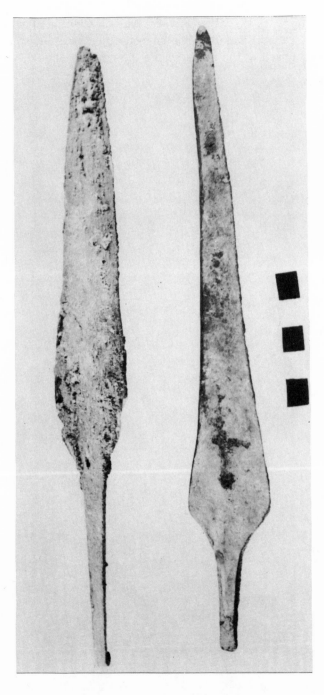

Figure 8. Bronze daggers.

and divided the object into two pieces. Both the size and shape of its "beak" repeated those of the first object.

Analogous stone objects were found by R. M. Munchaev in kurgans at the Uech I and II settlements in the Caucasus[10] and by N. Ia. Merpert in the Volgo-Ural interfluve.[11] However, both investigators did not determine their significance. Although we lack convincing proof, it seems to us that these objects were staffs symbolizing sovereignty. It is well known that the pharoahs of ancient Egypt[12] used bone and gold scepters of a somewhat different type.[13]

As opposed to other early agricultural sites in Central Asia, Sarazm contained numerous metal objects. So far, sixteen metal objects have been recorded among the accidental finds. These include a shaft-hole axe-adze (Figure 6), two-edged knives (Figure 7), and daggers (Figure 8). The significant quantity of crucibles and slag that was found in sounding 2 shows that metal was worked directly at the site.

Thus it has been clearly established that the inhabitants of Sarazm were occupied not only with agriculture and herding but also with metallurgical production.

Questions about the stratigraphy of Sarazm are still not resolved. The fact is that different chronological indices — the polychrome ceramics, the shaft-hole axe, and the weights — have been encountered among the surface materials and the accidental finds. By analogy with southern Turkmenian sites, they can be dated to the time of Namazga III and IV, i.e., to the Aeneolithic and Early Bronze Age periods, and also to the time of Namazga V.

The discovery of the extensive permanent agricultural settlement of Sarazm modifies a series of current conceptions concerning the range of cultures with painted ceramics. It is already clear that the Sarazm Culture also finds parallels over a significant territory of Central Asia, the borders of which stretch from the shores of the Indian Ocean to the Central Asian Mesopotamia.

Notes

1. The site was found in the fall of 1976. Archeological excavations began in 1977 and continued in 1978-79.

2. I. N. Khlopin, "Model' kruglogo zhertvennika iz Ialangach-depe," KSIA AN SSSR, 1964, no. 98, p. 48.

3. Ibid., p. 49.

4. B. A. Litvinskii, "Namazga-tepe po dannym raskopok 1949-1950 gg.,"

A. I. Isakov

Sovetskaia etnografiia, 1952, no. 4; B. A. Kuftin, "Polevoi otchet o rabote XIV otriada IuTAKE po izucheniiu kul'tury pervobytno-obshchinnykh osedlozemledel'cheskikh poselenii epokhi medi i bronzy v 1952 g.," TIuTAKE, vol. 7, Ashkhabad, 1956, pl. XXXI, 7; XXXII, 13.

5. V. I. Sarianidi, "Eneoliticheskoe poselenie Geoksiur," TIuTAKE, vol. 10, Ashkhabad 1960, p. 247, pls. III, IV, VIII.

6. V. M. Masson, "Raspisnaia keramika Turkmenii," ibid., p. 336, pls. XX, XXI.

7. R. Pumpelly, "Ancient Anau and the Oasesworld," Explorations in Turkestan. Prehistoric Civilizations of Anau, vol. 2, Washington, 1908, pp. 478-79, figs. 506-10.

8. V. M. Masson, "Eneolit iuzhnykh oblastei Srednei Azii," part 2, SAI, B3-8, p. 22, pl. XI, 10-13.

9. R. Ghirshman, Fouilles de Sialk, 1938; J.-M. Casal, Fouilles de Mundigak, Paris, 1961; V. A. Alekshin, "Kamennye giri s drevnezemledel'cheskikh poselenii Iuzhnoi Turkmenii," Sovetskaia arkheologiia, 1973, no. 4, p. 239, fig. 1.

10. R. M. Munchaev, Kavkaz na zare bronzogo veka, Moscow, 1975, p. 280, fig. 64, 16-18.

11. N. Ia. Merpert, Drevneishie skotovody Volzhsko-Ural'skogo mezhdurech'ia, Moscow, 1974, p. 75, fig. 10.

12. H. Carter, Grobnitsa Tutankhamona, Moscow, 1959, pls. 123 A and 141.

CHAPTER 13

Bronze Age Settlements of Southern Tadjikistan

L. T. P'IANKOVA

A large part of the territory of the Tadjik SSR is covered with high mountains. Only in the southwest of the republic is there an extensive low plain, the boundaries of which continue far to the south, beyond the borders of the Soviet Union. Geographically speaking, this plain belongs to the Southern Tadjik Province of the pre-Asian natural region.

The territory of the Southern Tadjik highland is intersected by a number of low ranges running from north to south. Between them run, also meridionally, the valleys of the right tributaries of the Pianj-Amu Darya: the Kafirnigan, Vakhsh, Kyzylsu, and their tributaries. In the south the valleys of these rivers merge into the Cis-Amu Darya Plain. In topography and natural conditions the territory of southwestern Tadjikistan resembles the adjacent districts of southern Uzbekistan and northern Afghanistan, where a considerable number of monuments of the Late Bronze Age have now been discovered and studied.

Systematic study of Bronze Age monuments in Southern Tadjikistan began in the 1950s with excavations of burial grounds in Beshkent Valley under the direction of A. M. Mandel'shtam. He investigated the Early Tulkhar and Aruktau burial grounds (Figure 1, 6, 7), where six different types of burial structures were found. Along with interment of the entire skeleton (contracted, on one side), which was the prevailing burial rite, cases of cremation were identified here, as well as burials of the bones of the dismembered skeleton. Mandel'shtam dates the Beshkent Valley

Figure 1. Diagram of Bronze Age sites in southern Tadjikistan. Key: I — cemeteries of pastoralist cultures; II — cemeteries with pottery ware of the settled farming type; III — settlements with materials of the settled farming and steppe type; IV — steppe Bronze Age site; 1 — Vakhsh I cemetery; 2 — Tigrovaia Balka cemetery; 3 — Oi Kul' cemetery; 4 — Dzhar Kul' cemetery; 5 — Makoni Mor cemetery; 6 — Rannii Tulkhar cemetery; 7 — Aruktau cemetery; 8 — Beshkent III cemetery; 9 — Beshkent I cemetery; 10 — Beshkent II cemetery; 11 — Isanbai cemetery; 12 — Zar Kamar cemetery; 13 — Tandyr Iul cemetery; 14 — Hissar cemetery; 16, 17 — Nurek cemeteries; 18 — Teguzak settlement; 19 — Kangurt-Tut settlement; 20 — site on Kirov state farm.

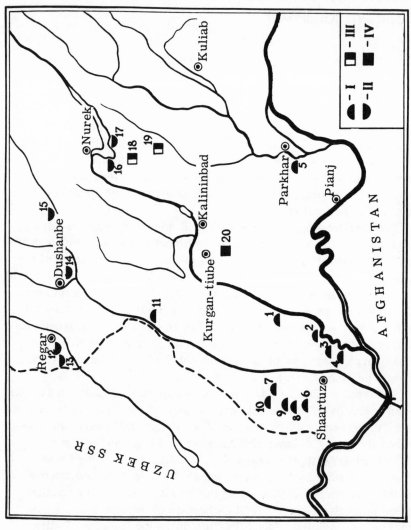

burial grounds to the fourteenth to thirteenth centuries B.C. Despite the repeatedly noted parallels in the Beshkent Culture materials with the ceramics and metalware of Margiana and southern Turkmenia sites of ancient agriculture, he prefers the northern ties of the ancient inhabitants of the lower reaches of the Kafirnigan, finding correspondences between their interment ritual and goods (chiefly metal products) in the cultures of the Andronovo group, Zamanbaba, and the Eurasian steppes.[1]

The 1960s saw the beginning of study of Bronze Age sites along the lower reaches of the Vakhsh and Kyzylsu. The work was conducted under the direction of B. A. Litvinskii. Despite special surveys no vestiges of settlements were found in those areas. A considerable number of burial grounds was discovered, five of which (Tigrovaia Balka, Oi Kul', Dzhar Kul', Vakhsh I, Makoni Mor [Figure 1, 1-5]) have been excavated in part or totally (a total of 240 mounds have been excavated). The burial grounds are characterized by uniformity of the burial structures, a single burial ritual, and identical material culture. As a result they have been classed as a single archeological culture, which Litvinskii named "Vakhsh."

The graves of the Vakhsh Culture lie in the upper foothill [adyry] terraces of the river valleys adjacent to the mountain ridge watersheds.

The burial structures of the Vakhsh Culture appear as round or oval heaped mounds of loess, although in some cases they are virtually rectangular or square differing in size (from 2 to 14 meters in diameter and 0.3 to 1 m high). A majority of these mounds or kurgans have a ring of stones forming a facing at their base. Sometimes this ring is on the slope of the mound. Some kurgans are surrounded by rings of stones beyond the limits of their piled mound.

All the burial structures, except a few in which children were interred, are graves of the chamber-lined catacomb type. The entry pit or dromos is filled with loess and packed with rocks of various sizes, usually very large. The chamber containing the interment is always filled with loess, except that sometimes single stones are found beneath the ceiling, which probably slid or fell there from the dromos.

The burial structures of the Vakhsh Culture grounds have dromoi of different shapes (Figure 2). The dromoi of most graves are oval-rectangular. But along with them every burial ground has structures with dromoi of approximately triangular, pear-shaped forms, and also in the form of arcs and the letters T and Π. They represent a negligible percentage of the graves.

The entry to the dromos usually consists of one or more small steps on the narrow side of the dromos.

The burial chambers are deep niches dug into the subsoil. The entrances are arched, while the floor is oval or segmented. The long axis of the catacomb is perpendicular to the long axis of the dromos, and these axes are parallel in chamber-lined arrangement.

The dromoi differ in size: lengths from 1 to 4 m, excluding the arc-shaped dromoi, which are up to 7 m long. Widths are 0.5 to 2 m; depths 0.5 to 3 m (in most cases 1.5 to 2). The maximum lengths of burial chambers are from 0.8 to 2.3 m, widths 0.7 to 2.5 m, height of entrance arch 0.5 to 2.1 m. No patterns in orientation of burial structure are evident.

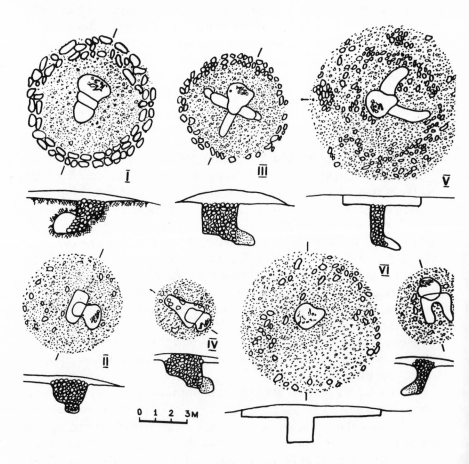

Figure 2. Types of burial structures of Vakhsh Culture.

All the burials were interments. The interred were placed in the chambers in the position typical during the Bronze Age: contracted and on one side.

Most of the burials are single. Males were almost exclusively laid on their right sides facing the entry of the chamber (there are rare exceptions). No definite pattern has been observed with respect to the position of female skeletons, although the same position with their faces turned toward the entrance position (in the majority of cases they are placed on their left side, but in a smaller number, on their right) has usually been found. There are fewer burials of women with their backs toward the chamber entry, and most of them are placed on their left side, fewer on their right.

Paired burials are rare in graves of the Vakhsh Culture. They divide into simultaneous burials and those in which interment was at different times. Most often such burials are of people of different sexes. In them a man and a woman are placed face to face, the woman's back toward the entrance. When two people of the same sex were buried together, both skeletons were in the same position.

While the orientation of the burials varied, nearly all fall within the west-north-east range, the northern orientation predominating. Orientations toward the south are rare.

The population that left the Vakhsh Culture burial grounds was of the Europeoid Mediterranean type, well known from many sites found in a wide belt from the Mediterranean Sea on the west to northern India on the east.

Grave goods are few. They consist of pottery and bronze, bone, and stone objects. Often an individual was accompanied only by a single vessel, more rarely by two, and in exceptional cases by three to five. The largest number of objects in a single grave, going as high as ten, was at the Makoni Mor burial ground. The grave goods were usually at the person's head, and more rarely at the feet, in front of the chest, or behind the back.

The major grave goods were pottery. The majority of vessels were shaped by hand (70 percent), and the rest (30 percent) were thrown on the wheel. However, the molded and thrown artifacts are sometimes strikingly similar in shape and very nearly the same size. But some shapes are represented only by handmade or only by thrown specimens.

Figures 3 and 4 present the classification of the ware. Figures 5 through 14 illustrate vessels from various burial grounds of the

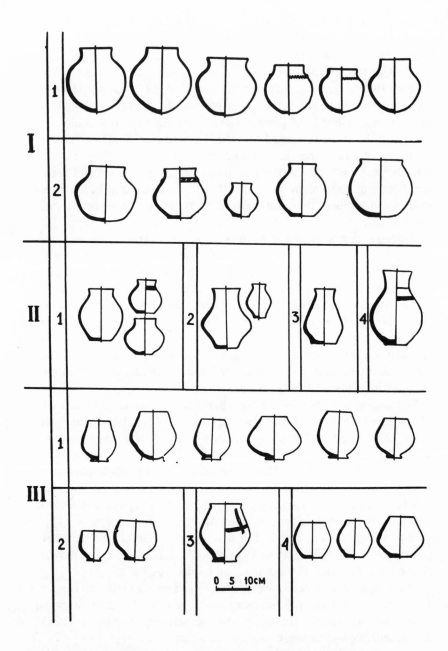

Figure 3. Classification of pottery ware from Vakhsh Culture cemeteries: I — pots for cooking food (1 — round-bottomed, 2 — flat-bottomed); II — jugs (1-4, various types); III — pot-shaped vessels (1-4, various types).

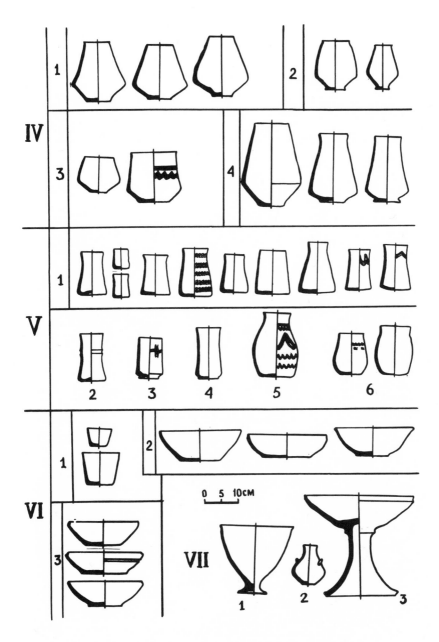

Figure 4. Classification of pottery ware from Vakhsh Culture cemeteries: IV — biconical vessels (1-4, various types); V — cylindrical vessels (1-6, various types); VI — saucers and dishes (1-3, various types); VII — vessels of individual forms.

Figure 5. Pottery ware from cemeteries of the Vakhsh Culture.

Vakhsh Culture. The vessel depicting a procession of goats from a grave, found at Dzhar Kul' (Figure 15), is unique.

Bronze ware consists of knives (Figure 16, 2-3), "razor"-type cutters (Figure 16, 4, 5, 8, 9), and mirrors both round (Figure 16,

Figure 6. Pottery ware from cemeteries of the Vakhsh Culture.

Figure 7. Pottery ware from cemeteries of the Vakhsh Culture.

10, 11) and with a handle on the side (Figure 16, 12). One specimen each was found of a pendant (Figure 16, 6) and a toggle or hair pin (Figure 16, 7). There was a unique find of a handled dagger from the Tigrovaia Balka cemetery (Figure 16, 1) resembling the daggers of the so-called "Asia Minor type," although there is

Figure 8. Pottery ware from cemeteries of the Vakhsh Culture.

Figure 9. Pottery ware from cemeteries of the Vakhsh Culture.

no exact correspondence. In the shape of the lower portion of the handle, the Vakhsh specimen is typologically comparable to knives with semicircles in relief on the upper portion of the blade. This analogy, however, is far from exact and this detail is most typical of the daggers of the Talysh region. Such daggers are also common in Iran, particularly in the northern and northwestern parts of the

Figure 10. Pottery ware from cemeteries of the Vakhsh Culture.

Figure 11. Pottery ware from cemeteries of the Vakhsh Culture.

country. The Vakhsh specimen differs in that its ricasso is not semicircular but a highly extended low arc in relief. Its blade is also different, since in cross section, the edges show a projection at approximately the half-way mark. One should note that for

Figure 12. Pottery ware from cemeteries of the Vakhsh Culture.

Figure 13. Pottery ware from cemeteries of the Vakhsh Culture.

thrusting weapons, such edges are more advanced than straight ones. The Talysh-Iranian type dagger is not a unique find in Tadjikistan. Another specimen, whose origin associates it with the same culture region, was found in the village of Ramit.[2] The particular paths by which Transcaucasian–Iranian-type daggers found their way to the territory of Tadjikistan are unknown to us. Similar daggers have not been found at the sedentary population sites of ancient Bactria or of Central Asia as a whole. But instances of their penetration far to the east have been repeatedly reported.

Stone artifacts are represented by two pin heads and by a series of flint shafted arrowheads, carefully worked with bilateral secondary retouch (Figure 17, 4-12).

Not only flint but bone arrowheads were used (Figure 17, 1-2). Bone is otherwise represented by awls and needles (Figure 17, 3) and polished thin sheets of unknown purpose (spoons?).

But for a few beads, ornaments are totally absent from the burials. A single bead has been found in some graves and apparently served as an amulet.

The Vakhsh Culture burial materials permit one to identify a number of cults associated with burial rituals. This is a reflection of a complex system of interwoven elements of concern for the dead kinsman and simultaneously of fear of him, expressed in the building of special barriers between the world of the living and that of the dead (for example, filling the dromos with large stones and setting up rings of rocks).

Figure 14. Pottery ware from cemeteries of the Vakhsh Culture.

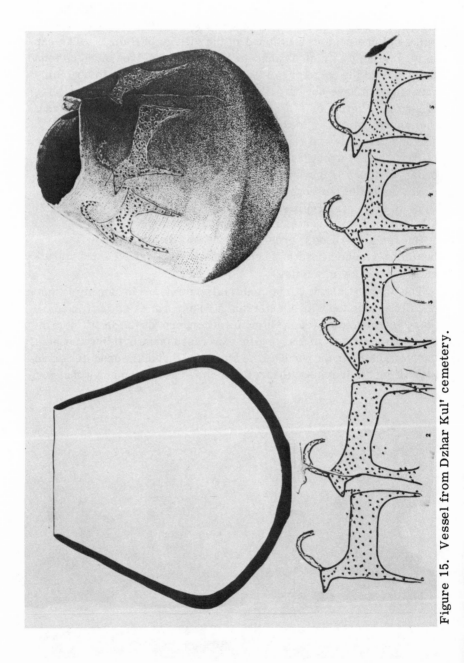

Figure 15. Vessel from Dzhar Kul' cemetery.

Fire worship is the clearest reflection of the beliefs of the ancient inhabitants of the lower reaches of the Vakhsh and Kyzylsu.

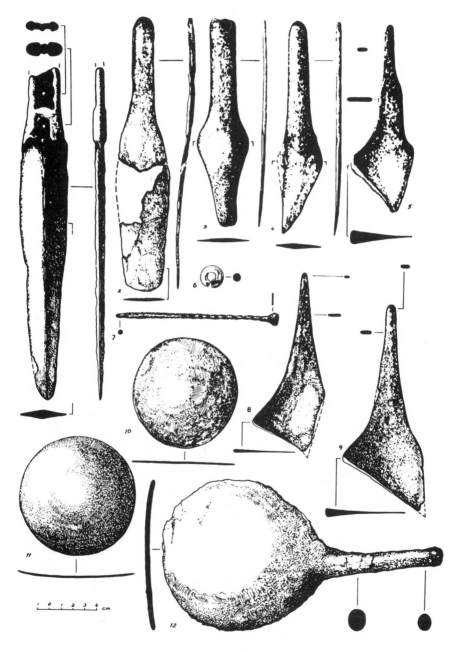

Figure 16. Bronze artifacts from Vakhsh Culture cemeteries.

Its traces are identifiable in the form of charcoal in graves, fires under the barrow fill, soot-covered vessels on small hearths in the chambers, and so on. The most vivid manifestation of the fire cult is in mounds 7 and 8 of the Tigrovaia Balka cemetery. They are the largest barrows in the burial grounds. Each is surrounded by a ring of set round stones (surrounding mound 7 there are 20 such placed stones, the ring having a total diameter of about 40 m; around mound 8 there are 41 stones, and the diameter of the ring exceeds 50 m. Beneath all the stones remains of fires that had burned in a ring around burials 7 and 8 respectively were detected. Judging by the size of the mounds, the grave goods, and the pomp of the burial rite, members of the clan-tribal elite of the ancient inhabitants of the Vakhsh (leaders or priests) are buried in these barrows. The burning of a fiery ring (or barrier) around their interments was evidently accompanied by some kind of sacrifice. Traces of libations poured onto the fire were discovered in the fires around mound 7, while small burned animal bones were found in the fires of mound 8. The ritual of putting out the fire with dirt

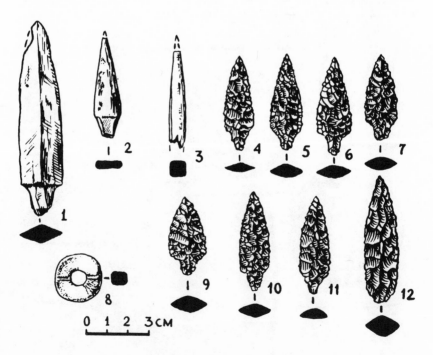

Figure 17. Bone and stone artifacts from Vakhsh Culture cemeteries.

might have been associated with the burial of the ancestral fire after the death of the leader. Mound 7 contained a single body, while mound 8 contained a couple, male and female, who were buried together.

Pastoralism was the basis of the economy of the Vakhsh Culture. The locality in which the cemeteries were found, which consisted of small and very rugged terrace outliers with pronounced slopes, was not suited to agriculture. Flood-plain thickets of mixed tree species and brush grew right up against the terraces. No traces of ancient irrigation were found anywhere in the low foothills, and the lands where the Vakhsh Culture cemeteries were found are used to this day as pastures, chiefly in winter. The materials associated with the burial grounds suggest that the herds of the ancient inhabitants consisted of sheep and goats, whose meat was placed in the graves as food for the dead. Pastoralism demanded a mobile way of life. The people of the Vakhsh Culture probably lived in temporary camps that might have been situated on the banks of the river, the traces of which have been washed away by the turbulent Vakhsh, which has frequently changed its course.

The material aspect of the Vakhsh Culture permits one to associate its origins with the centers of sedentary agriculture in ancient Bactria. Today two principal centers of that cultural region are known: one in southern Uzbekistan[3] and one in northern Afghanistan,[4] each having local features. The Vakhsh Culture more nearly resembles the latter. All the metal artifacts in the Vakhsh cemeteries came from ancient farming. Some of the forms of pottery ware were also widely prevalent in the entire region of settled agriculture of that period. However, analogies of all the typical forms of vessels making up the distinguishing feature of the Vakhsh Culture (pot-shaped, biconical, cylindrical, beaker vase [Figure 3, III; Figure 4, IV, V, VII, 1]) can be found in only one area — that containing Bronze Age sites of northern Afghanistan. Here one finds vessels identical to those of the Vakhsh Culture and others that could have served as genetic prototypes. Comparative analysis of pottery forms suggests that the most likely origin of the Vakhsh Culture was associated with the migration of late Bronze Age tribes from southern Bactria.

The material aspect of the Vakhsh Culture also displays a considerable similarity to that of the Beshkent pastoralists. This similarity applies particularly to hand-molded pottery ware. It was shaped by the chronological and geographic proximity of the cultures, as well as similar conditions of existence. However, the wheel-thrown pottery of the Beshkent cemeteries differs from that of the Vakhsh Culture. It is identical to the ware of the Molali stage of the Sapalli Culture and points to a genetic relationship between the Beshkent and Sapalli cultures.

The settled agricultural tribes that moved in the second half of the second millennium B.C. to the region of ancient Bactria from southwestern areas of Central Asia (the territory of present-day Turkmenistan), and also probably from northeastern Iran, had similar material cultures at various stages of their existence. However, by the final stage of the Bronze Age they had developed some local differences in the case of the tribes residing to the north and to the south of the Amu Darya. The pastoral Vakhsh Culture arose on the basis of the last Bronze Age assemblages of southern Bactria. The question of the relative chronology of the northern Afghan sites still requires further study. Late Bronze Age layers, synchronous with the Molali assemblages of southern Uzbekistan, have been found in Shortugai.[5] Here too there are the pottery shapes typical of the Vakhsh Culture, such as cylindrical and hourglass vessels. Ware identical to that of Vakhsh has been found at Dashly cemeteries 17 and 19 of the Dashly Oasis. Some vessel shapes have direct analogies in materials from Dashly 1 and 3.

On the other hand, the ancient farming assemblages of the Molali stage of northern Bactria were one of the components in the shaping of the pastoral Beshkent Culture. The handmade pottery of both the Vakhsh and Beshkent pastoralists, usually accompanying a mobile life style, was in many cases copied from wheel-thrown pottery brought from centers of settled agriculture — their "metropoli," as it were.

At the same time, one can also trace in the material aspects and burial rites of the pastoralist cultures of southern Tadjikistan the influences of steppe cultures that had arisen as a result of having been close neighbors and, evidently, having had contacts with them. Traces of the presence of steppe tribes in ancient Bactria can be followed more and more clearly to the present day. A steppe Bronze Age site has been investigated along the middle reaches of the Vakhsh River,[6] immediately adjacent to the living sites of the Vakhsh pastoralists (Figure 1, 20). The interesting settlements of Kangurt-Tut and Teguzak have very recently been discovered near the Nurek Reservoir (Figure 1, 18, 19).[7] Throughout their entire existence (the cultural layer is 1.5 to 2 m thick) there is observable in the material aspect of these settlements the

simultaneous existence of vessels made in the traditions of the
settled farming milieu (of the Molali type), on the one hand, and
pottery of the steppe Bronze Age on the other hand. In both settle-

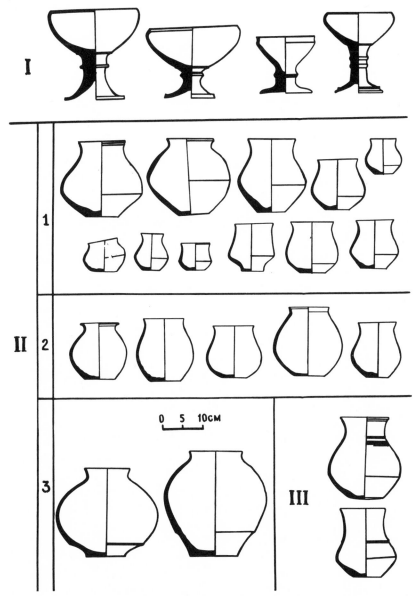

Figure 18. Classification of pottery ware from Nurek cemeteries:
I — vases; II — pots (1 — with hourglass body; 2 — with rounded
body; 3 — with truncated body); III — jugs.

L. T. P'iankova

ments two periods of construction have been identified, marked by
extensive use of stone in their architecture (a distinguishing feature of Late Bronze Age settlements in southern Tadjikistan),

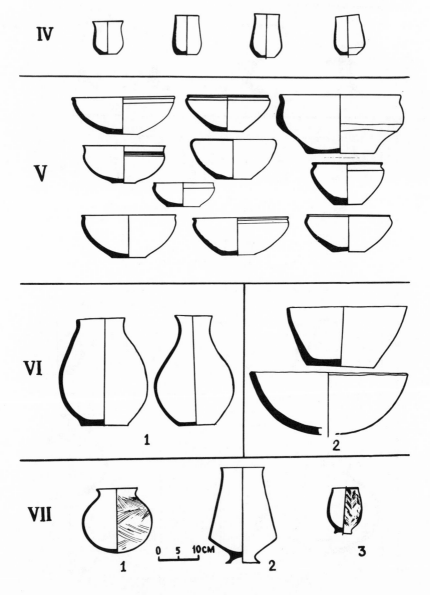

Figure 19. Classification of pottery ware from Nurek cemeteries:
IV — miniature cylindrical vessels; V — basin; VI — hand-molded
ware (1 — jugs, 2 — dishes); VII — vessels of individual forms.

306

while in the earlier period the adobe bricks characteristic of the format of the ancient Bactrian region of settled agriculture were found.

The influence of the pottery designs of the steppe tribes has been traced in kitchenware from the graves of the Vakhsh Culture

Figure 20. Pottery ware from Nurek cemeteries.

Figure 21. Pottery ware from Nurek cemeteries.

(Figure 3, 1). Similarities consist of cylinders, notches, and depressions.

The custom of burying the dead in graves of the chamber-lined catacomb type was widely prevalent among the ancient Bactrian settled agricultural populations, but such features of the burial structures as heaped mounds and stone cairns are characteristic of the cemeteries of the steppe tribes. Burials in stone boxes with goods of the steppe type have been discovered in the Beshkent II cemetery in the Beshkent Valley[8] (Figure 1, 10). Many features showing the influence of the steppe tribes have also been observed by A. M. Mandel'shtam in the cemeteries of Rannii Tulkhar and Aruktau. In the Beshkent Valley one observes a clear-cut mixing of diverse cultural traditions, including the penetration of Vakhsh pastoralists (into the catacomb graves of Rannii Tulkhar and the Beshkent I burial ground [Figure 1, 9]).

In the Hissar Valley of southern Tadjikistan and also in the vicinity of the Nurek Reservoir, cemeteries with material culture of the Molali type have been discovered (Figure 1, 12-17).[9] The burials consisted of interments primarily in earthen pits, considerably less often, in catacombs. The classification of the pottery ware from these cemeteries, based on the materials from the Nurek vicinity, is presented in Figures 18 and 19. The ware is almost exclusively wheel-thrown, but one also encounters vessels made by hand (Figure 19, VI, VII, 1, 2). Some vessels are shown in Figures 20 through 22. Animals are drawn on two pots from

Figure 22. Pottery ware from Nurek cemeteries.

Nurek: goats and horses (?) (Figure 23). Metal artifacts (chiefly knife fragments) and beads (including the azurite beads in the form of miniature axes characteristic of the Sapalli Culture) were also found in the cemeteries of this region. One of the Nurek burials contained a round gold pendant with turquoise pins and inset.

The path the bearers of the Sapalli Culture took into southern

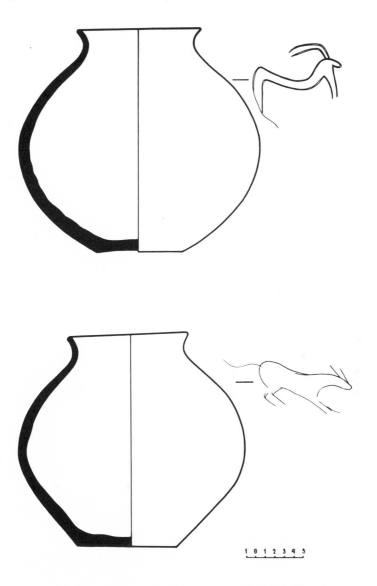

Figure 23. Vessels with depictions of animals from Nurek cemeteries.

L. T. P'iankova

Tadjikistan during the late stage of their existence is established beyond doubt: it is the Surkhan Darya Valley, which converges with that of the Hissar.

The data presented above in condensed form show how complex was the ethnocultural composition of the population of southern Tadjikistan during the Late Bronze Age. There was no unilinear development here, and the indisputable traces of the movement of various populations, representing one of the elements of those large tribal migrations characteristic of Central Asia in the second millennium B.C., have been identified here.

By archeological analogy all Bronze Age sites in southern Tadjikistan have been dated to the last quarter of the second millennium B.C. Chronologically they precede the assemblages with hand-molded painted ware (sites such as Kuchuk-tepe and Tillya-Tepe in Bactria, Yaz I in Margiana, Elken-depe, Ulug-depe, Iassy-depe, etc., in the foothill belt of the Kopet Dagh, and the Chust Culture in Fergana; a similar site, Karimberdy, has very recently been discovered in southern Tadjikistan as well). No sites of the early and developed Bronze Age have as yet been found in southern Tadjikistan. It is not impossible that the Neolithic Hissar Mountain Culture existed there until the final stage of the Bronze Age, but this question still requires separate investigation.

Notes

1. A. M. Mandel'shtam, Pamiatniki epokhi bronzy v Iuzhnom Tadzhikistane, Materialy i issledovaniia po arkheologii SSSR, no. 145, Leningrad, 1968.
2. B. A. Litvinskii, "Tadzhikistan i Indiia (primery drevnikh sviazei i kontaktov)," in Indiia v drevnosti, Moscow, 1964, fig. 10, p. 145.
3. A. Askarov, Drevnezemledel'cheskaia kul'tura epokhi bronzy iuga Uzbekistana, Tashkent, 1977.
4. V. I. Sarianidi, Drevnie zemledel'tsy Afganistana, Moskva, 1977.
5. H.-P. Francfort and M.-H. Pottier, "Sondage préliminaire sur l'établissement protohistorique Harappéen et post-Harappéen de Shortugai (Afghanistan du N.-E.)," Arts Asiatiques, vol. 34, Paris, 1978, p. 60.
6. B. A. Litvinskii and V. S. Solov'ev, "Stoianka stepnoi bronzy v Iuzhnom Tadzhikistane," Uspekhi sredneaziastskoi arkheologii, issue 1, Leningrad, 1972, pp. 41-47.
7. N. M. Vinogradova and the author of the present article are investigating these sites.
8. B. A. Litvinskii, T. I. Zeimal', and I. N. Medvedskaia, "Otchet o rabotakh Iuzhno-Tadzhikistanskoi arkheologicheskoi ekspeditsii v 1973 g.," Arkheologicheskie raboty v Tadzhikistane, issue 13, 1973, Dushanbe, 1977, pp. 85-90.
9. These cemeteries were investigated by N. M. Vinogradova, E. V. Antonova, and the author of the present article.

PART FOUR

Reproduction of Productive Activities: Techniques and Analysis

CHAPTER **14**

The History of Metalworking Production among the Ancient Agriculturalists of Southern Turkmenia

N. N. TEREKHOVA

The discovery of metal and the beginning of its production and processing were a turning point in human history. The very appearance of metal, usually associated with regions of ancient farming cultures, is regarded by science as an index of great potential for social development.

The metal artifacts at the sites of the culture of the so-called Anau tribes in southern Turkmenia are not only the oldest metal implements in our county, they are also important facts indicating, as do others, the position in the development of ancient farming cultures of parts of southern Turkmenistan.

From the beginning of their appearance, metal refining and

This dissertation abstract has been edited to omit references to structural and organizational features of the dissertation. The summary of Dr. Terekhova's review of the technical literature also was deleted. [For additional studies of early Central Asian and East European metals, including the results of technical analyses, see E. E. Kuz'mina, Metallicheskie izdeliia eneolita i bronzogo veka v Srednei Azii, SAI, B4-9, Moscow, 1966; E. N. Chernikh, "Nekotorye rezul'taty izucheniia metalla anauskoi kul'tury," KSIA, no. 91, 1962; N. V. Rindina, Drevneishee metalloobrabativaiushchee proizvodstvo Vostochnoi Evropy, Moscow, 1971; and, particularly, N. N. Terekhova, "Metallobrabativaiushchee proizvodstvo u drevneishikh zemledel'tsev Turkmenii," in Ocherki tekhnologii drevneishikh proizvodstv, ed. by B. A. Kolchin, Moscow 1975.])

metalworking were among the leading branches of all the earliest fields of production in the economy of ancient societies, and they determined the level of development of those societies. It is precisely in the area of such production that so complex a historical phenomenon as the process of the emergence of crafts occurred. The study of metalworking among the ancient farmers of southern Turkmenia makes it possible to trace this process in a concrete historical milieu.

In recent decades planned and systematic archeological investigations of the sites of ancient farmers in southern Central Asia, conducted by the South Turkmenistan Interdisciplinary Archeological Expedition jointly with the Archeology Sector of the Institute of History, Archeology, and Ethnography of the Academy of Sciences of the Turkmen Soviet Socialist Republic, allowed us to successively trace the history of these tribes. They shed detailed light on the nature of their material culture at various stages of its development and established a rigorous chronological periodization.

However, one of the most important aspects of the productive activity of the southern Turkmenistan farmers, metalworking, remains unknown to this day.

The absence from archeological assemblages of artifacts associated with metalworking makes it difficult to deal with this question using the standard techniques of archeology. Neither the sources nor the nature of metalworking is clear, nor are the patterns of its development among the ancient farmers of southern Turkmenistan.

This situation reflects the general state of the problem of the history of study of ancient metal production. The information available on this question is also quite fragmentary for the enormous world of the ancient farming tribes of the Near and Middle East, an integral part of which were the tribes of southern Turkmenia.

For these reasons the topic of the history of metalworking among the ancient farmers of southern Turkmenia would appear to be quite timely.

The object of our investigation is the processing of metal among the ancient agricultural tribes of southern Turkmenistan from the fifth to the second millennia B.C., i.e., over the entire course of the history of their culture, from the time the first metal artifacts appeared. Our objective is the investigation of the process of the development of this production on the basis of discovery of the technical and technological devices for the working of metal.

Metal artifacts themselves served as the objects of investigation. Appearing as the end result of metalworking production, the tangible product of human activity, metal artifacts represent a historical source of the very greatest value.

However, the traditional techniques of archeological research — morphological and typological analysis — cannot reveal their full meaning. Only utilization of the techniques of the natural sciences, particularly spectrographic and metallographic analysis, demonstrated what an extensive range of information had remained hidden from us.

Metallographic and, above all, micro- and macrostructural analyses are the most important techniques currently available for studying ancient implements and technology for metalworking.

They provide an opportunity to reconstruct the way in which metal products were made and to define their quality and the quality of the metal itself. On this basis it is possible to evaluate the suitability of procedures with respect to certain types of products, to estimate the amount of labor required, and in the final analysis, to gain some idea of the degree of work skills and the nature of the organization of production.

Techniques of micro- and macrostructural analysis of metal from south Turkmenistan formed the basis of the present investigation.

The materials studied came from the principal sites of the ancient farmers of south Turkmenia, investigated by V. M. Masson, I. N. Khlopin, V. I. Sarianidi, A. A. Marushenko, and O. K. Berdyev.

The collection is in the Institute of Archeology of the USSR Academy of Sciences, Leningrad Branch, and in a sector of the Institute of History, Archeology, and Ethnography of the Academy of Sciences of the Turkmen SSR.

All the principal types of metal products of the tribes of southern Turkmenistan — implements of labor, weapons, and ornaments — were represented among the materials studied.

Three hundred artifacts were subjected to laboratory study, of which 150 underwent macro- and microstructural analysis.

Metalworking Technology and Implements in the Aeneolithic

The earliest metal artifacts of the ancient farmers are associated with assemblages of the type of Anau IA (Mondjukly-depe, Chakmakly-depe, Kaushut). These artifacts already are marked by a high level of knowledge of metalworking. For example, different techniques of free forging have been identified (circular forging, producing a tetrahedral cross section, severance, flattening, bending, reducing) with the use of heat treatment — intermediate annealing.

It is suggestive that casting (an awl from Kaushut) was well known in the period under examination. The technique used made it possible for castings of good quality to be produced. The use of casting techniques presumes the ability to produce high temperatures (not under 1000° C). In chemical composition the artifacts were of copper, with trace impurities of lead, silver, nickel, and iron. In two objects (from Kaushut) a high level of arsenic was found: 0.5 and 3.0 percent.

The next period, that of Namazga I, witnessed the further development and elaboration of techniques already known. The technology for making figured pin heads with precise profiles and firm contours, the forging of which presumed the use of specialized and rather elaborate and delicate tools, demonstrates this development.

The flattening of metal, particularly the production of metal strips of uniform cross section and width, in the making of awls — another typical artifact — required high skill and experience not only in mechanical working but in selecting the proper temperatures.

The metal objects from the period of Namazga II characterize the distinguishing features of metalworking technology in the following period. Above all, the assortment of objects expanded, the techniques for working them became more varied, and new forms appeared (cold working of the working part of the object, material-softening annealing, and an attempt to use closed molds for casting).

It is significant that products of the same type, for example, knives and awls, were made with different technologies, i.e., one sees a search for the most suitable techniques in the light of the features of the raw material and the functional purpose of the tools. In the development of the plastic working of metal, perfection of the technique of the smith's work was decisive: improvement of the working qualities of the tools, and development of temperature sequences in accordance with the properties of the metal used — plumbous copper, which does not withstand high-temperature working. The raw material was copper with a high admixture of lead and a number of other impurities. In addition to copper, lead was known at that time.

Sharp changes in metalworking techniques are observable for the Late Aeneolithic period (Namazga III). There was a considerable increase in the overall volume of metal products and their qualitative diversity.

Innovations emerge most vividly in the appearance of more complex casting techniques — the use of closed molds and casting with a smelted model. The improvement in casting technique, and particularly the expansion of the potentials for modeling products by using for the purpose a plastic material such as wax, facilitated further development of metalworking.

The marked change in the technological process as such is significant. Now one sees a clear-cut differentiation and standardization of techniques for certain categories of products.

An important factor that improved the technological processing of metal was the utilization of an all-purpose blank made by casting. In our view the circular rods with a single thickened end functioned in this way. These rods, which in form and composition were identical with the remaining types of objects, appeared as semiprocessed products. The use of such cast blanks helped to considerably simplify and make more purposeful blacksmithing operations in fashioning an object.

In a number of cases one observes a different means of utilizing the raw material: a series of artifacts made of "pure" (lead-free) copper are noteworthy in this respect. In addition, products of arsenic copper become widespread. Silver and gold appear.

Knowledge in the field of metalworking was accumulated rapidly during the entire Aeneolithic period. As shown by technological investigation of the products themselves, the level of working the earliest metal artifacts assumes a long prior period of experimentation in this field.

Two major trends in metalworking — forging and casting — developed during the Aeneolithic period in southern Turkmenia. Various kinds of smith forging techniques were mastered: drawing down, flattening, bending, upsetting, twisting, the piercing of holes, severance, circular forging, shaping a rod to tetrahedral cross section, and cold working to improve the mechanical properties of the implement. Forging was performed either cold in combination with annealing or at a temperature at the recrystallization threshold. Heat treatment — annealing, which was initially used as an intermediate operation — came to be understood in the Late Aeneolithic as a necessary final operation for preparing certain types of products.

Basic changes in casting techniques are evident during the Aeneolithic — transition to complex forms of casting with the utilization of closed molds and to the technique of casting by smelted models.

N. N. Terekhova

Technology and Implements of Metalworking
in the Bronze Age

During the Bronze Age (Namazga IV-VI) significant changes occurred in the field of metalworking production. The general level rose, the very character of production became more complex, and technological processes were improved.

Metal products were distinguished by greater variety and the appearance of new types unknown in the previous epoch — daggers, spear points, shaving cutters, fish hooks, seals, and fibulae with complex figured heads. An accumulation of new methods can be observed in the implements and in the technology of making metal objects. Differentiation of techniques occurs. Products were now made with three principal techniques: smith forging of cast blanks (awls, needles, piercers, fibulae, bracelets); casting followed by finishing (flat implements: knives, daggers, adzes, razors); casting without finishing (seals, round rods with sculpted heads, sleeve-type implements, small tubes).

There were no significant changes in smith forging techniques. The operations used were already known in the prior period (severance, twisting, drawing down, bending, circular forging, strengthening by cold working, etc.), but careful elaboration of all techniques and the high professional standards of the artisans can now be seen. The temperature sequences of forging operations are strictly adhered to (cold forging was combined with intermediate annealing, which when necessary was also used as a final work-softening stage). The quality of the metal products shows that the smiths had mastered the properties of metals and consciously chose the most suitable raw materials. Thus they quite definitely tried to avoid copper with high lead content, as is shown by the sharp decline in the content of so harmful an impurity as lead in products made by forging (while it increased at the same time in casting alloys).

Quite novel changes occurred in casting technique, indicating that precisely this direction was fundamental in the development of metalworking. The improvement of casting technique went in two directions: the development of new process techniques, on the one hand, and the creation of synthetic alloys and the working out of formulas for various alloys, on the other. The period under examination is characterized by the use of various casting techniques: open molds, closed molds, smelted models, and forms with rods inserted to produce hollow objects. This last complex

318

technique appears in the time of Namazga IV and demonstrates an important stage in the development of casting techniques, making it possible to advance to the casting of metal vessels.

A key factor in the development of metalworking is the appearance of synthetic alloys used in casting. The following are known: (1) copper and silver (bilon); (2) silver and copper; (3) copper and lead (highest lead concentrations from 7.0 to 12.64 percent); (4) copper, lead, and arsenic (highest lead content 7 percent, arsenic 8.0 percent); (5) copper, lead, and tin (maximum lead 21.69 percent, tin 5.57 percent).

All these alloys have high casting properties and were used in making the specific objects that did not require further forging (seals, rods with complex sculpted heads).

The most common addition in the casting of alloys was lead. The very process of making the alloys presumes accumulation of special knowledge of the physical properties of metals. Thus a major role in the creation of synthetic lead alloys was played by the lengthy prior experience of using plumbous copper obtained from local ores.

The period of Namazga V saw the beginning of the mastery (not always successful) of the technology of making and working an alloy entirely new to the craftsmen of southern Turkmenistan — tin bronzes, which in fact did not become widespread.

Significant changes are to be seen in the production of the metal itself — the remains of traces of metallurgical activity (which I have attempted to reconstruct) at communities remote from the ore sources, which may indicate that metallurgical production as such could have been conducted separately from mining.

The assemblage of diverse data on the characteristics of the technology of metalworking in the Bronze Age, arrived at on the basis of metallographic study of various kinds of products with the use of the findings of spectroscopic analysis, permits us to say that that technology had reached a high level.

The development of new techniques and the introduction of synthetic alloys requiring special knowledge are an important indicator of the specialization of the craftsmen (smiths and foundrymen) and of improvements in procedures.

Stages in the Emergence and Features of the Development of Metalworking among the Ancient Farmers of Southern Turkmenia

1. We can identify five principal stages in the emergence of

metalworking in southern Turkmenia.

Stage I — the end of the fifth millennium B.C. (Anau IA) — is associated with the appearance of the first metal products on the territory of the Anau tribes.

Two main techniques — forging and casting — are used in metalworking.

Virtually all the most important operations of smith forging were already known. Heat treatment in the form of intermediate annealing was used.

The existence of thoroughly mastered casting techniques is notable and indicates long prior experience in working with metal, since casting marks a new stage in the development of metalworking.

The use of casting as a means of making metal products presumes the existence of special tools, casting molds, refractory crucibles to melt the metal adapted to pouring the metal, and most important, the presence of furnaces capable of providing temperatures in excess of 1000° C.

In all likelihood metal was obtained by refining. The sum of data on metalworking in this period suggests that this form of production had a clearly expressed specialized character from the very beginning of its appearance in southern Turkmenia.

Stage II — the fourth millennium B.C. (Namazga I-II) — is marked by the gradual emergence of local metal refining and working, including the search for and development of local raw materials, familiarization in practice with the new specific and distinctive features of the local metal due to the character of the ore, and the working out of new techniques for processing the metal, with consideration of its special qualities.

The oxidized copper ores worked at that time gave the metal obtained from them the characteristic lead additive.

In the course of the search for the best procedures, new techniques were discovered. The most important in forging were final work-softening annealing after cold forging and the strengthening of the working part of implements to improve its mechanical properties through increased hardness.

The first, albeit unsuccessful, attempts to advance to casting in closed molds were made. The very possibility that metalworking techniques could be improved and the intentional search for the most effective techniques presume, on the one hand, a definite level of development and, on the other, specialized human activity in this field, since only if all prior experience in metalworking had been well mastered would it have been possible to pose and solve new tasks.

Stage III — the late fourth and first half of the third millennia B.C. (Namazga III) — was marked by the organization of metalworking as an occupation at large settlements in the piedmont belt of southern Turkmenia.

There was a sharp increase in the quantity of metal products. The quality of their working was considerably improved.

When artifacts were made by forging, a general-purpose cast blank (bar-rod) was used the shape of which made it possible to form the required implements quickly using the simplest smith forging operations.

In casting technology the new stage of technological development was marked by the mastering of techniques of casting in closed molds shaped by means of smelted models.

The technological devices used were clearly correlated with the functional purposes of the products.

Standardization in the making of products of the same kind can be seen, along with clear differentiation of techniques for different categories of products.

The development of standard techniques indicates stability in the conditions of production, which could be achieved when specialized workshops were in regular operation.

The overall level of technique, the appearance of semifinished metal ingots, and the very appearance of centers of metalworking at communities far from sources of ore show that at this stage, metalworking became an independent field, i.e., that it had become separate from mining and refining. The possibility of and need for such a division resulted from the expansion and elaboration of specialized activity in both fields on the basis of a rather high level of technology.

Stage IV was in the second half of the third millennium B.C. (Namazga IV). The further development of technical knowledge in the metalworking field and further intensification of specialization in metallurgy led to separation of refining from mining. Metallurgical production was organized at settlements in the piedmont strip along the base of the Kopet Dagh which were far removed from the ore sources.

New techniques appeared in metalworking, and there were improvements in old methods. In forging, methods that had been well worked out in the preceding period were used. This utilization of earlier techniques reflected the stability of traditions in consolidating the most desirable technological means, on the one hand, and the genetic continuity of technical skills within a single culture area, on the other.

In casting, the appearance of so important a technique as the pouring of hollow objects by means of inserted cores indicates the attainment of a new level of development. Another achievement of major importance is represented by attempts to produce artificial alloys (bilon).

On the whole, this stage demonstrates the increased complexity of specialized human activity in such fields as mining, refining, and metalworking, which presumes a complex system of communication on the basis of a wide development of exchange.

Stage V covers the second millennium B.C. (Namazga V-VI). It was a period of the flourishing of metalworking crafts in southern Turkmenia, coinciding with a general upsurge in all economic fields.

New, significant achievements are observed in the implements and technology of metalworking.

In smith forging traditional devices were used, but they were worked out with greater care. A characteristic feature of development here is special selection of the material to be forged, the properties of which corresponded to technical requirements and facilitated the successful performance of various operations (plumbous copper, poorly suited to smith forging, went out of use, being replaced by arsenous copper). Casting developed at an incredible rate. Foundrymen created a variety of synthetic alloys with high casting properties. Lead came to be the most widely used alloying additive. The making of artificial alloys and the complex techniques of certain kinds of casting, particularly the pouring of highly artistic objects (amulet seals with complex designs and sculpted heads), show the further development of specialization. It would appear that at this stage casting was separated from forging, and it is possible that among the foundrymen themselves there were specialists in making objets d'art.

The total data obtained show the marked increase in complexity of the technical base and of a high degree of specialization in metalworking, which led to its ultimate emergence as an independent, socially and structurally distinct branch of the ancient economy — a craft.

As might have been observed, the principal stages in metalworking coincide with a chronological periodization of the southern Turkmenian ancient farming culture.

This fact seems quite natural, since cultural periods are identified on the basis of archeological assemblages reflecting a definite level of social development. However, the principal patterns, features, and tendencies of such development are revealed and manifested most clearly in productive activity, particularly in the leading branch of production of that day: metallurgy.

By the time metal appeared on the territory of the Anau tribes, at the end of the fifth millennium B.C., it was rather widespread among the ancient agricultural tribes of the Near East (Sialk, Tal-i Iblis, Tepe Giyan VB, Arpachiyyah, Chagar Bazar, Mersin, Beyçesultan, etc.), and metallurgy already had a history of at least 2,000 years.

The earliest metal products presently known date to the seventh millennium B.C. and come from sites in Anatolia (Cayönü-Tepesi, Catal Hüyük, and Suberde).

Finds of copper ore and, most important, metallurgical slag at settlements are significant. Among the metals copper and lead were already known.

In the sixth millennium B.C. metal appeared at sites of the earliest farmers in Mesopotamia (Yarim Tepe I, Tell Sotto, Tell es-Sawwan) and on adjacent Iranian territory (Ali-Kosh).

Finds of copper ore are also common in settlements of that time.

The unique find of a massive lead bracelet in the very lowest strata of the cultural levels at Yarim Tepe I (excavations by the Iraq Expedition of the Institute of Archeology, USSR Academy of Sciences, 1974) might indicate the development of metallurgy, particularly lead metallurgy.

In the fifth millennium B.C., not only copper and lead were known but silver (Beyçesultan) and, evidently, gold. The first treasures of metals appear.

Achievements in the metalworking field at early stages (fifth and fourth millennia B.C.) can be evaluated only from very fragmentary data (there have been only single instances of technological studies of the metal). However, one forms the impression that its level of development was quite high for the time. The early spread of casting techniques is suggestive (fifth millennium B.C. — Beyçesultan, the Amuq sites, Arpachiyyah, Tal-i Iblis).

There were various forging operations (flattening, severance, bending, circular forging, tetrahedral shaping, etc.).

Special operations utilizing heat treatment of metal — intermediate annealing and final material-softening — were well known. The working part of cutting implements was subjected to cold hardening that increased mechanical quality.

Analysis of the data at hand shows that the principal technological operations appeared at early stages simultaneously in various Near Eastern centers, including the territory of southern Turkmenia (for example, so important a stage in the development of casting technique as casting from wax patterns has been identified at the end of the fourth millennium B.C. at the Amuq sites and at sites in ancient Palestine, Mesopotamia, and southern Turkmenia).

In characterizing certain features of the development of metalworking, materials from sites in Syro-Cilicia (Amuq), one of the ancient centers of this kind of production, are significant. The very first products in this area (end of fifth millennium B.C.) are associated with developed metalworking techniques and technology. A sharp turning point in the gradual evolution of local production is evident roughly at the turn from the fourth to the third millennium B.C., which was followed by a more rapid, intensive development. The dynamics of the development of this metalworking production recalls the process among the Anau tribes, which perhaps reflects some general patterns in the development of this form of production.

Materials pertaining to the period when urban civilizations arose in the highly developed regions of Mesopotamia and Iran show the intense development of metalworking techniques (the painstaking workmanship and large number of forging operations, the complex and varied casting techniques, the development of formulas for synthetic alloys) and the high level of specialization there. It is precisely there that metal production very early emerged as a highly developed craft.

When one examines the metalworking of southern Turkmenia within the system of production of the Near Eastern tribes, one can see that in the Aeneolithic, new technical achievements spread fairly quickly and widely among the ancient farmers.

This suggests not only intimate contacts but, above all, similar technical levels of development. Only under these conditions was it possible to take up a new technical idea and carry it out in practice.

In the Bronze Age, when the unevenness of development of some regions became greater, technical contacts became more difficult.

In the regions making up the "second belt of civilization," the process of mastering new technical achievements was shifted in time, as it were, relative to the most developed countries.

CHAPTER 15

Ancient Reaping Tools and Their Productivity in the Light of Experimental Tracewear Analysis

G. F. KOROBKOVA

An increasing number of investigators in various disciplines have recently begun to study the problem of the origin and development of the earliest stages of agriculture. Specialized articles and monographs have been devoted to this subject, including treatments of the paleoeconomy of this important question. For studying the economics of early farming assemblages, the comprehensive investigation of the implements of labor associated with one of the critical branches of a productive economy — agriculture — is very important. The archeological literature contains studies of early farming implements from the standpoint of methods,[1] typology,[2] tracewear analysis,[3] and experimentation.[4] Nor have questions of sociological research on such tools been ignored.[5] Ethnographic comparisons are highly significant for research into the history of early agriculture. Published works have covered a considerable range of questions and problems associated with the origin of farming and the founding of an agricultural economy, the discovery of the patterns and technology of implements,[6] the identification of the nature of agriculture, the dynamics of development of agricultural implements,[7] and the examination of farming as a driving force in the economic revolution during the Neolithic period[8] and as an economic system containing the prerequisites for class differentiation and the emergence of civilizations.[9] In addition, a number of publications have dealt with questions of the technical, technological, and functional properties of various farm implements. However, the set of harvesting implements tested and

325

the size of the areas cropped were not representative enough to obtain stable criteria with which to characterize the productivity of any tool. [10] In this regard, interesting data were obtained in experimental expeditions led by S. A. Semenov. [11] The experiments were conducted over large areas, and a considerable number of different implements were used in working the land; rye, grasses, and feed crops were harvested on large parcels. The data on the productivity of digging tools were quite suggestive. This is less true of the harvesting implements, the number of which was limited in order to make comparisons among different types of sickles. Therefore it was not possible to trace any significant evolution within the set of types of implements tested. Identification of such evolution is particularly important, for without this it is impossible to understand the dynamics of development of a farming economy.

In recent years more and more materials descriptive of the earliest agricultural complexes in the Soviet Union have been discovered in the course of archeological research. The early farming zone embraces regions of Central Asia, Kazakhstan, the Caucasus, the south and southwestern Ukraine, and Moldavia. In this connection one of the important indicators of the level of development of farm work is the presence and character of harvesting implements identified by tracewear analysis of collections of ancient implements.

The most ancient sickles in Central Asia and Kazakhstan, using flint blades, come in a variety of types. The most common is the harvesting knife, consisting of two or three prismatic flakes, with no signs of secondary working, inserted in a straight wooden or horn holder (Figure 1, 6). This type is well known from materials from the early period of the Djeitun Culture[12] and the settlement at Ust'-Narym in eastern Kazakhstan, [13] and occasional finds were made in the roofing industry of the second level in the Hissar Culture site of Tutkaul. [14] In the late stage of the Djeitun Culture, the blade of the harvesting knife was given punctate toothed secondary flaking. This type of sickle is characteristic of the late Djeitun industry at Chagylly-depe, [15] and is also encountered in the Kelteminar Culture sites on the lower reaches of the Zeravshan. [16] During the Aeneolithic period of southern Turkmenia, harvesting knives with a toothed edge were still used, and a new type appeared: a single-bladed sickle with a notched working edge that was set at an oblique angle to a straight handle. [17] The sickles of the central Fergana Neolithic period look somewhat different. They were tools with a bent shape and a smooth, unretouched edge that consisted of microblades set into a handle, forming a notched line. It is interesting that in later periods the Fergana Valley was characterized by its own distinctive agricultural implements. In comparison with other regions of Central Asia, only in the Fergana Valley were ground stone, crescent-shaped sickles, unique in their manu-

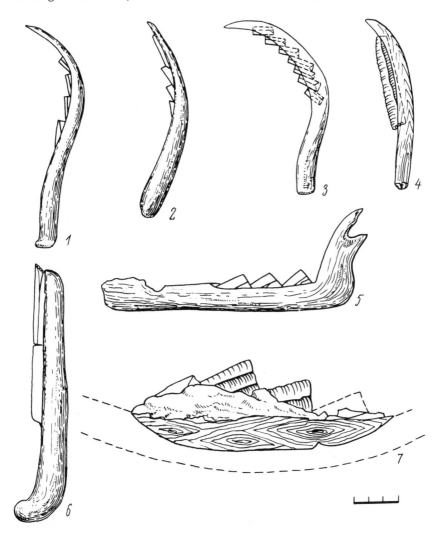

Figure 1. Earliest harvesting implements: 1, 2 — sickles from Karanovo; 3 — sickle from Luka Vrublevetskaia; 4 — late Tripolye sickle; 5, 7 — sickles from Shomu-tepe; 6 — harvesting knife from Chopan-depe.

G. F. Korobkova

facture, encountered.[18] Bronze sickles with a bent shape and lacking a notched edge appear during the Aeneolithic and Early Bronze
Age of southern Turkmenistan.

The sickles of the early farming cultures of the Caucasus also
consist of different types. Together with completely bent sickles
made of wood, antler, or most frequently, mandibles of large animals and set with obsidian inserts, primitive harvesting knives
occasionally appear. Such sickles are well-known in the materials
from Shomu-tepe,[19] Shulaveris-gora,[20] and other sites in this
group. As distinguished from Central Asian harvesting knives,
the blades of the Shomu-tepe sickles consist of obsidian or, less
frequently, flint inserts mounted in slots in the handle obliquely,
a feature that gives the working edge of such tools the form of a
large jagged edge set into a single plane. Moreover, sickles with
similar shapes are known from a series of Shomu-tepe culture
sites, e.g., Alikemek-tepesi,[21] that have edges of flint or, more
rarely, obsidian blades flatly fitted next to each other and occasionally worked with a notched retouch. The planes of sickles from
such sites as Kyul-tepe,[22] Ginchi,[23] and Khaturnakh[24] are completely different. These tools have a bent shape, but their working
edge consists of a single insert of a very large, elongated obsidian
blade with denticulate finish. The first copper sickles with crescent shapes appear during the Aeneolithic and Early Bronze Age
in the Caucasus.[25] Thus for the majority of early agricultural
sites of the Caucasus, bent-shaped sickles with a large-toothed or
smoothly set edge of three to five obsidian or, less frequently,
flint bladelets or chips, anchored with bitumen, were characteristic.

The southern Ukraine and Moldavia during the Neolithic and
Aeneolithic periods have analogous harvesting tools. However,
as distinguished from Central Asia and the Caucasus, where harvesting implements arose on a local basis,[26] the early sickles of
the Ukraine and Moldavia were probably borrowed from earlier
farming cultures in neighboring areas. This interpretation is completely natural considering that the agriculture of the Tripolye
Culture itself — in the opinion of several investigators — was
borrowed.[27] Here harvesting knives are not found. The Sorok
Neolithic complex of the Bug-Dniester Culture contains single inserts of sickles with a slanting sheen.[28] Such implements, which
are obliquely set into a bent shape, are characteristic only for the
early and middle Tripolye period (Figure 1, 3). Small and medium-
sized flint blades are used as inserts. Sickles of the Karanovo
type are exactly identical[29] (Figure 1, 1-2). Throughout the entire

development of the Tripolye Culture, the shape of harvesting
knives did not change. Only the inserted blades changed. During
the early stage they were used without having been worked in any
way;[30] during the second stage the cutting edges were subjected
to secondary flaking;[31] and in the late stage the multiple-insert
blades were replaced by one large one, finished with sawtooth or
wavy secondary flaking (Figure 1, 4).[32] At the same time, sickles
of the old shapes, with large-toothed blades, continued to exist
during the late stage. The provenance of the latter must be associated with Moldavia alone.[33] Typical late Tripolye sickles
were being used in the southern Ukraine at that time.[34] Thus the
differences between the late Tripolye sickles of Moldavia and the
Ukraine, noted above, are local in character.

When comparing Tripolye harvesting tools with the sickles of
synchronous sites in the Caucasus and Central Asia, one is immediately struck by the notable lag in their development behind
those of the latter two areas. When the first metal sickles were
beginning to appear in Central Asia and the Caucasus, pieced-
together stone tools of the Karanovo type, individual examples of
which had been found even at Neolithic sites, and single-flake tools
inserted in a slot in a bent handle continued to prevail in Tripolye.
This lag is apparently to be explained in terms of the differing
rates of development of the early farming-herding tribes of the
southern Ukraine and of Moldavia, on the one hand, and of Central
Asia and the Caucasus, on the other — in connection with the different bases of the economy.[35] A difference is also to be observed
in the quantitative composition of the harvesting implements. At
sites of the Tripolye Culture the sickles represent a comparatively
high percentage in the industry only of individual sites, while in
Central Asia and the Caucasus they are the most important single
category of tools (30-50 percent). But in most Tripolye sites sickles number 3-5 percent.[36]

From the example of the three early agricultural centers —
Moldavia and the southern Ukraine, Central Asia, and the Caucasus — one can see that while harvesting tools were functionally
identical, there were differences in the components of their blades.
Sickle shapes in the Caucasus, Moldavia, and the southern Ukraine
closely resembled each other, a fact to which a number of scholars
directed attention.[37] In addition, one still found in the Caucasus
sickles made from the jaws of large animals; but on the whole
their shapes were curved. However, the assembled blades of the
Caucasian and Tripolye sickles differed. In the former case they

were made of large, broad pieces of obsidian or, more rarely, flint, whose shapes were segmental or rectangular, and of flakes inserted into the holder at an oblique angle to make teeth or parallel to the slot to form a smooth cutting edge driven in tight and anchored with bitumen. In the latter case the tools were made solely of small pieces of flint, more often flint fragments, four or five being arranged at an oblique angle and fastened by means of some other binding substance. It could have been resin from cherry, plum, or pear trees mixed with water. Evidence of the use of vegetable resin to fasten inserts is provided by the Karanovo sickle finds,[38] with which the Tripolye harvesting tools display total identity.

If we consider data from the Caucasus and southern Ukraine of a later period, then one also sees some similarity in the shapes of sickle handles. As before there were the bent shapes, equipped, however, with a single large, elongated blade. However, in the Caucasus they were made of obsidian and shaped by secondary flaking into saw or toothed patterns, while in the Ukraine they were of flint, and the edge of the insert was finished with large sawtoothed or wavy secondary flaking.

The early Central Asian harvesting knives differ from the Caucasus and Tripolye sickles not only in the shapes of their blades and mode of attachment but in the handle as well. As observed above, the harvesting knives typical of Central Asia were straight, equipped with two or, more rarely, three medium-sized pieces of flint with beveled secondary flaking of their ends, or with four to six geometrically shaped microliths. It is not ruled out that they were fastened by means of a resinous vegetable substance, which is indicated by the absence of traces of bitumen on the blades or the surfaces of the surviving mount of the harvesting tool.

Thus comparative data on harvesting tools from Central Asia, the Caucasus, Moldavia, and the southern Ukraine during the Neolithic and Aeneolithic permit one to say that even in the presence of similar sickle handles, construction details of their equipment are indicators of local features in agricultural tools. The latter were intimately associated with technical traditions followed by a given group of tribes for many years, and they can be classed with the ethnic criteria characterizing large human communities in remote antiquity. This is also shown by ethnographic data from the study of farm implements in Moldavia.[39]

However, the evolution of harvesting tools within a single culture or cultural community did not follow the direction of development of the shapes of the handles, since they remained the same, but took the line of shaping the cutting edges of the inserted blades. If we compare the early harvesting tools, whether the knives of the Djeitun Culture or the curved sickles of the Shomu-tepe or early Tripolye type, the edges of the assembled blades are used without any secondary flaking, regardless of handle form (early Djeitun, Luka-Vrublevetskaia, Shomu-tepe). Tools from the subsequent stage of development already have secondarily flaked, sometimes toothed blades (Middle Djeitun, Polivanov Iar, Arukhlo). Sickles from the late stage are marked by the presence of a sawtooth working edge, produced by punctate toothed or wavy secondary flaking (late Djeitun, Khatunarkh, Usatovo).[40] These details of the blade-shaping technique provide dependable chronological criteria.

Entirely new information is provided by combined tracewear and experimental analysis of the harvesting tools. Today it has become possible in the course of experiments to identify the reason for the appearance of linear signs of wear on the working surfaces of sickles, which had been a point of lengthy scholarly dispute. Many investigators held that the appearance of linear scratches on the tools was associated with the presence of silica in the stalks of grain cultures.[41]

The erroneousness of this hypothesis was established by the studies of an experimental tracewear team that conducted its experiments in fields in Moldavia and Odessa Oblast. The experiments showed that linear signs of wear arose on tools used in cutting only domesticated grains raised on soil that had been turned. Despite the fact that the wheat stalks were cut at heights of 10-15 centimeters above the ground, the skin of one's arms, the wooden sickle handles, and the inset blades themselves were covered with a dense layer of dust and earth (Figure 2) from the dirt-covered stalks of the grain. The presence of abrasive particles on the stalks that were mixed with the juices of weeds in the course of the harvesting is what produced the linear traces readily evident on the tools under the microscope (Figure 3, 1, 2). Grass having a branching root system, however, forms a thick cover of turf protecting the plant against contamination by abrasive impurities from the soil due to rain, wind, and other natural causes. Therefore, when grass is reaped, the linear tracks on the tools are absent (Figure 3, 3). Wild grains, which form no dense turf, and those cultivated on soil that has not been turned have on their stalks individual particles of dust, barely visible under the micro-

331

Figure 2. Experimental harvesting tools: 1 — early Djeitun type; 2 — Yalangach-depe type; 3 — early Tripolye type; 4 — Hassuna type.

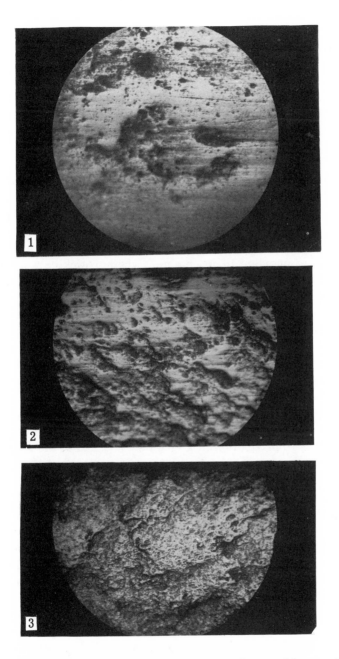

Figure 3. Microphotographs of working surfaces of harvesting tools: 1 — Djeitun harvesting knife; 2 — experimental tool used in cropping domesticated grains; 3 — experimental tool used in reaping grass.

scope, which leave only rare and barely perceptible linear traces on the sickle surfaces.

Thus it is possible to determine even now, on the basis of study of the character of traces of wear, what kinds of vegetation particular sickles were used for: grains, grasses, or reeds. The length of time tools were used can be determined from the degree of wear. The shape of the holder in which they were set can be determined from the location of signs of use on the surfaces of the inserts. The nature of the flaking observed on the working edges of the sickles can be used to explain its appearance: whether it was deliberately done before the tool was used, whether it appeared as a result of sharpening the tool while in use, or whether it was a result of using the tool in work. Experimental research made it possible to determine how long a sickle lasted. This point is particularly important in determining whether sickles were single-season tools or lasted through several seasons of work. [42]

In addition, the experiments made it possible to approach another very important question: was it possible to calculate the approximate size of the sown acreage by the degree of wear and the number of harvesting tools found in a given industry? Also central is the problem of the productivity of the harvest tools, without which it is difficult to form an idea of the dynamics of the development of sickles in the overall evolution of cultural history and technology. In addition, the productivity of harvesting implements is a rather instructive indicator of the level of development of the forces of production in a given society and of the agricultural economy as a whole, of which the implements of labor are a reflection.

All these questions were studied by physical modeling of the processes of production discovered from the data of tracewear analysis of agricultural implements from specific early farming assemblages. Toward this end, special tracewear and experimental studies were conducted in association with the Moldavian Neolithic Expedition. In the course of two field seasons, 1973-74, the Experimental Tracewear Division of the Leningrad Sector of the Institute of Archeology, USSR Academy of Sciences, conducted a multifaceted study of the system of economic techniques of Tripolye society by physical modeling and tracewear analysis of tools, [43] including agricultural implements. In addition, a number of experiments entailing research into harvesting implements were made by the present author as early as 1969. [44] Observing the conditions of experimentation was important in this regard. They had to resemble as closely as possible the conditions under which specific sites being studied at the given moment existed and they had to be done with tools quite similar to those being studied.

The experiments of the Experimental Tracewear Division were made in Moldavia and Odessa Oblast of the Ukraine in localities where Tripolye settlements had existed. Studying agriculture as a branch of the economy is impossible without reproducing so important a cycle of operations as the harvesting of grains. The objective of the party included comprehensive study of the implements of labor of the early agriculturalists to obtain standards of traces of wear on them, determination of the productivity of harvesting artifacts and of how long a sickle could function without whetting its cutting edge, identification of the differentiation of harvesting tools in accordance with their use with plants of various species — grains, grasses, and reeds — and acquisition of data for calculating at least the approximate dimensions of sown acreages. Seventeen types of all sorts of sickles were made to do the jobs devised. In addition, a contemporary metal sickle with a fine sawtooth blade was used for purposes of comparison. The harvesting tools made for the purposes of the experiment were produced on the model of sickles found in early agricultural assemblages of Central Asia, the Caucasus, Moldavia, and the southern Ukraine. Wood and horn were used to make the handles; and flints with no signs of wear, from Djeitun, Pessedjik-depe, Matveev Kurgan, and Floreshty, and obsidian pieces and flakes from Shomu-tepe, also bearing no signs of use, plus pieces of flint made for the experimental procedure, were used as blades. The inserts were fastened into the handle slot by means of natural resinous substances. In one case the juice from cherry, plum, and pear trees mixed with water was used; in another case ordinary tar with an admixture of sand was used.

The first harvesting implement was made along the lines of the harvesting knife of the early Djeitun type, constructed of two flint inserts with no secondary flaking (Figure 4, 2). The second specimen was a copy of the first but provided with three somewhat shorter inserts (Figure 4, 1). The third and fourth were analogous to the first two, except that they had cutting edges secondarily flaked to form teeth (Figure 4, 3, 4) and were made following the late Djeitun harvesting knives. The fifth was also a harvesting knife, but here the blade was made of one large piece of flint with a wavy, secondarily flaked edge. This type is found uniquely in the Shomu-tepe assemblage (Figure 4, 5). The sixth and seventh were made of obsidian pieces and flakes in the manner of the Shomu-tepe harvesting knives (Figure 2, 3; Figure 5, 1, 2). The eighth and ninth were made on the model of the single-piece blade-knives of the Stenald[45] and Yalangach-depe type, set into a holder at an oblique angle (Figure 5, 3, 4). Tools 10 and 11 were made on the model of the early Tripolye and Karanovo sickles (Figure 2, 4) with fine-toothed and large-toothed blades made up of five and four inserts respectively (Figure 6, 1, 2). Sickle 12 is a tool of the Shomu-tepe type with assembled obsidian working edge (Figure 6, 3). Sickles 13 and 14 are of horn with flint inserts driven in tight, as is characteristic of a number of sites of the

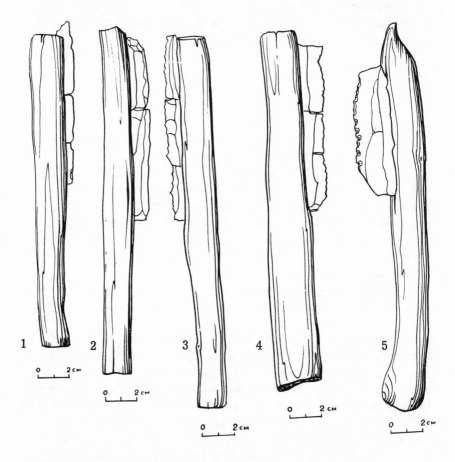

Figure 4. Experimental harvesting tools: 1, 2 — harvesting knives of the early Djeitun type; 3, 4 — harvesting knives of the late Djeitun type; 5 — harvesting knife of the Shomu-tepe type.

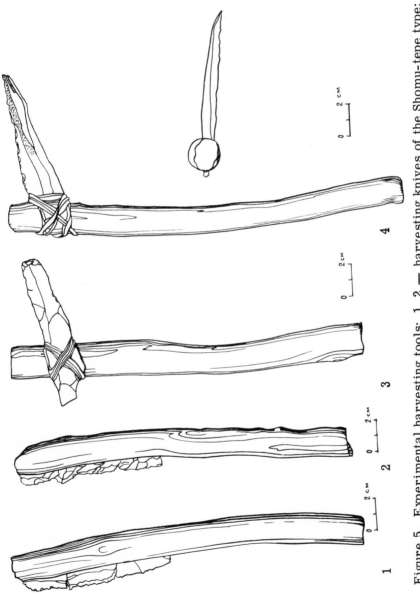

Figure 5. Experimental harvesting tools: 1, 2 — harvesting knives of the Shomu-tepe type; 3, 4 — harvesting tools of the Yalangach-depe and Stenald types.

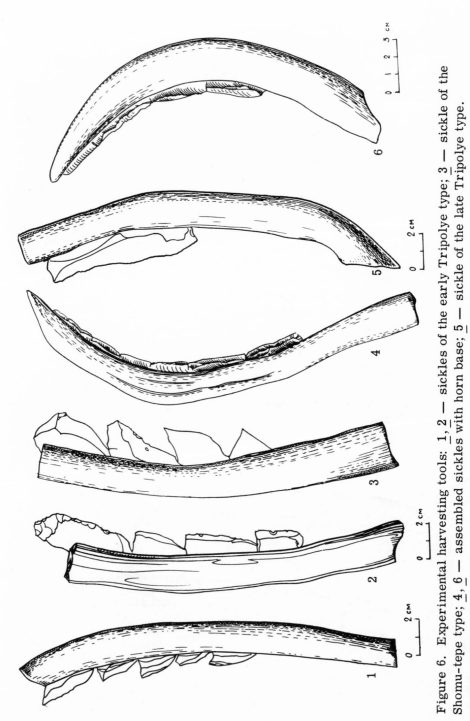

Figure 6. Experimental harvesting tools: 1, 2 — sickles of the early Tripolye type; 3 — sickle of the Shomu-tepe type; 4, 6 — assembled sickles with horn base; 5 — sickle of the late Tripolye type.

Shomu-tepe Culture, e.g., Alikemek-tepesi (Figure 6, 4, 6). Tool
15 is made on the model of the late Tripolye sickle with sawtooth
blade, also typical of certain settlements in the Caucasus, particularly Khatunarkha and Ginchi (Figure 6, 5). Sickle 16 is a tool
in the shape of a half-moon, made of cold forging of copper; sickle
17 is a modern metal tool with a fine sawtoothed edge, and 18 is a
piece of obsidian without secondary working and used without a
handle.

The tools were used on wheat, rye, oats, beans, reed, and
grasses cropped from an area of 8,204 square meters, or about
one hectare. Sample plots equal in quality and identical in area
were measured for the tests, and all the types of harvesting knives
and sickles were used on them. Male, female, and child labor was
employed, as well as the labor of professional reapers and of the
investigators. Experiments conducted on large areas made it possible to obtain not only specimens of tracks on the tools but to
learn how much time was required to reap a particular area, both
for signs of wear to appear and to obtain thoroughly dependable
indices for determining the productivity of the tools being studied.
In the course of the tests the required skills were gained, making
it possible to compare the work of the investigators and the professional reapers. That latter circumstance is particularly important for the purpose of obtaining data adequately comparable
to reality, since the ancient farmers were genuine professionals
on whose work the existence of the entire group depended. Using
muscle power at least approximating theirs, with professional labor put into the harvesting, makes it possible to attain sufficiently
reliable and firm results with respect to a whole series of questions associated with cutting the harvest, including the productivity
of the harvesting tools. However, in order to determine and compare the effectiveness of various types of harvesting tools, it is
necessary to apply equal physical force. Therefore, in order to
obtain more or less comparable standards for identifying the productivity of tools, each investigator tested all the types of sickles
on lots having identical properties and area (Figure 7). For comparison let us turn to the data from the experiments in harvesting
wheat.

It is clear from the table that of the assembled harvesting tools,
the most productive is the late Tripolye sickle, which is inferior
in productivity to the modern one by only a third. Next comes the
Shomu-tepe sickle with obsidian blade and the horn sickles made
with flint blades driven in tight, which are inferior to modern ones

	Type of Sickle	Area worked, sq m	Time worked	Average productivity, sq m per minute
1	Early Djeitun harvesting knife with two flint inserts	245	464	0.4-0.5
2	Early Djeitun harvesting knife with three flint inserts	308	571	0.5
3	Late Djeitun harvesting knife with two inserts finished with denticulate retouch	416	477	0.9
4	Late Djeitun harvesting knife shaped with three inserts by denticulate retouch	92	103	0.9
5	Harvesting knife with 2 single flint insert blades produced by large secondary flaking	138	228	0.6
6	Harvesting knife with three obsidian insert blades	262	489	0.5
7	Harvesting knife with five obsidian insert blades	52	81	0.6
8	One-piece flint sickle set at oblique angle into a straight handle	339	483	0.7
9	Analogous sickle	178	238	0.7
10	Early Tripolye sickle with four large flint insert blades	382	428	0.9
11	Early Tripolye sickle with five small flint insert blades	429	478	0.9
12	Shomu-tepe type sickle with obsidian insert blades	170	176	0.9-1
13	Curved horn sickle with tight-fitted flint insert blades	208	219	0.9-1
14	Analogous sickle but with longer blade	190	193	0.9-1
15	Late Tripolye sickle with saw-tooth secondary flaking on edge	476	431	1.1
16	Copper half-moon sickle	122	135	0.9
17	Contemporary metal sickle with fine sawtooth edge	202	120	1.9
18	Obsidian piece from Tsopi	34	85	0.4-0.5

by a factor of 1.7. Identical indices are yielded by the copper and the early Tripolye sickles and the late Djeitun harvesting knife. Their productivity is lower than that of a modern sickle by factors

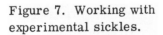

Figure 7. Working with experimental sickles.

of 1.9 to 2. The one-piece sickle that seems to represent a transitional stage from the harvesting knife to an implement of bent form, which is inferior to today's sickle by a factor of 2.5, also proved quite efficient. The lowest productivity was revealed by harvesting knives with multiple-part blades not given secondary flaking. In productivity they are 3.5 to 4 times inferior to the present harvesting implement. The obsidian harvesting knife, capable of 0.6 sq m per minute, is a bit better, or 2.8-3 times inferior to the metal sickle.

In order to verify the experimental data, the experiments with harvesting the wheat crop and other cultures were repeated dozens of times, making it possible to deduce average indices of productivity of the harvesting tools studied. In so doing the criterion of productivity of tools in our experiments was taken to be the ratio of the area of the harvested plots to the time required to harvest them. We also take into due consideration the fact that the labor productivity of man himself enters into these indices. However, when the experiments are performed by the same person, applying the same muscular strength, working under identical conditions, using different types of tools in sequence, and carrying out the experiments several times, the coefficient of productivity (S_1/t_1, where S_1 is the area of the plot cropped, and t_1 is the time required to crop it) proves extremely consistent and close to the ancient indices.

Thus three groups of harvesting tools emerge, as measured by productivity: group one — sickles whose coefficient of productivity is 0.4-0.5; group two — with coefficients of 0.6-0.7; and group three — with coefficients of 0.9-1.1 (Figure 8).

The data in the histogram confirm observations on the adoption by the early farming tribes of Moldavia and the southern Ukraine of harvesting tools of improved working shape and relatively high productivity. In the Central Asian and Caucasus centers, on the contrary, one sees a gradual development of sickles from inefficient to highly productive types. This explains the absence in Moldavia and the Ukraine of harvesting tools of the first group and their presence in Central Asia and the Caucasus.

It should also be noted that the data of our experiments agree with A. Steensberg's experimental findings, which he obtained with certain types of harvesting tools.[46] At the same time, it is difficult to agree with that scholar's conclusions with respect to the indices of productivity of the assembled type of flint sickle with the crescent shape and the flint harvesting knife. According to his data the productivity of both tools was identical, at 0.7 m^2 per minute. According to our data the latter tool is one half as productive as the former. Only the harvesting knife with toothed blade displays a productivity approximating that of the bent sickle without secondary flaking.

In the course of the experiments it became clear that a flint harvesting knife of the early Djeitun type lasted 20-25 hours of actual working time without retouching the edge. Therefore these tools are to be regarded as seasonal implements that were repaired from one harvest to the next by installing fresh blades, or sometimes simply replaced by new tools, for example, among the Djeitun farmers, as is shown by the absence of traces of any retouching

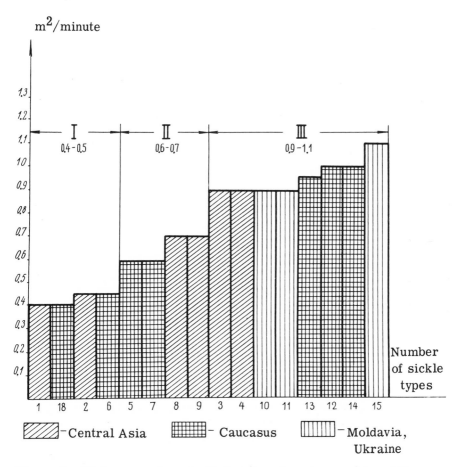

Figure 8. Histogram of productivity of various types of harvesting tools.

of the inset blades. The assembled flint sickles of the early Tripolye type show an entire different type of wear. They can be used for a longer period: several working seasons. For example, the early Tripolye sickle with which we experimented was used for two field seasons. During that period it was slightly repaired — one inset at the top end was replaced, and the entire assemblage of pieces had to be reglued with vegetable resin. It is interesting that it is specifically the first two inserts that wear out most intensively and require replacement or rearrangement or further retouching of the edges. This occurs because they undergo greater stress during the work than do the other inserts. Accordingly, the rate at which their surfaces wear is greater than that of the other pieces, as is shown by finds of sickle inserts at Tripolye sites that often have two worn working edges. This last point can hardly be explained by the early farmers' having large planted fields or by a shortage of flint. As the experiments show, the inserted blades of assembled sickles fastened without bitumen are very hard to put together so that the edges of the pieces forming the working blade fall into a single plane without a gap. Therefore it is easier to turn an old, worn-out insert onto the other edge than to match and replace it with a new one.

The results of the experiments we conducted are important in posing the question of the possible sizes of the field plots of the early farmers. The most favorable in that regard was the Neolithic site of Djeitun, which has been totally excavated at the second level of construction. Tracewear techniques resulted in the discovery in Djeitun industry of 1,054 totally worn out harvesting knife inserts that had been used only to cut grain. Judging by the handle of a harvesting knife found at Chopan-depe, the Djeitun sickle consisted of two prismatic pieces with no secondary flaking of the edge. Consequently there had been 527 tools at Djeitun.

Experiments done with the early Djeitun harvesting knife showed that it could last for a maximum of 20-25 hours of actual working time. We also know that a plot measuring 20-25 square meters could be cut with it in an hour. Thus knowing the maximum life of a Djeitun harvesting knife (20-25 hours) and the average area cut by it in an hour, it becomes possible to arrive at an approximate calculation of the size of the plot cut with his tool: $s \times t = S_1$, where s is the area one harvesting knife can cut in an hour, t is the maximum working life of the tool, and S_1 is the area cut with one harvesting knife during its life without repair. Substituting numbers in the formula, 20-25 m^2 × 20-25 hours = 400-625 m^2, we get the possible area worked with a single sickle. Having determined experimentally the size of the area cut by a single harvesting knife, and having identified the number of all sickles at Djeitun by tracewear analysis, it is possible to make an approximate calculation of the sown acreage of the Djeitun agriculturalists: $S_1 \times M = S$, where M is the total number of sickles in the settlement, and S is the total area of plantings: 400-625 m^2 × 527 harvesting knives = 210,800-329,375 square meters. Thus the average dimensions of the Djeitun fields might have been 20 to 30 hectares. It is interesting that similar figures were provided by calculations based on the population's annual need for grain.[47] This is particularly important, since the data on sown acreages at Djeitun were obtained by different researchers and by different means, while the conclusions proved to be similar. This agreement of findings makes it possible to regard the results of the experimental study of harvesting tools with greater confidence.

Of no less interest and importance are the conclusions regarding the differentiation of harvesting tools. The identification of differences in the signs of wear on sickles used in cropping quite different plants is of great importance in determining the character of the agricultural work they performed. Even now one can say that some of the harvesting tools belonged to true farmers who cut harvests of grains on a large scale; others belonged to gatherers of wild grains; a third category, to herdsmen who used sickles to cut grass for livestock feed; while a fourth group found wide use in daily life, being used in the gathering of reeds. Quantitative calculation of tools per site is quite important, for depending on the percentage relationships among functional groups of tools associated with a given branch of the economy and identified by the tracewear analysis, and taking paleoecological data into account, one can confidently identify types of household practices and local economic differences, even within the limits of a single culture or cultural community.[48]

The experiments also demonstrated that the flint sickles were quite sturdy, since they were capable of use for a very considerable period (20-25 hours for harvesting knives, and up to two seasons for early Tripolye and late Shomu-tepe sickles) without major retouching of the edges. And on the other hand, it proved possible to determine, by means of experiments, that not all the sickles were suited to the harvesting of crops. Thus, for example, one-piece sickles attached at a right angle to a straight handle are inconvenient for cutting grain because they do great damage, as indi-

cated by the fact that 50-60 percent of the plants came out with
their roots. Similar implements, but set in the handle slot at an
oblique angle, proved to be quite effective harvesting tools. Finds
of double-edged insets must be explained by the difficulty in finding
pieces that formed a smooth edge without gaps; it was therefore
easier to turn old pieces around, using the other edge, than
to replace them with new ones.

The experiments also showed that the productivity of sickles
bears a direct relationship to the shape of the handle and the way
in which the insets are worked. One can see two ways of increasing labor productivity, two courses of technical progress evident
among the early farming tribes. For example, the early Tripolye
sickle and late Djeitun harvesting knife demonstrated identical
productivity. However, the former achieved such high indices because of the improved shape of the handle, the latter because of
the toothed, secondarily flaked insert edges. Thus the highest
productivity would be that of a sickle of curved half-moon shape
whose edges are shaped by secondary sawtoothed or wavy flaking;
and this is seen in the late Tripolye, Khatunary, and Kiul'-tepe
sickles, which actually did show the highest productivity of all
flint and obsidian harvesting tools.

At the same time, the shape of the handle among early farming
tribes remained stable over the course of the entire existence of
a culture or a cultural community and served as an ethnic criterion. It is only the inserts themselves that underwent change.
Therefore the evolution of harvesting tools proceeds along the line
of changes in the dimensions and shapes of inserts, which finds
direct reflection in the productivity of the sickles.

The technical progress of harvesting implements was determined by the needs of specific forms of organization of agriculture.
Attempts to increase their effectiveness and productivity were
made on each occasion on the basis of local technical traditions,
which were an element in the ethnocultural features. Experimental tracewear analysis of the ancient sickles of the three early
agricultural centers in the southern USSR demonstrates this quite
concretely and definitely.

Notes

1. A. V. Artsikhovskii, "K metodike izucheniia serpov," TSA RANION, IV,
1928.

2. S. N. Bibikov, "Iz istorii kamennykh serpov na iugo-vostoke Evropy," SA, 1962, no. 3; V. A. Bdoian, "Zhatvennye orudiia v Armenii," IFZh, 1968, no. 3.

3. S. A. Semenov, "Zhatvennye kremnevye nozhi iz pozdneneoliticheskogo poseleniia Luka-Vrublevetskaia na Dnestre," SA, XI, 1949; idem., "Drevneishie kamennye serpy," SA, XXI, 1954; idem., "Keramicheskii serp iz drevnego poseleniia Eridu v Irake," SA, 1965, no. 3; idem., "Kamennye orudiia rannikh metallov," SA, 1968, no. 4; idem., Proiskhozhdenie zemledeliia, Leningrad, 1974, pp. 245-59; G. F. Korobkova, "Orudiia truda i khoziaistvo neoliticheskikh plemen Srednei Azii," MIA, no. 158, 1969, pp. 18-20, 29-31, 47, 48, 52, pls. I, X, XII, 4.

4. F. S. Spurrell, "Notes on Early Sickles," Archaeol. Journ., London, XLIX, 1892; A. Steensberg, Ancient Harvesting Implements, Copenhagen, 1943; J. R. Harlan, "A Wild Wheat Harvest in Turkey," Archaeology, 1967, no. 3; S. A. Semenov, "Pervobytnaia tekhnika," MIA, no. 54, 1957, p. 150; idem., Proizkhozhdenie zemledeliia, pp. 250-53; G. F. Korobkova, "Raboty eksperimental'noi gruppy Moldavskoi arkheologicheskoi ekspeditsii," AO — 1969, Moscow, 1970, pp. 350, 351; idem., "Eksperimental'noe izuchenie orudii truda tripol'skoi kul'tury," AO — 1973, Moscow, 1974, pp. 420, 421; idem., "Eksperimental'notrasologicheskoe izuchenie proizvodstv tripol'skogo obshchestva," AO — 1974, Moscow, 1975, p. 349.

5. A. V. Artsikhovskii, "Sotsiologicheskoe znachenie evoliutsii zemledel'cheskikh orudii," Trudy sotsiologicheskoi sektsii, vol. 1, RANION, 1927.

6. S. A. Semenov, "Obshchie zakonomernosti razvitiia zemledel'cheskikh orudii," Tezisy dokladov Vsesoiuznoi nauchnoi konferentsii po izucheniiu sistem zemledeliia (istoriia i sovremennaia praktika), Moscow, 1973, pp. 21, 22.

7. Iu. A. Krasnov, "Rannee zemledelie i zhivotnovodstvo v lesnoi polose Vostochnoi Evropy. II tys. do n.e. — pervaia polovina I tys. n.e.," MIA, no. 174, 1971; G. F. Korobkova, "Evoliutsiia zemledel'cheskikh orudii v drevnikh kul'turakh iuga SSSR," Tezisy dokladov Vsesoiuznoi nauchnoi konferentsii, pp. 23-25.

8. V. M. Masson, "Poselenia Dzheitun," MIA, no. 180, 1971, pp. 107 ff.

9. V. M. Masson, "Ekonomicheskie predposylki slozheniia ranneklassovogo obshchestva," in Leninskie idei v izuchenii istorii pervobytnogo obshchestva, rabovladeniia i feodalizma, Moscow, 1970, pp. 49-57.

10. A. Steensberg, op. cit., pp. 10-22.

11. S. A. Semenov, Proizkhozhdenie zemledeliia, pp. 192-203, 222-26, 253-56.

12. V. M. Masson, "Poselenie Dzheitun," pp. 82, 83; G. F. Korobkova, "Orudiia truda i khoziaistvo," pp. 18-20, 58.

13. G. F. Korobkova, "Orudiia truda i khoziaistvo," pp. 164, 168; S. S. Chernikov, "Vostochnyi Kazakhstan v epokhu neolita i bronzy," abstract of doctoral dissertation, Moscow, 1970, p. 8.

14. V. A. Ranov and G. F. Korobkova, "Tutkaul — mnogosloinoe poselenie gissarskoi kul'tury v Iuzhnom Tadzhikistane," SA, 1971, no. 2, p. 142.

15. O. K. Berdyev, Drevneishie zemledel'tsy Iuzhnogo Turkmenistana, Ashkhabad, 1969, p. 50.

16. Ia. G. Guliamov, U. I. Islamov, and A. Askarov, Pervobytnaia kul'tura i vozniknovenie oroshaemogo zemledeliia v nizov'iakh Zarafshana, Tashkent, 1966, p. 61, fig. 30.

17. G. F. Korobkova, "Kamennye i kostianye orudiia iz eneoliticheskikh poselenii Iuzhnoi Turkmenii," Izv. AN TSSR, Ser. oshchestv. nauk, no. 3, Ashkhabad, 1964, p. 82.

18. Iu. A. Zadneprovskii, "Drevnezemledel'cheskaia kul'tura Fergany," MIA, no. 118, 1962, p. 36, fig. 12; S. A. Semenov and T. Shirinov, "Kamennye serpy

G. F. Korobkova

chustkoi kul'tury," ONU, 1976, no. 10, Tashkent.

19. I. G. Narimanov, "Drevneishie serpy Azerbaidzhana," SA, 1964, no. 1; R. B. Arazova, "Kamennye orudiia epokhi eneolita Azerbaidzhana (obsidian i kremen')," abstract of candidate's dissertation, Baku, 1974, p. 24.

20. G. F. Korobkova and T. B. Kiguradze, "K voprosu o funktsional'noi klassifikatsii kamennykh orudii iz Shulaveris-gora," KSIA, AN SSSR, 1972, no. 132, pp. 53-54; T. B. Kiguradze, "Periodizatsiia rannezemledel'cheskoi kul'tury Vostochnogo Zakavkaz'ia," abstract of candidate's dissertation, Tbilisi, 1975.

21. F. R. Makhmudov and I. G. Narimanov, "O raskopkakh na poselenii Alikemek-tepesi," AO — 1971, Moscow, 1972, pp. 480-81.

22. O. A. Abibullaev, "Nekotorye itogi izucheniia kholma Kiul'-tepe v Azerbaidzhane," SA, 1963, no. 3, p. 159; I. G. Narimanov, "O zemledelii epokhi eneolita v Azerbaidzhane," SA, 1971, no. 3, p. 13.

23. M. G. Gadzhiev, "Drevnee zemledelie i skotovodstvo gornogo Dagestana," delivered at the conference "Formy perekhoda ot prisvaivaiushchego khoziaistva k proizvodiashchemu i osobennosti razvitiia obshchestvennogo stroia," Moscow, 1974, pp. 55-58.

24. R. M. Torosian "Nekotorye orudiia truda neolita i eneolita," IFZh, 1971, no. 3, Erevan.

25. E. V. Khanzadian, Kul'tura Armianskogo nagor'ia v III tys. do n.e.," Erevan, 1967, p. 59; L. Glonti, A. Dzhavakhishvili, G. Dzhavakhishvili, Ia. Kikvidze, and D. Tushabramishvili, "Nekotorye itogi polevykh rabot 1964 goda Urbnisskoi i Kviril'skoi arkheologicheskoi ekspeditsii," VGMG im. akad. S. N. Dzhanashia, vol. 25, Tbilisi, 1968, p. 5; K. Kh. Kushnareva and T. N. Chubinishvili, Drevnye kul'tury Iuzhnogo Kavkaza (V-III tys. do n.e.), Leningrad, 1970, p. 106; R. M. Munchaev, Kavkaz na zare bronzovogo veka, Moscow, 1975, p. 380.

26. G. F. Korobkova, "Orudiia truda i khoziaistvo," p. 64; I. G. Narimanov, "O zemledelii epokhi eneolita v Azerbaidzhane," p. 13.

27. S. N. Bibikov, "Rannetripol'skoe poselenie Luka-Vrublevetskaia na Dnestre," MIA, 1953, no. 38, p. 280; S. N. Bibikov, "Iz istorii kamennykh serpov," p. 23.

28. V. I. Markevich, Bugo-dnestrovskaia kul'tura na territorii Moldavii, Kishinev, 1974, p. 152.

29. V. Mikov, "Karanovo, Bulgaria," Antiquity, 1939, vol. 13, no. 51; F. Prošek, "Srpy z mladsi doby kamienne," Obzor Prehistoricky, vol. 13, Prague, 1946, pp. 86, 87.

30. S. N. Bibikov, "Iz istorii kamennykh serpov," pp. 3-5; idem., "Rannetripol'skoe poselenie Luka-Vrublevetskaia," pp. 87-78, pls. 9, 10.

31. T. S. Passek, "Tripol'skoe poselenie Polivanov Iar," KSIIMK, XXXVII, 1951, p. 53; S. A. Semenov, Pervobytnaia tekhnika, p. 146; I. I. Zaets, "Tripol'skoe poselenie Klishchev na Iuzhnom Buge (B/I — B/II)," SA, 1974, no. 4, p. 190, fig. 6, 8, 10, 12-14.

32. T. S. Passek, "Periodizatsiia tripol'skikh poselenii," MIA, no. 10, 1949, pp. 145, 147, fig. 80, 3, 4; S. N. Bibikov, "Iz istorii kamennykh serpov," p. 10.

33. V. I. Markevich, "Itogi polevykh rabot, provedennykh v 1969 g. Moldavskoi neoliticheskoi ekspeditsiei," AIM — 1968 — 1969, Kishinev, 1972, p. 50.

34. V. T. Movsha, "Pam'iatki tipu Kolomiishchina I," in Arkheologiia Ukrains'koi RSR, Kiev, 1971, p. 194.

35. G. F. Korobkova, "Perekhod k zemledeliiu i skotovodstvu i progress orudii truda (po materialam rannikh zemledel'chesko-skotovodcheskikh kul'tur iuga SSSR," Konferentsiia "Formy perekhoda ot prisvaivaiushchego khoziaistva k proizvodiashchemu," pp. 11-15.

36. G. F. Korobkova, "Lokal'nye razlichiia v ekonomike rannikh zemledel'-
chesko-skotovodcheskikh obshchestv (k postanovke problemy)," USA, 1972, no. 1,
pp. 17, 20.
37. I. G. Narimanov, "O zemledelii epokhi eneolita," p. 12.
38. G. Il. Georgiev, "Za niakoi or'diia proizvodstvo ot neolita i eneolita v
B'lgariia," Issledovaniia v chest na akad. Dimit'r Dechev po sluchai 80 godi-
shninata mu, Sofia, 1958, p. 370; F. Prošek, op. cit., fig. 2.
39. N. A. Demchenko, "Zemledel'cheskie orudiia kak material dlia izucheniia
etnogeneza i etnicheskoi istorii Moldavskogo naroda," in Materialy i issledovaniia po arkheologii i etnografii Moldavskoi SSR, Kishinev, 1964, pp. 35-61.
40. G. F. Korobkova, "Evoliutsiia zemledel'cheskikh orudii," pp. 24, 25.
41. F. Spurrell, op. cit.; E. Curwen, "Agriculture and the Flint Sickle in
Palestine," Antiquity, 1935; idem., "A Sickle Flint from Sussex," Anthrop. J.,
XVIII, 1938; A. Steensberg, op. cit.
42. S. A. Semenov, Proiskhozhdenie zemledeliia, p. 251.
43. G. F. Korobkova, "Eksperimental'noe izuchenie orudii truda tripol'skoi
kul'tury," pp. 420, 421; idem., "Eksperimental'no-trasologicheskoe izuchenie
proizvodstv," p. 439.
44. G. F. Korobkova, "Raboty eksperimental'noi gruppy," pp. 350, 351.
45. A. Steensberg, op. cit., p. 10; C. Blinkenberg, "Skaeftede Stenalders
Redskaber," Aarboger for nordisk oldkyndighed of Historie, vol. 13, Copenhagen, 1898, p. 141.
46. Ibid., pp. 10-22, figs. 3, 4.
47. V. M. Masson, "Poselenie Dzheitun," p. 102.
48. G. F. Korobkova, "Lokal'nye razlichiia v ekonomike."

CHAPTER 16

The History of Irrigation Agriculture in Southern Turkmenia

G. N. LISITSINA

Archeological study of sites in southern Turkmenia from the Neolithic to the Early Iron Age, along with special complex paleogeographic studies, has made it possible to reconstruct for that territory — more completely than for other centers of settled farming in our country — the history of the appearance and development of agriculture as the most important productive component of the economy. When one considers that the territory in question is in a zone of dry, subtropical climate, the history of farming becomes particularly interesting, for from the very earliest stages of habitation, i.e., since the sixth millennium B.C., it assumed the form of irrigation agriculture. The relative stability of the climate of the subtropics for the last eight to ten thousand years and the fundamental similarity of natural conditions, on the whole, during the Neolithic, Aeneolithic, Bronze, and Early Iron ages to present-day landscapes, confirmed by a series of paleogeographic studies, make it possible to state that the tribes of southern Turkmenia developed their economies in accordance with canons that were generally typical of the arid regions of Central Asia and the Near East.

As early as the Neolithic period, the distinctive character of the natural conditions of southern Turkmenia defined the basic emphasis of the economy, giving farming the leading role and pushing pastoralism into the background. Today, on the basis of an assemblage of archeological and paleographic materials applicable to the history of agriculture in that area, we can identify three consecutive stages in the development of modes of irrigation, reflecting

the continuous dynamics of the agricultural process on the basis
of the growth and changes in the productive forces and relations
of production: the most ancient, transitional period, marked by a
combination of dry and watered forms of farming; the period of
creation and intensive utilization of the simplest small irrigation
systems; and the period of creation of complex irrigation systems
making it possible to irrigate oases of considerable size (Lisitsina
1970).

Below we examine these three consecutive stages, considering
not only changes in irrigation methods but in the entire set of data
characterizing farming.

I. The earliest stage dates to the Neolithic and early Aeneolithic
(Djeitun Culture and the Namazga I period, extending from the sixth
to the middle of the fourth millennium B.C.). Sedentary farming
sites of the Neolithic are concentrated exclusively in the northern
foothills of the Kopet Dagh and thus far have not been found anywhere else, particularly at any considerable distance from the
mountains. They were associated in the past with the alluvial cones
of small mountain rivulets and streams, whose dried beds can be
traced by aerovisual techniques. Today these sites usually lie in
waterless desert regions, which is primarily the result of change
in the hydrographic network during the past 8,000 years.

The transition to settled farming in southern Turkmenistan occurred under very specific conditions, in the zone of so-called uncertain dry farming. Here plantings relying on rainfall yield very
low crops, but it is precisely in such areas that irrigated farming
can be developed on the flood plains of mountain streams and rivulets. Unlike dry-farming plantings, this agriculture yielded, even
with minimal labor outlays, rich harvests that provided real as-
surance of protein for the population. It was specifically this combination of dry and irrigated plantings, providing a stable guarantee
of the minimum required diet, that stimulated transition to stable
sedentary existence in this zone at the earliest date. One can assume that dry farming occurred in the foothills, where precipitation was higher, while irrigation agriculture was utilized in the
lower sections on the plains.

Initially the only irrigation used was a single flooding of the
fields under cultivation during high water by means of the simplest
structures to bar and drain the flow of water and also the diking
of lands intended for planting. Unfortunately, it has proved impossible to find these earliest irrigation structures because of the
rate at which alluvial-deluvial deposits accumulated at the foot of

the mountains. However, it is possible to trace other evidences of ancient agriculture, with which one must class, first, the remains of charred grains and also impressions of grain and grain stalks in the clay daubing of floors and in the adobe protobricks of the walls of houses at Djeitun. Among them soft and dwarf wheat and two-rowed barley have been identified. Finding a hybrid species like soft wheat indicates a lengthy prehistory of the process of cultivation.

In the soil horizons laid down near the Djeitun settlements, the typical genetic strata of soils of the desert type are underlain by loams of varying thickness preserving obvious signs that they had been used in ancient agriculture. We refer to the so-called archaic agroirrigated horizon, whose distinguishing features are a darker color due to elevated humus content, considerably increased density, lumpy-granular structure, presence of biogenic activity, and weak salinization.

Unmistakeable agricultural implements have been found in Djeitun Culture settlements: inset-blade sickles or knives for harvesting, whose handles were made of bone and, perhaps, of wood and numerous flint inserts for them; various objects of everyday life designed to process the products of agriculture: grain hullers, mortars, pestles, grindstones. No implements for cultivation of the soil were found, despite a considerable area of excavation. The reason for their absence probably lies in the nature of the soils, particularly the lightness of their physical composition. Such soils could have been worked with wooden hoes (Bukinich 1924), particularly tamarisk, the presence of thickets of which in the valleys and deltas of the rivulets and streams, as well as of other species of wood, is confirmed by a series of paleobotanical identifications of charcoals found at sites in southern Turkmenistan (Lisitsina 1968).

Rough calculations of the size of the population in the zone at the base of the mountains during the Neolithic, of the approximate areas under cultivation, and also of the yields of dry-farmed and irrigated cultivation permit the derivation of an approximate figure for the amount of grain per capita of population: 270 grams. Given the presence of livestock products and the results of the hunt, that amount could satisfy the most urgent requirements of the human organism, but it is obviously inadequate for any surplus to result. Only expansion of the irrigated fields and intensive development specifically of irrigation agriculture could assure a regular and steady rise in surplus product.

The following period, the Early Aeneolithic, saw something of
an extension of the geographic area of settled farming communities.
Instances are known of moves by parts of tribes from the zone beneath the mountains to the alluvial delta plain of the Tedjen River.
This factor is exceptionally important since it testifies to the final
establishment of irrigation agriculture as the leading component
of the economy. Whereas in the foothills zone dry farming served
as an additional source of grain, in the Tedjen Delta the cultivation
of fields could occur only by means of artificial watering. The fact
that the sites are in the "tail" portions of the branches of the subaerial river delta permits the assumption that in the early stages
of resettlement, people continued to follow the old tradition and
use primarily floodwater for irrigation.

No irrigation structures of that day have yet been found, nor
have any significant changes in the assortment of cultigens been
identified. Despite the appearance of metal, the implements of
labor continued as before to be represented by flint inserts into
harvesting knives of sickles and stone grain hullers, mortars, and
pestles. Two stone hoes similar in type to the hoes of Hassuna
(Berdyev 1968) were found at the Chakmakly-depe site. However,
this find does not in itself provide grounds for the belief that stone
hoes were widely used in farming. It would seem that the principal
farming implements continued to be made of wood. Ring-shaped
weights for digging sticks, which could be used, along with wooden
hoes, to cultivate light, loess-type and alluvial soils, are also found
at sites of that period.

II. The second stage in the history of agriculture, corresponding
to the periods of the developed and late Aeneolithic and the Early
Bronze Age (the time of Namazga II-IV, from the middle of the
fourth to the beginning of the second millennium B.C.), is characterized by the appearance of the simplest irrigation systems, which
were established through the efforts of individual settlements and
by means of which multiple waterings of planted lands were carried
out. Unfortunately, for the reasons already mentioned above (rapid
accumulation of precipitation in the zone at the base of the mountains), no irrigation structures of this period are known to exist.
The assumption that both dry and irrigated farming existed in these
districts, with irrigated agriculture predominating, continues to be
a valid hypothesis.

The general principles of design of the simplest irrigation systems can be determined following the example of investigations
of Aeneolithic settlements carried out in the Geoksyur Oasis in the

eastern part of the ancient subaerial delta of the Tedjen River.
With the aid of a specially designed aerial photographic survey
that covered a territory of 400 square kilometers, it proved possible to reconstruct the pattern of the archaic hydrographic network and trace the vestiges of the irrigation structures referrable
to the periods of the developed and late Aeneolithic periods at the
Geoksyur I settlement. For the period of Namazga II only small
fragments of aryks (or irrigation ditches) were discovered that
now are totally silted up and buried under later strata. Unfortunately, they did not provide an idea of the irrigation system as a
whole. The irrigation system of the time of Namazga III has been
the most completely identified. It consists of three parallel canals
drawn from a major branch of the delta. From these canals a network of small aryks branches off, delivering the water directly to
the fields, which extend in a narrow belt along the irrigation system. At sites located directly on major delta branches, the main
watering was done during flood season by a guidance system relying on diking of channels (Khapuz-depe). The appearance of the
first reservoirs in southern Turkmenia has been authenticated for
the same period (Mulali-depe).

Traces of ancient agriculture in the soil profiles can be found
both in the zone at the base of the mountains and in the alluvial
delta plains. Furthermore, in the lowlands beneath the mountains,
unbroken cultivation of the soil over many centuries led to the formation of an ancient agroirrigational level of considerable thickness — up to four meters and even more. Regrettably, chronological periodization of the buried layers of soil has proved impossible
thus far. This entire suite is characterized by the features already
referred to above: elevated humus content, packing, etc. It is only
the salinization that varies considerably, which might have been
due to various reasons, particularly features of the topography and
the system of irrigation flooding used in ancient times. The archaic agroirrigational horizons of the Geoksyur Oasis, unlike the
piedmont zone, are not thick, which can be explained by the fact
that these lands were comparatively briefly utilized under irrigated
agriculture and were highly salinized (Minashina 1969).

No significant changes in the mix of grains cultivated and in the
tools associated with the agricultural process have been observed.
Despite the widespread appearance of metal, no intact farm implements of metal have thus far been found. Occasional fragments
permit the hypothesis that both straight and curved sickles might
have been used in farming. The finding of miniature pottery wheels

for wagon models in layers from the late Aeneolithic and the Early Bronze Age provides indirect evidence that draft power was used in the economy (Masson 1960, p. 399; Sarianidi 1965, p. 39). Only a single complete clay wagon has been found so far. However, there is no direct evidence of the use of animal power specifically in cultivating the soil, and all arguments for the transition at this time to plow agriculture are profoundly hypothetical.

The increase in the area of irrigated land and the improvement of irrigation systems inevitably led to an increase in the crop yield and a general increase in the product obtained as a result of tilling the soil. In a number of places, particularly where there was a well-organized system of irrigation, it became possible to get two harvests a year. On the whole, under the conditions of relative lack of change in the areas under dry farming and an increase in irrigated land, the amount of grain per capita of population during this period might have increased, on the average, to 370 grams.

III. The third period in the history of irrigation agriculture, when the building of complex irrigation systems began, corresponds to the developed and Late Bronze Age periods and the Early Iron Age (the time of Namazga V and VI and the culture of archaic Dakhistan, i.e., the second and beginning of the first millennium B.C.). It is marked by significant changes in the material culture and economy of the settled farmers of southern Turkmenistan. During this period there was a considerable expansion of the geographic area of sedentary farming settlements, and the subaerial delta of the Murghab and the lower reaches of the Atrek River were brought into cultivation. The creation of extensive irrigation systems on the alluvial delta plains of the Murghab and Atrek is now associated with the taking of water from the main channels of the rivers, which was done by means of rather high-capacity water-elevating devices. These systems consist of large main canals that fed a branching network of secondary irrigation canals, while direct watering of the fields was done through aryks. The building of special inlet structures to regulate the water flow at the points where side canals are let into the main canals is characteristic. Work to exploit such complex systems required considerable labor power, and this led to the organization of oasis farming.

Many years of exploration along the lower reaches of the Atrek River, in the archaic delta plain now called the Meshed-Misrian Plain, demonstrated that in establishing irrigation systems, the ancient farmers used the features of delta topography, taking their main canals along the crests of the natural levees along the channels. This location of the main sources of irrigation on commanding heights helped in arranging gravity-flow irrigation, making possible the opening up of considerable areas of land to agriculture. The leftover irrigation water was discarded to low-lying areas, where solonchaks (or salt marshes) formed. Investigation of ancient agroirrigation levels permits the conclusion that watering was done with very great precision, for there are virtually no traces of secondary salinization in the territory over which sites of the ancient Dakhistan Culture are found. The insufficiency of the water raised from the Atrek made for the simultaneous utilization of local runoff water from the Western Kopet Dagh Range for irrigation and household needs.

In the piedmont zone crafts emerged as an independent branch of production; and the improvement of the irrigation systems, facilitating intensive irrigated farming, led to the emergence of large settlements of the protourban type (Masson 1967). Because the amount of runoff limited, to a certain degree, the expansion of irrigated land, supplemental sources of water were sought. This purpose was served by the kiariz [underground tunnels and wells to bring groundwaters to the surface], whose first appearance in the zone at the base of the mountains can be dated to the first millennium B.C. (Ulug-depe). The range of crops cultivated widened: soft and dwarf wheat, two-row and six-row naked and hulled barley, rye, and chick peas were sown. Grape growing developed. Considerable numbers of metal implements, particularly sickles, appeared. Numerous model wagons with the heads of camels and oxen molded into their fronts now offered more definite evidence of the use of draft power in farming.

An approximate calculation of crop yields during this period shows 450 to 650 grams of grain per capita of population. It is interesting that W. A. Fairservis arrived at a similar figure, 447 grams, for the people of the Harappa Culture in the valley of the Indus. It is obvious that at this level, intensive accumulation of surplus product, leading to significant changes in the structure of society, occurred. Over the course of all three periods described above, herding was the most important component of the ancient economy, along with the development of cultivation of the soil. The specific features of natural conditions in southern Turkmenistan, i.e., the composition and quality of pasturelands, shaped and gave impetus to the breeding primarily of sheep and goats.

Thus an uninterrupted growth of population is evident in southern

Turkmenia from the sixth to the first half of the first millennium
B.C. Its density increased, the area inhabited by the ancient sedentary farming tribes grew, as did the area of irrigated land.
The history of agriculture in the zone at the foot of the Kopet Dagh
Mountains and that of the alluvial-delta valleys of the Murghab,
Atrek, and Tedjen rivers differ somewhat from each other by virtue of specific climate conditions and other natural factors. In the
piedmont zone it proved possible to cultivate low-yield dry-farming
crops, whose area apparently did not change significantly over the
entire period under examination because they were rigorously
limited to a given zone. The increase in population density and
rise in number of settlements were a consequence of intensive development of the crafts and of irrigation agriculture,
which in turn was limited by the amount of runoff from the
mountains. Unlike in the piedmont zone, only irrigation farming was possible in the alluvial-delta plains, while improvement
in irrigation techniques inevitably had to lead in practice to
two crops a year, which facilitated the rapid accumulation of
surpluses.

In both areas agriculture was primarily of the oasis type. In
the two initial periods the creation of oases occurred primarily
on the geographical principle, i.e., it was caused by the need to
concentrate population in the areas most favorable to agriculture;
while in the third period, gathering at oases bore a socioeconomic
character and was determined by the generally high level of the
material base of agriculture.

The extremely approximate demographic calculations we have
performed for some areas show that population density in the
oases was very high and rose steadily as irrigation techniques improved. Thus, whereas during the first period it was 10 persons
per square kilometer, in the second it was 25, and in the third 80
to 90. However, the rise in population density in oases does not
signify a one-to-one increase in irrigated lands. That process
went considerably more slowly. The increase in agricultural produce was chiefly the result of development of techniques for cultivating the soil, working crops, and introducing multiple floodings;
improvements in seed, reflecting an unending process of selection
in the course of cultivation of some species; and the collection of
two crops per year. On the whole, a single type of economy, which
might be termed farming with herding, the emphasis being on irrigation agriculture, existed in southern Turkmenia for over 5,000
years.

G. N. Lisitsina

References

Berdyev, O. K. 1968 "Chakmakly-Depe — novyi pamiatnik vremeni Anau IA," in Istoriia, arkheologiia i etnografiia Srednei Azii, Moscow.

Bukinich, D. D. 1924 "Istoriia pervobytnogo oroshaemogo zemledeliia v Zakaspiiskoi oblasti v sviazi s voprosom o proiskhozhdenii zemledeliia i skotovodstva," Khlopkovoe delo, no. 3-4.

Lisitsina, G. N. 1968 "Rastitel'nost' Iuzhnoi Turkmenii v VI-I tys. do n.e. po dannym opredeleniia uglei," in Karakumskie drevnosti, vol. 2, Ashkhabad.

Lisitsina, G. N. 1970 Osnovnye etapy istorii oroshaemogo zemledeliia na iuge Srednei Azii i Blizhnem Vostoke, KSIA, vol. 122.

Masson, V. M. 1960 "Kara-Depe i Artyka," TIuTAKE, vol. 10.

Masson, V. M. 1967 "Protogorodskaia tsivilizatsiia iuga Srednei Azii," SA, no. 3.

Minashina, N. G. 1969 "Pochvy eneoliticheskogo oazisa Geoksiur," in Zemli drevnego orosheniia.

Sarianidi, V. I. 1965 Pamiatniki pozdnego eneolita Iugo-Vostochnoi Turkmenii, SAI, BZ-8, part 4.

CHAPTER 17

The Ecological Prerequisites for Early Farming in Southern Turkmenia

P. M. DOLUKHANOV

The evolution of early farming in southern Turkmenistan was a turning point in the development of the productive forces of the prehistoric population of the USSR. The mechanism of this process is of great importance from both theoretical and practical points of view. There is no doubt whatsoever that the evolution of agriculture was a complicated process shaped by both social and natural factors. On the one hand, this process largely depended on the social development of the population throughout a vast area embracing the Near and Middle East in the course of the Late Pleistocene and Early Holocene. On the other hand, it was stimulated by environmental conditions favorable to the emergence of ancient forms of agriculture in certain areas. The aim of the present article is an attempt to analyze the natural factors that favored the evolution of the earliest forms of agriculture in southern Turkmenia, and that imposed certain restrictions on its subsequent development there.

The article is based primarily on characteristics of the modern environment. Where possible, some adjustments for the conditions of the Middle and Late Holocene have been made. But the lack of reliable paleogeographic evidence remains the main source of problems in this field; it has prompted considerable controversy in the evaluation by some authors of general climatic trends. Thus G. N. Lisitsina (1965) thinks that climatic conditions in Central Asia were more or less stable throughout the Holocene. The majority of paleogeographers (Dolukhanov 1978 and 1980; Mamedov

1980) share the view that the climate during the Middle Holocene (6000-7000 B.C.) was moister than that of today. The latter opinion is further substantiated by evidence recently obtained for the whole arid belt of the Old World: in the Sahara (Petit Maire 1979); in the Arabian desert (McClure 1976) and in the Zagros piedmont (van Zeist and Bottema 1977).

Relief

The peculiarity of the relief in southern Turkmenia is largely due to the fact that the area lies within the border zone between two distinct tectonic units, namely, the Kara Kum Desert and the Kopet Dagh Mountains. The first had a marked subsidence trend throughout the Neogene-Quaternary; while the second, being the northernmost extension of the Turkmeno-Khorassan mountain system, is part of the Alpine geosyncline belt.

The Kopet Dagh forms an evenly folded arc, convex to the north. The structure of the northeastern belt is that of a nonsymmetrical anticline with an abrupt northeastern wing, in some cases overfolded and inclined to the north. Due to the undulation of its apex, the main anticline is divided into a number of brachyfolds running northwest, typical of the whole range. Each range corresponds to an anticline; intermontane depressions correspond to synclines. The following anticlines can be distinguished within the central and eastern Kopet Dagh: the main northern anticline situated between Ashkhabad and Bakharden; the Gyaur anticline; the main northeastern anticline. All three are formed by Cretaceous rocks. They are broken in the north by a system of folds. Important thermal springs are situated along this line.

The structural correlation between the Kopet Dagh and the southern Kara Kum is open to discussion. The greater part of the Kara Kum constitues part of a major depression known as the Kara Kum graben. On the basis of his studies M. K. Grave (1967) concludes that the northern limit of the Kopet Dagh is the line of the northern overfold. An intermediate zone situated to the north is regarded as an outer uplifted wing of the Kara Kum platform. Recent foldings within this zone are clearly marked; they die out to the north. These recent folds take the form of brachystructures extended along the main Kopet Dagh axis. They mark the areas of recent uplifting against the background of the subsidence trend typical of the piedmont strip. Three such areas can be noted: north of Kyzyl Arvat, the Kyzyldja-Bair hills, and a fault cutting the Adji-dere alluvial fan.

The northern piedmont of the Kopet Dagh is formed mostly by deposits: the marine facies in the west, continental ones in the east. Marine Akchagyllian deposits fill in the depressions [mul'dy] of the synclines. Marine deposits turn into continental ones east of Geok-Tepe. The latter consist mostly of colluvial rubbly rocks. Three stratigraphic units can be distinguished there (from bottom to top): (1) Karagudanian (red-brown sandstones interbedded with conglomerate), Upper Oligocene; (2) Kazganchainian (conglomerate interbedded with sandstone), Upper Miocene-Lower Oligocene; (3) Keshenbairian (conglomerate, sand, loam, clay), Upper Pliocene.

The piedmont plain is formed mostly by Quaternary deposits of different age and origin. One can distinguish there alluvial, deltaic-alluvial, and alluvial-proluvial facies.

Sands and clay forming the so-called Kara Kum formation and making up the surface of the Kara Kum lowland are the oldest among the alluvial deposits. This formation was deposited on the eroded surface of the marine Apsheronian and can be further subdivided into two units: (1) the lower one, consisting mostly of sand and loam (the last predominates), and (2) the upper one, consisting of sand interbedded with loam. The lower unit was formed mostly by the alluvium of rivers whose catchment basins were situated far away (Paropamisus, Hindu Kush, Pamir-Alai). The upper unit was formed by the deposits of nearby streams. The proluvial and alluvial-proluvial deposits formed by the runoff or terminal fans of seasonal and perennial streams overlie the Kara Kum formation within the piedmont strip. The oldest unit (Lower Quaternary) of the formation is represented by rubbly gravels exposed on the surface of low hills north of Bakharden.

Proluvial-alluvial deposits from the Middle Pleistocene are represented by the deposits of runoff or terminal fans in the areas where the mountain river valleys open onto the piedmont plain. These deposits are usually eroded by younger valleys: two terraces being formed on their slopes (depth of cut: 15-20 meters).

The proluvial-alluvial deposits from the Upper Pleistocene are the best preserved within the piedmont strip. They make up five lithological zones: (1) coarse rubble and pebbles along the slopes of the ridge; (2) loam with an admixture of rubble and pebbles north of the first zone; (3) loam and sand: the largest part of the piedmont strip; (4) loam and clay: northern outskirts of the piedmont strip; (5) clay: along the northwestern slopes of the Kopet Dagh.

One of the main peculiarities in the relief of the piedmont strip

is its being tilted in two directions: perpendicular to the main
axis of the Kopet Dagh and evenly to the northwest. The latter tilt
has been used in the construction of the Kara Kum Canal. Three
main types can be distinguished in the relief of the piedmont strip:
(1) a piedmont train, consisting of Lower Pleistocene fan deposits;
(2) a piedmont train, consisting of convex fans and depressions,
the general tilt being 3-4°; (3) the piedmont plain proper: leveled
alluvial fans formed predominantly by sand, loam, and loesslike
deposits (Grave 1952).

The Kara Kum lowland is a huge alluvial plain formed predominantly by the sands of the Kara Kum formation. These sands were
deposited by the streams of the Pra-Amu-Darya flowing toward
the Caspian Sea across the present-day Kara Kum. The sand was
bounded in the north by the deltaic deposits of the Tedjen and Murghab rivers. Their southern limits at the Ashkhabad latitude run
along the stretch of shory (closed depressions of inner drainage)
from the well of Bakhardok to Karry-Chirlé (90 kilometers north
of the railway line). The border turns to the south near Bezmein,
running 55.60 kilometers west of the railway line, and then goes
directly to the west. Unguz Cliff and the meridional stretch of the
Uzboi Valley form the northern border of the Kara Kum sands.
The period of formation of the Kara Kum sands ranges from the
Bakunian to the Khazarian (Grave 1957).

There is a general drop in the relief from east to west (from
300 to 50 meters above sea level). The modern appearance of the
lowlands is largely due to aeolian processes that led to the formation of ridges, thick ridges, and takyr surface types. Karst topography is widely represented (Makeev 1940; Luppov 1972).

The deltaic plains of the Tedjen and Murghab rivers lie east of
the Kopet Dagh piedmont strip. According to Grave (1957) the
oldest marginal portion of the Tedjen delta stretches far into the
Kara Kum lowlands. The oldest and more recent deltaic deposits
make up the "Tedjen formation." Transversely stratified fine and
middle grain sands typical of the deltaic deposits constitute the
lower part of the formation. Brown clays lie in the middle part of
the sequence. Takyrs have usually formed on the surface of such
clays. Deposits of the Tedjen formation are rich in freshwater
fauna, including subarctic species (Gyraulus ?). Summing up the
lithological, faunal, and geomorphic evidence, Grave (1957) comes
to the conclusion that the dimensions of the Murghab deltaic plain
are much greater than previously thought. The modern deltas of
both rivers are convex plains slightly sloping to the south. The

ancient river beds are badly preserved. Takyrs have developed in both the marginal and central parts, while sand dunes are numerous near the deltaic locks [zamok]. The floodplain is 1-2 meters high and is formed by loam, loamy sand, and sand. Both the Tedjen and the Murghab have four terraces from the Middle and Upper Pleistocene, which are preserved only in mountainous regions. Two lower terraces, 10 to 25 meters high, are of Upper Pleistocene and Holocene age.

Both rivers split at certain points into a number of streams, thus forming deltaic fans. The present-day Tedjen forms two such fans: one situated in the vicinity of the township of Serakhs, the second lying north of the township of Tedjen. The lock of the Serakhs delta is situated 20 kilometers south of the township; the depth of its deposits varies between 80 and 191 meters; their estimated age being Lower and Middle Pleistocene (Raevskii 1963). The lock of the Inklab delta is superimposed on that of the Serakhs. Its deposits are of Upper Pleistocene age; their depth varies between 2 and 39 meters. According to Lisitsina (1965) the settlements of the Geoksyur Oasis (fourth-third millennia B.C.) were situated on the streams of the Inklab delta. On the basis of her paleogeographic research, Lisitsina (1965) distinguishes three generations in the Tedjen streams: (1) Yalangach; (2) Geoksyur I; (3) Geoksyur II. The author reached the conclusion that there was a general trend in the displacement of the delta to the west and northwest.

Figure 1 shows the regional division of southern Turkmenia into geomorphic zones (after Makeev 1940).

Groundwater

Southern Turkmenia belongs among arid areas with an acute precipitation deficiency. Artificial irrigation was always essential for agricultural development. Groundwater is one of the main sources of irrigation. Southern Turkmenia in general and the piedmont strip in particular are rich in groundwater. The general storage of freshwater in the strip is estimated at 15,000 cubic kilometers. According to Grave (1957) the infiltration of rainwater into the rubbly deposits of the northeastern range is the main source of groundwater. Cretaceous rocks, predominantly of Neocomian [neokom] age, are the main water-bearing deposits. The main infiltration zones coincide with the transverse faults crossing the northeastern slopes of the range (a so-called "ther-

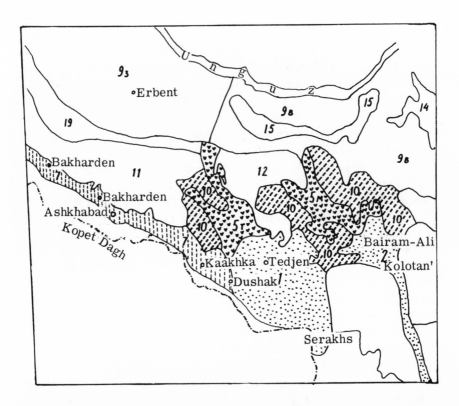

Figure 1. Geomorphological regions of southern Turkmenia.
1 — Tedjen alluvial plain; 2 — Murghab alluvial plain; 5 — dry
valleys of the Tedjen (5T) and of the Murghab (5M); 7 — Kopet
Dagh piedmont strip; 9 — western (93) and eastern (9B) areas of
central Kara Kum small ridges; 10 — small ridges and large
takyrs; 14 — loose sands; 15 — Chaghan sands (after Makeev
1940).

mal zone"). This zone is most amply supplied with water in the
piedmont. An uninterrupted water table exists within the rubble
zone. Rocks of poor penetrative quality prevent the infiltration of
water in the Archman-Sagadak area. The alluvial fans are generally poor in groundwater. The water there lies at great depths
(more than 30 meters) and is intensively mineralized (3-10 grams
per liter). The level of groundwater rises north of the railway
line, but its mineral content increases. The Ashkhabad area is
much better supplied with water. Numerous sources of thermal
water are situated along the main fault line. Most of this water is
filtered by the proluvial deposits. An artery of freshwater (less

than 1 gram per liter) flows along the mountain range at a shallow
depth. The capacity of groundwater springs in the Ashkhabad area
is about 100 liters per second. The table of groundwater in the
proluvial-alluvial plain lies at a comparatively shallow depth; its
salinity increases northward.

A powerful artery of groundwater exists in the Kaakhka area; its
level exceeds 25 meters. The artery feeds numerous <u>kyariz</u>
[qanat] wells; their heads are normally situated in the upper parts
of the alluvial fans. The total annual discharge of the kyarizes in
the piedmont strip is estimated at 2.5 cubic meters per second
(for 1954-56). The salinity of water increases within the alluvial-
proluvial zone (see Figure 2).

The Kara Kum lowlands have much less groundwater. Their
principal sources are rainfall and meltwater. Some water is provided by infiltration from the piedmont strip as well as from the
Murghab and Tedjen deltaic plains. As a result huge lenses of
both fresh and brackish water are formed within the lowlands.
These lenses feed numerous wells.

The valleys of the Tedjen and Murghab are sufficiently rich in
partly mineralized groundwater. On the upper branches of the Tedjen, the groundwater from the pebble bed is mainly used in the irrigation schemes (Kunin 1956).

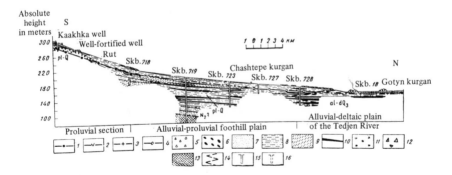

Figure 2. Schematic cross-section of the eastern section of the
Kopet Dagh piedmont strip. Levels of groundwater: 1-4 — fresh
(under 3 gr/liter); brackish (under 5 gr/liter); salty (under 20 gr/
liter). Lithology: 5 — rubble; 6 — pebbles; 7 — sand; 8 — interbedded loam, sandy loam, and sand; 9 — loam and sandy loam;
10 — clay; 11 — redeposited sand; 12 — sand with Khvalynian
fauna; 13 — conglomerate and sandstone (N2); 14 — supposed
contacts; 15, 16 — wells (after Grave 1957).

P. M. Dolukhanov

Rivers

Rivers provide the bulk of water for irrigation. There are only two large rivers in southern Turkmenia, namely, the Tedjen and the Murghab. According to V. L. Shul'ts (1965), the Tedjen is 1,124 kilometers long; its catchment area covers 70,620 square kilometers, predominantly in low mountains. The river is predominantly rainfall fed; the amount of snowfall in the catchment area is negligible. Due to this fact the variability of discharge values is enormous: from 25.9 cubic meters per second (1917) to more than 1,000 cubic meters per second (1956). In severely dry seasons the cessation of flow during the vegetational period can destroy an entire crop. Heavy floods often lead to inundation of huge areas of arable land. The floodwaters extend up to 60-70 kilometers (sometimes more) north of the railway line.

At present nearly all the Tedjen water goes to irrigation systems inside Iran. In summer the Tedjen dries out: only a chain of lakes fed by springs remains. Figure 3 shows combined curves for air temperature, rainfall, and water discharge from the Tedjen River, according to observation data of the Pulikhatum Station in 1932. The hydrological characteristics of the Murghab are similar to those of the Tedjen.

About fifty rivers and scores of small streams flow across the northeastern slopes of the Kopet Dagh. The following figures show the catchment areas of the most important rivers: Dorungar (Artyk) — 3,150 sq kms; Chaacha — 1,397 sq kms; Kazgok — 1,300 sq kms; Meana — 974 sq kms; Sakkiz — 949 sq kms. Discharges from these rivers are comparatively small. Groundwater plays a major role in feeding them; therefore their discharge is relatively stable. The maximum discharge falls in March to May; the minimum is from June to October (see Table 1).

Table 1

Months	Mar.	Apr.	May	June	July	Aug.	Sept.	Oct.	Nov.	Dec.	Jan.	Feb.
All rivers of the Kopet Dagh	11.9	12.6	12.9	11.7	10.9	11.4	10.3	10.2	10.3	10.8	11.0	10.0
Ashkhabadka, Keshinka, Karasu, Baghirka	1.48	1.58	1.65	1.61	1.61	1.59	1.58	1.53	1.54	1.51	1.50	1.50

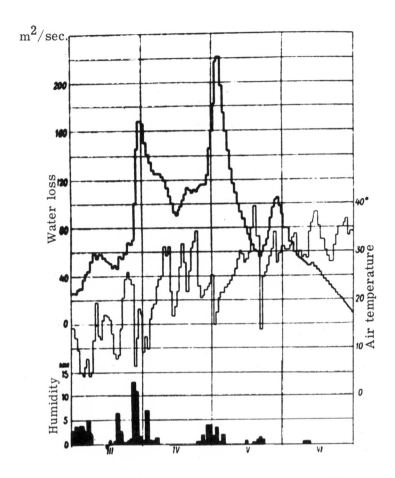

Figure 3. Combined curves of air temperature, precipitation, and water discharge of the Tedjen River, Pulikhatum Station, 1932 (Shul'ts 1965).

Climate

The climate of southern Turkmenia is continental and extremely arid. Winters are mild. January temperatures vary between –6°C (in the northeast) and 15°C (in the southwest). Intrusions of Siberian anticyclones during abnormally cold winters can make temperatures drop to –30-36°C. Summer is hot and dry. Southeastern areas (the Tedjen-Murghab watershed, the central Kara Kum) are the hottest. Mean July temperature there exceeds 30°C. The record registered in the southeastern Kara Kum is 48-50°C. Temperatures diminish with altitude. In the Kopet Dagh, at an altitude

367

of 2,000 meters above sea level, the mean temperature in July is 17.4°C.

Turkmenia has insufficient precipitation. The total amount of precipitation is small and unequally distributed. The Kopet Dagh and the piedmont strip are the moistest regions; their annual precipitation exceeds 250 mm. Nearly all the precipitation occurs during the winter and spring. In summer rainfall is practically nonexistent. The annual amount of precipitation varies between 24 and 564 mm. Sometimes the amount of rainfall in twenty-four hours exceeds monthly averages.

Seven agroclimatic areas can be distinguished for the entire territory of Turkmenia (Agroklimaticheskie resursy 1974). Three such areas are situated within the southern part: Murghab-Tedjen; Kopet Dagh-piedmontane; Kopet Dagh-mountainous.

The Murghab-Tedjen area: continental subtropitcal desert climate with very hot summers and mild winters (in the Murghab Valley winters are more severe). The climate here is moister than in surrounding areas, probably due to irrigation. The frequency of "vegetational" winters (with temperature over 0°C) is 70-80 percent. Annual precipitation is 139-249 mm.

Kopet Dagh-piedmontane area: mean annual temperature is 16.2°C; mean July temperature is 30-31°C. Winters are mild with weak frosts. The frequency of "vegetational" winters is 60 percent. Annual precipitation is 148-230 mm. The value of the hydrothermic coefficient varies between 0.16 (Kazandjik) and 0.24 (Ashkhabad).

To the Kopet Dagh-mountainous area belong ranges exceeding 500 meters above sea level. We can distinguish the following belts: hot, arid (440-570 m); hot, draughty (670-760 m); moderately hot, dryish (760-1010 m); very warm, dryish (1,010-1,335 m); warm, dryish (1,335-1,590 m); moderately warm, dryish (1,590-1,785 m); cool, dry (more than 1,785 m). The total positive temperatures in the belt from 760 to 1,010 m is about 4000°C; the frequency of sufficiently moist winters is 75 percent; that of vegetational winters is 56-53 percent. Presently such climatic features are regarded as favorable for dry farming of cereals (boghara). In the upper belt the frequency of sufficiently moist winters increases to 80-100 percent; the total of positive temperatures diminishes to 2200°C; the frequency of vegetational winters is practically nil. The values of annual precipitation are shown in Figure 4. Figure 5 shows the curves of precipitation, temperature, and moisture deficiency for several points in southern Turkmenia.

Vegetation

Vegetation in southern Turkmenia is of a desert or semidesert character. The plants are highly adapted to the lack of moisture. The tugai (bottomland complexes in river valleys) that have formed in the floodplains of the Amu-Darya, Tedjen, and Murghab are regarded by Shingareva (1940) as forest formations. The volume of

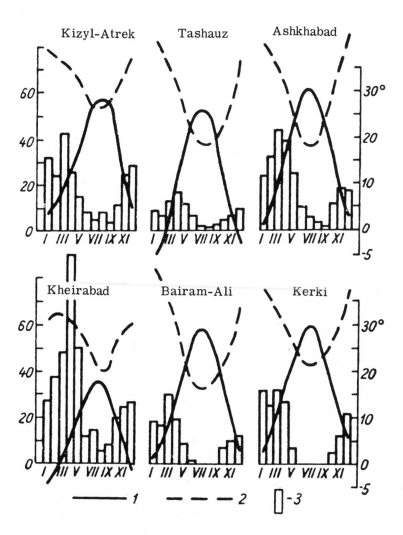

Figure 4. Annual temperatures (1), humidity (in %) (2), and precipitation (3) for different areas of Turkmenia (Agroklimaticheskie resursy 1974).

P. M. Dolukhanov

phytomass of these formations is 6-15, 0.5, and 1.0 tons per hectare correspondingly. Sedge (<u>Cyperaceae</u> and <u>Haloxylon</u>) woodlands with

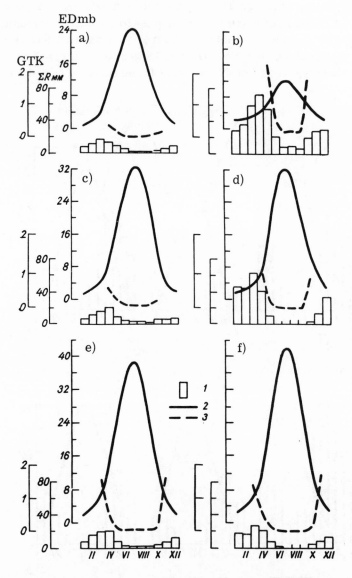

Figure 5. Annual average precipitation totals (1), humidity deficiencies (2), and values of hydro-thermal coefficient during the vegetational period (3): a) Tashauz; b) Kheirabad; c) Chaghyl; d) Lekker; e) Erbent; f) Uch-Adji.

tamarisk undergrowth have developed in the low stretches of the Tedjen and Murghab. Formations of sedges (Haloxylon-Cyperaceae) with saltwort and wormwood undergrowth grow on deltaic deposits. The phytomass volume of these formations is 108 and 75 kilograms per hectare correspondingly. These areas are normally used as permanent pastures of good quality. Within the piedmont strip one can distinguish: saltworm-wormwood formations; bluegrass-sagebrush ephemeral formations; saltworm ephemeral formations; and takyrs practically devoid of any vegetation. Piedmont strip regions are comparatively rich in phytomass and are normally used as seasonal (spring, autumn) pastures.

Various types of Haloxylon formations grow in the Kara Kum lowlands. These regions, rich in phytomass, are used as permanent pastures of good quality. Figure 6 shows the geobotanical subdivision of southern Turkmenia.

Agroclimatic Resources

There are reasons to assume that a formative period preceded the evolution of a stable agricultural economy in southern Turkmenia. This period, about which so far nothing is known, might have occurred during the Upper Pleistocene and Early Holocene. The western Turkmenian sites (the caves of Djebel, Chechme, and Kaylyu), which are often cited in this respect, cannot be regarded as representing a formative period: the environment of western Turkmenia being quite distinct from that of the southern regions favored a prolonged retention of a food-gathering economy (Dolukhanov 1980).

As had been stated above, conditions favorable for dry farming exist today only in the Kopet Dagh at altitudes over 760 m. A great variety of wild cereals has been reported from this area. There are reasons to assume that the earliest sites of incipient agriculture existed within this belt. These sites remain to be discovered.

The earliest agricultural sites known so far in southern Turkmenia belong to the Djeitun Culture. They date to the sixth and fifth millennia B.C. (Masson 1971; Berdyev 1969). The piedmont strip zone of loam and sand, where the sites of the Djeitun Culture are found, is not sufficiently endowed with rainfall. Some kind of irrigation was thus essential for the development of early farming in that area.

Rivers and small streams crossing the northeastern slope of the Kopet Dagh were the main source of irrigation. This accounts for the fact that all the Djeitun sites lie within the alluvial fans of the most important streams of the piedmont strip.

There are grounds to suggest that at that time, a system similar to estuary [liman] irrigation was in use. D. D. Bukinich (1924) reported such primitive irrigational devices, which he had observed in the Sumbar Valley and in the Kyuren Dagh in the 1910s. According to Bukinich small fields (less than 1.1-1.2 ha) were situated at the bottom of marl hills, which provided the crop with lime

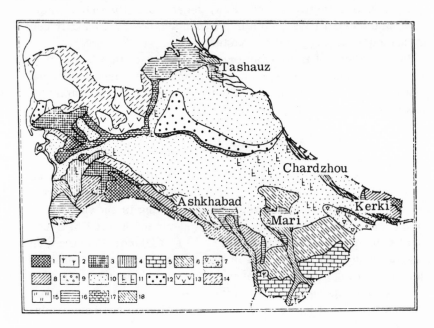

Figure 6. Vegetation of Turkmenia. 1 — steppe and forest-brush formations in mountains; 2 — pistachio formations of Badkhyz; 3 — sedge-bluegrass ephemeral formations; 4 — wormwood-saltwort ephemeral formations; 5 — sedge-bluegrass ephemeral formations of Badkhyz; 6 — sedge-sandwort desert with shrubs; 7 — mixed brush with sandwort-sedge cover; 8 — sedge-bluegrass ephemeral desert with sandwort-sedge cover; 9 — ephemeral sedge vegetation with saltwort formations; 10 — Haloxylon and psammophyte mixed brushes; 11 — Haloxylon formations; 12-14 — wormwood ephemeral vegetation of Transunghuz and Ust'-Urt plateaus; 15 — saltwort formations of Caspian shores; 16 — saltwort formations of river valleys; 17 — saltwort and shrub formations of shory; 18 — natural and manmade vegetation of river valleys (Agroklimaticheskie resursy 1974).

(natural fertilizer). The ground was usually flat; no additional leveling was necessary before watering. Around their plots farmers built small dams that retained water for some time.

In all probability similar devices were used by the ancient farmers in the piedmont strip. This area had several advantages for the early development of a farming economy. Among them Bukinich (1924, p. 129) notes the following: "mountains provide the crop with the necessary amount of water; there were no destructive mud flows (the catchment areas were small), or it was possible to position the fields in areas not affected by mud flows; the surface of the fans being flat, no additional leveling was necessary."

The last circumstance made it possible to irrigate considerable areas. But the size of a single field did not exceed 50 ha; this figure is accepted by G. N. Lisitsina for the fields of the Geoksyur Oasis, which were irrigated by streams of much greater capacity than those of the piedmont strip.

Simple calculations show that the discharge from the piedmontane rivers was sufficient for irrigation of such small plots. (In reality they were probably even smaller.)

There are several formulas for calculating the amount of water necessary for irrigation. One of the simplest ones is quoted by B. A. and B. B. Shumakov (1963) in relation to estuary irrigation:

$$R_{li} = C_{wc} \cdot H - 10\mu\sum P_1 - 10\mu\sum P_2, \qquad (1)$$

where R_{li} is the estuary irrigation rate; C_{wc} is coefficient of water consumption of a given plant (in cubic meters per ton); H is harvest (in tons per hectare); μ is the coefficient of rainfall use, which is calculated by the formula:

$$\mu = \frac{A}{-P}, \qquad (2)$$

where A is the amount of water dispensed to the compensation of groundwater losses per hectare; P is the precipitation total in millimeters. The μ coefficient is a function of climate, soil, the agricultural utility of land, precipitation, and surface features. $\sum P_1$ is the precipitation total during the vegetational period; $\sum P_2$ is that during the warm months of the year. The value of C_{wc} for cereals in the arid areas varies between 1,000 and 1,300 cubic meters per ton. The value of the μ coefficient for arid lands is 0.3-0.4.

The precipitation total for the vegetational period (monthly temperatures exceeding 10°C) in the piedmont strip is 81-102 mm, with a probability of 75 percent (Agroklimaticheskie resursy 1974).

The precipitation total for the warm months (above 0°C) is about
100 mm. According to Lisitsina and Sarianidi (1971) the crop harvest in southern Turkmenia during the Bronze Age was 2.0-2.2
tons per hectare. Consequently, the first part of formula (1) is
2,000-2,600 cubic meters per hectare. Taking P_1 and P_2 as 100
mm each, the second part of (1) will equal about 6,000 cubic meters,
This means that for a small harvest, the amount of existing precipitation is sufficient for the development of cereals. The necessity of irrigation was primarily caused by the instability and un-
equal distribution of rainfall.

Two-row barley (Hordeum distichum L.) and hexaploid wheat
(Triticum aestivum L.) were the oldest cereals to be cultivated at
the Djeitun sites (Lisitsina 1965, p. 135). The sowing season is
difficult to determine. According to Bukinich (1924, p. 107) sowing
was often continued throughout the winter (if the winter was sufficiently mild), so that winter and spring crops were practically
indistinguishable. In present-day Central Asia spring barley is
sown only in areas of dry farming, while winter barley is cultivated only on irrigated land. Winter barley is sown in August;
late autumn barley is sown in October-November; early spring
barley is sown in January-February (Lisitsina 1965, p. 137). The
resumption of vegetational development occurs when the temperature exceeds 3°C, which usually happens in southern Turkmenia
between February 3 and 8. The phase of initial swelling of winter
barley occurs in the middle of March. Water requirement are
greatest for the period between swelling and flowering; these requirement are usually met with water held in the soil. Ear formation usually occurs by the end of April or beginning of May. The
milk-ripe stage begins in about thirteen to seventeen days. The
yellow-ripe stage occurs by the end of May or the beginning of
June; the full-ripe stage is achieved in two to nine days. During
these final stages the water deficiency is very acute since rainfall
is negligible at that time (Agroklimaticheskie resursy 1974). The
water needs of a plant in relation to the humidity of the soil determine the number of waterings needed. In modern agricultural
practice this number varies between three and five.

Another factor necessitated the building of irrigational systems:
namely, a considerable fluctuation in the annual precipitation in
southern Turkmenia. Dry years occur when the amount of rainfall
is particularly small. In these years the normal growth of cereals
is impossible without irrigation.

Small rivers crossing the piedmont strip were the main source of irrigation. These rivers are fed mostly by groundwater and therefore have a stable discharge pattern. Although during the sixth and fifth millennia the spring floods were more pronounced (due to greater rainfall and to denser vegetation on mountain slopes), stable discharge from these rivers was assured because they were fed by groundwater. Irrigation systems based on these rivers could provide stable watering even during the hottest months.

Development of Agricultural Systems

1. The Djeitun Culture

As stated above, the settlements of the Djeitun Culture within the piedmont strip were located on the alluvial fans of the most important streams crossing the northeastern slope of the Kopet Dagh. The densest concentration of these sites is observed in the Central Oasis (Akhala). The westernmost sites are situated 30 kilometers west of Kyzil Arvat Township. The large settlement of Bami (ca. 4 hectares) belongs to this cluster. The site is located on evenly sloped plain dissected by numerous dry valleys (Berdyev 1969, pp. 28-29). A number of sites located between the Meana and Chaacha rivers (e.g., Mondjukly, Chagylly) form the eastern cluster.

Judging from the available evidence, the earliest sites of the Djeitun Culture were situated in areas comparatively distant from the mountain chains. Bukinich (1924) first observed this peculiarity. The earliest agricultural settlements were situated in the marginal areas of the alluvial fans, where the water flow was slow, and where it was easy to build dams. The site of Djeitun itself is typical in this respect. The settlement is situated 30 kilometers north of Ashkhabad, within the southernmost sand ridge of the Kara Kum Desert. Special investigations (Lisitsina 1965) have shown that the settlement was situated on the alluvial fan of the Kara-su River; a high sandy ridge crossed the waterway near the site. A small depression that could have served as a natural tank was located immediately to the south. The fields of the Djeitun farmers were probably ranged along its banks. A layer of buried soil that probably corresponded to the time of the settlement (sandy loam with patches of humus and gley) was found beneath the takyr formations in a test pit (Lisitsina 1965, p. 24).

During the following stages settlements arose within the Central

P. M. Dolukhanov

Oasis and moved both west and east. In all cases comparatively
small settlements were located in a similar setting: along the
banks of perennial streams with a constant discharge assuring
constant watering of the crop. The settled area was restricted to
the central and eastern sections of the piedmont strip.

2. The Aeneolithic (4500-2500 B.C.)

During the Aeneolithic period a further development of agricultural systems based on the achievements of the preceding stage
occurred. This development was carried out mostly within the
oases reclaimed during the Djeitun stage. The population density
rose considerably, which led to the evolution of huge tells, the size
of which reached several hectares (e.g., Namazga: 50 ha; Kara-
depe: 6-8 ha; although the whole area was not inhabited simultaneously).

The rise in population density created demographic stress,
which was overcome by segmentation and budding off of some of
the surplus population.

The increase in population density was created primarily by the
rise in agricultural productivity. This was achieved in the first
place by an increase in the extent of arable land. There was a
clear tendency to shift settlements to the middle stretches of pied-
montal rivers. The situation of Namazga-tepe is typical in this
respect. The settlement is located in the Kaakhka section of the
proluvial-alluvial zone of the piedmont strip. Three perennial
streams fed by groundwater springs run there. All the rivers
have considerable catchment areas and pronounced spring floods.
Moreover, there is a network of seasonal springs. The fields of
the Aeneolithic farmers were probably distributed among these
streams.

The spring floods of these streams were much more pronounced
than they are now. Sowing was possible after flood waters receded
in April or in May. Due to the constant feeding of the streams by
groundwater, watering was possible throughout the vegetational
period.

The appearance of agricultural settlements on the deltaic plains
of the Tedjen was an important point in the development of agriculture in southern Turkmenia. The first settlements made their appearance there by the end of the Namazga I stage (about 3700
B.C.). According to I. N. Khlopin (1964), this was connected
with the segmentation and budding off of some of the surplus

population from the piedmont strip.

The ancient farmers, having penetrated to the Tedjen delta, found themselves in an environment quite different from the one with which they had been dealing in the piedmont. The difference lay primarily in the hydrological pattern of the Tedjen River. Unlike the streams of the piedmont, the Tedjen was fed mainly by rainfall. This resulted in huge fluctuations in its discharge, which clearly depended on the amount of rainfall (see Figure 3). While in moist years heavy floods could cause the inundation of huge territories, during droughts the river could completely dry out. This peculiarity made agriculture in the Tedjen delta much more precarious than in the piedmont strip.

As noted above, the Tedjen delta consists of numerous streams. According to G. N. Lisitsina (1965) the streams along which agricultural settlements arose during the fourth and third millennia B.C. belonged to the Inklab delta. The lock of this delta was situated near the present-day township of Tedjen. In all probability the Aeneolithic farmers populated the whole area of the Tedjen delta, but stable settlements evolved only along the streams whose discharge pattern guaranteed a stable harvest. There was a clear trend in displacement of the settlements (following the shift in the delta) from northeast to southwest.

There are reasons to assume that in their earliest settlements, the Tedjen farmers used the piedmont model: they sowed immediately after the recession of water; simple irrigation works of the estuary type were used for irrigation. These earliest settlements lay on the outskirts of the deltaic plain, where water was easier to retain. The instability of water supply had forced Aeneolithic farmers to shift their settlements to the full-water arteries in the middle part of the delta, e.g., to the Geoksyur Oasis. The same considerations induced the Tedjen settlers to devise more complicated irrigational systems to regulate the discharge pattern and to supply their crops with water throughout the vegetational period.

As follows from the observations by Lisitsina (1965, p. 74) the streams chosen by the Geoksyur farmers were "sufficient but not particularly large." Thanks to air reconnaissance and to field investigations, Lisitsina was able to trace the remnants of rather complex irrigational systems, which she linked with the Aeneolithic settlements. The most complex network was established in the vicinity of the Geoksyur I settlement. Three main canals have been traced a distance of up to 3 kilometers; there were numerous branches that supplied water directly to the fields (Figure 7). This system resembles a "valley type of irrigation" (Glebov 1938).

Archeological investigations carried out by Khlopin (1964) have led him to conclude that the Aeneolithic population of the area was unstable. Khlopin has singled out three stages in the development of the Geoksyur Oasis. At each stage there existed no more than three settlements. There were no more than two settlements on each stream (Figure 8). A clear-cut hierarchy of size can be established. Comparing the size of the settlements, Khlopin (1964, p. 142) has concluded that from the beginning of the agricultural settlement until the middle of the Yalangach stage (Namazga II, ca. 3500 B.C.), the population had grown about one and a half to two times. During the following stage the population became stable and later declined.

According to Lisitsina and Sarianidi (1971, pp. 20-21) the fields of the Geoksyur settlers lay along the canals. Two fields ca. 25 hectares each lay both in the head and in the tail sections of the irrigation system. It should be noted that the system was not particularly effective. The head race of the canal ran nearly perpendicularly to the main stream, so that it could be fed water only during floods. The insignificant thickness of alluvial deposits in the cross-sections of the canals points to their low capacity.

By the end of the fourth millennium B.C., life in the Geoksyur Oasis had gradually faded away. The reason for this remains to be found, although in my opinion, one main factor was the instability of agriculture in the Tedjen delta. Several droughts in succession causing severe famines could have forced the entire popu-

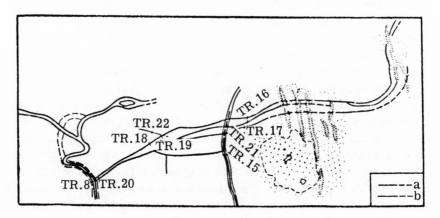

Figure 7. Irrigation canals in the vicinity of Geoksyur 1: a — Geoksyur network, b — Yalangach network (Lisitsina 1965).

lation to abandon the area. Another reason is perhaps the result of primitive agriculture: an increase in the salinity of soils and destruction of irrigation devices. The last point might be at least

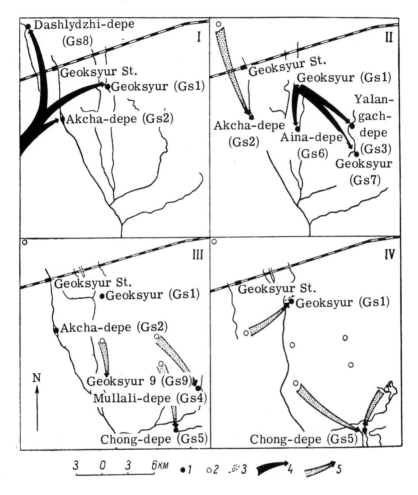

Figure 8. Development of agricultural settlements in the Tedjen delta. I — colonization of the delta and founding of first settlements; II — segmentation of main group and formation of secondary settlements; III — transfer of subsidiary settlements to new sites; IV — desertion of the oasis and concentration of population in two settlements. 1 — existing settlement; 2 — abandoned settlement; 3 — artificial canals; 4 — direction of settlements; 5 — direction of migration (Khlopin 1964).

partly connected with an increase in mud flows due to the deforestation of mountain slopes.

3. The Bronze Age (2800-1000 B.C.)

This stage corresponds to the flourishing (Namazga IV: 2500-
1800 B.C.) and the following recession (Namazga V-VI: 1800-1000
B.C.) of prehistoric agricultural settlements in the piedmont. It
should be noted that for a considerable part of this stage, the piedmont strip was the only region in Turkmenia where productive
agriculture existed.

During Namazga V and VI there arose a well-defined spatial
patterning of settlements. Only one large center of a protourban
type existed within every agricultural oasis (Namazga-depe; Altyn-
depe; Ulug-depe). Aside from them we note medium-sized (about
10 ha) and small settlements. The mean distance between large
settlements was about 55 kilometers. The settlement pattern had
not essentially changed compared to the previous stage. The
settlements lay on the alluvial fans, in areas rich in water. Thus
the large settlement of Altyn-depe was located on a joint alluvial
fan formed by the Meana and Chaacha rivers. This combined fan
stretches far to the north, coming close to the deltaic plain of the
Tedjen.

The spatial pattern of agricultural settlements of the piedmont
strip reveals, on the one hand, the high degree of adaptation to the
environment attained by the local population and, on the other,
rather high productivity of agriculture. The efficiency of this agricultural system is further demonstrated by the fact that a settlement pattern similar to the ancient one prevailed in the area, with
some minor changes, until the beginning of the twentieth century.

A marked change in the settlement pattern coincided with the
beginning of Namazga VI, about 1650 B.C. (1350 B.C. according
to Khlopin). The settled area at Namazga was restricted by that
time to the "Tower," about 2 hectares. There appeared another
settlement of Namazga-Tower size (Tekkem), and a number of
smaller settlements. R. Biscione (1977) interprets this change
as a shift from a protourban to a village type of settlement.

There are reasons to link this change to the growing aridity of
the climate. Archeological deposits at Tekkem and those from
the smaller hamlets are often interstratified with layers of silt.
The deposition of silt was a result of repeated mud flows due to
the deforestation of mountain slopes. It was connected with both

the increasing aridity of the climate and the growing importance
of stock breeding in the piedmont strip.

In the course of the second millennium B.C., a network of agricultural settlements genetically connected with those of the piedmont appeared in the Murghab delta. New investigations (Masimov
1979) have shown that the settlement pattern of these settlements,
synchronous with the Namazga V stage, was similar to that of the

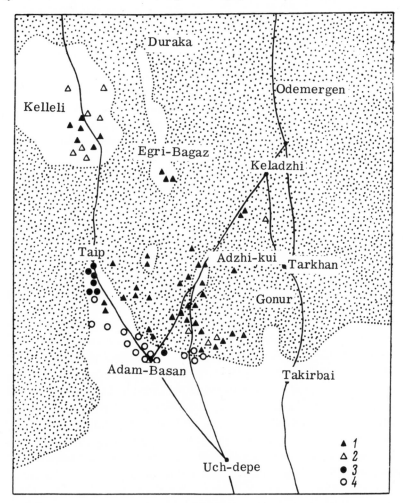

Figure 9. Bronze Age settlements in the Murghab delta.
1 — Bronze Age settlements; 2 — unidentified settlements;
3 — Yaz I stage settlements; 4 — Yaz 2 and 3 settlements
(Masimov 1979).

Tedjen delta. The sites in the area of Kelleli are the oldest and date to the first half of the second millennium B.C. (Masimov 1979, p. 130). The settlements lying to the south date to the middle of the second millennium. All the settlements lie along the ancient streams of the Murghab delta. Traces of a canal have been found in the vicinity of one of the settlements. Inside each oasis there existed one large (up to 28 ha) and a number of smaller settlements (Figure 9). All the sites are one-layered; the quantity of archeological deposits is low. All this indicates a comparatively short term of occupation. The considerable dynamism of the Bronze Age population in the Murghab delta was probably due to the instability of the hydrological pattern of the river.

By the end of the third and the beginning of the second millennium B.C., a network of agricultural settlements arose in Bactria, on the piedmont plain of the Hindu Kush. These settlements were irrigated by the southern and northern tributaries of the Amu-Darya (Sarianidi 1977; Askarov 1977).

By the end of the second millennium B.C., agricultural settlements appeared on the Meshed-Misrian plain and in the southeastern Caspian area (Masson 1954). Special investigations have shown (Lisitsina and Prishchepenko 1972; Lisitsina 1978) that this area was an important center of agriculture based on irrigation systems using the waters of the Atrek and Sumbar valleys.

Investigations by I. N. Khlopin (1977) in the Sumbar Valley have revealed the existence of sites (settlements and cemeteries) ranging in time from the fourth to first millennia B.C. These sites were genetically connected both with the piedmont strip and with the southeastern Caspian area.

Changes in the demography and in the settlement pattern in the whole area of southern Turkmenia were primarily caused by the dessication of climate. This dessication, which started about 2000 B.C., reached its climax by 5000 B.C. It reduced the agricultural productivity of arable land, causing relative overpopulation. This, in its turn, caused a decrease in population density, a shift from the protourban to the village type of settlement, and a general exodus of the population to the east and west.

Conclusions

On the basis of the evidence presented above, one can draw the following conclusions as to the ecological prerequisites for early farming in southern Turkmenia.

1. A formative stage of incipient agriculture restricted to the mountainous area of the Kopet Dagh probably preceded the evolution of the known agricultural sites in southern Turkmenia.

2. The Neolithic stage in the development of early farming (sixth-fifth millennia B.C.) was restricted to the central and eastern sections of the piedmont strip. Comparatively small settlements were situated on the alluvial fans of rivers with a stable discharge pattern. An estuary type of irrigation is evident.

3. The Aeneolithic and the Bronze Age (fifth to the end of the second millennia B.C.) correspond to the flourishing and the subsequent decline of early farming in southern Turkmenia. Successful adaptation to the environment caused a considerable increase in population density and the evolution of a network of settlements showing a hierarchical structure.

The area of agricultural settlement had considerably increased. The following zones of settlements are clear: (1) Kopet Dagh piedmont strip (fifth-second millennia); (2) deltaic plain of the Tedjen (fourth-second millennia); (3) deltaic plain of the Murghab (beginning-middle of the second millennium); (4) Sumbar Valley (fourth-second millennia); (5) Hindu Kush piedmont plain (end of the third-middle of the second millennia B.C.). Among all these zones the most stable agricultural systems existed within the Kopet Dagh piedmont strip. This was primarily due to the fact that the Kopet Dagh rivers fed by groundwater had a more stable discharge pattern.

4. During the middle and the second half of the second millennium B.C., the agricultural settlements in southern Turkmenia gradually faded away. While in the Kopet Dagh piedmont strip there was a shift from the protourban to the village type of settlement, the agricultural sites in the Tedjen and Murghab deltas disappeared completely. After a short-lived efflorescence the agricultural settlements disappeared from the Hindu Kush piedmont and from the southeastern Caspian area. In all probability the settlements within the densely forested Sumbar Valley lasted longest. The gradual disappearance of early agriculture in southern Turkmenia was caused by a disturbance of the equilibrium in the eco-social system induced by the growing aridity of the climate and by the resultant decline in agroclimatic potential.

References

Agroklimaticheskie resursy Turkmenskoi SSR, Leningrad, 1974.

P. M. Dolukhanov

Askarov, A. 1977. Drevnezemledel'cheskaia kul'tura epokhi bronzy na iuge Uz-bekistana, Tashkent.

Berdyev, O. 1969. Drevneishie zemledel'tsy Iuzhnogo Turkmenistana, Ashkhabad.

Biscione, R. 1977. "The Crisis of Central Asian Urbanisation in the XI millennium B.C. and Villages as an Alternative System," in Le Plateau Iranien et l'Asie Centrale des origines a la conqête islamique, Paris, pp. 112-27.

Bukinich, D. D. 1924. "Istoriia pervobytnogo oroshaemogo zemledeliia v Zaka-piiskoi oblasti v sviazi s voprosom o proiskhozhdenii zemledeliia istokovod-stva," Khlopovoe delo, no. 3-4, pp. 92-135.

Dolukhanov, P. M. 1977. "Evolution of Eco-social Systems in Central Asia and in Iran in the Course of Upper Holocene," in Le Plateau Iranien et l'Asie Centrale, Paris, pp. 13-22.

_____ 1980. "Paleography and Prehistoric Settlement in the Causasus and in Central Asia during the Pleistocene and Holocene," in Annali Istituto Univers. Orientale, Naples.

_____ 1980. "Razvitie ekosotsial'nykh sistem na territorii Iugo-Zapadnoi Azii v verkhnem pleistotsene i golotsene," in Kolebaniia uvlazhennosti Aralo-Kaspiiskogo regiona v golotsene, Moscow, pp. 126-32.

Grave, M. K. 1957. Severnaia podgornaia ravnina Kopet-Daga, Moscow.

Khlopin, I. N. 1964. Geoksiurskaia gruppa poselenii epokhi eneolita, Moscow-Leningrad.

_____ 1977. "Sumbarskie mogil'niki — kliuch sinkhronizatsii pamiatnikov epokhi bronzy iuga Srednei Azii i Irana," in Le Plateau Iranien et l'Asie Centrale, Paris, pp. 143-54.

Kunin, V. I. 1955. Ocherki prirody Karakumov, Moscow.

Lisitsina, G. N. 1965. Oroshaemoe zemledelie epokhi eneolita na iuge Turk-menii, Moscow.

_____ 1978. Stanovlenie i razvitie oroshaemogo zemledeliia v Iuzhnoi Turkmenii, Moscow.

Lisitsina, G. N., and L. V. Prishchepenko 1977. Paleoetnobotanicheskie na-khodki Kavkaza i Blizhnego Vostoka, Moscow.

Lisitsina, G. N., and V. I. Sarianidi 1971. "Zemledelie i agrarnye otnosheniia v Turkmenistane v epokhu pervobytno-obshchinnogo stroia," in Ocherki istorii zemledeliia i agrarnykh otnoshenii v Turkmenistane (s drevenishikh vremen do prisoedineniia k Rossii), Ashkhabad.

Luppov, N. P., ed. 1972. Geologiia SSSR, vol. 22, Turkmenskaia SSR, Geologi-cheskoe opisanie, Moscow.

McClure, H. A. 1976. "Radiocarbon Chronology of Late Quaternary Lakes in the Arabian Desert," Nature, no. 263, pp. 755-56.

Makeev, P. S. 1940. "Fiziko-geograficheskii ocherk Nizmennykh Karakumov," in Prirodnye resursy Karakumov, I. P. Gerasimov, ed., Moscow-Leningrad.

Mamedov, E. 1980. "Izmenenie klimata sredneaziatskikh pustyn' v golotsene," in Kolebaniia uvlazhennosti Aralo-Kaspiiskogo regiona v golotsene, Moscow, pp. 170-74.

Masimov, I. S. 1979. "Izuchenie pamiatnikov epokhi bronzy nizov'ev Murgaba," Sovetskaia arkheologiia, no. 1, pp. 111-31.

Masson, V. M. 1956. Pamiatniki kul'tury arkhaicheskogo Dakhistana v iugo-zapadnoi Turkmenii, Trudy IuTAKE, vol. 7.

_____ 1971. Poselenie Dzheitun, MIA 180, Moscow-Leningrad.

Petit Maire, N. 1979. "Cadre écologique et peuplement humaine du littoral Ouest-Saharien depuis 10,000 ans," L'Anthropologie, vol. 83, no. 1, pp. 69-82.

Raevskii, M. I. 1963. "Chetvertichnye otlozheniia del'ty r. Tedzhen," Izv. AN Turkmen. SSR, seriia fiz.-tekhn., khim. i. gumanitar. nauk.

Sarianidi, V. I. "Drevnie zemledel'tsy Afganastana," Materialy sov.-afgan. ekspeditsii 1969-1974 gg., Moscow.

Shingareva, E. A. 1940. "Rastitel'nost' i kormovye resursy Tsentral'nykh i Vostochnykh Karakumov," in Prirodnye resursy Karakumov, I. P. Gerasimov, ed.

Shul'ts, V. L. 1965. Reki Srednei Azii, Leningrad.

Shumakov, B. A., and B. B. Shumakov 1963. Limannoe oroshenie, Moscow.

van Zeist, W., and S. Bottema 1977. "The Pleniglacial, Late Glacial and Early Postglacial Vegetations of Zeribar and Their Present-day Counterparts," Palaeohistoria, no. 19, pp. 19-85.

Afterword

C. C. LAMBERG-KARLOVSKY

If, as Morton White has written, "historical explanation explains facts prevailing at one time by reference to facts prevailing at an earlier time," then this statement would seem to be doubly true for archeological explanation.[1] Like history, archeology is dependent upon a particular data base and a particular theoretical conceptualization. The absence of either, data base or theoretical construct, results in the writing of a dictionary: words defined but resulting in a book with neither plot nor meaning.

This book underscores the importance of a new data base and presents conceptual frameworks that profoundly impact on our understanding of "an earlier time." For decades archeologists have concentrated on the primacy of the great riverine civilizations of the Old World: Egypt, Mesopotamia, the Indus, and China. These four areas were seen as ones of "pristine civilization," where urban manifestations evolved essentially independently and where developments in other areas were seen as secondary and of lesser significance. In the past decade and a half the results of archeological research in Central Asia and the Iranian Plateau have challenged this simplistic view, making it increasingly difficult to distinguish between what is a "pristine" and "secondary state" or a "primary urban generation" from a "secondary urban generation."[2]

Since 1965 a number of archeological excavations from the Mediterranean to the Indus have provided new data requiring new conceptual models; alternatively, new conceptual models motivated

386

excavations in search of new data. Thus, prior to the 1960s the evolution of complex society (the state or civilization) was believed to be restricted to Mesopotamia, Egypt, and perhaps the Indus, which many still perceived as a secondary civilization ultimately derived from Mesopotamia. The archeological cultures of the Iranian Plateau, as well as those of Central Asia (the Namazga Civilization of this book), were thought to be essentially autochthonous and less developed.

Active field programs, from the middle 1960s to the late '70s, challenged the accepted view and replaced it with Mesopotamia forming part of a greater interacting whole. The earlier restricted world view (with specific reference to the Indus Civilization) is indicated in Sir Mortimer Wheeler's classic The Indus Civilization.[3] There is not a single reference to, let alone recognition of, our present concern for the extent and nature of interaction which brought the Indus Civilization into contact with Central Asia. By 1970 archeological excavations had reported: Jemdet Nasr pottery, of Mesopotamian type, from tombs in Oman;[4] Proto-Elamite tablets, cylinder seals, and sealings from Tepe Yahya in distant southeastern Iran;[5] the large-scale processing of lapis lazuli at Shahr-i Sokhta in Seistan;[6] and possible Proto-Elamite signs on figurines in Central Asia.[7] This last parallel was to become more convincing as years later (1977) a Proto-Elamite tablet was recovered at Shahr-i Sokhta in a context in which 40 percent of the painted wares are of Central Asian (Namazga III) type.[8] Additionally, the well-known corpus of carved chlorite vessels, so fully documented by Dr. Kohl, were shown to have several centers of production but with identical parallels in shape and design from Mari in Syria to Mohenjo-daro on the Indus.[9] It was becoming increasingly clear that in our earlier efforts to understand the extent of interaction from the Mediterranean to the Indus, we had been looking into the wrong end of the telescope, seeing but part of the area.

By the early 1970s it was no longer possible to pass off the Iranian Plateau and Central Asia as cultural backwaters stimulated only by diffusion from Mesopotamia. In recent years the emerging picture has become even more complex. The discovery of Indus settlements on the banks of the Amu Darya in northern Afghanistan is paralleled inversely by the discovery of graves and cenotaphs of Bronze Age Turkmenian types (Namazga V/VI) near Mehrgarh in Pakistan Baluchistan.[10] The work of the past decade has made it the more imperative "to adopt a more complex model which sees southeastern Iran, the Persian Gulf, Baluchistan, Turkmenistan, the Indus and Mesopotamia as already separate polities ca. 3500-3000 B.C. with each of the above areas a separate 'interaction sphere' ... establishing its own administrative centers and social organization."[11]

The papers collected in this volume attest to the prehistoric and protohistoric significance of Central Asia and to the productive results of Soviet archeological research. The processes which directed the formation of agricultural communities and the development of urban centers in Central Asia provide both contrasts and similarities to better-known areas. This volume provides the reader with the significance of this little known area and, in doing so, allows Central Asia to take its place beside other regions in enriching the development of a comparative science which examines the multilinear processes involved in the evolution of complex societies.

One is struck, however, by the absence of anthropological models that discuss the relevant importance of population pressure, irrigation agriculture, settlement patterns, competition and warfare, economic exchange and religious integration which so characterize American writings dealing with the rise of complex societies. This, one suspects, is clearly not because of an absence of evidence bearing on the above issues but the result of different academic traditions in which the archeology of Central Asia is pursued by scholars concerned with the historical-descriptive rather than the analytical-explanatory models that characterize archeological research in this country.[12] The extraordinarily successful research of the past few decades in Central Asia nevertheless requires us to focus on the complexity of such issues as the role of diffusion, nomadism, "core," "periphery," and ethnic boundaries when dealing with archeological evidence at the regional and interregional levels. Cultural relations between distant areas or contiguous cultural regions may or may not be the result of similar adaptive strategies in overcoming environmental needs or of similar organizational bureaucracies controlling production. Adequate methods to distinguish between different processes have yet to be developed. That some form of cultural relations existed between the Namazga Civilization, the Indus, the Iranian Plateau, and Mesopotamia, however, cannot be denied. It is extremely rare that we can support from the archeological record evidence suggesting the presence of mutually understood ideologies. That they nevertheless existed interculturally can be suggested by the following examples which, in turn, point to a method that derives an understanding of the nature and extent of the communication systems that existed (at different times) over this broad area.

From Ur Sir Leonard Woolley recovered a cuneiform text, of an Old Babylonian copy, recording a gift to Ibbi-Sin (2028-2004) of a red-dog from Meluhha (commonly thought to be the Indus Civilization).[13] Ibbi-Sin is said to have made an image of the dog and called it "Let him Catch." This recalls the well-known apotropaic dogs whose function of warding off evil spirits is understood from Mesopotamian texts and inscriptions. The longevity of this belief is further attested at Nineveh, where small bronze dogs were placed beneath thresholds of Assur-nasir-pal's palace; one was inscribed "Don't stop to think, bite him."[14] From Ibbi-Sin to Assur-nasir-pal is a period of over one thousand years of continued belief in apotropaic dogs. What is far more surprising and significant, however, is that this belief may have been understood by the person from Meluhha who offered Ibbi-Sin the red-dog as a gift. This suggests that the pattern of communication between the Indus and Mesopotamia was far greater than indicated by the rare discovery of similar objects, i.e., seals recovered from excavation, and that between at least the elites of Mesopotamia and the Indus there was a considerable understanding of belief systems. This need come as no surprise, however, as written texts point to the acculturation of Meluhhan traders in Mesopotamia in the late third millennium.[15] The intimacy of communication between the Indus and Mesopotamia is further underscored by the much overlooked and very significant cylinder seal (Figure 1) first published almost a hundred years ago by De Clerq.[16] This extraordinary Akkadian seal depicts an official Meluhhan interpreter sitting on the lap of the king, who is receiving two petitioners. Fortunately for us the inscription on this seal clarifies the role of the personages depicted. This seal, as the gift of a red-dog to Ibbi-Sin and additional evidence of its kind, offers an opportunity to resurrect the signs and symbols of political communication: the political semiological system. Thus the Meluhhan gift of a red-dog suggests not only a mutually comprehended symbol[17] but, more importantly, a concern for the safety of King Ibbi-Sin by providing him a gift for warding off evil spirits. Similarly, the above-described cylinder seal places the Meluhhan translator on the king's lap, a position which, on the one hand, is physically close and, on the other, subservient and childlike. It is also clear that the king thought sufficiently highly of his affairs with Meluhha to employ an official translator.

The evidence cited above and numerous instances of comparable

Figure 1. Akkadian cylinder seal with Meluhhan translator (Artist: W. Powell).

evidence provided in this volume, i.e., the Indus-type seals from Altyn Tepe, suggest a communication system which at different levels of meaning and significance, and at different times, brought the distinctive cultures over this broad area into contact.

Years ago Lévi-Strauss suggested that communication proceeds at three different levels: (1) exchange of women, (2) exchange of goods and services, and (3) exchange of other types of messages.[18] Archeologists, given their limited evidence, have been mute on the first instance and most energetic in reconstructing the second manner of communication. It is the third which I believe can be more persuasively pursued. The "exchange of other types of message" systems can be divided into three types, for each of which I provide limited examples.

Formal/Structural Messages

Formal/structural messages entail information in which the meaning of the symbols (their sequence and association) is fully comprehended by those using them. Thus the symbolism on the carved chlorite bowls, so identical in shape and motif from Mari to Mohenjo-daro, suggests a specific grammar of meaning understood throughout the area of their principle use. It is clear that we have yet to understand the meaning conveyed by these bowls. That they assumed a special place and communicated specific information can hardly be doubted. One of the most frequently depicted motifs is the so-called "hut-pot" design depicting the facade of a single building. The identical representation of this building supports the presence of a shared meaning and raises the question whether such a building physically existed. Since they were manufactured in several centers, we might eliminate their being "souvenirs" of visits to the actual building. It is not unlikely, however, that they depict a single building of exceptional significance in an especially "sacred" pilgrimage city — such a community might be Nippur. The distribution of their use and production, from Tepe Yahya in southeastern Iran to the island of Tarut in the Persian Gulf and Mari on the Upper Euphrates, isolates three points at which the meaning of these vessels was fully comprehended; this in spite of the absence of other material remains which would signify culture contact. Other examples can be pointed out, some referred to in this volume, i.e., the Altyn Tepe ziggurat and its suggested similarity to Mesopotamian sacred buildings suggest a formal similarity and/or adoption of specific religious beliefs. Such a hypothesis becomes the more probable, however, if the similarity of form is complemented by a similarity of either (preferably both) technology of construction or similarity of associated material remains.

A clear example of a formally structured sharing of a complex ideological religious belief can be seen on one of the cylinder seals from Tepe Yahya (Figure 2). This seal depicts a winged goddess of vegetation wearing a horned helmet next to another partially nude figure with sprigs of vegetation sprouting from the body.[19] Dated to the middle of the third millennium, the seal is of a local, distinctive style believed to characterize the production of seals in southeastern Iran.[20] In a discussion of this midthird millennium seal, Pierre Amiet recalls the Mesopotamian deity Ningishzidda and parallels the seal to Akkadian glyptic depicting paired goddesses evoking the legend of Etana.

Thus Amiet feels that this seal represents the translation of a popular Mesopotamian myth into a distinctive southeast Iranian glyptic style.[21] A far more convincing parallel for this seal exists in equating the horned, winged female figure with Inanna, a common manner of depicting this deity in Akkadian times.[22] This possibility is reinforced by the identity of the second figure — clearly a male — which we believe to be the husband of Inanna, Dumuzi. This seal from Yahya is clearly reflected, if not partially described, in the following quotes involving Inanna and Dumuzi:

> In the marriage of Inanna to "the wild bull Dumuzi"
> of the cowherds in Nippur the rite was essentially
> a fertility rite of spring, the king's potency in the
> consummation of it being coincident with the shooting
> up of the flax, the grain, and the verdure of the steppe.[23]

Figure 2. "Inanna and Dumuzi" cylinder
seal from Tepe Yahya, ca. 2500 B.C.
(Artist: W. Powell).

The unfinished seal of Pl. XXc shows the god producing corn, not only around him but on his robe
and from his hands, his head and his shoulders.
Here is the "garment of grain-heads," mentioned
in a Sippar cult-tablet, with which Marduk was
clothed in the ritual of the New Year's festival,
and which may have symbolised his coffin, since
the god of vegetation dies with the ripening and
harvesting of the corn. Often a god wearing this
"garment" is shown worshipping the goddess of
fertility (Pl. XXk). On other occasions care is
taken that the plants sprouting from his body should
be of different kinds in order to express a more uni-
versal dominion over vegetable life (Pl. XXj).[24]

One further observation adds credibility to this hypothesis: gods
and goddesses of vegetation are often depicted sitting on top of, or
emerging from, mountains: "The god of fertility is seated upon his
throne, well characterized by the plants which sprout from his body
or his mountain."[25] In the seal from Tepe Yahya vegetation sprouts
from both body and underlying "mountain." The "mountain" has
incised chevrons, perhaps symbolizing grain mountains, on which
the texts state fertility gods and goddesses rested.

Informal/Unstructured Messages

The literature focusing on the interrelations that characterized
the regions bounded by the Kara Kum, Indian Ocean, Mesopotamia,
and the Indus have centered on individual object classes, seals,
ceramics, and metal types, etc., for the purpose of (1) building a
comparative stratigraphy and (2) proving that contacts took place.
Such an approach, though providing little understanding of the
underlying reasons that bring about culture contact, does support
the contention for random contact between distant areas. The random material remains discovered provide informal/unstructured
messages without meaning, other than the existence of "foreign-
ness." Thus the study of the distribution of etched carnelian beads
(long thought of Indus manufacture) characterizes this approach.
Whether dealing with distributional studies of simple material
types (informal exchange of carnelian beads or formal adoption of
ziggurat forms), their significance lies in their meaning within the
cultural context in which they are found. In recognizing this it is

equally clear that change in meaning and change in form are separate phenomena which depend on each other but do not necessarily coincide.

Technical Messages

The communication of technical information can be determined by the scientific analysis of archeological remains. Two recent examples may be cited which are of significance in suggesting the degree of technical communication which flowed over this wide area.

Recent studies have indicated that the production of lithic drill heads and microdrilling techniques which characterized the technology at Shahr-i Sokhta were identical to those of contemporary Hissar and later Chanhu-daro.[26] It is of significance to note that very little in the material assemblage (i.e., ceramics, metals, small finds, etc.) of Hissar can be related to Shahr-i Sokhta. Nevertheless it seems clear that these sites shared an identical technology in the production of specific tools which were also to characterize the later Indus site of Chanhu-daro. Such evidence suggests a shared communication in the method of stone tool production not otherwise evident in their distinctive material culture.

A second example pointing to a communication of technological knowledge in another direction involves the metallurgical production that characterized Central Asia (the Namazga Civilization) and Shahr-i Sokhta. This evidence complements the ceramic parallels which tie Shahr-i Sokhta with Namazga III.[27]

Examination of spectographic analyses and other metallurgical results from Susa, Yahya, Sialk, and Hissar distinguish their metallurgical technology from that of Shahr-i Sokhta and Central Asia.[28] On the former sites copper objects were produced of oxide and carbonate ores, while on the earliest occupation at Shahr-i Sokhta and on contemporary sites in Central Asia (early third millennium), specific nonferrous sulphide ores were used to produce metal objects. Sulphide ore technology is not evident on the Iranian Plateau until a later date, suggesting a different sphere of shared technological communication in the production of metal objects from that of Shahr-i Sokhta and Central Asia.

From the Mediterranean to the Indian Ocean the social landscape of the Bronze Age was extremely fluid, forming ever-shifting patchworks of fragmented polities. It is extremely doubtful that the segmented social pyramids that we refer to as "city-states" engaged in "foreign affairs" across defined territorial boundaries. It is equally unlikely that such concepts as "citizenship" existed to bind one to given territorial units or that "hierarchically tiered villages" situated in specific political units formed "emic" realities within the population. The cultural framework provided entirely permeable social units allowing farmers, nomads, and craftsmen alike to move from place to place depending on ecological and social conditions. Within the social framework it is likely that only the "elites" formed tightly integrated, politically uniform kinship groups. It is the interaction of this class which we see taking place in the gift to Ibbi-Sin from Meluhha and on the cylinder seal depicting the Meluhhan translator on the king's lap. Similarly the carved chlorite bowls are invariably recovered from elite contexts: temples, palaces, royal tombs, etc., over the broad area of their distribution. The absence of mundane material remains in everyday contexts (i.e., ceramic types) underscores the fact that intercultural relations between major segments of the population were neither frequent nor formalized within sociopolitical or economic hierarchies. When centralizing tendencies did appear, both within and between given areas, they appear to have been less the result of coercive administrative efforts for economic exploitation than the result of channeling sociocultural patterns into shared ideological bonds.

The recognition and isolation of the distinctive systems of communication which at different times, and for different reasons, connected this large area appear as "different ways of signifying the relationship of the human consciousness to the world it confronts in different degrees of certitude and comprehension."[29] Certain it is that the publication of this book expands our understanding of the complex cultural relations which existed between distinctive geographical areas and serves notice on those who perpetuate the restrictive biological analogy of seeing Mesopotamia as the cradle and/or heartland of civilization and/or cities.

Notes

1. Morton White, "Historical Explanation," Patrick Gardner, ed., in Theories of History, Glencoe, Ill., Free Press, 1959, p. 357.

2. For three recent books with collected essays bearing on this question see: J. Freidman and M. J. Rowlands, eds., The Evolution of Social Systems, University of Pittsburg Press, 1978; Ronald Cohen and Elman R. Service, eds., Origins of the State, Philadelphia, Institute for the Study of Human Issues, 1978; Henri

J. M. Claessen and Peter Skalnik, eds., Origins of the State, Mouton, 1979. See also Elman R. Service, Origins of the State and Civilization, W. W. Norton, 1975; and Morton H. Fried, The Evolution of Political Society, Random House, 1967.

3. Sir Mortimer Wheeler, The Indus Civilization, Cambridge University Press, 3rd ed., 1967.

4. K. Frifelt, "Jemdet Nasr graves in Oman," Kuml, pp. 374-83, 1970; see more recently Serge Cleuziou, "Three Seasons at Hilli: Toward a Chronology and Cultural History of the Oman Peninsula in the 3rd Millennium B.C.," Proceedings of the Seminar for Arabian Studies, vol. 10, pp. 19-32, 1980.

5. C. C. Lamberg-Karlovsky, "The Proto-Elamite Settlement at Tepe Yahya," Iran, pp. 87-96, 1971; for a detailed summary of the third millennium at Tepe Yahya, see D. Potts, "Tradition and Transformation: Tepe Yahya and the Iranian Plateau in the Third Millennium," unpublished Ph.D. dissertation, Department of Anthropology, Harvard University, 1980.

6. M. Tosi, "The lapis lazuli trade across the Iranian Plateau in the Third Millennium, B.C.," Gururajamarjarika, ISMEO, Rome, 1974; "On the Route for lapis lazuli," parts 1 and 2, The Illustrated London News, January 24 and February 7, 1970.

7. V. M. Masson and V. I. Sarianidi, Central Asia, Thames and Hudson, 1972, pp. 128-31.

8. C. C. Lamberg-Karlovsky and M. Tosi, "Shahr-i Sokhta and Tepe Yahya: Tracks in the Earliest History of the Iranian Plateau," East and West, vol. 23, 1973; see also R. Biscione, "Dynamics of an Early South Asian Urbanization: The First Period of Shahr-i Sokhta and its Connections with Southern Turkmenia," in N. Hammond, ed., South Asian Archaeology, London, Duckworth, 1973.

9. For an expansive treatment of these carved chlorite vessels, including physical-chemical analysis, see P. Kohl, "Seeds of Upheaval: The Production of Chlorite at Tepe Yahya and an Analysis of Commodity Production and Trade in Southwest Asia in the Mid-Third Millennium," unpublished Ph.D. dissertation, Department of Anthropology, Harvard University, 1974. For a brief summary, see P. Kohl, "The Balance of Trade in Southwestern Asia in the Mid-Third Millennium B.C.," Current Anthropology, vol. 19, no. 3, pp. 463-92, 1978.

10. The excavations of these tombs were undertaken in the seasons of 1979 and 1980 and remain largely unpublished. My thanks to the excavator Jean Francoise Jarrige for his discussing and showing slides of this most important discovery. For mention of it, see Jean-Francoise Jarrige and Richard Meadow, "The Antecedents of Civilization in the Indus Valley," Scientific American, vol. 243, no. 2, pp. 122-33, 1980.

11. C. C. Lamberg-Karlovsky, "Tepe Yahya 1971: Mesopotamia and the Indo-Iranian Borderlands," Iran, vol. 10, pp. 89-101, 1972.

12. Gordon R. Willey and Jeremy A. Sabloff, A History of American Archaeology, W. H. Freeman, 2nd ed., 1980. See particularly the discussions of chapters 7 and 8.

13. Edmund Sollberger, Ur Excavation Texts: Royal Inscriptions, vol. 8, Interdocumentation, Zug, Switzerland, 1980. N. E. 436, No. 1; reference 37, u. 1. Copy pl. VI.

14. Sir Max Mallowan, Nimrud and Its Remains, London, Collins, pp. 103 and 146-47.

15. S. Parpola and R. H. Brunswig, Jr., "The Meluhhan Village," Journal of the Economic and Social History of the Orient, vol. 20, pl. II, pp. 13-165.

16. This seal is published in Collection De Clercq, Catalogue methodique et raisonné, Paris, 1888, vol. 1, pl. 9, no. 83. It is discussed briefly in Leo Oppen-

heina, Ancient Mesopotamia, rev. ed., 1977, p. 64. My thanks to Professor Gregory Possehl for providing me with a photo of this cylinder seal.

17. We note that dogs do not appear on the glyptic of the Indus Civilization but are a frequent occurrence in excavations, in the form of sculpted clay. In most instances these models of dogs are painted red!

18. Claude Lévi-Strauss, Anthropologié structurale, Paris, 1958, p. 326.

19. Lamberg-Karlovsky, op. cit., 1971, pl. VI.

20. Pierre Amiet, "Antiquities du desert de Lut," Revue Assyriologique, vol. 68, no. 2, pp. 97-110.

21. Ibid., p. 106.

22. R. M. Boehmer, Die Entwicklung der Glyptik wahrend der Akkad-Zeit, Berlin, Untersuchungen zur Assyriologie und vorderasiatische Archaeologie 4, p. 66.

23. T. Jacobsen, "Mesopotamian Gods and Pantheons," in W. Moran, ed., Toward the Image of Tammuz and Other Essays on Mesopotamian History and Culture, Harvard University Press, 1970, p. 29. For a comprehensive discussion of Inanna and Dumuzi, see T. Jacobsen, The Treasures of Darkness, Yale University Press, 1976, pp. 23-75 and 135-43. Jacobsen takes this myth to be a metaphor, a mythopoetic explanation which provided the Sumerians with an understanding of their cosmos. Thus Inanna, goddess of fertility, Queen of the Heavens, storehouses, and thunder, and Dumuzi, shepherd, "Lord of the Bulls," represent a coalescence of a dual economy, agriculture and herding. Similarly the marriage of Inanna and Dumuzi is seen as a call for nations to multiply which can be seen as a metaphor of Mesopotamian political expansion. We might further suggest that the adoption of such a myth at distant Yahya represents not only evidence for political expansion but a transformation to a new technological base of agricultural production — symbolized in the metaphorical meaning of the myth.

24. H. Frankfort, Cylinder Seals, London, MacMillan, 1939, pp. 114-16.

25. Ibid., p. 115.

26. See Marcello Piperno, "Micro-drilling at Shahr-i Sokhta; the making and use of lithic drill-heads," in Norman Hammond, op. cit.; "Grave 66 at Shahr-i Sokhta: Further Evidence of Technological Specialization in the Third Millennium B.C.," East and West, vol. 26, pp. 9-12, 1976; with M. Tosi, "Lithic Technology Behind the Ancient Lapis Lazuli Trade," Expedition, vol. 16, no. 1, 1973.

27. See the references cited in Note 8.

28. Dennis Heskel, "Metallurgical Technology on the Iranian Plateau: Fourth-Third Millennium," tentative title of unfinished Ph.D. dissertation, Department of Anthropology, Harvard University.

29. Hayden White, "The Irrational and the Problem of Historical Knowledge in the Enlightenment," in Harold E. Pagliaro, ed., Studies in Eighteenth Century Culture: Irrationalism in the Eighteenth Century, 1972, p. 315, Case Western Reserve University, Cleveland.

ABOUT THE EDITOR

Philip L. Kohl is Associate Professor of Anthropology at Wellesley College. Educated at Columbia and Harvard Universities, he is the author of numerous articles on the early history of Central Asia: Iran, Afghanistan, and their Soviet neighbors. Professor Kohl has done field work in Iran (Tepe Yahya and the Darreh Gaz plain), Turkey, Afghanistan, and, almost uniquely among Western archeologists, Soviet Central Asia.